The History of Bear Island

****

Vignettes on

Other Islands and Lake Topics

By

John A. Hopper

ISBN: 978-0-692-10937-3
ISBN: 0692109374

Front cover picture: Aerial view of Bear Island taken by Bill Hemmel of Laconia, NH.

Wood Ridge Publishing
Center Harbor, New Hampshire

Dedication

***

This book is dedicated to my parents,
Helen and Stanley Hopper,
*whose vision and pioneering spirit
brought us to Bear Island
all those many years ago.*

*I read each misty mountain sign,
I know the voice of wave and pine,
And I am yours, and ye are mine.*

*Life's burdens fall, its discords cease,
I lapse into the glad release
Of Nature's own exceeding peace.*[1]

---

[1] Thomas Starr King: "Summer by the Lake-side," White Hills (1860), p. 49.

Table of Contents

PART III: From the Farming Era to the Summer Tourism Era

PART IV: The Summer Vacation Era and Bear Island

PART V: The Post-war Vacation Boom: 1950 - Present

PART VI: Related Topics

Part VI: The Early History of Other Islands

Appendix: Family Trees

Preface

I recall as a young boy being fascinated by the cellar holes and stone walls found all over Bear Island. Their presence was a constant reminder that others had lived there long before my parents had the great good fortune to buy a summer cottage on the island in 1945. Yet I never took the time to explore the history. This shortcoming became apparent to me when, as one of the 'older-timers', I was increasingly being asked questions about the island's history. I had very few answers, and my initial efforts to find some proved to be unsatisfactory. Most of what was available was fascinating, but it was anecdotal and incomplete. There just did not seem to be much in-depth research available about Bear, especially the early history.

Thus, I decided to explore more deeply. This book began as a modest effort to unravel the early settlement history of the island. After a little research, it became apparent that the historiography was very limited and quite fragmented, not only of the island but also Lake Winnipesaukee, Meredith, and the Lakes Region. Moreover, hardly any of it was recent. The more recent histories were based largely upon studies written during the period from 1880 to 1930.

I quickly came to a realization that this lack of original research was quite understandable. Original historical information is itself quite sparse and extremely fragmented. It also became readily apparent that there would be no shortcuts to unraveling the history of Bear Island. Even finding answers to the most basic of historical questions proved difficult. This made the task of gathering it very time consuming and tedious. It was the proverbial jigsaw puzzle but without knowing what it might look like; having very few pieces with which to begin; and not clearly knowing where to find additional pieces.

In previous decades, I would have given up the challenge of tracking down this history because family and work would have taken precedence. But in 2014, the happy coincidence of retirement, my love for the island, and my historical interest conspired to make the task appealing. The further coincidence of the digital age made it possible to cover far more ground than was ever possible before. As one result, the breadth of the project expanded continuously from its initial limited scope.

Despite the advantages of the digital age, the results of my research still proved to be challenging. There are few, high quality pieces of original information available. In the absence of old letters and diaries, the core of the research was based upon a limited range of sources. The most important were the real estate deeds that documented all land sales within New Hampshire. These contain the most reliable information for understanding the early history. In many cases, they also contain additional tidbits of information that add color and/or key links to the underlying history. Often I relied upon these links to connect the proverbial dots in the puzzle, although this process is fraught with danger when the inferences are stretched too far.

In addition to the deeds, other insightful information was gleaned from various original records that have survived the passage of time. These include Masonian records, township proprietary records, state legislative records, and Meredith town records. There are several great repositories around the region that have copies of these records, including the Meredith Historical Society, the Meredith Town Hall, the Laconia Gale Library and Historical Society, and the New Hampshire Historical Society in Concord among others.

Original documentation research was supplemented by genealogical information found in census reports and marriage, death, and birth records accessed through Genealogy.com. The process was further complemented by the broad search powers of the internet which in many instances provided biographical information as well as more detailed insights into virtually any topic of interest no matter what the era.

The end result is a far larger book than originally contemplated. It is by intent very heavy in detail about its main focus, i.e. the settlement on Bear Island across more than 200 years. In that regard, its primary audience includes all of those people who have lived or spent time on the island and have come to love it so dearly.

But the book should have much wider appeal as well. Anyone interested in the history of the lake and the islands will find an array of new information that will enlighten one's knowledge and understanding of Winnipesaukee's history. At yet another level, anyone interested in the early history of Meredith (and, for that matter, New Hampshire) will also find that the history of Bear Island and Lake Winnipesaukee correlate closely with the broader history of the town and the state. New Hampshire's State Architectural Historian, James Garvin, once wrote that "New Hampshire's history is the history of much of the United States writ small."[1] Well, one can also say that the history of Bear Island—this narrow slice of Americana-- is the history of New Hampshire writ smaller.

There is a great deal more research that needs to be done, but that is for another time. It is my hope that this book will lead others to discover sources of information that I overlooked or just did not know existed. My apologies for any errors, misinterpretations, omissions, or misunderstandings found herein. They are entirely my responsibility. I would greatly welcome corrections, reinterpretations, new information, etc. from anyone wishing to do so.

I can be contacted at *Bearislandhistory7@gmail.com*.

---

[1] James Garvin, "New Hampshire's Cultural Landscape," www.james.garvin.com.

Introduction

Amidst the astonishing natural beauty that is the setting of Lake Winnipesaukee, Bear Island stands as one of its crowning jewels. The second largest island in the lake, Bear is home to nearly 190 summer cottages that ring its shoreline. Many of these homes have occupied its waterfront for more than 100 years. The interior of the island, on the other hand, is entirely undeveloped except for the iconic presence of the stone chapel called St. John's on-the-Lake. It too is fast approaching 100 years of existence.

While the interior of the island is undeveloped, one can hardly take even a short walk back from the shore before encountering the hard work of the early New Hampshire farmers who once made this island their home. The island is lined with stone walls that speak to the pioneers who opened this region to western settlement and paved the way for those who occupy it now.

In surveying these walls and other remains, one cannot help but pause to wonder: Who built them? When did they do it? Where were they from? What brought them to settle on the island instead of the mainland? These questions in turn lead to others: What happened to them? When did they leave? How and when did the island become a vacation paradise? What were the forces that drove the transition? And when and how did the island evolve to its current situation?

These and other questions like them have been hanging in the winds and waves for decades. This book attempts to answer them, unraveling the history of this small but magnificent slice of Americana.

New Hampshire Towns important in the Founding of Meredith

Bear Island Locations of Note[1]

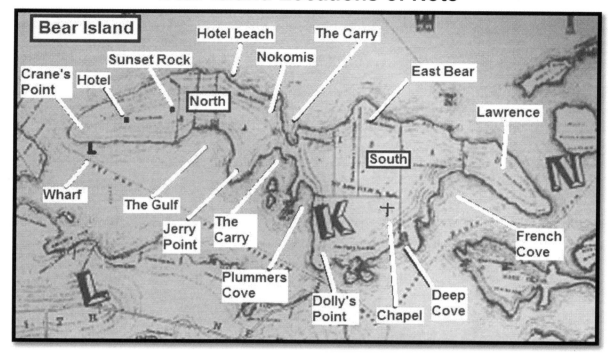

Bear Island Lot Numbers delineated in 1819

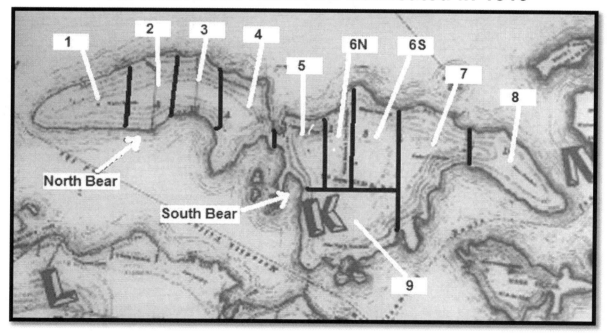

[1] This is a snapshot taken from a map of the lake completed by William Crocker in 1858. This remarkable map is used throughout the book to help identify locations.

5

Meredith Neck Locations of Note

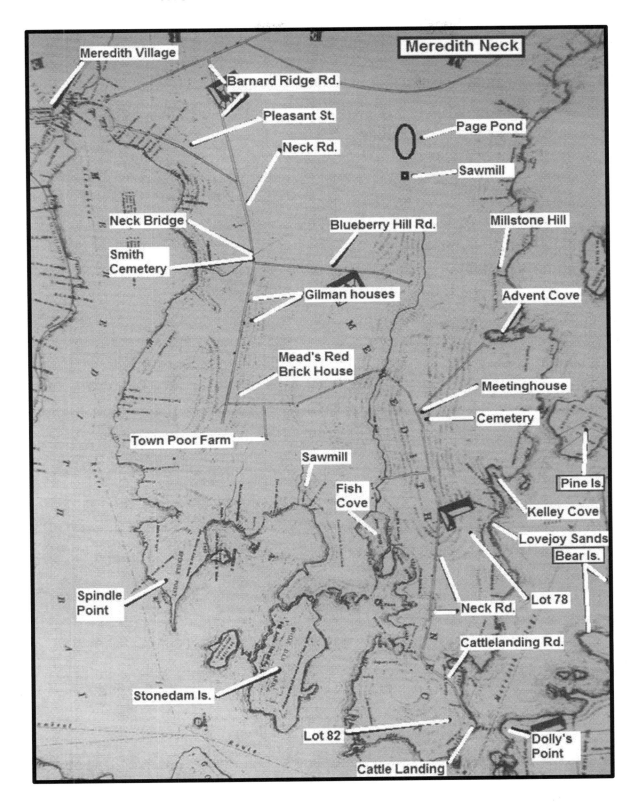

Part I:

The

Founding

Of

Meredith

Chapter One

The Early New Hampshire Colony[1]

Bear Island is located less than 60 miles from the seacoast city of Portsmouth, New Hampshire, where the first European colony in the state was established in 1623. Yet 140 years passed before the initial, tiny colonial foothold on the coast evolved into a thriving body-politic capable of expanding into the interior of New Hampshire and settling the Lakes Region.

European expansion in the New World was a major preoccupation of England and France during the early 1600s. In the first two decades of the century, the monarchies of these two European powers became engaged in a struggle for supremacy of North America that was believed to hold untold riches. In 1620, King James I chartered the Council for New England to promote English colonization in the New World. It was given authority to grant lands in an area they called New England, i.e. the land between the 40th and 48th parallels. The first English foothold was at Plymouth, Massachusetts in 1620 when the Pilgrims founded a tiny colony. Expansion into what would become New Hampshire followed in 1623. The Council granted two of its most prominent members, John Mason and Fernando Gorges, the swath of land between the Merrimack River in the south and the Kennebec River in the north. Subsequently, Mason and Gorges divided this tract, with Mason taking ownership of the area between the Merrimack and the Piscataqua Rivers. The division of the territory between the two men was formalized in 1629 when the Council for New England gave Mason a grant (or patent) for these lands that extended 60 miles inland. Lake Winnipesaukee and Bear Island fell within this territory. The royal grant to Mason was one of the most significant events in the history of New Hampshire and ultimately directly affected the pattern of settlement in Meredith and Bear Island.

John Mason was an avid colonialist. He was generally familiar with the region, having previously served seven years as governor of Newfoundland before returning to England in 1622. Mason created his own company, the Laconia Company, to manage his efforts in the region that he now dubbed New Hampshire, after the county of Hampshire in England where he once lived. Mason earnestly set to work developing his grant. His interests were entirely commercial in nature. He invested the huge sum of 22,000 pounds into the colony, establishing two settlements along the Piscataqua River that became the towns of Portsmouth and Dover. The commercial pursuits of fishing, trapping, trading, and forestry were the focus of the small number of company men who occupied the two locations. Mason made no effort nor had any inclination to bring in families of colonists to expand the settlements.

Interestingly, Mason never had the opportunity to actually set foot in his colony. He died in 1635 while still in England, just prior to his first scheduled visit. His patent retained its legal

---

[1] The discussion of early New Hampshire history is largely drawn from: C. Clark, Eastern Frontier, and J. Daniel, Colonial New Hampshire.

existence after his death, but over the next 100 years, its legitimacy and the ownership of it were subject to constant challenge.

In the decades after Mason's death, the colony of New Hampshire experienced very limited growth. Only the towns of Exeter (1638) and Hampton (1639) were added to the first two commercial settlements. Both were very different from the two original towns. They were established by colonial families that migrated north from Massachusetts, looking for relief from Puritan control. They were predominantly farmers, in contrast to the commercial focus of the first two settlements.

By 1640, the entire colony still had only some 1000 inhabitants. Moreover, the four towns functioned independently of each other. There was no central leadership that knit them together with any sense of unity. As a result, the coastal area where the settlers lived was less a unified colony than a group of small, satellite settlements on the periphery of the much larger Massachusetts colony which provided government oversight for the Crown.

The colonies south of New Hampshire had grown in numbers far beyond those in New Hampshire. In 1628, the Puritans established the Massachusetts Bay Colony. During the 1630s, the Great Migration of religious dissidents from England brought more than 20,000 new settlers to southern New England, with half of them settling in Massachusetts.

While the colonies to the south expanded, the tiny New Hampshire settlements remained confined to the coastal area. There were no overarching designs of expanding inland. With its small population, there was only modest pressure to move beyond the existing bounds.

The economy also remained largely commercially oriented. The commercial focus led the colonists into direct contact with the western Abenaki, the Native Americans who lived in the interior of the colony.[1] The Abenaki had occupied these lands for upwards of 12,000 years. Their territory spanned northern New England and southern Canada. They lived in relatively small groups consisting of extended families. In central New Hampshire, the family group of the western Abenaki, known as the Penacook, occupied the region from the Concord area north through the Lakes Region.

The Abenaki lived harmoniously with each other. Each family group (or tribe) resided in roughly contiguous territories. Villages were most often established near lakes and the mouths of rivers. Their activities and movements were driven by the seasons. They were not nomadic, but shifted seasonally for planting, fishing, hunting, and enduring winter. Winnipesaukee was a favorite summer location for them. Aquadoctan, now known as the Weirs, was the primary

---

[1] The summary of the Abenaki is derived from: John and Donna Moody, "Town by Town, Watershed by Watershed: Native Americans in New Hampshire," presentation given April 10, 2017, Moultonborough, NH; J. Daniels, Colonial New Hampshire; C. Clark, The Eastern Frontier.

fishing ground of the Penacook and others. Penacook hunting parties frequented other parts of the lake, including the islands, in search of game.[1]

Prior to 1600, Abenaki numbers in New Hampshire and Vermont may have approached 50,000 people. But the population decreased drastically in the late 1500s and early 1600s. First, they suffered heavily from incursions made by their traditional enemy, the Mohawks, one of the five nations that made up the Iroquois Confederation in northern New York. Then, just prior to the arrival of English settlers, the Abenaki and all of the Native Americans along the New Hampshire and Maine coastal area fell victim to a multi-year epidemic that wiped out a huge proportion of the population. Estimates suggest that from 75% to 98% of the coastal Abenaki died during the epidemic which lasted from 1616 to 1619.[2] The epidemic was an unintended consequence of contact with the earliest European voyagers who carried diseases to which the Abenaki had no immunity. As a result, when English and French colonists began arriving in New England, they found only small Native American societies residing in New Hampshire, amounting to perhaps as few as 2000 people.

The first colonists in New Hampshire developed good relations with the Penacook. Regular trading patterns were established in which the Native Americans exchanged furs (especially beaver pelts) for metal goods, blankets, and liquor. The Penacook played a key role in the trading process. They traded directly with the English but also often acted as middlemen, buying pelts from other tribes and then trading them to the English. The future Concord area became the center of this trading activity. The friendly trading relationship lasted until the late 1680s.

While the period from 1640 through 1680 was one of very limited growth for the New Hampshire colony, the period served to entrench the norms and institutions that characterized colonial society for decades thereafter. The family formed the nuclear unit of society, with the universal expectation that children would marry and continue the process. Religion provided the second leg of the social order, with the 'meeting house' and Sunday services a core part of life. The fundamental organizational and governing structure was the town.

While these institutions were being developed, however, the political affairs of the colony were in constant flux as various factions jockeyed for control of the colony. These included some of the wealthier colonists themselves, the English provincial authorities, and the colony of Massachusetts. One of the biggest issues facing the colonists was the actual ownership of the land they occupied.

There were overlapping claims to the territory between Mason's heirs and the colony of Massachusetts. After Mason's death in 1635, his patent was inherited by his nephew, Robert

---

[1] As far as we can tell, they never established anything more than hunting camps on the islands.
[2] New Hampshire Historical Society, Online "Time Line" segment.

Tufton Mason, but he was still a minor. His representatives let enforcement of the grant lapse. Massachusetts sought to take advantage of the situation by claiming ownership of much of New Hampshire. The original Massachusetts charter, imprecisely written, defined its northern border as running three miles north of the Merrimack River. Massachusetts colonial leaders further interpreted the grant to mean that its border was located three miles north of the <u>source</u> of the river. This interpretation suggested that a huge portion of New Hampshire and even some of Maine belonged to Massachusetts.[1] In an effort to formalize this claim, Governor Endicott of Massachusetts sent surveyors up the Merrimack River in 1652 to find its source. They determined that the Winnipesaukee outlet at the Weirs was the source of the river, marking the spot by engraving the stone known as Endicott Rock.

The land dispute continued to fester for decades as the ultimate arbiter, the Crown, was preoccupied with other matters. But the Crown began to make its weight felt more directly in New Hampshire in 1679 when English authorities finally declared New Hampshire to be a royal colony. It was separated from Massachusetts, and a provincial governor was installed to run it, supported by an Assembly comprised of local colonists. The boundary issue, however, remained unresolved.

Soon after, events in Europe brought an abrupt end to the several decades of stability in New Hampshire. England declared war on France in 1688, starting the first of four wars between the two arch enemies that took place over the next 75 years. All four of these European wars spilled over into the New World and northern New England, preventing any colonial expansion into the interior of the colony.

The first conflict was called King William's War (1688-1697). It began a 20 year period of sporadic but bitter conflict. The French aligned with the Abenaki, who by this time were becoming aggrieved by the actions of some English settlers. The English allied with the Iroquois. During the war, the Abenaki raided Dover and Portsmouth, killing or capturing several hundred colonists. The fighting was very nasty. Neither side gave any quarter to women and children, and both sides paid bounties for scalps.

After a lull, a second outbreak of war, known as Queen Anne's War, occurred in 1703. It lasted until 1713 when a peace agreement ended the fighting but failed to resolve the overlapping ambitions of the English and French in the New World. At the beginning of this war, the Abenaki retreated to French-held territory in northern Maine and eastern Canada; but their retreat and the peace treaty in 1713 still did not open central and northern New Hampshire to any sort of colonial settlement. Those territories remained a no-man's land through which bands of hostile French and Abenaki still traveled.

---

[1] See New Hampshire Historical Society eNewsletter, January 2017. The authors of the original Massachusetts charter presumed that the Merrimack River ran simply ran east to west. They were not aware of the sharp northerly turn the river takes some 35 miles inland, the turn that leads it the Lakes Region. See map, p. 4.

Another outbreak of war occurred in northern Maine in 1722, again pitting the French and the Abenaki against the English and the Iroquois. It too was characterized by nasty fighting with scalps taken by both sides. The English finally claimed victory in 1725, pushing the French and Abenaki out of Maine and parts of southeastern Canada.

At the conclusion of this war, the New Hampshire colony still consisted of only seven townships, all located in the seacoast area. These included the four earliest towns, along with three additions: New Castle (1693), Kingston (1694), and Stratham (1716). But by the 1720s, colonists were champing at the bit to expand. Some of pressure came from Colonial authorities in both New Hampshire and Massachusetts anxious to establish new towns on the periphery where they could serve as an outer defensive ring. Colonists were interested because the population had grown fairly rapidly despite the extended years of conflict. Prior to 1690 or so, the colony's population had amounted to only about 6000 people. By 1702, the number of settlers was estimated to have reached 10,000. By the mid-1730s, it was up to about 25,000.[1] The vast majority of these newcomers were farmers who needed land. Young families especially were anxious to develop their own homesteads, and established farmers were interested in additional land.

As a result, during the 1720s and 1730s, numerous new towns were incorporated in New Hampshire, if not always actually settled. Some of this township expansion resulted from the overlapping claims to the ownership of the land between Massachusetts and New Hampshire officials. Massachusetts established some 16 new towns during the 1730s in the part of New Hampshire it claimed to serve as border protection against potential raids. The New Hampshire provincial government countered by establishing other towns, often nearby.[2]

The border issue with Massachusetts finally came to a head in the early 1730s in what was one of the major turning points in New Hampshire history. At the urging of various parties, the Privy Council in England established a commission to resolve the dispute. New Hampshire interests were led by an oligarchy of wealthy seacoast merchants who were closely tied to the provincial Governor, John Wentworth. They hired a wealthy English merchant, John Thomlinson, to handle their case in London. Thomlinson's efforts carried the day in dramatic fashion. The commission ruled in favor of New Hampshire, ultimately defining the border between New Hampshire and Massachusetts more favorably than even the colonists had hoped. In a landmark decision finalized in 1741, the border was established as it still exists today. Implicit in the boundary decision, the Masonian Patent was reaffirmed as legal and binding.

---

[1] See Clark, Eastern Frontier, p. 170 footnote; Gazetteer of 1817, p. 59; Daniels, Colonial New Hampshire, p. 140. Much of the growth resulted from natural reproduction, the rate of which was increased by gradually increasing life expectancies, improved standards of living, and the propensity for large families (it was not unusual to find six to 12 children per family). Population growth also continued to benefit from immigration. Some of it came from England and the West Indies, but the bulk came from the colonies in southern New England that were experiencing very rapid population growth.

[2] The most notable case of competing townships involved the founding of Rumford (i.e. Concord, 1725) by Massachusetts and Bow (1727) by New Hampshire. One of the other new towns established by the NH province was the town of Gilmanton (1727). It theoretically brought the northern boundary of the colony to Lake Winnipesaukee (the current town of Gilford was part of Gilmanton). But Gilmanton was not actually settled until about 1770 as a result of the conflicts with the French and Abenaki.

Chapter Two

The Masonian Proprietorship

With the legality of John Mason's patent established, its then-owner, John Tufton Mason, was approached by various parties that wanted to purchase it. After first agreeing to sell it to Massachusetts interests, he reversed course and sold the patent to a group of the leading New Hampshire seacoast merchants. The 12 men who comprised the group became known as the Masonian Proprietors. They were something of a Who's Who in colonial politics at the time. Nearly all of them were either related to the provincial Governor, Benning Wentworth, or to each other or both. In all cases, they came from the wealthiest and 'best' families in the province. All of them had served in the provincial government in one position or another for many years, including the Governor's Council and the Assembly (known as the General Court). According to one historian, "they *were* the Royal government of New Hampshire."[1]

The Proprietors (and some of their interconnections) were:

Mark Hunking Wentworth	Brother of the governor, Benning Wentworth
John Wentworth	Brother of the governor
Theodore Atkinson	Married to a sister of the governor
Jotham Odiorne Jr.	Cousin of Mark Wentworth's wife
George Jaffrey	Nephew of the governor
Richard Wibird	Brother-in-law to another Wentworth sibling
Thomas Packer	Married to a sister of the governor
John Rindge	Son of Thomas Packer's second wife
Joshua Peirce	His brother was married to John Rindge's sister
Nathaniel Meserve	Married to a sister of Jotham Odiorne Jr.
John Moffatt	No known relationships with the others
Thomas Wallingford	No known relationships with the others

[2]

The purchase was not finally closed until 1746. The primary reason for the delay was the reemergence of conflict between England and France. The War of the Austrian Succession, which broke out in Europe in 1740, leaked into North America in 1744 in the form of King George's War. The immediate territory of New Hampshire went largely unscathed in this war, but its frontier towns were on constant alert. Canterbury, for example, dealt with a number of small raiding parties as did other locations. Major fighting was forestalled thanks to the forts built on the perimeter, including one in 1746 in what is now the town of Tilton. The war ended with a peace treaty in 1748, but it was hardly conclusive. As with earlier periods, the New World conflicting aspirations of both England and France remained unresolved.

---

[1] State Papers, Vol. 28, p. 256.
[2] "The Mason Title", State Papers, Vol. 28, pp. 256-257. Interestingly, despite the close family ties, Governor Wentworth was actually irate that these men had made the purchase. He had personal aspirations to control all of the unoccupied land in New Hampshire.

The Masonian Proprietors took their first official step in 1746 when they issued clean titles of ownership to the 16 towns that were previously granted by the provincial governor within the geographical bounds of the patent.[1] These included New Hampshire's earliest towns as well as others such as Bow and Canterbury that were created by the provincial authorities in 1727.

The Masonian Proprietors did not turn to the task of distributing the massive acreage they had purchased until May 1748 when they convened their first meeting in Portsmouth. They wanted to establish a process by which the colony of New Hampshire could expand and thrive. They understood implicitly that they would prosper from the overall success of this process, eventually if not immediately. Their initial focus rested entirely upon establishing the criteria by which they would parcel out new townships. They adopted, in somewhat modified form, the long established blueprint of township creation that was used in the earlier expansion of New Hampshire.[2]

The Masonian Proprietors formalized the ground rules for establishing a new township during subsequent meetings held over the summer of 1748. The first requirement was the formation of groups of colonists committed to developing new townships. Each group was expected to consist of 82 men who would become the 'township proprietors' willing to undertake and underwrite the development of a new township. A specific geographical area of some six miles square would be identified for each new township. The township proprietors would then be required to survey the prospective land, creating three geographical divisions within it. Each division was to be divided into 100 lots, containing 100 acres or so each.[3] The lots were then to be allocated to individual owners (comprised of both township proprietors and Masonian proprietors) through a 'drawing' of lots. The breakdown in each division would result in 82 of the 100 lots belonging to township proprietors; 15 belonging to Masonian proprietors; and three being allocated for a Meeting House, a minister, and a school.[4]

The approach was well received by colonists interested in becoming township proprietors for two primary reasons. Many got involved for purely speculative reasons. Real estate was one of the few potentially lucrative investment alternatives available to them. On the other hand, it appears that just as many embraced the new townships as opportunities for their children to establish themselves. Population growth had placed real pressure on previously available lands, and there were increasing concerns about how younger generations were to establish

---

[1] The Proprietors made an initial effort to sell the patent to the provincial government for the amount they had paid for it. However, they were not able to reach an agreement due to conflicting interests within the provincial General Assembly.

[2] See the article by James L. Garvin, "The Range Township in Eighteenth-Century New Hampshire, " Dublin Annual Proceedings 1980, pp. 47-68. The Proprietors' authority, however, ran only to the granting of lands for potential new towns. The authority to actually grant the status of 'town' resided with the provincial Governor and the General Assembly.

[3] Given the rugged and unevenness of the land in New Hampshire, the idea was that owning large, separate lots would give each proprietor a better chance to end up with at least some farmable property.

[4] The Masonians drew 15 lots rather than 12. The three additional lots were allocated individually or jointly to key compatriots, including John Thomlinson, Daniel Peirce, Samuel Moore, John Tufton Mason, Samuel Solly, and Clement March. Each had played an important part in the acquisition of the Masonian patent. The Masonian Proprietors would also collectively own any township land (called 'common land') that was not included within the surveyed lots for whatever reason.

themselves. Regardless of motive, very few of the township proprietors themselves had any interest in actually relocating to the new settlements.[1]

By late summer 1748, some 30 different groups of petitioners had begun discussions with the Masonians.[2] Some of them had identified locations they wished to settle, but most of them had not. The groups were all comprised of better heeled colonists from the seacoast towns. In some cases, all of a group's members came from the same town, while in others the members were drawn from several towns.

---

[1] It was also very easy to sign up with a group. Since it was a new undertaking, few had any inkling of what the expenses might be. Initially at least, there was little or even no upfront cost to join one of the groups.
[2] State Papers, Vol. 27, pp. 234-237.

Chapter Three

The Granting of the New Town[1]

The group of colonists who founded the town that became Meredith was among the first to seek approval for a new township. From the outset, it worked jointly with another group that would ultimately establish the township of Sanbornton. Both contained contingents drawn predominantly from Exeter, Stratham, and to a lesser extent Hampton. Moreover, the groups were cross-pollinated with different family members belonging to one or the other.[2] Initial planning meetings were held together, and the elected officers at each meeting included individuals from both groups.

The combination also made sense in that the territories the two groups sought were contiguous, located on either side of the Pemigewasset River.[3] Precisely how they arrived at this specific region and divided it between themselves is not clear; but several men in the two groups were among the militia stationed at Fort Atkinson along the Winnipesaukee River (Tilton) in 1746 under the command of Colonel Theodore Atkinson (one of the leading Masonian Proprietors). Their wartime duties included scouting the Winnipesaukee region for hostile French and Abenaki.[4]

The combined groups, with John Sanborn of Sanbornton taking the lead, met with the Masonian Proprietors in the early fall of 1748. The early leaders chosen by the Meredith group were Ensign Oliver Smith and Joseph Rawlins, both of Exeter. They found a willing audience among the Masonians who clearly encouraged the joint effort. At this point, neither of the two groups had decided upon a name for their proposed townships. Initially the Masonians referred to them simply as the "first town" (i.e. the future Sanbornton) and the "second town" (i.e. the future Meredith). The Masonians urged the groups to develop their plans further. As a result, in November the groups appointed a committee consisting of two members from each "to go up to lay out" the preliminary bounds of the two townships.[5]

Upon completion of this step, the group leaders met again with the Masonians on December 8th to address next steps. The meeting resulted in a potential roadblock. Each group had only 60 township proprietors, while the Masonian Proprietors insisted that the number should be 80 each. The Masonians proposed that the two groups each add 20 new proprietors

---

[1] This chapter is largely drawn from the records of the Masonian Proprietors found in: State Papers, Vol. 27, pp. 418, 476-488; re Sanbornton, see pp. 228-229

[2] Most of the Meredith group was from Exeter (25) and Stratham (25). Exeter men came to dominate the leadership. Half of the Sanbornton group came from Stratham (30), but the leadership, under John Sanborn, came from Hampton.

[3] Interestingly, a group from Hampton had petitioned the provincial Governor and Council for a township on the Pemigewasset in the early 1740s but was unsuccessful. The group again petitioned the Governor and Council in 1749 with a similar request, perhaps trying to go around the Masonians. It was not granted. The Masonians eventually granted them the township that became Moultonborough in 1763. See State Papers, Vol. 13, p. 80; Vol. 12, p. 616.

[4] Potter, p.89. A block house had also been built in 1736 on the (now) Gilford side of the Weirs channel, but it was almost always unoccupied. By this period, the Weirs area had long been abandoned by the Abenaki, but many of the primary pathways south went through the area. Another blockhouse had been built in Alton at the same time in an effort to provide protection for farmers on the frontier.

[5] Proprietors Meeting, Nov 10, 1748.

from a separate group of Hampton colonists that was seeking a township.[1] But this proved to be a non-starter when the Hampton group refused to be divided.[2] John Sanborn met again with the Masonians on December 20th, requesting that no additional proprietors be added to the two groups. In making his argument, he noted that the prospective townships were too small to provide each proprietor with the standard 300 acres of land presumed by the six square mile township model developed by the Masonians. In particular he told them they would "find that in the 2d township (i.e. future Meredith) there is one 4th part water" which would especially diminish the potential land holdings of each proprietor. Sanborn's appeal fell on deaf ears. The Masonians granted townships to the two groups on December 31, 1748, but the grant specifications still called for 80 township proprietors in each case.[3]

The issue of proprietor numbers continued to dominate the township proprietors' dealings during 1749 to the detriment of everything else. Perhaps uncertain about what to do next, it was not until June that they finally decided that John Sanborn should re-approach the Masonians about the issue. Finally, in October, Sanborn presented a petition to them, again inveighing that each group not be required to add 20 new members to their proprietorship numbers.[4] The Masonians relented.[5] The final list of 60 township proprietors remained unchanged thereafter.[6]

With this concurrence in hand, the township proprietors finally turned their attention to the practical aspects of developing their townships. Still operating jointly, as a first step they voted in November 1749 to send a committee into the granted territory to determine the boundary line between the two prospective townships.

Separately, the 'Meredith' contingent on the joint committee was also instructed to identify a place for a saw mill and a center square.[7] When this apparently did not happen, another committee was chosen in June 1750 to establish a location for a saw mill and a center square. At the same time, Jonathan Longfellow was tasked with formally surveying part of the new township and laying out lots. The committee's work was completed by early July.[8] Longfellow's survey focused upon the southern-most region of the new town which became known as the First Division. He divided it into 82 numbered lots containing 100 acres each.[9] A Town Square was also set aside. Due to the irregularity of the land, the division also contained some smaller, unnumbered parcels.

---

[1] See State Papers, Vol. 27, p. 476.
[2] State Papers, Vol. 27, p. 322.
[3] State Papers, Vol. 27, pp. 476-482, Masonian Records, December 20 and 31, 1748.
[4] State Papers, Vol. 27, p. 482.
[5] See Proprietors Records, June 21, 1749. In June 1750, John Sanborn was paid 30 shillings for "giting eighteen men omitted." In fact most of the first 30 township proprietor groups had fewer than the requisite 80 members.
[6] These names were on both the 1753 Plan and the 1770 Plan of Meredith. State Papers, Vol. 27, between pp. 488 and 489.
[7] Proprietors Records, November 14, 1749.
[8] Proprietors Records, June 21 and July 10, 1750
[9] The 82 lots were less than the original 100 established by the Masonians because of the fewer number of township proprietors in the group. The layout of the First Division proved to be quite different from the subsequent layout of Second and Third Divisions. It was divided into seven ranges that ran north to south. The lots in each range were numbered from one up to 11. There were two other areas in the First Division that were also divided into lots but were not labeled as ranges. The largest was the Point Lot that included the future downtown Laconia and Lakeport. It had 14 individual lots. The other area included the Weirs and the head of Paugus Bay. It had only four lots.

In December 1750, representatives traveled to Portsmouth to meet with the Masonian Proprietors to undertake the formal process of drawing the 82 lots in the First Division. This was the means by which individual ownership of the land was determined. Sixty of the 82 lots were drawn to the names of Township Proprietors, and 15 were drawn to individual Masonian Proprietors. Four of the remaining six were designated simply as 'proprietors' lots owned jointly by Masonian Proprietors. The remaining three were designated for a church, a parsonage, and a school. A few smaller, unnumbered parcels became 'common land'.

Neither of the two townships had been given a specific name by late 1750. The Masonians simply listed the names of the township proprietors when referencing the townships. In the case of Meredith, the first name on the list was Samuel Palmer Esquire of Hampton, so the Masonians referred to the township as 'the tract of land granted to Samuel Palmer, Jonathan Shaw, etc.' or as 'the tract of land granted to Samuel Palmer and Associates'. In mid-1750, the description was apparently reduced to 'Palmer's Town' by the surveyor, Jonathan Longfellow, on his survey map of the First Division.[1] Palmer's Town, however, was never an 'official' name for the new town. Jonathan Longfellow was virtually the only person who ever used it. Just months after Longfellow's first survey, the township proprietors formally voted to name it Salem.[2]

The inspiration behind the choice of this name is not known. None of the proprietors came directly from Salem, Massachusetts, as some historians have suggested.[3] All of them were from New Hampshire, and all but ten were from Exeter and Stratham. The name was selected perhaps because of its Biblical prominence (it means 'peace'). Regardless, the proprietors had to change the name to New Salem in 1753, presumably after discovering that the name 'Salem' was already adopted by another New Hampshire town incorporated in 1750.[4]

Notwithstanding this flurry of activity around the name, no additional steps were taken to develop the township during 1751 and most of 1752. The township proprietors continued to hold

---

[1] I am not aware that any copy of the original 1750 survey exists so the use of the name at that date cannot be verified. The only place that this name seems to actually occur in any of the contemporary records is on a second survey completed by Longfellow in 1753. The only other use of the name in the early documents was the 1764 granting of a petition to enlarge the town of Sandwich signed by the Governor. It references the town's border with "Palmers Town, or New Salem." State Papers, Vol. 25, p. 512.

[2] Salem first appears in: Township Proprietor Records, December 26, 1750. Samuel Palmer's role in the township group was apparently quite minimal. There are indications in the documents that he may have been brought into the group by other members rather than his personally seeking a role in it. For example, his early 'dues' were paid by Joseph Rawlins. His inclusion gave the group much greater visibility with the Masonians. He was well known to the Masonians, having served numerous terms in the colony's Assembly with several of them and having worked with some of them on various provincial affairs. He was a respected member of the seacoast community and the New Hampshire province. But he played only a very minor role in the actual Meredith petition process that led to the grant. The only direct reference to him in the records was made in 1748 when the two groups voted to consult with him regarding the sufficiency of land within the boundaries of the Masonian grant. Thereafter, his name is nowhere to be found in the active deliberations of the Meredith township proprietors, although his name continued to be listed on the rolls for years afterwards. Either he or a namesake became an active member of a Hampton group that petitioned for its own township. Palmer died c. 1764. See 'Meredith' Proprietors Records, Nov 10, 1748; State Papers, Vol. 12, p. 322 and Vol. 13, p. 80.

[3] See, for example: Isaac Hammond's editorial introduction to Meredith, State Papers, Vol. 12, p. 581. He may have derived that idea from a document about the founding of Salem, NH, thinking it was in reference to the future Meredith.

[4] The first reference to New Salem is found in: Township Proprietors Records, June 29, 1753. The obvious formal naming of the township begs the question of why Jonathan Longfellow still insisted in 1753 on calling it Palmer's Town on his second survey. The town of Salem, NH was originally just a portion of the northern parish of Methuen, MA. The area became part of New Hampshire when the Massachusetts border issue was settled in 1741. The new town was not formally incorporated until 1750 when it adopted the name of Salem from the town in Massachusetts from which many of the inhabitants had originally come.

sporadic meetings, but the main point of concern seemed to be the collection of unpaid 'taxes' levied on the township proprietors to cover the costs of the organization.[1]

Whatever the delays, the township proprietors finally refocused on their new town in November 1752. They voted to send another committee led by Longfellow up to the township to lay out the remaining land in the grant (i.e. the Second Division).[2] The committee presented its work to the group of township proprietors in July 1753. The layout again included 82 lots, but the results apparently suggested each lot only contained 80 acres each.[3] The plan was approved, and representatives were selected to go to Portsmouth for a drawing of these lots.[4] However, following the results of the Second Division survey, the New Salem proprietors were disappointed in the limited size of the lands they had received from the Masonians. The original expectation of each township proprietor was that he would receive 300 acres, comprised of three separate lots. The New Salem surveys had resulted in two lots per proprietor amounting to 180 acres. With that in mind, the proprietors agreed in January

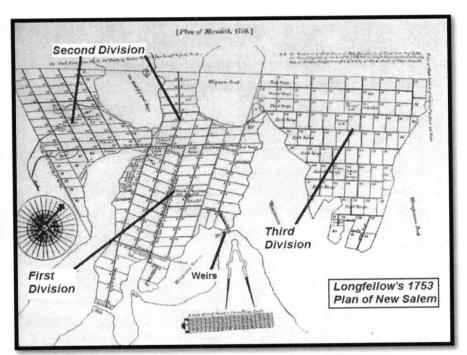

1754 to retain Jonathan Longfellow as their agent in an effort to get more land for the township from the Masonian proprietors. The New Salem group agreed to pay him a fee of one shilling for every additional acre of land he could get added to the township.[5]

Thereafter, Longfellow revised his 1753 survey map to incorporate in it ungranted Masonian land east of and contiguous to New Salem. Most of this land included what became Meredith Neck. In May 1754, he traveled to Portsmouth to present a petition to the Masonian

---

[1] Collecting monies always proved to be a problem. Levies were only authorized by vote at group meetings, but even then the group had no real leverage to collect from reluctant proprietors. The group frequently threatened to revoke a proprietor's rights if payments were not made, but the township proprietors actually lacked the authority to enforce the threat. The Masonian proprietors had retained the power to approve or disapprove of all township proprietors.

[2] 'Meredith' Proprietors Records, November 2, 1752.

[3] This figure comes from the 1753 map prepared for the Masonian Proprietors when Longfellow petitioned to get more land for the new township. His map of the Second Division did not include all of the land granted to the township. As discussed below, he had every incentive to underestimate the acreage.

[4] 'Meredith' Proprietors Records, December 26, 1752; June 29, 1753 and July 12, 1753.

[5] 'Meredith' Proprietors Records, January 1, 1754.

Proprietors, asking that these lands be added to New Salem as the Third Division.[1] The Masonians agreed, stating that the additional land should have been part of the township in the first place. A "clerical error" made in the original description of the township had led to its omission.[2]

The addition of the Third Division was the last substantive accomplishment of the New Salem proprietors during the 1750s. The fourth and final round of warfare with the French broke out in 1755. This was known as the Seven Years' War in Europe. In North America it was called the French and Indian War, again pitting the colonies of New England against those of New France. The New Salem proprietors undertook no meaningful steps while the war ran its course over the next six years. It was not until 1761 that the English won a complete victory over the French. With the Treaty of Paris in 1763, the English took total control of Canada and North America east of the Mississippi River. The end of the war removed the final impediments to the settlement of New Salem.

---

[1] Longfellow's 1753survey showed lot sizes of 80 acres each in the Second Division and 125 acres each in the prospective Third Division. The map omits township lands around Lake Pemigewasset. A 1770 re-survey of these divisions by Ebenezer Smith found that the Second Division lots were 125 acres in size and the Third Division lots were only 95 acres.

[2] State Papers, Vol. 27 pp. 485-486: Masonian Records, May 3, 1754. In November 1754, a meeting of the New Salem proprietors voted to pay Longfellow 420 pounds for his services. Not surprisingly, the group was unable to raise all of the monies to fulfill the obligation. In September 1755, Longfellow sued the proprietors for the shortfall. There is no information about how the suit was resolved. Regardless, Longfellow soon after sold his original rights in the new town and joined another group. State Papers, Masonian Records, Vol. 27, PP.485 – 487. 'Meredith' Proprietors Records, November 12, 1754.

Chapter Four

The Settlement of New Salem

At the conclusion of fighting in 1761, the New Salem proprietors once again took up the task of township building. The group was beginning anew some 13 years after they had received the initial Masonian grant. By then, some of the original members were dead, while others had simply dropped out due to disinterest, poor finances, and/or misfortune. They were now replaced by other seacoast colonists who purchased or inherited the 'Original Right' to the lots of land drawn in 1750 by the 'first' township proprietors. This was an important transition, because several of these 'new' men (or 'second' proprietors) took the lead in the eventual settlement of the town. They saw New Salem as their means to advance in life, and they were fully committed to the process. The most prominent among them were Ebenezer Smith, Abraham Folsom, and John Odlin who joined with two original holdovers, Josiah Sanborn and Ephraim Robinson, to form the leadership of the reconstituted New Salem proprietors' group.

Ebenezer Smith was by far the most noteworthy. He rose to become the driving force behind the ultimate development of the new town. Born in 1734, Smith spearheaded the settlement process, committing himself and his future to the new township. The third son of a fairly wealthy Exeter tradesman, Smith was already seeking to find his way in the world through the Masonian grant process by the time the French and Indian War ended. Before his involvement with New Salem, he was one of several colonists who had posted a bond to establish a farm in the still unsettled township of Gilmanton. But Smith obviously saw a much more appealing opportunity in New Salem. He purchased the Original Right of Jacob Longfellow in 1759 and became a township proprietor.[1]

In late 1761 or early 1762, Smith purportedly led a group of six colonists to scout out the new town.[2] Simply to reach the new township, Smith and the others had to follow the only route available, a 26 mile path with room for only a single horse that began in the town of Epsom and ended at the Winnipesaukee River (now downtown Laconia). After most of the men returned to their homes, Ebenezer is said to have remained and begun clearing his homestead lot in the First Division, near Lake Opechee.[3]

The following year, Smith and the other active proprietors began to step up the process of township development. They voted to cut a road (really a cart path) from Canterbury to New Salem, connecting at the saw mill lot on the Winnipesaukee River (now downtown Laconia).

---

[1] Ebenezer's father, Daniel Smith, was an original New Salem township proprietor who had died in 1752. It was not until 1761 that Ebenezer purchased his right as well. Over time Ebenezer purchased numerous original rights in Meredith and was responsible for getting these lands occupied. Smith was typical of leaders found in other new towns who made their fortunes by investing their lives in them. See, Clark, Eastern Frontier, pp. 238-239.

[2] See, for example, Old Meredith and Vicinity, p. 67. There is nothing in any of the proprietors' records about this trip.

[3] The lot was D1/Point/ L10, the Original Right (OR) of Jacob Longfellow. The First Division was the only option for settlement at this time. It was the only division with the lots actually laid out on the ground. The backbone of the First Division contained some of the best farm land in the township and was home to the sawmill grant. At the time, Lake Opechee was known to the colonists as Round Bay.

Another road from the center of Gilmanton to the saw mill site was voted in December of 1762. Further, they voted to have the saw mill built. They also voted to build a bridge across the Winnipesaukee River at the saw mill grant (hence the later name, Meredith Bridge, for that location).[1] To finance the roads and the saw mill, the township proprietors voted an assessment of 30 pounds from each member. Despite the good intentions, the initiatives barely got underway during 1763, with only the Canterbury road being cut.

In December 1763, the proprietors again made an effort to encourage additional settlement activity in New Salem. They voted once again to have the saw mill built and the bridge constructed. In addition, the proprietors voted at the January 1764 annual meeting to provide a sizeable monetary incentive for people to actually settle in New Salem. They agreed to create an incentive pool of 4000 pounds (an assessment of about 66 pounds per proprietor) that would be shared by the first 20 proprietors who settled or had their right settled.[2] The township proprietors set specific standards that had to be met to qualify for payment. These included at least six acres felled of trees within one year; three acres of cleared land fit for planting or mowing within 16 months; and an 18' by 14' house suitable for dwelling within 20 months. Additionally, a proprietor or his hired settler had to live there for four years. Settlement standards were all to be met by the fall of 1765. Any interested proprietor was required to post a bond to support his commitment, promising to pay 30 pounds sterling if he did not comply with the terms.[3]

While this program was rolling out, Ebenezer Smith and another influential 'second proprietor,' William Mead, undertook the task of building the saw mill. Along with almost everything else in the new township, Smith was the driving force behind it. He personally hauled all of the iron for it from his home town of Exeter to New Salem. Thanks to his efforts, the saw mill was completed by mid-December 1765. Smith and Mead were given a three year contract to operate it.[4]

As a result of these steps, a nascent township with a dozen farms emerged in New Salem during 1765 and 1766. The first settlement undertakings were naturally modest. In September 1766, a committee of township proprietors reported on the progress of these first settlers.

---

[1] See Township Proprietors' Records, Sep 6, 1762, Dec 18, 1762 and Dec 14, 1763. On a side note, various publications about early Meredith erroneously locate the first saw mill at the Weirs channel. The error was apparently picked up from The History of Merrimack and Belknap Counties, edited by D. Hamilton Hurd, in 1885, p. 810. Interestingly, the correct location, at Laconia, is actually given in a separate chapter in the same volume of Hurd's history on p. 835.

[2] Proprietors' Records, Jan 2, 1764. Incentives like this were not unusual in convincing would be settlers to take the plunge. When response to the incentive program proved to be tepid, the proprietors voted to extend the time frame allowed for settlement for another year. Further, they voted to allocate 1000 pounds of the original 4000 pound incentive pool to be paid to 10 previously uncommitted proprietors who met the settlement criteria within 18 months of the meeting. Proprietors' Records, Oct 7, 1765.

[3] For example, see details in re a bond posted January 1764 by Daniel Gale: see "Meredith Town Records," Miscellaneous, 1754-1803, NH State Archives. Despite the bond, Gale's lot (D1/R6/L3) was not among those developed in the first wave.

[4] Proprietors' Records, Jan 6, 1766. Control of the saw mill was one of the few keys to wealth in the early settlements. Every new house was built out of boards cut at the mill. Smith and Mead received half of the lumber that was sawn there.

The table below lays out the details of the committee's findings against the criteria established by the incentive program:

#	Settler Name	Lot	House	Clear	Fell	Lot Proprietor/Owner
1	Abraham Folsom Jr. (son)	D1/Point/L14	Built	10 acres	3 acres	Abraham Folsom Sr. (2nd Proprietor)
2	James Quimby	D1/R3/L9	Built	3 acres	7-8 acres	Abraham Clark (Original Proprietor)
3	(Jacob) Eaton, wife, 7 children	D1/R2/L2	Built	3 acres	8-9 acres	Eliphalet Rawlings (Original Proprietor)
4	(Samuel) Torrey, wife, 6 children	D1/R1/L3	Built	3 acres	6 acres	Jonathan Shaw (Original Proprietor)
5	Robert Bryant	D1/R3/L4	Built; frame	3 acres	6 acres	Joseph Robinson (Original Proprietor)
6	(Ebenezer) Pitman	D1/R6/L5	Partly built	1/2 acres	5 acres	Samuel Goodhue (2nd Proprietor)
7	William Mead	D1/R5/L3	2 Built	6 acres	16 acres	William Mead (2nd Proprietor)
8	(Reuben) Marston Jr.	D1/R6/L8	Built	3 acres	6 acres	Josiah Sanborn (Original Proprietor)
9	George Bean, wife, children	D1/R6/L2	Partly built	3 clear	6 acres	Ebenezer Smith (2nd Proprietor.)
10	(Job) Judkins	D1/R6/L2		1 acre	6 acres	Ebenezer Smith (2nd Proprietor)
11	Ebenezer Smith and family	D1/Point/L10	2 houses; barn	1 8 acres	25 acres	Ebenezer Smith (2nd Proprietor.)
12	(Thomas) Danford	D1/Point/L7	Built	2 acres	6 acres	Ebenezer Smith (2nd Proprietor)

Among other things, the report underscores the leading role played by Ebenezer Smith. The amount of progress he had made by 1766 in clearing land and felling trees was far ahead of anyone else, reflecting his early and full commitment to New Salem. Not only had he relocated his own family, he had recruited three other men (Danford, Judkins and Bean) to develop other land rights that he had purchased.

This initial group of settlers did not include any 'original' or first township proprietors, but it did include two 'second' township proprietors, Ebenezer Smith and William Mead. Another settler, Abraham Folsom Jr., was the son of a 'second' township proprietor, Abraham Folsom Sr. Five Original Right holders hired men to settle their lands, while Ebenezer Smith hired three others to settle some of his other lands. Another 'second' township proprietor, Samuel Goodhue of Stratham[1], also hired someone to settle one of his lots. The standard arrangement in hiring

---

[1] Samuel Goodhue is an example of someone who bought in as a real estate speculator. He acquired several Original Rights in the 1760s and 1770s. In 1769, he sold the Division 1 lot to Ebenezer Pitman along with parts of Division 1 and Division 2 lots originally granted to Daniel Clark. See BCRI, B/P 1/128.

someone entailed the proprietor either giving or more often selling (usually years later at a very low cost) the hired settler 50 acres or more of land in exchange for his work.[1]

Robert Bryant was noteworthy among the men hired by a proprietor to open up New Salem. From the seacoast area town of New Market (originally part of Exeter) and only 22 years old, Bryant had somehow connected with Joseph Robinson, the Original Right holder of Lot 4 in the Third Range of Division 1 (D1/R3/L4). Robinson hired Bryant to settle his lot for him so he, Robinson, could earn the incentive. In exchange, Robinson agreed to sell Bryant half of his lots in the First and Second Division.[2] Bryant flourished in the new town, and as we shall see below, he became the first person to settle on Bear Island.

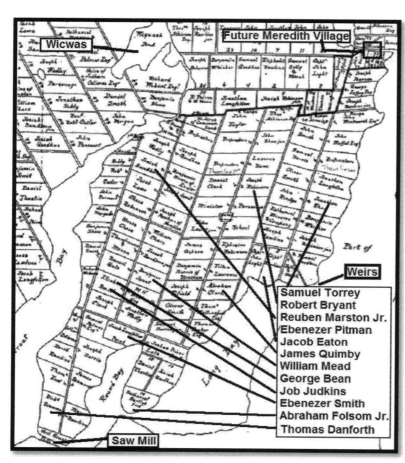

William Mead also stands out among the early settlers who had later ties to Bear Island. He had apparently purchased his proprietorship right in 1765.[3] He became one of the most important men, along with Ebenezer Smith, in developing the new town.[4] His sons and grandsons became large land holders on Meredith Neck. One son later owned the north end of Bear Island for a short period, and a great grandson owned a vacation place in the Carry during the early 1900s.[5]

Once the first homesteads were underway and the infrastructure was improved, the number of settlers in New Salem gradually increased. By mid-1768, there were "17 Families now

---

[1] **Note:** the blurred names in each lot on the map are those of the original township proprietors and Masonian proprietors who drew the lots in 1750. Only one of them, Chase Robinson, ever actually lived in the town. A number of them were already dead by the time the town was first settled in the 1760s and many others had long since dropped out of active participation in the goup..

[2] BCRI, B/P 1/120. The actual sale, as was typical for all 'hired' settlers, took place several years after settlement. In the case of Bryant, it was Joseph Robinson's son, Jonathan, who finally made good on the deal in December 1772 on behalf of his father who had passed away. The northern border of Bryant's D1 lot was not far from present day Roller Coaster Road.

[3] William Mead's name first appears in the Proprietors' Records on Oct 7, 1765.

[4] Among other things, he was voted Moderator at the town's first Annual Meeting in 1768.

[5] Another of the early settlers, Jacob Eaton, did not have any direct connections to Bear Island, but in later years his son also settled on Meredith Neck. His descendants became huge land holders in the area that includes Spindle Point. Eaton Avenue was named after his lineage.

resident…and four other Families (were) now preparing to go & reside there."[1] The total population of the town amounted to about 120 people. Despite this modest size, Ebenezer Smith and David Lawrence[2] petitioned the General Court for incorporation as a town. In December 1768, the Governor and Council approved the request for incorporation, but the Governor insisted upon calling the town 'Meredith' in honor of an influential friend and long-time member of the English parliament, Sir William Meredith, 3rd Baronet.[3]

Vignette

Early Settler Life

The challenge undertaken by these pioneers was daunting to say the least, but their hopes and dreams drove them. As young men, they surely viewed this as their best (if not their only) chance to establish their own farms and provide for the futures of their families. There were no shortcuts in the process. Like Ebenezer Smith a few years earlier, the pioneer settlers would have spent most of 1764-65 simply clearing the best pieces of land for farming on the 50-100 acre parcels they or the proprietors owned.[4] It was done inch by inch, tree by tree, and rock by rock. Along the way, their first steps undoubtedly included establishing small gardens and preparing small fields for crops and grazing. They also planted small orchards.

It was an arduous and lonely process. The settlers would have returned to their families back in their seacoast towns during the fall of 1764. In the spring of 1765, they would have returned to continue the work on the new homesteads. Once there was shelter and a small, operating farm, they would have been joined by their families. Since each farm was largely self-sufficient with regard to food and clothing, the added labor was was absolutely necessary to make life sustainable. The families would have worked individually much of the time, but a collective effort among neighboring farmers was necessary to complete such things as hauling logs and haying as well as building log homes, barns, and eventually houses.

In time, increasing numbers of farming families joined the first pioneer settlers. But even with increased numbers and the passage of time, the vast majority of farms remained small, family affairs. Planted fields and cleared pastures seldom exceeded five to 10 acres. The labor requirements would not permit anything more. Fields were planted with wheat, oats, rye, and other grasses. Gardens were planted with carrots, peas, lettuce, radishes, and onions. Potatoes and corn were other farming staples. All had to be hardy to withstand the vagaries of the

---

[1] Petition for Incorporation from Ebenezer Smith and David Lawrence, June 16, 1768, State Papers, Vol. 12, p. 582.

[2] David was a son or brother of the Original Township Proprietor, Tilton Lawrence.

[3] State Papers, Vol. 25, pp. 332-334. Sir William Meredith served in the House of Commons from 1754-1780. In 1768, he was a representative from Liverpool. Governor John Wentworth's connections to Meredith are not clear. Perhaps Wentworth saw Meredith as a supporter of colonial interests. For example, Meredith had voted against the Stamp Act in 1865. See: Sir William Meredith, ww.historyofparliamentonline.org. The primary benefit of incorporation as a town was that townspeople were now in charge of all decisions facing the town. Previously, these decisions rested with the township proprietors and the Masonian proprietors. The township proprietors were happy with the change because it meant they were no longer solely responsible for supporting the settlement financially and they no longer were beholden to the Masonians.

[4] It is said that the early farmers could determine the best quality soil by the types of trees that were found there.

weather, and farmers faced the constant challenge of timing their planting and harvesting times. The chores that accompanied the annual farming cycle were unrelenting. Among them, there was spring tilling and planting followed by multiple summer harvests, regular weeding, haying, mowing, raking, forking, and threshing, all of which carried through the fall.[1]

"The dull routine of work in which their lives…were passed"[2] could only be accomplished by many hands dividing up the labor and providing assistance to one another. Women's lives were consumed by an innumerable array of chores that never ceased. These included (but were hardly limited to) cooking, cleaning, spinning, weaving, making clothes, knitting stockings, cobbling shoes, and making candles as well as tending gardens, caring for the few animals each owned, and preserving foods for the winter, not to mention raising the children. Men were occupied with work in the fields that perpetually dominated a farmer's calendar from spring planting through fall harvests. Children were all required to help and even take responsibility for as much as possible. The work never ended.

During the winter months, the primary focus of the men was cutting wood. In those days, wood was perhaps second in importance only to food when it came to survival. Wood supply was one of two reasons early farms were so large.[3] One could not endure without a constant supply. Access to wood was an overriding concern of New Hampshire settlers through most of the 1800s. Most important, wood was the settler's sole source of heat and energy for cooking. There was a never ending demand for cord wood. All early houses and barns were made of wood. It was also used for just about everything else. All wagons and tools were made of wood. The by-products of wood—especially potash and pearl ash—were important necessities for making soap, baking goods, dyes, and gunpowder among other things. Timber (for boards) was a major trading product, while potash and pearl ash were also useful trading commodities in an economic system that was largely driven by barter.

During the early years in New Salem, goods that were not locally produced were quite scarce. Things such as salt, sugar, molasses, spice, and especially rum only sporadically made their way north with itinerant traders or as a result of rare visits to the seacoast by settlers. In the absence of these things, the early settlers turned to hard apple cider and maple syrup to sooth their aching limbs, sweeten their meals, and numb their minds.

Life was indeed challenging for them all. But this was the world they inhabited. They chose the challenge and labored long and hard to make the best of it.

---

[1] There are many sources of information about the farming cycle. One that is locally rooted is Early New England Farming: Tools and Techniques, Harold Wyatt, Meredith Historical Society (1999)
[2] Ethel S. Bolton, Farm Life a Century Ago, (1909), at babel.hathitrust.org.
[3] The other reason was that it required a big enough parcel within which to find sufficient cultivatable land given the relative inhospitality of New Hampshire's terrain .

Chapter Five

The Growth of Meredith: 1769 - 1800

By the end of 1769, the key ingredients for additional growth in Meredith were in place. There were 29 separate homesteads in various stages of development in the new town. The saw mill was well established at Meredith Bridge, and a grist mill was in place along the outlet stream of Lake Wicwas at what became known as Meredith Center.[1] There was also a small network of roads that traversed the First Division and led into the Second Division. At this point, however, almost all of the settlement had occurred in the First Division, with the primary exception of the grist mill.

While the township was poised for further growth, the possibility of expansion into the Second and Third Divisions was still constrained because the lots in those two divisions had not actually been laid out on the ground. Jonathan Longfellow's original surveys in the early 1750s had defined the outside boundaries on the ground, but his division of the lots was only a paper exercise (and a very inaccurate one, at that). Thus in June of 1768, the proprietors voted to send a committee led by Ebenezer Smith and William Mead to resurvey the Second and Third Divisions. Their work was completed by early 1770.

The resurvey resulted in some major changes in the layout of both divisions. Among other things, the size of the lots in the two divisions was flip flopped. In 1753, Longfellow had assumed 125 acre lots in the Third Division and 80 acre lots in the Second Division. When Smith and Mead remapped the area, the Third Division lots were reduced to 95 acres each, and the Second Division lots were increased to 120 acres each. In addition, the irregularities of the shorelines around lakes Winnipesaukee and Waukewan (then called Measley Pond) resulted in several Third Division lots being smaller than the standard of 95 acres per lot declared, leading Smith and Mead to create seven "addition lots" or "amendment lots" from the common lands (i.e. unassigned proprietors' land) in what became Meredith Village. In 1770, the latter area was just uninhabited land.[2]

More interestingly, Smith and Mead changed the ownership of every lot except one in the Second and Third Divisions from the initial lot drawing that had occurred in 1754 (i.e. the original names were all the same but their lot assignments were almost all different). The rationale for this de facto 'redrawing' is not known, but it is conceivable that Smith and Mead orchestrated the changes in a case of enlightened self-interest. The two men were the unquestioned leaders of the new town. The changes gave them an opportunity to control some of the parcels critical to the growth of the town. Perhaps the best example of this was Smith gaining ownership of

---

[1] As early as 1764 the township proprietors voted to build a grist mill on the outlet stream between Wicwas and Winnisquam. Like the other slow developing initiatives, it was not completed until 1769. In colonial times, a grist mill and a saw mill were the sine qua non of settlement.
[2] The errors and omissions in Longfellow's 1753 survey map suggest that he might have purposely distorted it to ensure approval of his request for additional lands by the Masonians.

Addition Lot 20 in what became Meredith Village. The lot controlled the stream running from Lake Waukewan to Lake Winnipesaukee, conferring the critical water rights to Smith for future exploitation.

The revised plan was approved by the township proprietors who by this time had fully hitched their wagons to whatever Ebenezer Smith wanted. Smith took the new plan to Portsmouth where it was approved by the Masonian Proprietors.[1]

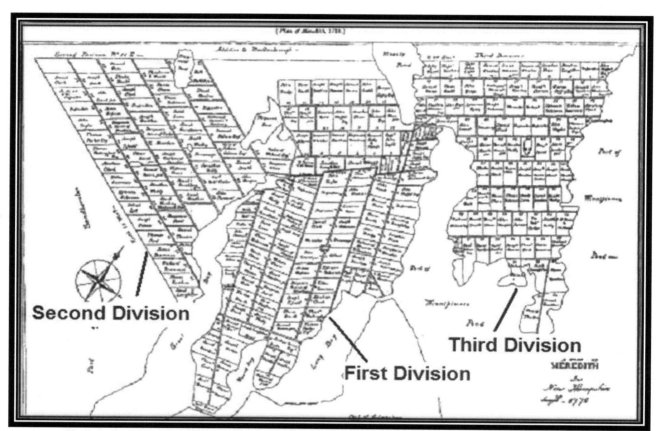

Ebenezer Smith's 1770 Division and Lot Plan of Meredith.[2]

With the new plan in place, settlers moved into the new town in increasing numbers. The growth in Meredith was part of a colony-wide phenomenon. The entire province had entered a period of extremely rapid population growth after the end of the French and Indian War in 1763. In large part this was fueled by a substantial migration of farmers from the larger colonies south of New Hampshire, coupled with continued natural growth.

---

[1] Proprietors Meeting, June 1770. The Masonians were not going to quibble with Ebenezer Smith about his changes. The town was established and growing which meant the Masonians had some prospect of reaping benefits from it.

[2] Each lot in divisions two and three contains a number from 1 through 82 and the name of its owner. The names were the same as those who originally drew lots in 1749, i.e. they included the original 60 township proprietors and the original 15 Masonian lots. By 1770, many of those people were dead and their rights to Meredith lots had been inherited by others or sold to others, including people such as Ebenezer Smith.

Population Growth: 1770 - 1800[1]

Date	1770	1775	1790	1800
New Hampshire	52,000*	82,000	141,000	183,000
Meredith	128	259	881	1609

*Figure actually for 1767

As the population increased, the settlers gradually began to establish farms in the Second and Third Divisions. Most of the initial wave of settler expansion in the Third Division occurred in the upper or northern half, encompassing lots one through 39. This area stretched east from Lake Waukewan to the township border with Moultonborough. Large portions of it consisted of good, relatively flat farmland. As early as 1773, there were enough settlers there that "a large number" of them petitioned Meredith town officials to have a road built from the Province Road in the First Division, through what later became Meredith Village, to "the dwelling house of Joseph Senter Esq." at what later became Center Harbor village.[2] By the end of the 1790s, 26 of the 39 lots were occupied by farmers.[3]

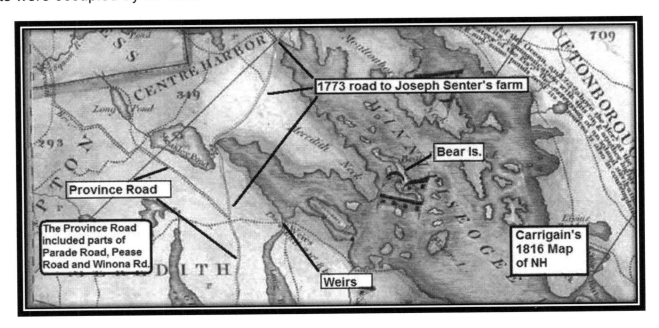

1773 road to Joseph Senter's farm
Bear Is.
Province Road
The Province Road included parts of Parade Road, Pease Road and Winona Rd.
Weirs
Carrigain's 1816 Map of NH

---

[1] For state totals, see, Gazetteer of 1817, p. 45. In re Meredith figures, 1770 total based upon: State Papers, vol. XXIX, pp. 395-397; other totals, see vol. VII, p. 753. The timing and extent of Meredith's growth were generally mirrored in all of the Lakes Region towns, whether Gilmanton, Sanbornton, Moultonborough or Wolfeboro. All of them went through the early formative stages during the 1760s or early 1770s before settlement really took off in the 1770s.

[2] Meredith Town Records, handwritten extracts of Vittum's Copy, December 1773, Meredith Historical Society. All of this territory belonged to Meredith in 1773, including half of the waterfront in today's Center Harbor village (Moultonborough owned the other half). Joseph Senter's farm, located behind where the Center Harbor library is located today, was not part of Meredith. It was part of the Moultonborough Addition (later New Hampton and later still part of the town of Center Harbor established in 1797) and bordered Meredith.

The new road followed the current Parade Road north, came down Ladd Hill and connected with Main St. in Meredith Village; it followed Main St. down the hill, turned left on to Plymouth St. and ran up to where the present Meredith Cemetery is located; it then turned east and connected with what is now True Rd.; it followed True Rd. to its current intersection with now Rte. 25 and then became Old Center Harbor Rd. near the Towle House; it continued to Senter's farm, entering that area where the main street runs today in front of the Center Harbor Town Hall and fire department. See: Road Histories of Meredith, NH by Harold Wyatt, 2004 for details on the various parts of this route.

[3] This is based upon a fairly comprehensive review of the deeds for each lot.

Early Settlement of lower Meredith Neck (Lots 40 – 82)

The completion of the road to Joseph Senter's place in 1774 also helped to open up the

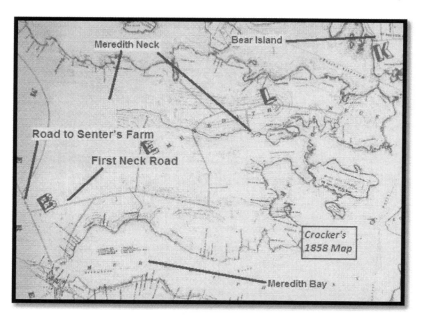

lower part of Meredith Neck (i.e. Third Division Lots 40 – 82). The path of the Neck road followed in close proximity the range way (now Barnard Ridge Road) that ran south between Neck Lots 36/37 and 40/41. This became the primary access route south to the lower Neck.[1]

Portions of the lower Neck were very attractive to the growing settler population, although like so many other places in the town, the desirability was diminished in places by natural impediments like Page Pond and its extensive flowage area as well as by Pinnacle Hill and other rocky terrain around the irregular shoreline.

Despite the improved access, there was almost no actual settlement undertaken on the lower Neck during the 1770s. Only Samuel Carr could be found on Lot 54 by 1774, and he was still in the initial phase of clearing it of trees. Carr's lot was located only a mile or so down the range way.[2] During the latter 1770s, little further expansion on the Neck occurred because almost all able bodied men had volunteered to fight in the Revolutionary War. The families of these men had all they could handle in keeping their existing farms going while the men were away.

During the 1780s, at least five additional settlers moved on to the lower Neck, and in the 1790s another eight or so joined them. These settlers represented the economic spectrum of Meredith inhabitants. On one end were the poorer colonists, similar to Carr, who were encouraged, or perhaps recruited, by Ebenezer Smith to settle on his lands in exchange for the opportunity later on to buy the lots or sell the improvements they made to the lots. These men included Phillip McCrillis, William Dockham and David Wiggin, all of whom settled on Lots 78 or 79.[3] On the other end of the spectrum were offspring of established settlers. William Mead Jr.

---

[1] It was not until 1833 that a road, now Pleasant Street, was built at the base of Meredith Bay and out to the Neck. The long period between the occupation of the Neck and the building of the road was due in large part to the quagmire that was Hawkins swamp at the base of Meredith bay. Winnipesaukee Street, across the base of the bay, was not built until the 1810 – 1820 period. Wyatt, p. 219. See Chapter 11 Vignette for more about the building of Pleasant Street and the Meredith Neck Bridge.

[2] BCRI, B/P 1/19. Not surprisingly, he had purchased the lot from Ebenezer Smith.

[3] BCRI, B/P 4/91; 4/122; 4/192; 4/123.

and Jacob Eaton Jr. staked out some of the best land on the Neck and ultimately acquired large land holdings with the help of their families.[1] Another early Neck settler was James Gilman who only arrived in town in 1789. He built his homestead on Lot 57. He prospered there and went on to become one of the wealthiest of all the residents on the Neck.[2] Decades later, members of his family became large land owners on Bear Island.[3]

Two other lower Neck settlers from this period are noteworthy. One was Chase Robinson who was the only original township proprietor to settle in Meredith. While his homestead farm was in the First Division (D1/R6/L6), he used his own Neck Lot 58 seasonally for grazing.[4] The other was Theophilus Dockham who was occupying part of Lot 76 in the mid-1790s.[5] He later had the misfortune of becoming a prisoner during the War of 1812 before returning to the Neck. His four children all subsequently played major roles during the farming era on Bear Island, although he himself had little involvement on it.[6]

By the mid–1790s then, there were more than a dozen families living on the lower Neck. At the time, there was a reasonable road that extended down the Barnard Ridge range way, past James Gilman's home on Lot 57, and then continued on to William Mead Jr.'s farm on Lot 67. In 1795, Neck residents petitioned the town to have the road extended further south on the range way between Lots 75 and 76. The work was undertaken and completed within a year or so, opening up more of the Neck to additional occupation. Nevertheless, the lowest end of the Neck

---

[1] BCRI, B/P 2/381. William Mead Jr. bought Lot 67 from his father in 1791, B/P 1/19. Jacob Eaton Jr. bought Lot 73 in 1794. Some early histories of Meredith list Jacob Eaton Sr. as one of the earliest settlers on the Neck. He in fact always lived in the First Division.

[2] B/P 2/169; 2/168. Gilman initially bought Lot 51 in 1789 but moved to Lot 57 in 1790.

[3] See below, Chapter 17, *Vignettes: The 1860s*.

[4] Robinson fought in the Revolution with the other Meredith men. Afterwards, he played a very prominent role in town politics.

[5] See Town Records, Nov 1795. There is no deed showing a purchase by him. He was probably encouraged to occupy the land by Ebenezer Smith. His presence there is noted in the discussion of an extension of the Neck Road. See Meredith Records, Nov 1795.

[6] Some histories erroneously mention him as one of the earliest settlers on Bear Island. He lived on the island only for a brief period in the late 1840s and/or early 1850s.

(Lots 76 -82) was still largely unoccupied in 1800.[1] Not surprisingly, just a little way across the water from the lower Neck, Bear Island also remained unoccupied.

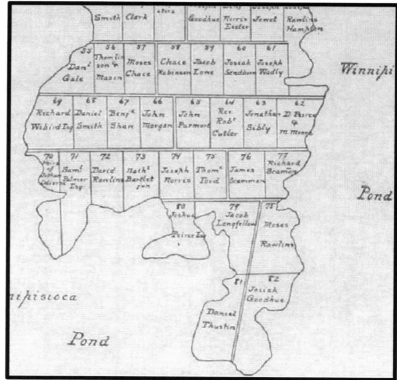

Lower end of Meredith Neck on the 1770 survey. Lots 78 and 82 faced Bear Island. The names listed on the survey are those of the original township proprietors who drew those lots. Moses Rawlins owned the 'original right' to Lot 78 and Josiah Goodhue had the 'original right' to Lot 82.

Vignette

The Settlement of Meredith Village

The area that became Meredith Village was initially made accessible by the new road completed in 1774 to Joseph Senter's farm on the Moultonborough border. But the area did not attract any inhabitants until the 1780s.[2] It did not make for good farm land, nestled as it was among the hills, bookended by Lakes Waukewan and Winnipesaukee, and bordered at the head of the bay by the largely impassable Hawkins swamp.[3]

---

[1] Lots 76-82 were unoccupied except for three 'tenants' on Lots 78 and 79 who did not own the land. The early ownership trail of these lots is very difficult to track. It is telling that Ebenezer Smith owned Lots 76, 77, 78, and 82 before his death in 1807. Lots 77, 78, and 82 all faced Bear Island. Cattle Landing was part of Lot 82. The lowest end of the Neck, Lots 81 and 82, were not purchased by local farmers until 1817 and 1818. Lot 80 was still in the hands of the heirs of the Original Right holder until 1822. ·

[2] By the early 1780s, only one Asa Foster apparently was squatting along the outlet stream that connected Lake Waukewan to Winnipesaukee. See John Jenness to Samuel Jenness in 1792, regarding Amendment Lot 20. BCRI, B/P 5/80.

[3] At the time, the base of Meredith Bay was a quagmire. Access across it was not accomplished until the first two decades of the 19th century. The swamp is still quite visible behind the buildings and shopping mall near the base of Meredith Bay and along Rte. 25.

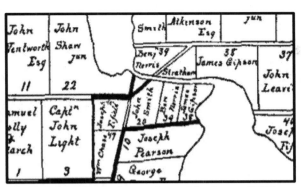

Meredith Village Amendment Lots on 1770 survey.

By the 1780s, the lots that comprised the eventual core Meredith Village area had been acquired by Ebenezer Smith who recognized the strategic value of its water power. Smith took the first substantive step in developing the village area in 1787 when he sold the 40 acre Amendment Lot 20 to John Jenness. With the help of Smith, Jenness became the first developer of the future Meredith Village. From the outset, the two men planned to build mills along the stream between the two lakes.[1] A saw mill was in operation by 1788, although it was actually built on the northern side of the stream on Amendment Lot 38 that was still owned by Smith. Jenness built his home and barn on Lot 38 as well.[2] He did not actually buy the lot from Smith until years later. By 1792, Jenness also built a grist mill nearby.[3] These were the first substantive steps in the development of what became Meredith Village.

---

[1] BP 3/606; 2/499. In his deed of sale to Jenness, Smith retained one half part of the saw mill rights. Smith's prominence in developing the mill there was evident from a 1788 petition from Third Division farmers who referred to this area as "Col Smith's Mill". See State Papers, Vol. 11, pp. 276-277, Petition for Incorporation.

[2] The house and mills were located along today's Lang St., up behind the town fire department.

[3] BCRI, B/P 2/515, E. Smith to J. Jenness, Sep 1795.

Part II:

The

Farming Era

On

Bear Island

Chapter Six

The First Farmers on Bear Island

Before 1800, the islands of Lake Winnipesaukee were hardly considered of any value. But they did not go entirely unnoticed during the early years of colonial expansion in New Hampshire. In 1727, for example, the provincial Assembly voted to have a survey undertaken of the islands, although nothing ever came of the vote until 1745 when one Tim Clements undertook the task.[1] His work was probably commissioned in conjunction with the building of Fort Atkinson in Tilton during the French and Indian War.[2]

The following year, the Masonian Proprietors became the owners of record of the islands when they completed the purchase of John Mason's patent. But the islands were not a priority of the Masonians, since they had some two million acres of mainland to be allocated.[3] When it came time to parcel out townships, the islands were such an afterthought that they were not included in any of the tracts of land granted to the new townships around the lake. They remained separate entities unto themselves. Finally in 1750, the Masonians took brief notice of them and voted that all of the islands should at least be allocated amongst themselves.[4] Yet once again there was no follow up on this resolution.

It was not until 1770 that the Masonians again took up the question of establishing individual ownership of the islands. They commissioned another survey of them, this time to be undertaken by James Hersey, one of the earliest settlers of Sanbornton.[5] The issue had been pushed to the forefront after the new Provincial Governor, now John Wentworth, established an estate, called Kings Wood, in the area that became the town of Wolfeboro in 1767.[6] He had also taken a fancy to Governors Island which, back in the 1720s, had apparently been promised to his grandfather, then Governor John Wentworth. To assuage the Governor, the Masonian Proprietors granted Governors Island to John Wentworth in 1772 under the rationale that he had "greatly encouraged and promoted the Settlement of the Lands about said [Winnipesaukee] Pond…" [7]

Hersey's survey and map later became the basis for the future allocation of the islands among the Masonian Proprietors. His work also included giving names to eight of the larger

---

[1] State Papers, Vol. 4, p. 477; Vol. 18, pp. 421-422.
[2] No report of Clements' findings was found in the records.
[3] The total land area of New Hampshire is 5.75 million acres, so the Masonians controlled about 35% of the total. Of course, in those days, Governor Wentworth claimed that the future state of Vermont was part of New Hampshire.
[4] State Papers, Vol. 29, p. 439.
[5] The Hersey Mountain Forest in Sanbornton was named after this family.
[6] John Wentworth had acceded to the Governorship in 1766, replacing his uncle Benning Wentworth (Governor from 1741-1766). John was the son of the Masonian Proprietor, Mark Hunking Wentworth, and the grandson of the colonial NH Lieutenant Governor, John Wentworth, who oversaw the colony from 1723 – 1730. Prior to taking over as Governor in 1766, John Wentworth was an original township proprietor of Wolfeboro, a township first granted by the Masonians in 1759.
[7] State papers, Vol. 29, p. 553. Of note, Governor Wentworth never actually did anything with Governors Island.

islands.[1] He was the man who bestowed the name of Bear Island. It derived from an encounter that he and his party had with several bears there during the surveying expedition. Little else is known about his trip to the lake other than the map he made.[2]

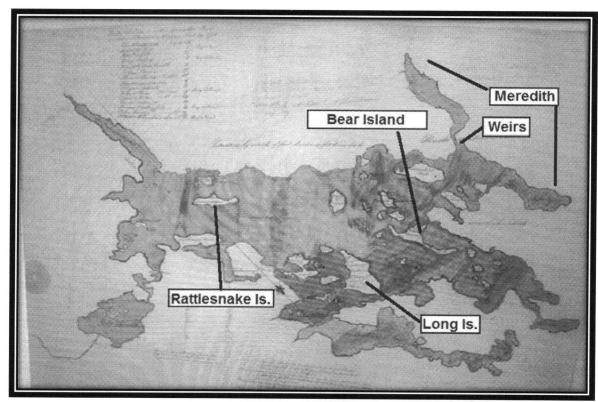

Copy of Hersey's 1772 map of Winnipesaukee.[3]

Despite Hersey's survey, the Masonians still did not immediately address the issue of allocating ownership of the islands. Finally, in 1781, they got around to dividing them amongst themselves. The 35 largest islands were separated into 15 lots, mirroring the original 15 shares established by the Masonians for lot drawings in 1748. The largest islands such as Bear, Cow, Rattlesnake, and Long Island were split into more than one lot, while the smaller islands were grouped into various other lots. The plan was designed so that the Masonian Proprietors would own about 225 acres each.

Bear Island was divided into two lots, numbered 10 and 11. The heirs of Theodore Atkinson, drawing lot #11, received ownership of the northern end of the island and part of the southern end, and the heirs of Thomas Packer, drawing #10, received the rest of the southern end of the island.[1] This formal allocation of ownership among the Masonians, however,

---

[1] Of the eight islands named, only four retain those names today. They are Bear, Long, Mark, and Rattlesnake. Three of the other four were changed and the other one was later given to another island.

[2] Edgar H. Wilcomb, Out-Door Life in New Hampshire, "How Big Bear Got Its Name," c. 1923, pp. 32-35; Boston Globe, Aug 21, 1936. There is an occasionally repeated story that the island was named in the mid-1800s after two Neck farmers got into a fight with bears on the island. See, for example: Old Meredith and Vicinity, p. 94; and The Lakes Region NH, A Visual History, p.49. The story of the fight was probably true. Both men involved owned property on Bear for awhile. But the island's name was given to it in 1772.

[3] True copy was made in the mid-1800s. Map held in the NH State Archives.

however, did not change anything on the ground in the near term. In 1781, there were still too few settlers and too much other land to make Bear or the other islands of any interest.

A big part of the reason for the disinterest was that, despite being allocated among the Masonians, the islands were still not incorporated into any of the towns that had been granted around the lake. The neglect finally came to a head in 1799 when their orphan status reached the level of state politics. The issue might have been prompted by Eleazer Davis of Alton who purchased Governors Island that year. The New Hampshire Assembly stepped in and allocated six of the largest islands to the nearest towns. Legislators probably recognized that island farmers could not be taxed if they were not part of a local municipality. Governors Island became part of Gilmanton. Bear and Stonedam were annexed to Meredith. In addition, Long Island was incorporated into Moultonborough; Cow became part of Tuftonboro; and Barndoor Island was tied to Alton.[2]

While the state action established municipality, it did not change the legal ownership of the land on the islands. Theodore Atkinson's right on Bear was inherited by his cousin, George King Sparhawk. The right of Thomas Packer was inherited by his widow, Molly Packer. In 1796, she sold her interest in Bear to John Peirce, who subsequently sold half of it to Nathaniel Appleton Haven. All three of these men (Sparhawk, Peirce, and Haven) were highly successful Portsmouth residents with familial ties to the Masonian Proprietors.

Of the three, Nathaniel Appleton Haven had the biggest impact on the settlement of Bear. Born in 1762, he was a physician and merchant who had served as a ship's surgeon during the Revolutionary War. He had graduated from Harvard in 1779 and later was elected to the United States House of Representatives in 1810. He used his family's ties and his own skills to acquire various 'original rights' from the heirs of Masonian Proprietors who passed away.[3]

Bear, of course, was still unsettled by colonists at the time Haven, Sparhawk, and Peirce acquired ownership of it. Moreover, it had probably not been settled by anyone for many, many decades (if ever). It had surely attracted Native American hunting parties, and fishermen certainly plied the waters around it. Undoubtedly, there were parties that had periodically camped on the island for relatively short stays. But in the vast expanse of New Hampshire, Native Americans found far better lands for farming, far better places for fishing (i.e. the Weirs), and far larger tracts for hunting.

---

[1] See State Papers, Vol. 29, unnumbered page found between pp. 585-586.
[2] Laws of New Hampshire, Vol. 6, Second Constitutional Period 1792-1801, pp. 620-621(State Archives). Governors Island later became part of Gilford when it was subdivided from Gilmanton until 1812.
[3] As an entrepreneur, Nathaniel Haven was involved in a diverse range of interests throughout New Hampshire. In 1817 and 1818, for example, he purchased ownership shares in the Meredith Cotton and Woolen Factory that was built by Stephen Perley in Laconia around 1811. See, Meredith Cotton and Woolen Record Book, (Meredith Historical Society).

The Purchase of Bear Island, 1801

The neglect of Bear Island came to an end in October 1801. Robert Bryant, one of the founding settlers of Meredith, purchased the island in separate transactions from Sparhawk and Peirce/Haven. Bryant paid the former $200.00 for an estimated 176 acres, and he paid the latter $850.00 for an estimated 200 acres on the southern end.[1] The specifics of these transactions are confusing. First, the island in total actually amounts to some 780 acres of land, so the deeds' reference of 376 acres, based upon Hersey's 1772 survey, account for less than half of the total.[2] The extent of the shortfall in estimated acreage suggests that Hersey never actually completed a full survey of the island, probably due to being distracted by the encounter with the bears. Second, the payment to Peirce/Haven was three times the amount paid to Sparhawk, although the acreage on the map was only 14% more. The premium is perhaps attributable to the awareness of Haven and Peirce of the actual size of the island as well as the recognition that the southern end of Bear had far more favorable farming land.

Bryant's purchase had another important aspect to it as well. He simultaneously took an $850.00 mortgage loan on the island from Peirce and Haven. The loan consisted of three notes each to Peirce and Haven payable over three years in amounts ranging from $100.00 to $200.00 each year. Significantly, all six of the notes were co-signed by another First Division settler, John Bickford.[3] John Bickford's family came to play a predominant role on Bear during the 19th century.

Robert Bryant

In 1770, Robert Bryant was living on his First Division farm with his wife, Joanna Stevens Bryant, and their two sons, John (born 1769) and Robert Jr. (born c. 1770). A third child, Dorothy ("Dolly"), was born about 1777. The farm was located not too far from the intersection of Parade Road (Rte 106) and Roller Coaster Road. It was Bryant's 'homestead' in Meredith. In subsequent years, he bought and sold other acreage nearby, but he always lived on the original farm until he moved to Bear Island.[4]

In 1776, Bryant had joined with virtually every other able bodied townsman to fight in the Revolutionary War. He rose to the rank of Ensign, a rank adopted from the English military and akin to sergeant and standard-bearer. Bryant was engaged on at least two occasions during the Revolution, including the battles of Bennington and Saratoga in 1777.[5] After the war, Bryant

---

[1] B/P 37/335 and 37/336. Original copies of these deeds are located at the New Hampshire Historical Society, Peirce Papers, Box 22. Transcribed copies can also be found at the Strafford Registry in Dover. Neither can be found online as both were omitted from the online deeds accessible through the Belknap County Registry of Deeds.

[2] This acreage total appears on the map used by the Masonians when they drew their island lots. The discrepancy accounts for why Bear was only divided into two lots while Long Island, which at 1186 acres is only 52% bigger than Bear, was divided into five lots. Of course, one can readily appreciate the challenges of getting accurate measurements in those days.

[3] SCR, B/P 37/271

[4] BCRI, B/P 3/601. When he sold it in 1802, Bryant described the place as "the whole of my homestead farm on which I now live."

[5] State Papers, Vol. 14, pp. 15, 296, 432; Vol. 15, pp. 163, 171; Vol. 17, p. 215. See also, Vol. 30, p. 93 for a list of those from Meredith, including Bryant, who signed the 1776 loyalty oath, termed the "Association Test".

returned to Meredith and played an active role in town governance. Among other things, he was elected by residents to serve as auditor and as assessor in the 1770s and 1780s. In the 1790s and early 1800s, he was elected to the office of "fish warden" on at least five separate occasions.[1]

It was perhaps his fish warden duties that led to Bryant's initial intrigue with Bear Island. He may have begun scouting the island during the late 1790s. By 1800, he probably had made the decision to move there. Drawing on his earliest New Salem experience, he perhaps spent some of 1800 and 1801 starting the clearing process on the island. Even while wintering at his mainland home, he would have returned to the island throughout the year to continue the process. In fact it was easier for him and his sons to travel across the ice during the winter months to continue the clearing. His motivation for moving to the island is unknown. He may have discovered, after some 35 years of farming the same land, that he had exhausted the soil of his farm and needed fresh lands. With the rapid population growth of Meredith during the 1780s and 1790s gobbling up available lots, perhaps he identified Bear as having the best remaining farmland at a reasonable cost.

Bryant (now 57) probably relocated permanently to the island not long after he purchased it in October of 1801. Less than three months later, in January 1802, he sold his First Division homestead farm and his other mainland pasture for $700.00.[2] Bryant settled on the southern section of Bear that is now known as Dolly's Point. This area had a large swath of good farmland,[3] and it was the closest part of the island to Meredith Neck. Initially, he built a small cabin on the point.[4] Subsequently, according to oral tradition, he built a more elaborate house located on the highest point on that end of the island. This is the spot where the St. John's on-the-Lake Chapel now stands.[5] Bryant's well, still in good shape today, is is

Robert Bryant's well.

---

[1] See Meredith annual meeting records for 1779, 1786, 1794, 1797, 1799, 1800, 1801, and 1802.

[2] BCRI, B/P 9003/601. An 1851 article suggests that Bryant moved to the island in 1804. "Bear Island-Aunt Dolly," Boston Evening Transcript, July 28, 1851, p. 1

[3] An outside observer noted in 1858, for example, that "the soil (on Bear Island) is very good, and its crops are said to average better than corresponding acres on the main; often yielding fifty bushels of shelled corn to the acre." "Picnic on Bear Island," Independent Democrat (Concord, NH), September 16, 1858, p. 3.

[4] "Bear Island-Aunt Dolly," Boston Evening Transcript, July 28, 1851, p. 1.

[5] Letter, Hugh Kelsea to Nathaniel Haven and the heirs of John Peirce, 1819. Peirce Family papers, box 22, New Hampshire Historical Society. Kelsea's report on island inhabitants, as well as later deeds, clearly show that Bryant settled on the south end of the island. Oral histories maintain that Bryant settled on the highest spot on the island. The Chapel location is the high spot on the southern end. Early historians

found about a quarter mile down the hill from his likely old home site.

Robert Bryant settled on the island with his wife, Joanna, and probably his son, Robert Jr. (c. 34). By this time, the latter was married to Abigail Bickford and had a young daughter, Nancy. In addition, Robert Sr. and wife may have had other children living with them. The 1800 census shows that there were seven youngsters in their household, two boys under the age of nine, and two boys and three girls aged 16 to 25. None of these youngsters were the children of Robert and Joanna; but it is likely that they were Bryants.[1]

Meanwhile, Bryant's other two children, John and Dolly, remained on the mainland. John owned his own farm in the First Division where he became a solid member of the community.[2] Dolly had married Joseph Nichols, but almost nothing is known about them during these early years.

John Bickford

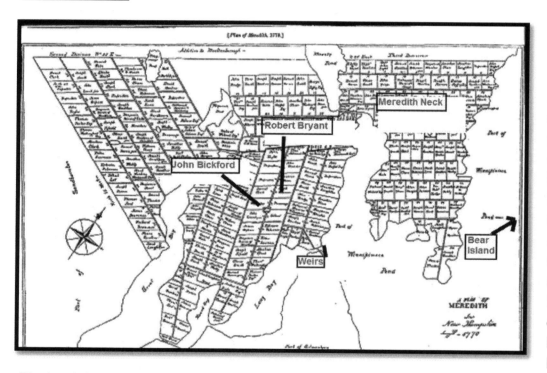

Robert Bryant's partner in the Bear Island venture was John Bickford, the co-signer of Bryant's mortgage notes in October 1801. Bryant had known the Bickfords for at least a decade. Born 1742, John Bickford was about the same age as Robert Bryant, but he had not been one of the early arrivals in Meredith. John Bickford and his wife, Phebe Johnson, were Epsom residents who moved to Meredith around the mid-1790s.[3] In 1799, John Bickford purchased a First Division lot (D1/R1/L5) along the shore of Meredith Bay, across from Pinnacle Hill on Meredith Neck.[4] This became his homestead farm.

---

assumed erroneously that the spot chosen by Bryant was on the north end near where the old hotel was later located. See, for example, Old Meredith and Vicinity, p. 94.

[1] This is suggested by the multitude of Bryant women who later married Bear Islanders from the Nichols and Bickford families.

[2] BCRI, B/P 9001/614; 9003/333. John's homestead was on D1/R3/L2, the Original Right of John Shaw Jr.

[3] BCRI, B/P 9003/241. John Bickford's first identifiable land purchase in Meredith occurred in 1796, a small strip of the Ministerial lot in the First Division.

[4] BCRI, 9003/285. Lot 5 was located just north of the long established, former Longridge Farm (now Picnic Rock Farms) on US Route 3 in Meredith.

The Bickford's had four children. Their daughter, Eleanor (b. 1770), had established the first connection between the Bickfords and the Bryants in 1791 when she married Robert's oldest son, John, while the family was still living in Epsom. Eleanor relocated to Meredith after the wedding.[1] Two of the Bickford's three sons, John Jr. (b. 1768) and Eleazer (b. 1780), came to Meredith with their parents c. 1795. Their oldest son, Jonathan (b. 1766), moved to Meredith in 1797, when he purchased a First Division farm along Meredith Bay.[2]

John Bickford never personally moved permanently to Bear Island, but he clearly had some specific plans in mind when he co-signed Bryant's mortgage notes. It is likely that he viewed the island as an opportunity for his sons to establish their own farms.

The Lives of the First Farmers on Bear Island

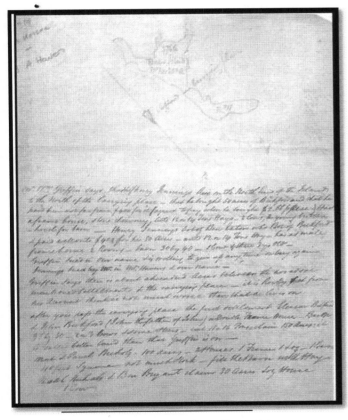

Lamentably, there is almost no information about what happened on Bear Island during the first seventeen years after Robert Bryant purchased it. It was not until 1819, when a Center Harbor surveyor named Hugh Kelsea was sent to the island, that a firsthand report was given about the farmers there.[3]

Hugh Kelsea's Report. Note the faint sketch of Bear at the top.

At the time of Kelsea's visit, he found seven distinct farms there. Two of these farms were located on the northern end, and the other five were on the southern section. The two farms on the northern end were occupied by Henry Jenness and William Griffin. Jenness was located on the northern-most end where the hotel was eventually built. Griffin was

---

[1] Epsom Genealogical website at *Epsomhistory.com*.
[2] BCRI, B/P 9002/619. The farm purchased by his parents in 1799 was next door.
[3] Report of Hugh Kelsea to Nathaniel Haven and John Peirce heirs, undated (1819) and unsigned, Peirce Papers, Box 22, New Hampshire Historical Society. Kelsea was a prominent person in Center Harbor, among other things serving as a Selectman and Clerk after the incorporation of the town in 1797. Kelsea Avenue in Center Harbor is named after his family. See Center Harbor, (15th Anniversary publication), p. 9. Kelsea's 1819 report was unquestionably written by him when he was hired that year by Nathaniel Haven and the heirs of John Peirce to survey and lay out lots on the island. The Kelsea report provides us with a baseline from which we can speculate about what may have happened during the previous years. In the almost two decades following Bryant's 1801 purchase, there are no first hand records indicating who was on the island, much less where, when or why. But there are snippets of information that give us some insights into this puzzle (such as census, birth, death, and marriage reports). Seventeen years is a long time, and the picture undoubtedly changed with some frequency as individuals and/or families moved on to and off of the island. Some of this movement was probably seasonal, as all Meredith farmers maintained summer grazing pastures apart from their homestead farms. Some of the movement was permanent, resulting from the natural ebb and flow of families as children were born, grew up, married, and moved; or as some may have decided the island just was not their cup of tea. Unfortunately there are huge gaps in our understanding, mysteries that perhaps will find some light of day in the future.

located just south of Jenness, encompassing an area that would have included Sunset Rock. To the south of Griffin and all of the way to the Carry, the island was uninhabited. Griffin told Kelsea that he had purchased his farm from John Bickford, and he said that Jenness had purchased his from Benjamin Eaton who had previously purchased it from John Bickford.

The farms of the two men were substantial, suggesting that they had lived there for some years. Jenness claimed some 50 acres. According to Kelsea, he had built a small frame house with two rooms; had built a barn that was 30 feet by 40 feet; annually cut 12 to 14 tons of hay; and had one cow and three other cattle. Griffin also claimed 50 acres for his farm. He had built a frame house with a stone chimney; had a "hovel" (an open shed) for a barn; cut 12-14 tons of hay; and had two cows and a couple of other stock animals.

There is very little additional information about either of these men. Henry Jenness was an established farmer in Meredith by 1808. In December of that year, he paid John Roberts $700 for 85 acres of Neck Lot 64 (known later as Boardman Hill and the Meetinghouse lot). In that transaction, he also acquired an adjoining 25 acres on Lot 76. The 1810 census listed him as head of a family of four. Henry farmed Lot 64 until 1814. By June of that year, he was apparently experiencing financial difficulties. He borrowed a combined $288.80 from two mortgage lenders, securing the loans with his farm. He sold Lot 64 in December 1814 presumably to pay off his debts. He likely moved out to Bear in the spring of 1815, using the net proceeds from the sale of his farm to buy the property.[1]

There is even less information about William Griffin. William was probably living on Bear in 1810, as the census of that year, organized geographically, lists him just after Robert Bryant Jr. and various Neck families. At the time, William had a wife and family of three boys and one girl. His forebears are unknown. There were only a couple of Griffins in early Meredith. One, Jeremiah Griffin, was a Revolutionary soldier from Chester, New Hampshire, who fought with Meredith men during the war. He moved up to Meredith after the conflict was over. William was perhaps a son.

On the southern section of the island, Kelsea found five separate farms. The occupants included people from three extended families: the Bryants, the Bickfords, and the Nichols. Moving geographically southwards, Kelsea identified the first farm, said to be 150 acres, as

---

[1] BCRI, B/P 9007/253; 9006/610; 9006/611; 9005/332. The Jenness name is well known in the annals of Meredith history. There were several Jenness families who lived on the upper Neck and near Meredith Village. Jenness Hill Road was named after members of the family. John Jenness was the settler who built the first saw mill and grist mill in what became Meredith Village in the latter 1780s. Very little is also known about Benjamin Eaton, reported to have sold the land on north Bear to Henry Jenness. The Eaton family had a heavy presence on Meredith Neck dating to the 1790s, but Benjamin did not appear to be closely associated with them. In 1812, he was one of 30 First Division farmers who petitioned the state Assembly for permission to build a wing dam at the Weirs. He only appears in the deeds in a back-to-back real estate deal in 1817 in which he bought part of Neck Lot 65 from John Eaton for $150.00 and sold it two days later for $200.00. Similar to the latter transaction, one might presume he purchased part of North Bear Island from John Bickford and quickly sold it to Henry Jenness. He was perhaps one of the many settlers who were real estate investors that took advantage of situations as they presented themselves. In any case, there is nothing to suggest that he actually lived out on the island.

belonging to John Bickford (c. 77 years old) and his son, Eleazer (then about 40). Next to them, he found Paul Nichols (c. 56) and his son, Nathaniel (c. 23), who claimed 100 acres. Nearby, Noah Nichols and Benjamin Bryant had settled on 30 acres. At the far end of the island (the Camp Lawrence area), John Bickford's oldest son, Jonathan Sr. (c. 51), had laid claim to 50 acres. And finally, Robert Bryant (c. 75) and his son, Robert Jr. (c. 49), claimed 100 acres on the crown of the southern end, extending westerly toward Meredith Neck (later known as Dolly's Point).

Most of these farms were also well established but with some interesting distinctions.

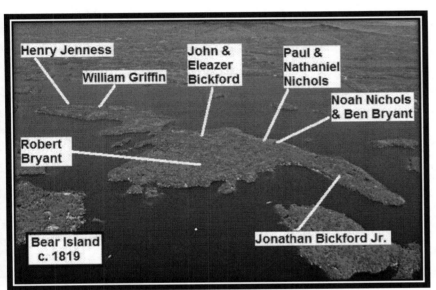

John and Eleazer Bickford had built a barn that was 36' by 30'; had two or three cows and some steers; and had cut 15-16 tons of hay. But interestingly, there is no report of a house, an omission found nowhere else among the Bear settlers. This indicates that they used the island for seasonal purposes only. In contrast, the farm of Paul and Nathaniel Nichols included two houses—one frame and one log; a 40' square barn; enough hay to fill the barn; but not much stock. Their near neighbors, Noah Nichols and Ben Bryant, were reported as having only a log house and one cow to show for themselves.[1] A little further south, Jonathan Bickford Sr. had only a log house, a log barn, and one cow. Robert Bryant and his son, Robert Jr., on the other hand, were reported as having a good house, a 30' by 36' barn, considerable hay, and four cows. The better quality of the house suggests that they had been on the island longer than any of the others.

Very little is known about the occupants of the smallest farm, Benjamin Bryant and Noah Nichols. Both disappeared from the records after 1819. Benjamin Bryant was assuredly related to Robert Bryant. He, or perhaps his father, was listed in the 1790 Meredith census, but he was not listed in either the 1800 or 1810 census. He also does not appear in any real estate transactions. Like the northern end settlers, he too apparently moved out of Meredith shortly after Kelsea's visit. Of Noah Nichols, we only know that he was living on Bear in 1818-1819. His relationship to Paul Nichols is unknown. Presumably still a young man, Meredith town records

---

[1] It was common practice to build a log home as a first residence, later building a frame house using boards once a farm was established and sawn wood could be bought. Around this time, there were at least three options for saw mills, including Meredith Village, the Weirs, and at the western edge of Moultonborough very near the border with Meredith and Center Harbor. The first saw mill on the lower part of Meredith Neck was not built until the 1820s. In the early 1800s, the lumber was very likely brought to the island during the ice-in season since it was easier to pull it by horse or oxen over the ice than to haul it by boat (not to mention that there were very few boats on the lake during the early 1800s).

show that Noah Nichols of "Baire Island" married Susan Bryant in 1819. The couple's relationship to the other Nichols and Bryants on the island is not known. They do not appear to have been children of the settling families. They too moved out of Meredith after Kelsea's visit.

Jonathan Bickford Sr., on the other hand, left an indelible mark on the history of Bear Island. After moving to Meredith in 1797, he lived on his Meredith Bay homestead farm until March of 1806 when he sold it to Levi Berry.[1] It appears that Jonathan and his family moved to Bear Island about this time. He made no other recorded purchases of land in Meredith thereafter. Like Robert Bryant before him, he perhaps had already been clearing his section of the island for some time and had built the log cabin there.[2]

Jonathan and his wife, Abigail Page, had a very fruitful marriage, spawning eleven children who were all born between 1789 and 1814. Almost everyone in this nuclear family spent large parts of their lives on Bear Island, and in any accounting, they would be considered the 'first' family of the island. As many as four of their children-- James S. (1805), Abigail (1810), Mahala (1812), and Eleanor (1814)—may have been born on Bear Island.

The Nichols family as well had a fairly long and extensive tenure on Bear Island, though nothing to rival the Bickfords. Paul Nichols (1763-c.1855) was the man who led the family out there. He was probably the son of Lt. James Nichols, a Brentwood blacksmith who moved to Meredith in 1781 after serving in the Revolution. James had purchased part of First Division Lot 1 in the 5th Range (D1/R5/L1) from Jonathan Clark when he arrived in town. He expanded his holdings there during the 1780s, putting him in close proximity to Ebenezer Smith and Ensign Robert Bryant. In 1784, he was among the first settlers to purchase land on Meredith Neck, acquiring half of Lot 68, which he most likely used for seasonal grazing. In 1797, James subsequently sold his farm to Ebenezer Smith's nephew, Daniel.[3]

Like James Nichols, Paul Nichols (b. c. 1763) was also born in Brentwood and was also a blacksmith.[4] He had established his own household by 1790 with his wife, Elizabeth Bryant, and a daughter, Moore.[5] In 1792, Paul purchased 30 acres of common land very near Meredith Village and built his homestead farm there.[6] He lived on and improved this land "for sundry years" before selling it to Israel Gilman in 1796.[7] In 1810, Paul was still living in the First Division.[8] By this time, his household unit consisted of twelve people, including four boys and four girls all under the age of sixteen. In 1812, he was among a group of First Division farmers

---

[1] BCRI, B/P 9004/473.

[2] It is difficult to pin down the timing of Jonathan's move to the island. On one hand, his son, James, told William Puffer in the mid-1880s that he had been born on the island in 1805. On the other hand, Hugh Kelsea reported in 1819 that Jonathan only had a log cabin, meaning he had not taken the obvious next step of building a house yet.

[3] BCRI, B/P 9001/201, 9001/234, 9001/291, 9001/621, 9002/568. James' relationship to Paul is not clear. Some genealogical records suggest that Paul's father was named Nathaniel.

[4] BCRI, B/P 9004/272. The combination of Brentwood and blacksmith provide the suggestion that he was the son of James Nichols.

[5] 1790 Census.

[6] BCRI, B/P 9004/272.

[7] BCRI, B/P 9004/272. Thereafter, the information gets sketchy. Paul did not appear in the 1800 census.

[8] 1810 Census.

who petitioned the state Assembly for the right to build a wing dam at the Weirs.[1] He was apparently still living in the First Division as late as 1814.[2] Sometime after 1814, Paul Nichols made his way out to Bear Island, presumably purchasing his farm on South Bear from either Robert Bryant or John Bickford. He settled there with his wife and his sons, Nathaniel (b.1796), John (b.1804), and Parker P. (b.1807).

There were two additional people who lived on Bear during the early 1800s. They were Robert Bryant's daughter, Dolly (b. 1777), and her husband, Joseph Nichols (b. c. 1770). Dolly married Joseph sometime before 1800.[3] Joseph was probably the brother of Paul and the son of of Lt. James Nichols. Dolly and Joseph had at least three children, two sons and a daughter, before moving to the island. It is not clear when Dolly and Joseph moved out to the island, but it was probably after 1812 and around the same time that Joseph's brother, Paul, did so as well.[4] Oral history tells us that Dolly and Joseph did not go out there to be farmers. Rather they moved into the small house on the point originally built by Robert Bryant when he first moved to Bear.[5] It It was located at the nearest point to Meredith Neck.[6] Joseph and Dolly established a ferry business that carried people and livestock between Bear and the Neck.

Bryant, Bickford and Nichols Intermarriages

The three extended families that lived on the southern end of Bear—the Bryants, the Bickfords, and the Nichols—were extremely close. One statistic will suffice to illustrate just how close they were. During the first four decades of the 19th century, there were at least 14 intermarriages between members of the three families. Seven of the 14 were between Bickfords and Bryants, and five of those involved sons of Jonathan Bickford Sr. Three marriages took place between Bickfords and Nichols, and three marriages were between Bryants and Nichols. All of Robert Bryant's children as well as a grandson married Bickfords or Nichols.[7] The picture could not be clearer; the three families on the southern end of Bear Island were very closely knit!

---

[1] Petition, June 6, 1812, State Archives.
[2] BCRI, B/P 9007/451.
[3] The 1800 census listed Joseph Nichols as the head of a household that included a woman (Dolly) aged between 26 and 45 along with two children, a boy and a girl, under the age of 10.
[4] There is nothing to confirm and very little to infer that Joseph Nichols was the son of Lt. James Nichols, but the connection makes sense within the context. For what it is worth, he and Dolly named their first son, James, and their second, Robert. Joseph Nichols was among the First Division farmers who signed the Weirs dam petition in June 1812. This does not suggest a man who was running a ferry business between Meredith Neck and Bear Island at the time. Petition, June 6, 1812, State Archives.
[5] "Bear Island-Aunt Dolly," Boston Evening Transcript, July 28, 1851, p. 1.
[6] In reference to the house location, see Ripples Around the Lake, July 1919, p. 20.
[7] The first intermarriage was that of his son, John, to John Bickford's daughter, Eleanor, in 1791. Robert Jr. married Abigail Bickford of the extended Bickford clan before 1800. Dolly married Joseph Nichols, likely a son of James Nichols and brother of Paul Nichols, also before 1800. Robert Bryant Jr.'s son, Abram, married Jonathan Bickford Sr.'s daughter, Mahala. Jonathan Bickford's son, Jonathan Jr., married Priscilla Bryant, the daughter of John and Eleanor Bryant.

Bryant, Bickford, and Nichols Intermarriages

#	MAN	WOMAN	FATHERS
1	John Bryant	Eleanor Bickford	Robert Bryant Sr. John Bickford Sr.
2	Joseph Nichols	Dolly Bryant	James Nichols Robert Bryant Sr.
3	Robert Bryant Jr.	Abigail Bickford	Robert Bryant Sr. Unknown
4	Brackett Bickford	Mary Bryant	Jonathan Bickford Sr. Unknown
5	Jonathan Bickford Jr.	Priscilla W. Bryant	Jonathan Bickford Sr. John Bryant
6	Oliver Bickford	Julia A. Nichols	James S. Bickford Nathaniel Nichols
7	John P. Bickford	Nancy Bryant	Jonathan Bickford Jr. Unknown
8	John Nichols	Priscilla Bickford	Paul Nichols Jonathan Bickford Sr.
9	James S. Bickford	Lucinda Bryant	Jonathan Bickford Sr. Unknown
10	Abram Bryant	Mahala Bickford	Robert Bryant Jr. Jonathan Bickford Sr.
11	Thomas B. Nichols	Climena Bickford	Nathaniel Nichols Brackett Bickford
12	Ebenezer Bickford Jr.	Almira Bickford	Brackett Bickford Eleazer Bickford Sr.
13	Paul Nichols	Elisabeth Bryant	James Nichols Unknown
14	Noah Nichols	Susan Bryant	Unknown Unknown

Extensive intermarriage between family members living in close proximity was typical in New Hampshire, especially during the first six decades of the 19th century. Quite aside from the natural imperative to find a mate, a basic pillar of the small farming communities was the family. There were few opportunities available for single people outside of the family setting. Moreover, children by custom and practice remained at home until they married. They were naturally anxious to set up their own farms and households. Opportunities to meet potential mates were few and far between due to the dispersed nature of farming. The combination of desire, opportunity, and necessity resulted in numerous matches among neighboring families. The process was very often perpetuated by the settlement of newly formed families in close proximity to their parents and siblings.

The Demise of the First Farming Era on Bear

In 1819, life on Bear Island changed dramatically. Ownership of the entire island reverted back to Nathaniel Haven and the heirs of John Peirce.[1] There is nothing in the historical records that shows what specifically led to this reversion of ownership. The only logical explanation is that a foreclosure occurred. None of the earliest settlers retained ownership of the farms they had developed. Hugh Kelsea's report made clear that the island farmers were fully reconciled to the situation. All of them willingly left the island, suggesting that they accepted that they did not have clear title to their farms. Indeed, Kelsea wrote that Eleazer Bickford, Brackett Bickford, and Nathaniel Nichols all expressed their willingness to purchase parcels on the island. The rules of real estate law were fully embedded in society. The Bear Islanders would have understood that any unpaid mortgage, which preceded their purchases, gave Haven and the Peirces the right to take the property.

The deeds show that Robert Bryant legitimately purchased Bear Island. They also show the first mortgage agreement signed by Bryant and co-signed by John Bickford. There are no deeds for the presumed sales of the parcels on the island to the other settlers who were out there before 1819. But this would seem to be more an issue of record keeping rather than deceit. In the absence of any other information, it seems that Haven and the Peirce heirs must have foreclosed on their 1801 mortgage. This obviously suggests that Robert Bryant and John Bickford did not comply with the terms of the mortgage. One would guess the two men extended the mortgage before the initial payment dates came up. Sometime along the way, they reached a point at which they could not make payments and could no longer get an extension. Perhaps 1816, the year without a summer, put the final nail in the coffin. It took until 1819 before Haven and the Peirces marshaled the resources to enforce a foreclosure.

---

[1] Peirce had died in 1814, so the Bear properties became part of his estate, the heirs to which were Mark, Joshua and Daniel Peirce.

Chapter Seven

The Aftermath for Some of the First Farmers

Ensign Robert Bryant Sr.

The foreclosure and subsequent fate of Robert Sr. cast something of a pall over the early history of the island. As one of the original settlers of the town, he earned a meaningful place in its history through his courage and hard work. By all indications, he was a well respected settler, having served his country in the Revolution and having served his town in many official capacities over the years. His venture out to Bear was completed through a seemingly clean purchase of the island. But somehow it all came apart.

Unfortunately there is very little information about Robert's life after the foreclosure.[1] It is possible that he continued to live on Bear. There was no apparent pressure to move off; his farm remained unsold until 1831. And there is nothing in the records or deeds to suggest that he moved anywhere else.

In the 1820s, Robert Sr. probably split time between the island and Meredith Neck. His only mention in the town records occurred in 1825 when the town gave him a $1.51 rebate on his taxes.[2] By 1830, at the age of 86 and with his health failing, his longtime friend, Paul Nichols, was helping to take care of him.[3] He died in 1831.[4]

It is generally accepted in Meredith historiography that Robert Sr. was buried in the Meetinghouse cemetery on Meredith Neck; but there is really nothing to substantiate the claim. There is no original marker for him. The existing Revolutionary headstone honoring him was not placed there until 1925 through the efforts of Mary Hanaford, a genealogist seeking to recognize all of the town's Revolutionary veterans.

The linking of Robert Bryant Sr. to the Meetinghouse cemetery seems to have arisen exclusively from a misinterpretation of the memories of two of Robert's great granddaughters, Mrs. C.P. Cushing and especially Harriett Dolloff. Harriett was the daughter of Abram Bryant and his wife, Mahala, and the granddaughter of Robert Bryant Jr. and his wife, Abigail.[5] Harriett told Mary Hanaford in 1925 that her "grandfather" was buried in the Meetinghouse cemetery next to

---

[1] Unfortunately, the US Census for 1820 was destroyed by fire. Bryant is not listed in the 1830 Census. There is no mention at all about the life of his wife, Joanna.

[2] Meredith Treasurer's book, copies of reports 1806 – 1867, black bound volume (Meredith Historical Society Archives).

[3] Meredith Town Records, 1832. Paul was paid $16.00 by the town for his care of Bryant in 1830. Paul and his son Parker were living on their farm on Neck Lot 74 not too far from Fish Cove during this period.

[4] Caleb Lovejoy built Bryant's casket. Meredith Town Records, 1831. Caleb was paid $2.00 for this service. His farm was located on Lot 78, near where the public parking lot of Shep Brown's is now located.

[5] Abigail Bryant and her daughter, Nancy Clark, were buried in the Meetinghouse cemetery. Despite some references to the contrary, Robert Jr.'s son, Abram, and his wife, Mahala, were not buried there. Their graves can be found in the Meredith Neck (aka Smith) cemetery located a bit south of the intersection of Barnard Ridge Rd. and Pleasant St. Abram purchased plots there in the 1859. BCRI, B/P 33/420. Harriett Dolloff and her husband, John Dolloff, were buried in the Smith cemetery as well. Their headstones clearly identify them. John Dolloff was killed at Cold Harbor, VA during the Civil War.

other family members.[1] It was assumed that she was referring to Ensign Robert Bryant, but in fact it was to Robert Bryant Jr.[2]

As a result, there is no evidence to link Ensign Bryant to the Meetinghouse cemetery. At the time of his death, the Meetinghouse building had still not been built. The land was a farm owned by Stephen Boardman who had bought it in 1829.[3] The timing of the cemetery is unknown, although it predated Robert Sr.'s death. There are three headstones in it that date to the 1820s and one to 1816. But it was not a public cemetery; there were none in those days. Burying grounds were all typically family or neighborhood affairs.[4] In 1831, it would have been unusual for Robert to be interred in the Lot 64 cemetery as the Bryants had no apparent connections to Boardman or that part of the Neck in those days.

The Bear Island Burying Ground

The uncertainty surrounding Robert's final resting place leads to the suspicion that he was actually laid to rest in the burying ground that can still be found on Bear Island. This cemetery is located very near where his daughter, Dolly, was living at the time of his death.[5] An 1858 visitor to Bear wrote in a newspaper article that Bryant had indeed died on the island: "The first settler is said to have been a man named *Bryant*, who closed his life upon the island."[6]

Given its location, the obvious conclusion is that the burying ground was built by the Bryants and Nichols. Old island lore holds that perhaps as many as nine people were buried there, although there are no headstones to indicate who might be interred. Indeed, there are only a few flat, surface stones that are believed to be grave markers. Nevertheless, it seems quite plausible that Ensign Bryant was buried there, perhaps joined by his wife, Joanna, along with Dolly's husband, Joseph, and two of her children who died at early ages.[7]

Robert Bryant Jr.

The fate of Robert Jr. after the foreclosure is also unclear. Only the smallest traces of him exist after 1819. There are no records of him purchasing any real estate in Meredith. He was rumored to have moved to Holland, Vermont in 1830,[8] but if so, he was back in Meredith by the

---

[1] Old Meredith and Vicinity, p. 39.
[2] Conflation of early colonial names is very common in colonial histories due to the repetitive usage of first names down through the generations. In early Bear Island history, the confusion is most apparent in the cases of Robert Bryant and Theophilus Dockham.
[3] BCRI, B/P 9012/349. This lot, # 64, was one of the most actively farmed during the first three decades of the 1800s.
[4] The Smith family, for example, had established a cemetery down the road on Lot 53 before 1816. BRCI, B/P 9007/67.
[5] While it is generally agreed that the stone enclosure on Dolly's old property is/was a burying ground, the determination is open to some dispute. One 1887 visitor referred to it as a sheep pen (W. Hawkes, Winnipesaukee and About There, p. 34) and others as a pound. Most believe it to be a cemetery, and the style of its construction would seem to support that belief.
[6] "Picnic on Bear Island," *Independent Democrat* (Concord, New Hampshire), September 16, 1858, p. 3.
[7] Other than Dolly and her family, no one else lived permanently on this section of Bear Island until the vacation era began there in 1898. Some of the purported graves may belong to extended family members who joined the Bryants and Nichols on the island during these early years.
[8] A Robert Bryant is listed in the 1830 census for Holland, Orleans, Vermont. Interestingly, another man perhaps from Meredith Neck, an elderly William Mead (70ish), is listed right above him in the Vermont census. One of the Neck's William Meads did in fact move to Vermont, but the identifying details have not been traced.

latter 1840s. The brief references available suggest that he lived on the Neck, probably staying with friends and family. Both his son, Abram, and his daughter, Nancy, had married and lived on the lower Neck during this period. Anecdotal reports indicate that he helped at least two lower Neck families build barns on their properties.[1] Town reports also show that Neck residents H.B. Plummer and B.B. Rollins provided care for him in 1848 when his health was apparently failing.[2] He probably died soon thereafter. As referenced above and according to his granddaughter, he was buried at the Meetinghouse cemetery (although there is no headstone for him).[3]

Dolly Nichols

Dorothy 'Dolly' Nichols—often referred to as Aunt Dolly—is the best known settler of Bear Island. She became something of a legend and was often caricatured in the literature about the lake and the island.[4] Although she never personally owned any land on Bear, Dolly lived on the island for almost 40 years. She and her husband, Joseph, were the first 'service providers' to island residents when they began their ferry service between the island and the Neck around 1814.

Original sign for Dolly's Ferry (Meredith Historical Society)

After the 'foreclosure' in 1819, Dolly continued to reside on the western tip of South Bear, across from the Neck, where she maintained her ferry and provisions business. By the late 1820s, she was alone, her husband having left the family; two of her children apparently having died; and her third child, Robert, having moved to the mainland to earn a living.[5] She maintained "a little shack that neighbors had built for her. Here she fished and furnished food and drink to those who came that way."[6]

Dolly lived a vigorous but difficult life. She persevered in her own version of the great American survival story. Her presence and services were indispensable to fishermen as well

---

[1] Old Meredith and Vicinity, pp. 95, 96.

[2] Meredith Town Report, 1848.

[3] Old Meredith and Vicinity, p. 39. Robert Jr.'s wife, Abigail Bryant, outlived her husband by many years. She lived with their daughter, Nancy Clark, on the lower Neck Lot 79 until she died in 1865. Abigail Bryant, Nancy Clark (d. 1888) and her husband, Thomas Clark (d. 1881) were all buried in marked graves at the Meetinghouse cemetery.

[4] See, for example: Elizabeth Wilkin, Winnipesaukee Whoppers (1949). In the 1850s, her renown was the inspiration for the character Dolly Plot in Isaac Scribner's Laconia; or, Legends of the White Mountains and Merry Meeting Bay.

[5] There is no documentary confirmation of these deaths. In re her husband's departure, see: The Boston Atlas, August 3, 1849, p. 2. See also: Briggs, Meredith Neck; S. Colby, "Aunt Dolly Nichols," in Early Meredith, p. 68.

[6] Old Meredith and Vicinity, p. 91. One publication, The Lakes Region New Hampshire: A Visual History, p. 88 says her place on Bear was named "Fisherman's Haven" although we found no historical support for the name.

as to the island farmers. The ferry service was vital during the first half of the 1800s because boats large enough to transport live stock to the island were few and far between. She supplemented her income by rowing (in summer) or walking (in winter) to the Weirs where she picked up supplies that she sold to island residents and visitors. The most prized of these supplies was rum, which found its way to the Lakes Region from the West Indies or from seacoast distilleries. She obtained her supplies initially from the Nathaniel Davis farm on Governors Island, but beginning around 1840, she could avail herself of a new store, known as the "old red store", that was built at the Weirs very near the channel bridge.[1]

The Old Red House seen here to the left of Weirs bridge. (Courtesy of David Ames.)

Dolly became "a locally famous character" probably as a result of the 1849 arrival of the steamboat, the *Lady of the Lake*.[2] The *Lady's* regular travel route took it past Dolly's cabin on the point at least a couple of times a day. The boat's pilot was Dolly's island neighbor, Eleazer

---

[1] For early commerce on the lake, see van Veghten, The History of Meredith Bay, pp. 16-23. In re 'the old Red Store', see Huse, The Weirs, p. 26; and Wilcomb, Rambles About the Weirs, pp. 1-4. A review of the deeds suggests the store was not built until after 1840. BCRI, B/P 18/210. Dolly is also said to have purchased liquor at "the old Hoyt tavern" on the easterly (i.e. Gilford side) of the Weirs channel. Meredith News, Nov 28, 1928.

[2] Meredith News, Nov 28, 1928.

Bickford Jr., who undoubtedly told his passengers about Dolly as part of his informal travelogue.[1] One 1849 traveler wrote (without particular accuracy):

> "Upon one of the small islands which we passed, resides an elderly lady, named Nichols, familiarly called Aunt Dolly. She has been an inhabitant of the island for upwards of 20 years, and it has been cultivated during that period, under her sole direction. She had a quarrel with her husband and separated from him and a large family, which fact caused her hermit-like life."[2]

Depiction of Aunt Dolly (by Jackie Roy)

Her reputation became so widely known that a newspaper correspondent from Springfield, MA, made a special trip to Bear Island in 1851 just to meet her. He referred to her as "a celebrated old woman, in whose history I expected to be interested" and as "the greatest female attraction of Bear Island."[3]

It was an arduous and lonely life, but one she seemingly endured pretty well. As her 1851 visitor observed, "Aunt Dolly is a true philosopher in her way—and a pattern to others for energy and contentment." In describing the interior of her cabin, he noted "in one corner is a *beaufet* full of china, where her tin quart mugs are seen to shine as bright as the old-time silver tankards. Over her bed hangs a defaced canopy of chintz, and sundry other less conspicuous 'remains' may be noticed in this old homestead." She grew corn, potatoes, and cabbage in a little garden. She provided passing fishermen with drink as well as occasional lodging when the weather forced them to take refuge on the island. She apparently enjoyed the winter season more than the summer (she felt "quite lively" then), because there were a great many more people going across the frozen lake than there were during the summer in this era of very limited boating.[4]

---

[1] One newspaperman wrote, regarding Eleazer's commentary, that he "gives many interesting incidents, in travel across (the lake)..." The Boston Traveler, August 11, 1857, p. 4. Aunt Dolly also received mention in an 1852 article about steamboat travel across the lake. The Boston Recorder, August 12, 1852, p. 130.

[2] The Boston Semi-weekly Atlas, August 4, 1849, p. 2.

[3] "Bear Island- Aunt Dolly," Boston Evening Transcript, July 28, 1851, p. 1. This article may be the only first-hand interview with Dolly that exists. As such it is like a very rare stamp! My sincerest thanks to Leslie Hopper Keeler for finding it.

[4] "Bear Island- Aunt Dolly," Boston Evening Transcript, July 28, 1851, p. 1. The reporter had sailed to Bear from Center Harbor. It took four hours for the visiting reporter's party to maneuver their sailboat back to Center Harbor from Bear due to a strong northwest wind.

Dolly had relatives living on the lower end of the Neck with whom she often visited. One was a niece, Nancy Bryant Clark, the daughter of Dolly's brother, Robert Jr. Nancy was the wife of Thomas Clark, who owned part of Lot 79.[1] Dolly's sister-in-law, Abigail Bickford Bryant, lived with the Clarks during some of these years.

Dolly's fortunes took a turn for the worse right around 1850. The beginning of her downfall occurred when she was robbed by a lodger who had taken shelter at her place during a stormy night. The thief took "with him all Aunt Dolly's hoard of money—the savings of long years and much self-denial." In discussing the theft a year or so later with a reporter, Dolly lamented:

> "I hain't had much luck in life. It seems as if fate went strongly agin me sometimes, but arter all, I've had as much as I could eat and drink, and I've got it all honestly, and that's more than some on 'em can say, may be."[2]

With advancing age, Dolly's health began to fail in the 1850s. By then in her mid-70s, she began to receive more extensive care from friends and family on the Neck. In 1853, she left the island for good and entered the town's Poor Farm located on Hatch Road in the Second Division. She also received medical care from Dr. John Sanborn, who was paid by the town as part of its external care program.[3] In 1856, she was moved back to Meredith Neck when the town purchased a new Poor Farm (or Alms House) on Lot 73.[4] Dolly died in late 1857 at the age of 81. She was buried at the Poor Farm cemetery, but the burial site was disturbed many years later by a land owner expanding his property. The graves were subsequently moved to an unknown, unmarked location nearby.[5]

Little remains to commemorate this most legendary of Bear Islanders. The only physical reminder of Dolly's domain is the old cemetery near where her shack stood on the western tip of South Bear. While her old well, cellar hole, and some chimney bricks were still readily identifiable in the late 1880s,[6] no trace can any longer be found. The three Dolly Islands nearby, named in her honor, also remain to commemorate this early settler.

The Nichols Family

The lives of the Nichols were much more visible than the Bryants after the 'foreclosure'. Paul Nichols may have stayed for several years on the island during the early 1820s, just as Ensign Robert Bryant perhaps had. There was no pressure to move off Lot 7 since it was not sold until the early 1830s. In 1826, Paul's oldest son, Nathaniel, bought a 50 acre farm on the

---

[1] Thomas Clark and his brother had a blacksmith shop and a wood working shop there for years. The old wood working shop apparently still stands (#387 Meredith Neck Road). Tommy's Cove was presumably named after him.
[2] "Bear Island- Aunt Dolly," <u>Boston Evening Transcript</u>, July 28, 1851, p. 1.
[3] Town Records, 1854. Dolly's age is listed as 77. P. 11. (Meredith Historical Society.)
[4] BCRI, B/P 25/376. L. Babb to D. Vittum. The Poor Farm was located on what is now Old Hubbard Road.
[5] Colby, "Aunt Dolly," <u>Early Meredith</u>, p. 69.
[6] See: news article, <u>Springfield Republican</u> (MA), October 1, 1887, p.8. A picture of her old well is found in <u>Old Meredith and Vicinity</u>, p. 92.

Neck Road, spanning parts of Lots 65 and 66.[1] Two years later, in 1828, Paul and his son, Parker, moved to the lower Neck. They jointly purchased Lot 74 from Washington Smith, one of Ebenezer Smith's sons.[2]

In the years thereafter, two of Paul's sons, John and Parker, and his nephew, Robert M. Nichols (Dolly's son), each returned at different times to Bear Island. As for Paul, in 1845 he sold his half interest in the Lot 74 farm to Parker and then entered into a lease-back transaction for the remainder of his life. He remained an active member of the community until his death in the mid-1850s. There is no record of where he was buried. His wife, Elizabeth Bryant Nichols, continued to live with Parker on Lot 74.

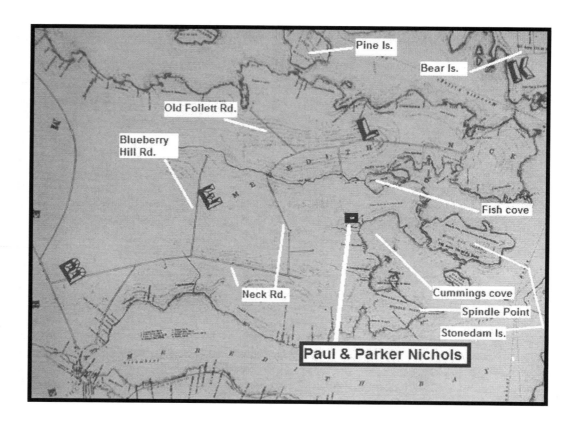

[1] BCRI, B/P 12/381. This farm is now 206 Meredith Neck Road. Nathaniel later died in 1855 in the collapse of the Meredith town hall. His son, Thomas, continued living in the house until 1868 when he sold it to another Bear Islander, Oliver Bickford. B/P 47/583. On another side note, Nathaniel Nichol's son, Nathaniel, was part of the 9th NH Regiment during the Civil War. He died in service.
[2] BCRI, B/P 15/461. Washington Smith also died in the collapse of the Meredith town hall in 1855.

Chapter Eight

The Second Phase of Settlement: The 1820s

Hugh Kelsea's mission in visiting Bear in 1819 was to survey the island and divide it into lots that Nathaniel Haven and the heirs of John Peirce could sell. In completing his survey, he marked out nine separate lots on the island, the boundaries of which still remain clearly evident today in almost every case. Not surprisingly, his lots mirrored in many respects the established outlines of the earliest farms.

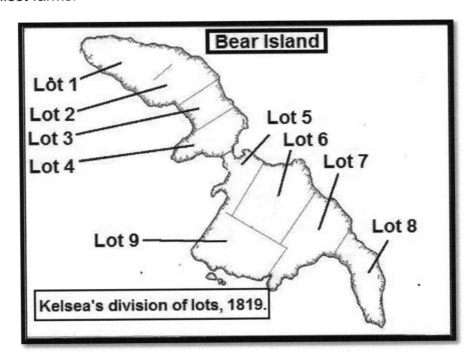

Kelsea's division of lots, 1819.

Kelsea began his survey at the northern tip of the island and worked south along the eastern side of it. He gave sequential numbers to eight parallel lots (1-4 on North Bear, 5-8 on South Bear). The ninth lot, Robert Bryant's land, was sectioned off last on the west side of the island. His report listed the size of each lot:

Lot 1:	51 acres	**Lot 4**:	55 acres	**Lot 7**:	95 acres
Lot 2:	62 acres	**Lot 5**:	47 acres	**Lot 8**:	58 acres
Lot 3:	66 acres	**Lot 6**:	116 acres	**Lot 9**:	79 acres

<u>**Total**</u>: 629 acres

Nearly all of the stone walls that divide the nine lots were constructed during the years following the survey. As detailed just below, they still define the boundaries between all of the lots except between lots 1-2 and 5-6:

-<u>Between Lots 1 and 2</u>: there is no single dividing wall between these two lots. There is a section of wall that runs east-west across the hiking trail in the middle of the island located somewhat south of the hotel cellar hole. This was likely the dividing line between the two lots. If the wall were to continue down to the water on either side of the island, it would reach the shoreline in close proximity to the current house addresses of #32 on the eastern shore and #420 on the west side.[1]

-<u>Between lots 2 and 3</u>: there is a shoreline to shoreline wall that begins near #48 on the east and ends near #396 on the west.

-<u>Between lots 3 and 4</u>: there is a shoreline to shoreline wall that begins just south of #63 on the east and ends near #382 on the west.

-<u>Between lots 4 and 5</u>: there is a short shoreline to shoreline wall in the Carry that begins near #93 in the cove on the east and ends in the cove on the other side of the island near #354.

-<u>Between Lots 5 and 6</u>: there is no single wall dividing these two lots. A dividing wall begins on the east at #114. There are various fragments of walls in the interior but no clear delineating wall. The lot line ends in the vicinity of #331 in the cove on the western facing shore.

-<u>Lot 6</u> was subdivided into northern and southern parcels (to be called Lots 6N and 6S) in the early 1820s. There is a long dividing wall between the two parcels that begins on the east side of the island near #125 and runs up near the Chapel where it intersects with the wall that divides Lot 6 from Lot 9.

-<u>Between Lots 6 and 7</u>: there is a dividing wall that runs from the shoreline at #140 on the east to an intersection with the wall that divides Lot 6 from Lot 9 behind and just south of the Chapel.

-<u>Between Lots 7 and 8</u>: there is a dividing wall that runs from the shoreline at #165 on the east to the shoreline at #232 on the west. This wall defines the northern boundary of Camp Lawrence.

-<u>Lot 9 is divided from Lot 6</u> by a long wall that starts near the rear of the Chapel and runs northwesterly towards house #331 in the cove on the northwest side of Dolly Point. The wall ends well short of the shore line, but the continuation of this boundary line is apparent from the remnants of old barbed wire fencing employed in the latter 1800s to enclose the area. The end point of this lot line was at an intersection of Lots, 5, 6N, and 9. Lot 9 also is separated from Lot 7 by a short stretch of wall that is almost a continuation of the dividing wall between Lot 6 and Lot 7, running down from its starting point behind and south of the Chapel to Deep Cove.

The 'Resale' of Bear Island: 1820s

As a result of the 'foreclosure', Nathaniel Haven ended up owning all of Bear Island except for half of Lot 6 and Lot 9 which were owned by the sons of John Peirce. In 1821, Haven turned over control of his lots to his son, Nathaniel A. Haven Jr.[2] Haven Jr. began to market the properties fairly quickly but the process moved unevenly. The first parcel to be sold after the

---

[1] See B/P 105/97, Lovejoy to Nye, 1900. The deed makes reference to the 'second stone wall' from the steamboat landing. The first wall was located between (now) #433 and #432. It was not built until after 1873. See below, John Crane, Chapter 20.
[2] Formalized by deed in 1822. BCRI, BP 9010/36.

'foreclosure' was Lot 2 on the northern section of the island. It was purchased in November 1821 by Stephen Boardman Sr. The deed of sale states that it was "the same formerly occupied by William Griffin" and "northwest of Lot No. 1 or the Jenness lot." Boardman bought the land for seasonal grazing and/or speculative purposes. He had no intention of moving out to the island permanently.[1] Boardman was an established Meredith farmer who had purchased Lot 71 and part of Lot 68 on the Neck in 1814 when he moved to Meredith from Stratham. His farm was located at the end of the road that became Eaton Avenue.[2] During the early 1800s, that area was known as Boardman's Cove. Decades later, the area became known as Cummings Cove, although the name Boardman's Point still appears on maps.

A month after Boardman bought Lot 2, Haven Jr. sold Lot 1 on North Bear to William Mead Jr.[3] Like Boardman, Mead made the purchase for seasonal grazing purposes and probably for speculation. He never planned to move out to the island. As we saw, Mead was a son of one of the original Meredith settlers. He had moved to the Neck in the 1790s where he and his brother, Joseph R. Mead, became two of the wealthiest and most prominent members of the Neck community. Their homes were built on Lots 67 and 66 in the area where current day Eaton Avenue and Old Hubbard Road intersect with Meredith Neck Road.[4] In addition to their homestead farms, the Meads routinely acquired other parcels of land on the lower Neck for seasonal grazing and speculative purposes. At various times in the early 1800s, they owned all or parts of Lots 64 through 68, 73, and 76 through 82. The Bear Island purchase, their only foray out to the island, was simply an extension of this pattern.

Neither Mead nor Boardman held on to their Bear Island properties for very long. John Batchelder bought Lot 2 from Boardman in 1822 and Lot 1 from Mead in 1823. In both cases, the sellers made small profits on the transactions. Unlike his predecessors, John Batchelder was not a lower Neck farmer at that time.[5] Having lived in Meredith since at least 1819, he was a blacksmith who also owned a farm in the upper portion of the Third Division (Lots 2 and 18) near Lake Waukewan (known as Measley Pond in those days) as well as a piece of the 'mill lot' in growing Meredith Village. He bought the land on Bear for seasonal grazing and held onto it for the rest of the decade.

Lots 1 and 2 were the only parcels on North Bear that were sold during the 1820s. Lots 3 and 4 were not purchased by anyone. From the earliest days of settlement on Bear, these lots were considered to be the least desirable on the island.[6]

---

[1] BCRI, B/P 9/336. During this period and years later, almost all of the deeds make specific mention of Hugh Kelsea's lots.
[2] BCRI, B/P 7/345.
[3] BCRI, B/P 9009/632.
[4] The still existing Brick House was built by Joseph Mead on Lot 67. The Mead family cemetery can still be found across the Neck Road from the Brick House. William Mead built his house just south of the Brick House, past Old Hubbard Road and up the hill. This location became known as Mead Hill.
[5] In the 1830s, Batchelder established a farm on Neck Lot 40 near the intersection of Barnard Ridge Road and the Neck Road. It is located at 37 Meredith Neck Road. In 1836, Batchelder also bought part of Lot 81 on the lower Neck for seasonal grazing purposes.
[6] William Griffin had told as much to Hugh Kelsea in 1819 in explaining why they were unoccupied at the time of Kelsea's visit.

The situation on South Bear was quite different. Nathaniel Haven Jr. found an immediate market for lots 6 and 8 among the Bickford family who had lived on the island prior to the 'foreclosure'. In December 1821, Haven sold his undivided half ownership of Lot 6 to Eleazer Bickford Sr.[1] Lot 6 was the largest of the nine island lots (116 acres) laid out by Kelsea, and it contained the best farm land on the island. The other undivided half was owned by the sons of John Peirce. As an undivided half, Eleazer was theoretically not able to lawfully set aside or define 'his land'. Half of wherever he settled would continue to be owned by the Peirce estate.

There did not seem, however, to be any confusion on Eleazer's part. He settled on the best section of the property, the southern end of the lot (henceforth Lot 6S). This was the location of his farm during the pre-foreclosure days, and he had expressed an interest in buying it when Hugh Kelsea was on the island in 1819.[2]

Unlike the settlers on North Bear, Eleazer and his wife, Sarah, moved out to the island permanently, establishing their "homestead seat" there.[3] They had only one child, Charles (12), at the time. Two more children, Eleazer Jr. (b. 1822) and Almira (b. 1825), were born in the next four years. Eleazer Sr. was the farmer who dug the cellar hole still to be found on Lot 6S.[4] There are footprints for several outbuildings nearby the cellar hole as well. Moreover, there is also an old dug well a short ways down the hill from the cellar hole.

Eight months after Eleazer Sr. acquired lot 6S, his nephew, Jonathan Bickford Jr., purchased Lot 8 from Haven Jr.[5] Encompassing the southern point of the island that is now Camp Lawrence, Lot 8 was estimated to contain 58 acres. Prior to 1819, the farm was occupied by Jonathan's father, Jonathan Bickford Sr., and his large brood of 11 children. Jonathan Jr. (and perhaps many of his siblings) had remained on the island following the 'foreclosure' period.[6] Jonathan Jr. was 29 years old when he bought Lot 8. He was married to Priscilla Bryant, the oldest daughter of Ensign Robert Bryant's son, John Bryant.[7] They lived on Bear for decades after the purchase. Yet the only visible reminder of his presence is the shore-to-shore stone wall that divided Lot 8 from Lot 7. There are no cellar holes or wells any longer extant.[8]

---

[1] B/P 11/403. Half of a lot was referred to as a 'moiety' in the deeds.
[2] Kelsea report, 1819. "Mr. Eleazer Bickford offers to purchase 100 acres he is upon south (of the) Carrying Place but immediately at $2 p(er) acre."
[3] BCRI, B/P 9012/521.
[4] Now largely overgrown, it can still be found next to the Chapel trail and the old logger's road that comes up from East Bear. It is one of eight cellar holes that have been located on the island.
[5] BCRI, B/P 9009/484.
[6] BCRI, B/P 9009/484. There is some uncertainty about this. The deed clearly states that Jonathan Jr. was the purchaser. But in the description, it states that Jonathan Bickford (without the 'Jr.") was "still in the occupation" of it.
[7] Priscilla was Jonathan's first cousin, her mother being Jonathan's aunt.
[8] In years past a cellar hole was said to be easily found. It may be that it was covered over by one of the camp buildings.

There were no further land sales on South Bear until five years later. In 1827, Eleazer sold "part of (of his) homestead seat whereon I now live and improve" to his nephew, Brackett Bickford.[1] Brackett was also an island veteran, the oldest son of Jonathan Bickford Sr. Back in 1819, he and Paul Nichols' oldest son, Nathaniel, had expressed an interest to Hugh Kelsea about buying and dividing the estimated 100 acres located between Eleazer and the Carrying

Old well on Lot 6N.

Place (i.e. Lot 5 and part of Lot 6).[2] That transaction never happened, perhaps because of the muddled Peirce ownership of an undivided half of Lot 6. By 1827, Brackett decided to plunge ahead by purchasing the land from his uncle. Brackett assumed ownership of the northern half (58 acres) of the parcel (henceforth Lot 6N). The old cellar hole of his house can still be found as can his dug well located near the still functioning spring on that part of the island.[3] The 36 year old Brackett was married to Mary Bryant,[4] and they had four children, including Thomas, Ebenezer, George S., and Climena. While it is not clear where they were living before the purchase, Lot 6N became their homestead farm for more than 20 years.

In December 1827, shortly after Brackett's purchase, a third son of Jonathan Sr., James S. Bickford, purchased Lot 5 from Nathaniel Haven Jr.[5] The lot was estimated to contain some 47 ½ acres. It included the Carrying Place and the beautiful beach on the northeast side of the island. James was married to Lucinda Bryant,[6] and the couple came to have nine children, many of whom were born on the island. They made Lot 5 their 'homestead farm' and lived there year-round. It was James who dug the cellar hole still to be found along the power line behind #111 Bear Island. There are numerous building footprints in the vicinity of the cellar hole. He was also most likely responsible for digging the now-defunct spring still found near the cellar hole.[7]

Elsewhere on South Bear, Lots 7 and 9 were not sold during the 1820s. Dolly Nichols continued to live on the point of Lot 9. As conjectured previously, there is some likelihood that Robert Bryant and Paul Nichols also continued to live or spend time on those two Lots during the 1820s.

---

[1] BCRI, B/P 9012/521. The deed refers to half of Lot 6 as well as 'part' of Eleazer's ownership interest.
[2] Kelsea's report, 1819.
[3] The cellar hole is near the 'old' Chapel trail and largely overgrown. The spring is owned by Jocelyn DeGroot whose great grandmother, Lina Pearsall Earp, bought it in 1914. BCRI, B/P 140/262.
[4] Mary Bryant's family connection to Robert Bryant is not known, but she was undoubtedly a relative.
[5] BCRI, BP 9011/503.
[6] Lucinda Bryant's family connection to Robert Bryant is also not known, but again it is highly likely that she was a relative.
[7] This spring was utilized by Bear Islanders and campers well into the twentieth century.

Summary

Thus by the end of the 1820s, Bear Island was occupied by four Bickford families, including three sons of Jonathan Sr., that were living permanently on the southern end. Dolly Nichols was also living year-round on the southern end of the island. In stark contrast, North Bear had no permanent farmers living there. Half of it was being used seasonally for grazing by its Meredith Village owner, while the rest remained unsold and unused.

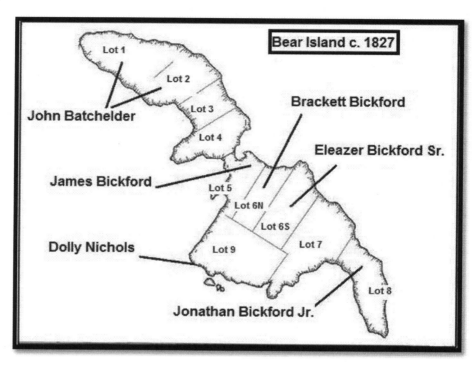

Chapter Nine

The Stone Walls and the Sheep Craze

Like everywhere else in New Hampshire and New England, Bear Island is crisscrossed by stone walls that were built by the early farmers. The island's walls form but a tiny part of the more than 250,000 miles of stone walls in the Northeast. The amount of labor that went into building all of these walls was staggering. By one estimate, it would have taken 15,000 men, working 365 days each year, 243 years to build all of the walls.[1] But build them they did. The question is, why?

The primary answer to the question is the economic phenomenon known as the 'sheep craze' that transformed the economy of the Northeast between 1810 and 1850. Of the thousands of miles of stone walls that traverse New England, it is estimated that 90% of them were built during this era. The walls were built to enclose new pasture lands that were carved out of the forests for flocks of sheep. This was the period when most of the deforestation of the region occurred. Around 1810, only some 30% of the region was open agricultural land; by 1840, the amount had leaped to 80%.[2]

The history behind the sheep craze is fascinating, a product of some of the dramatic changes that characterized the entire era. The craze played a dominant role in converting the interior New England region from a predominantly locally oriented farming economy to a market driven economy. Wool emerged as an overriding cash crop, taking a dominant role from 1820 to 1850.

Prior to the sheep craze, the first farmers who settled on Bear Island, like those in the rest of Meredith and most of New Hampshire, were self-sufficient farmers. All of a family's needs were met primarily through home industry and neighborly support. They owned very few sheep. The wool of the early breeds of sheep was of very poor quality, although of necessity, it was still used by the women of each household to make clothing.[3]

While these early settlers owned large tracts of land, the actively farmed portions were rather small.[4] They typically plowed only two to three acres for crops; cleared perhaps six acres for pasture; and had small gardens and tiny orchards. Most had an ox or two to assist with the hard work of plowing, hauling and clearing. They usually also owned a couple head of dairy

---

[1] Susan Allport, Sermons in Stone, p. 18. Her information is drawn from the Report of the Commissioner of Agriculture, "Statistics of Fences in the United States," 1871, pp. 497-513.

[2] "Tom Wessels on sheep fever," www.sentinelsource.com, August 17, 2006; Tom Wessels, Reading the Forested Landscape: A Natural History of New England, (1997), p. 59. Wessels is an ecologist and the director of the Environmental Biology Program at Antioch New England Graduate School. The deforestation was also a product of the basic demand for wood which was used for everything from buildings to fire wood to trade.

[3] Sheep were introduced into America by the first colonists in the early 1600s.

[4] Lots in the early New Hampshire towns averaged about 100 acres for two primary reasons: first, large tracts were needed to ensure each landholder got enough good farm land in light of the unpredictability of land quality (hills, swamps, rocky terrain, etc,); and second, they gave settlers ownership of vital wood supplies.

cattle used for milk, butter and cheese; but the number of cattle was small because maintaining them was too costly and time consuming for most early farmers. Sheep were so insignificant that town officials did not bother including them in annual tax inventories.[1]

This way of life began to change in the early 1800s. The Industrial Revolution brought factories, mass production, and the initial phases of urbanization during the first three decades of the 19th century. The Northeast was in the vanguard of the changes, benefitting from its entrepreneurial spirit and the presence of abundant water power on rivers like the Merrimack. The textile industry especially felt the revolution's early impact. As methods of processing raw wool and cotton increasingly became automated and centralized, cotton and woolen mills were built all over the Northeast. By 1831, some 500 of the 801 cotton mills in the country were in the six New England states.[2] A loosely affiliated group of Boston entrepreneurs (referred to as the 'Boston Associates') led the way, introducing to the United States the first large mill complexes that integrated the previously fragmented processing techniques. The first of these mills was built in Waltham, MA in 1813. Thereafter, the Boston entrepreneurs expanded their efforts, building additional mill complexes along the Merrimack River in Lowell, MA (1822), Manchester, NH (1825), Nashua, NH (1836), and Lawrence, MA (1845).[3]

The Industrial Revolution was accompanied by very rapid population growth. Over the four decade period between 1800 and 1840, the population of the United States more than tripled in size: New England grew 81%, New Hampshire increased 60%, and Meredith doubled.

Population Figures: 1800 - 1840

Segment	1800	1810	1820	1830	1840
United States	4,879,820	6,584,231	8,972,396	11,930,987	15,908,376
New England	1,233,011	1,471,973	1,660,065	1,954,717	2,234,822
New Hampshire	177,431	205,688	235,203	262,020	284,352
Meredith	1,609	1,940	2,416	2,683	3,344

Urbanization accompanied the Industrial Revolution as people, especially women, increasingly moved off of the farms to work in the new mills. The process was augmented by large numbers of immigrants who came to this country to find work. Many came from Canada where worn out soils forced them to seek alternatives.

The combination of population growth and expanding production created an ever increasing demand for raw materials, especially wool and cotton. Almost all of this need historically had been met through imports, largely from England where higher quality wool had a very long history. Around 1800, a few enterprising Americans began to focus upon raising better

---

[1] Early taxation calculations were based upon the productive capacity of the land, not pure acreage. Productivity was then translated into acreage calculations for tax purposes. In addition, the total number of horses, oxen, cows, cattle, and neat stock were tabulated. See, Heyduk: Stories in the History of New Hampshire's Lakes Region, p. 60. See, for example, the Meredith Tax Inventories, 1828 and 1829 (Meredith Historical Society Archives). Earlier town inventory records were not found.
[2] "New England Textile Mill Villages in the Early 19th Century," Roger N. Parks (1967).
[3] See Dalzell, Enterprising Elite, chapters 1 - 3. This book provides a good introduction to the Industrial Revolution in the U.S. in general and Massachusetts and New Hampshire in particular.

quality sheep to meet the demand for wool.[1] However, the effort was miniscule as most farmers were fully preoccupied with simply meeting the daily demands of their existence.

In 1802, the first inkling of a domestic wool solution began to emerge from an entrepreneurial Vermonter, Colonel David Humphreys.[2] He was the US ambassador to Spain. During his tenure there, he was introduced to the famed Spanish merino sheep that were world renown for their very high quality wool that grew in much larger quantities per sheep (triple the productivity of American sheep, apparently).[3] The Spanish nobility outlawed export of the merinos to protect their home industry, but Humphreys was able to import a small number from Portugal.[4] This was a tiny but important first step.

The interest in finding an American solution to the supply problem took on real urgency in 1807 when the Napoleonic Wars in Europe began affecting the United States. The war between England and France led President Jefferson to pass an Embargo Act in 1807, barring trade with either of the two warring countries. The embargo necessitated that American mills had to source all of their wool and cotton supplies from producers in the United States.

GROUP OF SPANISH MERINO SHEEP.
Spanish merino sheep.

These circumstances led another American diplomat, William Jarvis, to finagle the importation of a far larger number of merino sheep into the country in 1811. Jarvis was the US Consul to Portugal at the time. Spain was then in dire conflict with Napoleon, and the Spanish nobility feared for the future of their prized flocks. Jarvis convinced the Spanish to sell him some merino sheep, and he shipped 4000 of them to a new farm he started up in Weathersfield, Vermont, just across the border from Claremont, NH.[5]

Jarvis was in the forefront, but he was not alone in this importation. During 1810 and 1811, at least 106 vessels arrived at east coast ports, bringing some 15,767 merino sheep to the United States.[6] The outbreak of war between the United States and England in 1812 served only

---

[1] Special Report on the history and present condition of the sheep, US Bureau of Animal Husbandry, Dr. D.E. Salmon, Washington (1892), pp. 131-217.
[2] Merrill and Merrill, Gazetteer, 1817, p. 73.
[3] "The Rise and Fall of New Hampshire Sheep Country," Carol Robidoux, The Derry Ink News Link, March 1, 2011, www.derryinklink.com.
[4] The US was not the first in seeking merino sheep. In 1797, for example, some were imported into Australia.
[5] Jarvis was a New Yorker but had relatives in Charlestown, NH. The region was perfect for sheep raising.
[6] Spanish Merino Sheep, Vermont Breeders' Association (1879), p. 31. New York was the biggest port of entry by far, with 9349 sheep off-loaded there. Massachusetts ports of entry were second with 2379 merino sheep.

to reinforce the demand for domestic supplies. The price for wool surged dramatically, more than doubling to $1.50 per pound. As a result, the sheep craze gathered even greater momentum.

Part of the reason why New England farmers jumped so heavily into the craze was the discovery that the merino sheep were extremely well suited to the northeast, including southern and central New Hampshire. The merino's cleft upper lip allowed them to thrive on the sparse grasses that grew on the thin, rocky lands of northern New England. The sheep were very low maintenance animals that could be turned loose in the fields in early spring and left to graze until late fall. This flexibility led the farmers to open up new, more extensive grazing areas where there were none before.

Moreover, wool growing proved to be a very democratic enterprise. Almost anyone with a farm could participate. Annual Meredith inventory reports from the first half of the 19th century show that perhaps half of all the farmers in town acquired small flocks. There were only a few with more than 20 head, while the majority owned from as few as one or two to the low teens.[1] The profitability of even a single sheep was apparently so high (relative to other cash crops) that it enabled those with small farms to partake successfully in the business.

By the end of 1812, there were already an astounding 364,892 sheep in New Hampshire.[2] Meredith farmers were active participants in the craze, owning 2836 sheep in 1812.[3] Noting the obvious, observers in 1817 remarked that "sheep have greatly multiplied, and are considered the most profitable stock that can be raised on a farm."

Wool growing and the manufacturing economy in the Northeast naturally flourished during this period as domestic suppliers replaced both raw materials and finished goods previously obtained from England. But the end of the war in 1814 led to a sharp reversal of the process when English goods flooded back into the US market. Among other impacts, the price of wool plummeted to 40 cents a pound.[4]

With the nascent Northeastern economy imperiled, Congress responded in 1816 by passing a tariff on wool imports. This was the beginning of an extended protectionist phase designed to bolster American industry. Tariff rates were raised again in 1824 and 1828 reaching nearly 50%. Each tariff resulted in sharp increases in domestic wool prices. The three tariffs refueled the sheep craze. By the latter 1820s, wool production took on even greater importance

---

[1] See, Meredith Annual Inventory & Tax Reports, for each year from 1831 forward, (Meredith Historical Society Archives). 1831 was the first year that town officials broke out sheep counts as a separate inventory and tax category. Gilford Town Inventories also show the same pattern during the 1840s and 1850s (Gilford Inventory records, Gilford Town Hall).
[2] Merrill and Merrill, Gazetteer, 1817, Table III. The compilers indicated that this was a conservative accounting, having reached out to town Selectmen for their information but not getting responses from all of them. Table III also shows many towns without any sheep at all.
[3] Merrill and Merrill, Gazetteer, 1817, pp. 16 and Table III.
[4] Robert Blaivet, "The Vermont Sheep Industry: 1811-1880," in Vermont History, January 1965, Vol. xxxiii No. 1, p. 243.

for New England farmers because their other market products were becoming increasingly uncompetitive with those from western farms.[1]

The domestic wool industry entered its golden era following the enactment of the 1828 tariff. The period was 'golden' because demand outstripped supply, and foreign competitors were boxed out of the market.[2] Vermont led the way in raising sheep among New England states, but the craze was apparent throughout the Northeast. Statistics for this period are spotty at best, but the growth pattern between 1836 and 1840 is quite apparent as the table below shows:

Sheep population, 1836 vs.1840[3]

	NH	VT	New England
1836	465,000	1,099,000	2,895,000
1840	617,000	1,682,000	3,820,000
% Change	33%	53%	32%

The farmers in Meredith continued to participate along with the rest of New Hampshire in taking advantage of the opportunity. By 1832, the number of sheep in the town had increased to 3423. The number peaked in 1840 at 3826.[4]

The sheep craze certainly played an important role in the settlement of Bear Island after the 'foreclosure' in 1819. Prior to it, the first farmers on the island had not raised any sheep.[5] During the second phase of settlement of the island that began in the 1820s, most, if not all, of the island farmers raised sheep during their years on Bear. The detailed Meredith inventory and tax reports for 1830s and 1840s show that virtually all of the permanent and seasonal farmers on the island had small flocks.[6]

Bear Island was a very attractive place for sheep farming. In addition to its relatively large acreage and favorable grazing attributes, farmers realized that, thanks to the frontage on the lake, they only needed to build containment walls on two sides in most cases to control their flocks, rather than four or more on mainland farms. The most obvious examples are the

---

[1] Western lands (especially Ohio) were far better suited for farming. Their rich, deep soils and vast flat lands enabled them to farm on a much greater scale than New England where the relatively poor farm lands had been over-worked for decades already. The completion of the Erie Canal in 1825 was the real beginning of the end for New England farmers, cutting the transportation costs of western products such that they became cheaper than local supplies.

[2] Chester Whitney Wright, "Wool-growing and the tariff," by Cambridge (1910), p. 93. Despite the 'golden' label, the market for wool was still quite volatile throughout the 1830s. Annual prices over the ten year period from 1827 to 1836 moved as follows: .36, .40, .29, .405, .58, .41, .525, .50, .57, and .58. Benton and Barry, A Statistical View of the Number of Sheep, 1836, p. 122.

[3] Wright, "Wool-growing and the tariff," p. 90. Massachusetts was not a big participant in the wool growing industry. Sheep totals in 1836 and 1840 were only 373,000 and 378,000. On the other hand, sheep totals were very high in the larger states of the Northeast. In 1836 New York had the most, 4,299,000, followed by Pennsylvania and Ohio had 1,714,000 and 1,711,000, respectively. Per capita, however, Vermont was the largest sheep raising state in the country.

[4] Meredith Annual Inventory & Tax Reports, 1831-1840. (Meredith Historical Society Archives). The town's involvement in the craze was in the middle of the pack compared with other towns throughout the state. By far the towns with the highest counts were all located along the western side of the state. The three largest in 1836 were Walpole, Lebanon, and Hanover where sheep counts ranged from 11,000 to 15,000. The three western counties of New Hampshire accounted for 57% of the sheep in the state. Meredith had the fourth highest sheep count of the 34 towns in (then) Strafford County, behind Gilmanton (4313), Sanbornton (3892), and Sandwich (3344). Numerous towns in the state had fewer than 2000. C. Benton and S. Barry, A Statistical View of the Number of Sheep... in 1836, Folsom, Wells, and Thurston (1837), pp. 10-21.

[5] Hugh Kelsea's report, 1819 details the numbers of other stock held by the first farmers, but there is no mention of any sheep.

[6] Meredith Annual Inventory & Tax Reports, (Meredith Historical Society Archives).

shoreline to shoreline dividing walls between Lots 2/3, 3/4, 4/5, 6/7, and 7/8. These large stone 'sheep' walls were almost the only ones built on Lots 3, 4, 7, 8, and 9.[1]

Some of the other islands on the lake provided even greater convenience. Few or no walls, for example, were required on Pine Island, which was owned for sheep grazing by Caleb Lovejoy from 1828 until his death in the early 1840s.[2] Lockes Island, Welsh Island, Timber Island, and Cow Island were similarly known as seasonal pastures for sheep. In the 1820s and early 1830s, Cow Island in fact became home to so many Spanish sheep that it was called "Mereno Island" by its owner before the name was changed back in the 1830s.[3]

The 'golden era' of sheep farming came to an end in the 1840s. Enhanced competition entered the supply side of the market. First, the advent of the railroad in the 1830s enabled wool to flood in from the West.[4] Then, the protective tariffs were reduced in 1842 and eliminated in 1846. These developments opened the market to imports from countries such as Argentina, Australia and New Zealand where wide open spaces had fostered the growth of huge herds.[5] Prices fell dramatically from 57 cents/pound in 1835 to 25 cents/pound by the late 1840s. The New England market never recovered, and the size of flocks plummeted. By 1851, the total number of sheep in Meredith had declined to 2017. Vermont's flocks dropped from a peak of 1.7 million sheep to 1.0 million in 1850, while New England in total declined from 3.8 million to 1.8 million.[6]

Left behind by the sheep frenzy was the remarkable and enduring legacy that we continue to marvel at today: the stone walls. The craze could not have occurred without them. The walls were necessitated by the nature of sheep. The merinos and their derivatives were hardy animals that roamed anywhere they could in search of food. Unprotected crops and gardens were particular favorites. Sheep were also difficult to contain as they constantly tested walls for openings or jumped over them if they were not high enough.[7]

Before the sheep era, the first settlers built most of their fences out of wood, usually rails, stumps and brush collected as part of the clearing process. These fences were only built around

---

[1] Not coincidentally, all but Lot 8 were probably never used as permanent farms after 1819, although Lot 9 had a brief period of year-round farming.

[2] Meredith records show that Caleb owned from 12 to 18 sheep during the 1830s. Meredith Inventory and Tax Records (Meredith Historical Society Archives).

[3] BCRI, B/P 9014/191, John Prince to Henry Andrews et al, April 1834; Mulligan, Gunstock Parish, p. 265. See below, Chapter 36, for a short history of Cow Island.

[4] The cost differential between New England and the West was huge. In Vermont, the cost to produce wool was $1-2.00 compared with $0.25 to 1.00 in the West. Whitney, "Wool-growing and the tariff."

[5] Australia, for example, became the largest exporter of wool to England by 1849, shipping a staggering 16,300 tons of wool. "Industrial Revolution in Australia," Museum of Applied Arts & Sciences, March 31, 2016.

[6] Whitney, "Wool-growing and the tariff." Prices witnessed something of a rebound during the Civil War when woolen uniforms and blankets for northern soldiers raised the demand, but sheep farming in New England continued to ebb. Nevertheless, several Bear Islanders continued to raise sheep into the 1880s. By then they had moved to Meredith Neck where they maintained small flocks. See Meredith Annual Inventory & Tax Report, 1880 and 1881. By 1882, there were only 536 sheep in the entire town. Meredith Selectmen's Report, 1882, State Archives.

[7] Susan Allport, Sermons in Stone: The Stone Walls of New England and New York, (1990), p. 95.

their cultivated fields, gardens, and orchards.[1] But the nearby wood lots became exhausted relatively quickly because wood was a multipurpose resource in constant demand. It was used voraciously for heating and in the construction of homes, barns, roads, and many other things. Moreover, it was also burned extensively for potash and pearl ash that were used in making soap, glass, and fertilizer.

Even before the sheep craze, some stone walls were built around cultivated fields. The glacier had left ample field stones everywhere. The annual plowing for crops simply added to the supply in a process that played out over and over again with each passing year. These small stones were sandwiched between larger stones in the walls built around the plowed fields. As a result these walls are easily identifiable because they are much thicker than the stone walls used to fence in sheep.[2]

On Bear, these thicker walls are most prevalent on Lot 6 where there were three separate permanent farms active during the 1830s. This concentration of farms also accounts for the well-defined sheep runs that are still quite evident on both halves of Lot 6.

Sheep run on Lot 6N

In contrast to the thicker walls, those built to contain sheep resulted in a different, simpler design. Using oxen, the farmers gathered nearby large stones to build the walls around their much larger sheep pastures that came to encompass almost all of a farmer's land holdings. These types of walls are far more ubiquitous as they were built along property boundaries as well as around internal fields used only for sheep grazing.

---

[1] The early farmers did not build walls specifically to mark the boundaries of their properties. They had more than enough to do without adding to it.
[2] When no more walls needed to be built around plowed fields, the farmers often simply made piles of surface stones here and there to keep them away from the plows. These piles are particularly noticeable on Bear Island Lot 6S, for example. During the 20th century, vacationer lore held that the largest of these piles were 'Indian burial grounds'.

Chapter Ten

Bear Island: The 1830s

The 1830s were important years in the history of Bear Island. The era of ownership by speculators linked directly to the Masonian Proprietors came to an end. The four previously unsold lots on the island finally found ownership among men who lived in Meredith. Moreover, the first members of two of the more venerable families in island history acquired property during the decade.

North Bear

On the north end of Bear, Lots 1 and 2 continued to change hands several times during the 1830s. In 1833, John Batchelder sold them to Stephen B. Dockham in a transaction that began the multifaceted history of the Dockham family on Bear Island.[1] Stephen was the eldest of the four children of Theophilus Dockham Sr. and his wife, Abigail.[2] Little is known about Stephen, but at the time of the purchase he was living in Meredith and considered himself to be a "Gentleman" (rather than a Yeoman or Husbandman as most others did).[3] He presumably bought the lots on Bear for seasonal pasturage for sheep.[4]

Stephen owned Lots 1 and 2 for six years. In 1837, he sold them to his brother, Nathaniel, but the following year, he bought them back.[5] Stephen sold them again in 1839 to a Gilford farmer, John Blaisdell Jr.[6] At about the same time, Stephen purchased two lots in Gilford from Eliphalet Blaisdell, the father of his wife, Charlotte.[7]

Meanwhile, a little further down North Bear, the neighboring Lots 3 and 4 were sold for the first time. During the early 1820s, these two lots were owned by Nathaniel Haven Jr. But he had passed away in 1827, and the lots remained in his estate. In 1830, Haven's wife sold all of his Bear Island holdings (Lots 3, 4, and 7) to Stephen C. Lyford, a very influential Meredith Bridge (later Laconia) attorney, real estate speculator, and entrepreneur.[8] In 1833, Lyford finally found local buyers for Lots 3 and 4 on Bear. In separate transactions, he sold undivided halves in each of them to Caleb Lovejoy Jr. and his son, David R. Lovejoy. This purchase marked the

---

[1] See Appendix for the Dockham family tree.

[2] For detail on Theophilus Dockham, see 'Vignettes' at the end of this chapter. Abigail was referred to as Elsy or Alse in various old documents.

[3] BCRI, B/P 9014/365. The location of his mainland homestead is not known as there is no prior record of any land ownership in his name.

[4] He does not appear in the inconsistent Meredith Inventory and Tax Records until 1839 when he is listed as owning 17 sheep.

[5] BCRI, B/P 9016/612. The latter sale appears to have resulted from Nathaniel having identified and then purchasing about 70 acres of Lot 75 on the Neck from Richard Plummer. The lot was next door to the Meetinghouse cemetery. The land extended down to the lake opposite the western side of Pine Island and eventually included the point that forms part of Kelley Cove.

[6] BCRI, B/P 9018/365. Like those before him, Blaisdell purchased the Bear lots for summer pasturage, also primarily for his sheep. As part of the sales agreement, Stephen reserved ownership of a six acre crop of rye grass he had sewn in the fall.

[7] BCRI, B/P 9018/366. John Blaisdell was probably part of the same family.

[8] The actual deeds of sale to Lyford were not located. For more on Lyford, see Chapter 11, 'Vignettes'.

introduction of the Lovejoy family to Bear Island.[1] Caleb and David subsequently divided their ownership in the two lots with Caleb taking Lot 3 and David Lot 4.

Caleb Lovejoy was a 'joiner' (aka carpenter) who moved to Meredith from Pembroke in 1813 when he bought 37 acres on the northern end of Neck Lot 78.[2] This farm ran roughly from the entrance of Kelley Cove on the north to what is now the public parking lot at Shep Brown's on the south. As such, the lot was located directly across from the northern end of Bear. The Bear purchase was not Caleb's first acquisition of island property. Some six years earlier, in 1827, he had purchased Pine Island from the heirs of one of the original proprietors, Jotham Odiorne.[3]

David Lovejoy was Caleb's first son, born in Pembroke in 1805. Not long after his purchase of the property on Bear, David acquired his own Neck farm in 1835 when he paid off a mortgage loan that Caleb had taken on a 50 acre parcel on Lot 79 that ran from the Neck Road to Fish Cove.[4]

David kept Lot 4 until 1839 when he subdivided it and sold it in separate transactions to two full-time Bear Island residents. He sold the western half (Jerry Point) to James S. Bickford whose year-round homestead was next door on Lot 5. He sold the remainder (the Camp Nokomis portion) to Thomas Bickford, the son of Brackett Bickford who owned the eastern half of Lot 6N.[5]

South Bear

On the southern end of the island, there was quite a bit of change during the decade. In 1830, Brackett Bickford subdivided his homestead on Lot 6N, initially selling off the interior half of it to his neighbor and younger brother, James S. Bickford,.[6] But within months, Brackett bought it it back and quickly sold it to his brother-in-law and former Bear Islander, John Nichols.[7] Nichols was a son of the early island settler, Paul Nichols, and he had spent some of his youthful years living on the island. By 1830, John was married to Brackett's sister, Priscilla Bickford.[8]

---

[1] BCRI, B/P 9017/204; B/P 9003/140. See the Appendix for the Lovejoy family tree.
[2] BCRI, B/P 9007/227. The copy of the deed incorrectly says he bought 87 acres. Later sales for Lot 78 make it clear the parcel was approximated 37 acres.
[3] BCRI, B/P 9011/405. For more information about Pine Island, see Chapter 37.
[4] BCRI, B/P 9017/195. See also, B/P 9014/37.
[5] BCRI, B/P 9006/502; 9005/261. Both deeds say he sold 36 acres to the respective buyers, for a total of 72 acres. The lot was generally believed to contain about 50 acres. This was David Lovejoy's only foray out to the island. He remained very active in Meredith affairs in the ensuing years. Among other things during the 1850s, he was the town tax collector for the Neck on two occasions, and he served as a Selectman for the town during two other years.
[6] BCRI, B/P 9013/93.
[7] BCRI, B/P 9013/142; 9014/303.
[8] John and Priscilla were the settlers responsible for digging the large cellar hole still found not too far from the boundary wall between Lot 6N and Lot 9. The rough outline of an old well and rudimentary footprints of several out buildings are also visible around the cellar hole.

The subdivision and sale of Lot 6N were fraught with potential legal issues. Brackett had originally purchased his half of Lot 6 from his uncle, Eleazer Bickford. While that sale implied that Eleazer was the owner of the entire lot, in fact he only owned an undivided half of Lot 6. Hence,

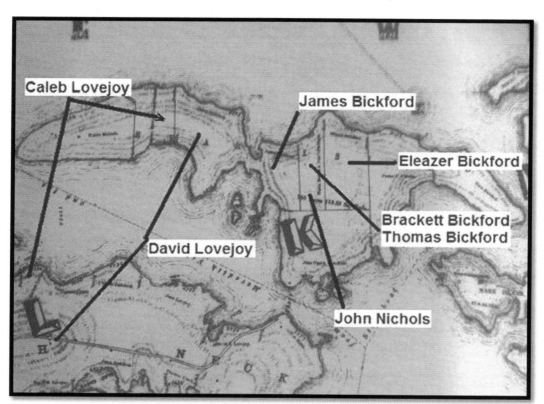

Brackett legally owned only an undivided half of Eleazer's undivided half. Brackett's sale to John Nichols simply extended the equation. Meanwhile, the other undivided half was still owned by the heirs of John Peirce.

The ownership issue was finally resolved the next year. In April 1832, Eleazer's son, Charles Bickford, purchased the Peirce's "undivided moiety or half part" of the 116 acre Lot 6.[1] Charles (only 23) was unmarried at the time and was still living with his parents on Lot 6S. This transaction legally resolved the ownership structure of Lot 6 on the ground. Eleazer and Charles jointly owned Lot 6S (58 acres). Brackett Bickford owned and occupied the eastern half (29 acres) of Lot 6N, and John Nichols owned and occupied the interior half (29 acres) of Lot 6N. Once resolved, that ownership structure remained in place for many years thereafter.[2]

While Lot 6 was being sorted out, the two remaining, unsold lots on South Bear, Lots 7 and 9, finally found a new owner. Both of these lots were purchased in 1830 by Stephen C. Lyford. He bought Lot 7 from the estate of Nathaniel Haven Jr. (along with Lots 3 and 4), and he purchased Lot 9 from the heirs of John Peirce.[3] In early 1831, Lyford sold both Lots 7 and 9 to Nathaniel Davis, the long-time owner of Governors Island.[4] Davis bought the lots for their timber

---

[1] BCRI, B/P 15/360.
[2] BCRI, B/P 9018/86. In 1838, Charles Bickford left the island for the Neck. He purchased the farm of Mac D. Lovejoy on Lot 78, just down the shore from Caleb Lovejoy. His shorefront began south of Shep Brown's Boat Basin and reached about to Camp Menotomy. By then he was 29 years old and married to Augusta Chase. The island farm remained in his name, but his parents and two younger siblings, Eleazer Jr. and Almira, remained living on Lot 6S on Bear.
[3] See BCRI, B/P 9017/195.
[4] BCRI, B/P 9017/195.

and grazing possibilities. He was the son of Eleazer Davis, the Alton (and later Gilford) settler who had purchased Governors Island in 1799 and sold it to his son, Nathaniel, in 1802.[1]

Nathaniel Davis retained ownership of Lot 7 for many years, but he quickly decided to sell Lot 9. In 1833, Dolly Nichols' son, Robert M. Nichols, purchased the 87 acre parcel and the buildings thereon from Davis.[2] The sale represented the return of Robert who had left the island home in 1829. Through his own hard work on the farm of Daniel Wiggin near Advent Cove, Robert had successfully earned enough money to purchase the property.[3]

Robert held on to Lot 9 for only a little more than two years. Whatever reconciliation he might have attempted with his mother did not work out. In 1836, he sold a one acre piece, abutting Lot 7, to Charles Bickford, giving the Lot 6S owner direct access to the lake at Deep Cove.[4] About the same time, he sold the rest of Lot 9 to MacDaniel Lovejoy.[5] Robert M. Nichols was the last full-time farmer to occupy this section of Bear Island.

McDaniel Lovejoy (Mac D. in deeds and familiarly) was the son of Benjamin Lovejoy, a former Pembroke farmer who had originally moved to a 70 acre farm on the lower end of the Neck (Lot 76) in 1808.[6] His relationship to Caleb Lovejoy, who arrived in 1813, is not clear, although both were from Pembroke, NH. Mac D. (b.1802) spent much of his youth on the Neck. In 1823, he married Martha P. Lovejoy (b. 1807), the daughter of Caleb Lovejoy. Beyond these details, Mac D.'s early years in Meredith are quite murky. His father, Benjamin, had sold the family's Neck farm in 1817[7] and disappeared from the Meredith records. Mac D. had purchased a 50 acre piece of Lot 78 in 1824, adjoining Caleb's property, where he established his homestead with his new bride.[8] Lot 9 provided seasonal grazing for his livestock.

Mac D. owned Lot 9 on Bear for only two years. In 1838, he sold it to brothers, John Neal and Joseph Neal Jr.[9] The Neal boys were sons of the early Meredith settler, Joseph "White Oak" Oak" Neal.[10] Their family farm was located in the First Range of the First Division along Meredith Bay, looking across the bay towards Pinnacle Hill and Meredith Neck.[11] They bought Lot 9 for its timber and seasonal grazing. The property stayed in the Neal family for the next 30 years. They were the last 'landlords' who allowed Dolly Nichols to live on the tip of the property.

---

[1] BCRI, B/P 9005/304; 9006/424. See below, Chapter 37, for a brief history of Governors Island.
[2] BCRI, B/P 9014/400.
[3] For further details about Robert's life, see Chapter 11, Vignettes.
[4] BCRI, B/P 9018/87. This parcel is now part of the St. John's on-the-Lake Chapel property.
[5] BCRI, B/P 9015/514.
[6] BCRI, B/P 9005/246.
[7] BCRI, B/P 9008/103.
[8] B/P 10/441. The seller was the former Neck resident, William Mead, who was living in Derby, Vermont at this time. BCRI, B/P 11/365.

[9] BCRI, B/P 9017/5. Deep in debt, he also sold his Neck farm to Bear Islander, Charles Bickford. BCRI, B/P 9018/86. Thereafter, Mac D. and his family moved to Moultonborough.
[10] Joseph "White Oak" Neal had a cousin of the same name who developed a farm in the Third Division. He was known as Joseph "Red Oak" Neal. See Hanaford, Annals, pp. 356-358.
[11] Neal Shore Road got its name from this family. The Neal family bought some of its First Division land from John Bickford, the progenitor of the Bear Island Bickfords. See, for example, BCRI B/P 9003/401.

Summary

Thus by the end of the 1830s, all of Bear Island was owned by local farmers, and all but one of them were from Meredith. The entire northern end of the island was still only being used for seasonal pasture and timber. The same usage was being made of Lots 7 and 9 by that time as well.

There were five permanent farms on the southern end of the island, four owned by Bickford family members. The year-round Bickfords were brothers James, Brackett, and Jonathan Jr. Their uncle, Eleazer, and his son, Charles, were the owners of record of the fourth. The fifth farm was owned by John Nichols, whose wife was the sister of the three Bickford brothers and a cousin of Charles.

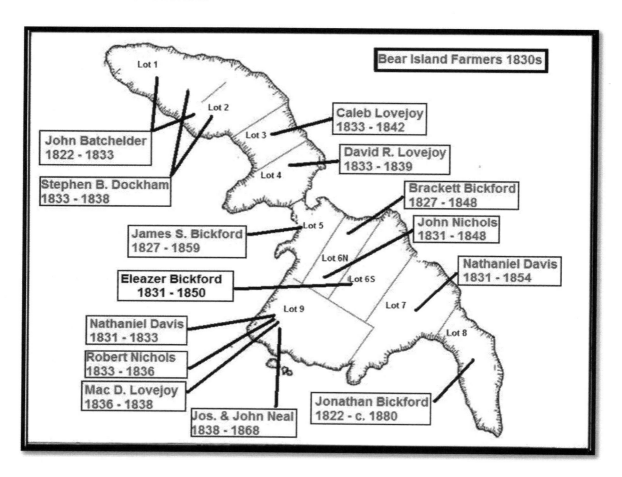

Chapter Eleven

Vignettes from the 1830s

Theophilus Dockham Sr.

Arising from the conflation of names, Theophilus Dockham Sr. was often mistaken in earlier histories as one of the first settlers on Bear Island. He was not. In fact, he only lived there briefly during the late 1840s and early 1850s when his son, Theophilus R., bought property on the island.

The early life of Theophilus Sr. is difficult to trace. He was very likely related to the three Dockhams (Thomas, John and William) who were living on Meredith Neck in the 1780s and 1790s (perhaps even the son of one of them and the brother or nephew of the other two?). His forebears were likely among the earliest settlers in Meredith history, as the Dockham name is found in the town annals in the 1760s. By the mid-1790s, Theophilus Sr. had carved out his own homestead on the lower part of Meredith Neck on parts of adjoining Lots 64 and 76. He did not own the land at the time; he occupied it at the grace of Ebenezer Smith. But he was able to establish himself by parlaying Smith's benevolence with his own hard labor. He sold his initial 'squatters' homestead with his improvements in 1804, but it is not clear where he moved thereafter. In 1813, he served in the military and fought in the War of 1812. He was taken captive during the war, but he returned to Meredith afterwards.

He and his wife, Abigail, had four children, including Stephen B., Theophilus R., Nathaniel, and Abigail. During the early 1840s and probably well before, Theophilus Sr. was living on the Neck. By 1850, it appears that he had moved to Bear Island with his son, Theophilus R., who had purchased Lot 6N in 1848.[1] Theophilus Sr. died c. 1851. His burial site is not known. After his death, his wife, Abigail, remained on Bear Island. She moved in with her daughter, also named Abigail, who was married to Waldo Meloon.

Robert M. Nichols

Oral tradition tells us that Dolly's youngest son, Robert, left the family's Bear Island home in 1819 when he was 12 years old because he was dissatisfied with the situation there. He was purportedly taken in by Daniel Wiggin who lived near Advent Cove. This oral history, however, has two major flaws. Daniel Wiggin was only about 15 years old in 1819, and he did not buy his farm near Advent Cove until 1829. It is more likely that Robert left home in 1829 at the age of 22, joining Daniel Wiggin on his new farm to help him develop it.[2] He used the money he earned

---

[1] See 1850 Census.
[2] In re Daniel's age, see Census of 1850. He was born in 1803 or 1804. For the 1829 purchase of his farm on Lot 61, see B/P 11/552. See also: Briggs, <u>Meredith Neck</u> (1957). Daniel Wiggin came from the wealthy line of Wiggins—Bradstreet, Chase and Chase Jr-- who arrived in Meredith in the 1780s. Coincidentally, Daniel was married in 1830 to Sarah Robinson, the grand-daughter of the Meredith proprietor who

working for Wiggin to buy Lot 9 on Bear in 1833. In late 1836, Robert used the proceeds from the sale of Lot 9 to acquire a 50 acre homestead farm spanning parts of Third Division Lots 8 and 13 near Center Harbor village.[1] By all indications Robert enjoyed a very successful life thereafter. He acquired additional lands nearby, including some waterfront on Winnipesaukee in 1856 that he used for pasture.[2]

Robert married Huldah Fogg c. 1840. They had three children.[3] In 1870, Robert, 63, moved to Meredith Village, acquiring a house on Lang Street.[4] Here he became a next door neighbor of Eleazer Bickford Jr., who had grown up on Bear Island, overlapping some of the years that Robert was living there. Robert died in 1873 and was buried in the Meredith Village Cemetery. His wife was buried there as well in 1879.[5]

In a classic case of 'small town boy makes good', Robert's son, James E. (picture below), grew up to become hugely successful.[6] Born in 1844 and schooled in Meredith, James left home for Boston in 1864, at the height of the Civil War. He first worked as a clerk at the department store, Jordan Marsh, before becoming a traveling salesman for the Franklin (NH) Woolen Mills in the latter 1860s.

James thrived as a salesman, becoming financially sound and savvy. His travels took him to New York City on numerous occasions, and he finally moved there. In 1879, he met Robert Austin, co-owner of the Fitts & Austin spice and coffee trading business. Austin convinced James to invest in Austin's dream of expanding into the wholesale grocery business. A new company named Austin, Nichols & Co. was incorporated by the two men. James became CEO when Austin died in 1885,. Thereafter, the company flourished as the wholesale grocery industry grew dramatically. In time, Austin, Nichols & Co. became the world's largest wholesale grocer.

James accumulated considerable wealth. He diversified into real estate and banking among other things. He became a Director of the Irving National Bank, the Broadway Trust Company, the Fidelity Trust Company, the Childs Company, and the Merchants' Refrigerating Company. Outside of business, he was an avid horseman and traveled extensively on big-game

---

originally hired Robert Bryant in 1765 to clear his lot in the First Division. See <u>Sons of the American Revolution</u>, Applications, 1889-1970, pp. 186, 189. The Wiggin family traced its history in New England back to the 1630s, including some of the governing families in Massachusetts.
    [1] BCRI, BP 9016/90. In 1873, it became part of the town of Center Harbor when the eastern-most section of Meredith, including the waterfront and wharf area on Winnipesaukee, was annexed to Center Harbor by the state legislature.
    [2] BCRI, B/P 18/206, 27/155, 31/283.
    [3] Hanaford, <u>Genealogies</u>, pp. 366-367.
    [4] BCRI, B/P 51/377.
    [5] BCRI, B/P 64/597. In 1879, another Bear veteran, George Bickford, bought Robert's house. He was a son of Brackett Bickford (Lot 6N) and just five years younger than his neighbor and cousin, Eleazer Bickford Jr. Their lives would have overlapped by several years on Bear where they lived on neighboring lots.
    [6] The information regarding James is drawn from: Granite Monthly, 1914, p. 267; <u>NY Times</u>, Aug 19, 1914; Walter, Frederick: <u>The History of Austin, Nichols & Co. Inc., 1855-1955</u>, p. 11; Austin, Nichols website; Blog, *Daytonian in Manhattan*, March 22, 2012; The 1900 James E. Nichols House, March 2012, website.

hunting expeditions. He also supported the polar expeditions of that era, providing them with stocks of food from his business.

In the area of real estate, James left his mark in Manhattan in 1900 after purchasing an East 79th Street property that was under construction. Located in the exclusive 'Cook Block', he built a five story mansion with numerous architectural flourishes. The original budget for the house was $105,000, a huge amount in those days. The New York Times praised it as "magnificently furnished, being especially notable for the splendid collection of wild animal heads gathered by Mr. Nichols."[1]

James did not forget his roots in New Hampshire. In 1910, he donated a new library building with all of its furnishings to the town of Center Harbor.[2] The classic structure was named the James E. Nichols Library in honor of its benefactor.

The fairy tale came to end for James in July 1914 when he died suddenly of heart disease while traveling in Austria. Shockingly, only a year later his wife was murdered by jewel thieves in their Manhattan home.

James' passing marked the end of the line for the Robert Nichols family. James had no children; his older brother, George, had died of illness in 1862, shortly after his Civil War enlistment ; and his sister was also childless. James life was a remarkable bookend to the legacy of his forebears: his great grandfather, Ensign Robert Bryant, the early Meredith settler who became the first Bear Island settler; and his grandmother, Dolly Bryant Nichols, the quintessential survivor in a world dominated by men.

Stephen C. Lyford

Stephen C. Lyford (1788 – 1869) was a Meredith Bridge (Laconia) attorney and entrepreneur who played a particularly prominent role in the region during the first half of the 19th century. Real estate investment was just one of his many activities, involving numerous purchases and sales throughout the Lakes Region. In 1829, he was given an honorary A.M. degree by Dartmouth College. In 1848, he was called "one of our most estimable citizens" by the Freemasons.[3]

He had his hands in a wide range of entrepreneurial endeavors. In 1831, Lyford helped found, along with Ichabod Bartlett, the steamboat company that built the *Belknap*, the first steamer on the lake.[4] During the same year, he was one of the founders of the Meredith Bridge

---

[1] New York Times, July 18, 1904.
[2] BCRI, B/P 129/217. The animal heads still on display in the library were part of James' collection.
[3] The Freemason's Monthly Magazine, Vols. 7-8, Feb 1, 1848.
[4] Blaisdell, Paul H., Three Centuries on Winnipesaukee, pp. 23 – 24; Blackstone, Edward H., Farewell Old Mount Washington, pp. 9-10.

Savings Bank.[1] He was its first Treasurer. He also operated a saw mill at Lake Village in the 1830s. In 1848, he was a charter member of the Winnipesaukee Steamboat Company that built the *Lady of the Lake*.[2] Lyford Street in Laconia was named after him.

The Meredith Neck Bridge

During the 1830s, the lower Neck witnessed several key improvements that involved future Bear Islanders. These developments are still quite visible today, bearing witness to the many talents of these early farmers. The Neck Bridge is perhaps the most important but least recognized of these developments. Its construction in 1832 led to the building of Pleasant Street, a quicker route to the lower Neck. Prior to the 1830s, the route to the Neck from the First Division and Meredith Village was a much longer one. The 1774 road to Center Harbor had provided the initial access route, running through the Village, up Plymouth Street, then east near the current Village Cemetery to True Avenue. From there settlers reached the Neck by dropping down to the range way that became Barnard Ridge Road. Travelers followed Barnard Ridge to where it intersects with the current Neck Road and Pleasant Street, but then the road dipped down towards the lake to flatter ground where it crossed the little stream that impeded travel above. The road followed fairly close to the lake before turning back up across the field where it resumed its current path near the intersection of Blueberry Hill Road and the Neck Road.

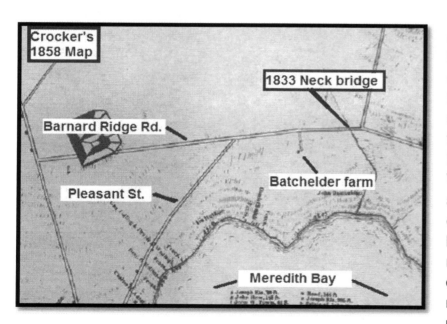

By about 1830, a shorter route for reaching the Neck had become feasible when the town completed a new road across the base of Meredith Bay. This area had defied travel for decades because of the quagmire caused by the Hawkins swamp that emptied into Winnipesaukee there.[3] A road across the base of the bay, now part of Rte. 25, gradually evolved between 1810 and 1820 from a narrow path, that was impassible during mud season, to a corduroy road. It was finally improved into a more finished product by 1830.[4]

---

[1] The bank became the Laconia Savings Bank and is now called the Bank of New Hampshire.
[2] Early Meredith and Vicinity, p. 48.
[3] The swamp or 'wetlands' are still quite evident behind the buildings and shopping plaza today. In fact, in 2015, new steel pilings had to be put in place to keep some of the buildings there from sinking any further.
[4] Wyatt, Road Histories, p. 219. This new road was built across Third Division Lot 38. It gave easier access to the Center Harbor Road via the Neal or Center Harbor hill (now often referred to as High School hill).

With the base of the bay conquered, Neck residents petitioned the town to shorten the route to the Neck Road by having a new road built from the base of the bay to an intersection with the Neck Road about where Barnard Ridge Road meets it today. Town officials agreed to do this, but they insisted that Neck residents first build a bridge across the brook next to the Smith Cemetery, so the Neck Road could be straightened.

Neck residents agreed, and the bridge was completed by 1833. There proved to be one hitch, however, in the completion of the new road. After the Neck residents finished the bridge, town officials reneged on their agreement to build the connecting road. The Neck farmers sued the town, initially without satisfaction. They then took their suit to the Strafford County court in Dover where they won a complete victory.[1] Modern day Pleasant Street—originally called the Meredith Neck Road--was completed in 1833.[2]

Stone work of the Neck Bridge

Their work was a remarkable accomplishment. The bridge is still in use today, some 184 years later. Anyone who travels the Neck road drives across it, probably unwittingly. Because of the layout, travelers cannot see the level of engineering that went into it. The granite foundation is not readily visible from either direction while heading towards it or passing over it. The massive granite stones used to build the bridge speak volumes to the ingenuity and perseverance of these early farmers.

---

[1] Wyatt, "Stone Bridge on Meredith Neck," in loose leaf binder (Meredith Historical Society Archives).
[2] The name was changed to Pleasant Street in the 1970s when the town took ownership of it from the state. Meredith Neck Road is a state owned road. Wyatt, Road Histories, p. 171.

Page Pond Saw Mill

The Page Pond saw mill on the Neck was another remarkable feat of engineering by some of the farmers during the 1830s. Saw mills and grist mills were the two essentials for survival and growth in the early towns of New Hampshire. In the 1820s, the grist mill needs of the Neck were being met by the mill in Meredith Village that was developed in the late 1780s. Saw mill needs were also met either there or further down the Neck;[1] but given the weight and aggravation of moving logs and lumber, proximity was always important.

In May 1830, Sewall Leavitt purchased a one acre parcel on the outlet stream of Little Pond (later renamed Page Pond) on Lot 51 from James Gilman.[2] The parcel was located on the range way between Lot 51 and Lots 44 and 45. As part of the purchase, Leavitt also acquired the right to dam up the stream each spring so he could create enough water power for a saw mill.[3] Thereafter, Leavitt built two dams to create his water supply. The larger of the two was almost 100 feet long, 16 feet wide, and 18 feet high at the spillway.[4]

Like the Neck Road Bridge, the large dam and sluice were constructed using huge blocks of granite. The engineering and perseverance were again remarkable, and they have stood the test of time quite well.

Mill Stone Hill

The construction of the bridge and the saw mill raise the obvious question of where the farmers quarried the granite blocks for them. Surprisingly, the question has not been definitively answered. The deeds from the 1830s and thereafter do not mention a quarry in that or any other area.[5] By the early 1900s, a 'traprock' quarry located on Lot 45 (off Quarry Road on land formerly owned at the time by the Leavitts when the mill and bridge were built) was developed not too far away; but it was used for crushed stone for roadways.[6] There is only speculation that the granite blocks were quarried there. Harold Wyatt, arguably the most informed Meredith historian, noted

---

[1] The first Neck saw mill was built on Lot 75 at the lower end of the Neck by Richard Plummer at least as early as the 1820s. Plummer acquired the lot in 1817. It included a shingle mill as well. See BCRI, B/P 9009/57; 9016/136.

[2] BCRI, B/P 9013/382. Gilman had purchased that lot in 1789 when he moved to Meredith.

[3] The right he acquired allowed him to "flow (i.e. flood) the land" of Jeremiah Morgan until May 20th of each year.

[4] "Page Pond and Forest: A History and Guide," by Dan Heyduk, p. 16. This paper is an excellent source of information about Page Pond. This is town land, and there are several well marked hiking trails that include loops to the pond and the mill site.

[5] A fairly comprehensive search yielded nothing.

[6] Heyduk, "Page Pond," pp. 16, and footnote 13 on p. 25.

some years ago that he did "not know where the stone came from…" but was told it had originated from the quarry on Leavitt's property.[1]

Against the backdrop of this uncertainty, there was another site where the granite blocks were more likely quarried. This is a location that was specifically named "Mill Stone Hill" before 1858.[2] It was part of Lot 61 that abutted Advent Cove on the lake. The northern end of the lot was bound by the range way that became Blueberry Hill Road which would have provided good

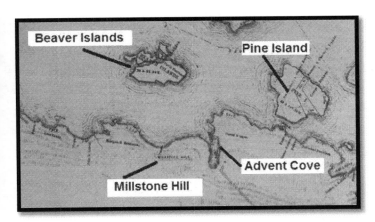

access to the mill location and the bridge.[3] In 1830, the lot was owned by Daniel Wiggin.[4] Millstone Hill must have been an especially significant location to have been given a name. Throughout the entire settlement era of Meredith, very few locations were ever given names. Only those places that had clearly defined importance were labeled. The name in this case speaks volumes to the likelihood that it was the source of the granite for the saw mill and the bridge.

Meredith Neck Meetinghouse

The Meredith Neck Meetinghouse is one of the most visible legacies of the farming era that remain on the Neck. In July 1839, a group of 41 Neck residents petitioned the Meredith Village Free Will Baptist Church, requesting approval to break away from it to establish their own meetinghouse. The rationale was simple: it would be far more convenient for them. The Meredith Village Free Will Baptist Church had itself only broken away the year before from the original Free Will Baptist Church that was built on Oak Hill (Winona Road) in 1802 by Simon Pottle.[5] After much rancor, permission was granted.[6] The land for the new meetinghouse was donated by Stephen Boardman Jr. and his wife, Sarah, who owned the parcel where the meetinghouse now sits. The small lot had an ideal location at the top of what was known as Boardman Hill. There was a small cemetery already established next to the parcel.

---

[1] Wyatt, "Stone Bridge on Meredith Neck," loose leaf binder, Meredith Historical Society.
[2] Crocker's map of Lake Winnipesaukee shore front owners, 1858. (State Archives.)
[3] In those days, the range way (now Blueberry) continued straight ahead for quite some distance past Lots 51, 50 and 49 rather than curving sharply to the right as the paved road does today. Much of the old range way still exists in the form of a logging road.
[4] BCRI, B/P 9011/552. Also B/P 9013/198. Wiggin bought it jointly with Stephen Boardman Jr. in 1829, and then Wiggin bought out Boardman in 1830. This is the same Daniel Wiggin with whom Robert Nichols lived when he left his mother, Dolly, on Bear Island. Daniel's farm was on the southern half of the lot very near Advent Cove. The stone house at 28 Little Road is on that property. The hill is to the north and located at the end of Advent Cove Road.
[5] "Meredith Neck Church," Cawley, in Hanaford, Annals (1932), Fractions of History 81; "History of Meredith," History of Belknap County, McClintock, pp. 848-850; Wyatt, "Meredith Neck Church," loose leaf binder, Meredith Historical Society. The Pottle Meetinghouse still stands and presently houses the Farm Museum of the Meredith Historical Society on what is now Winona Road. The Meredith Village arm of the Free Will Baptist church was organized in October 1838.
[6] Histories of Meredith always refer to the residents on the Neck as being a community apart from the rest of the town. This episode probably contributed a great deal in establishing this frame of reference.

The seven leading signers of the petition included Bear Islanders Eleazer Bickford Sr. and John Nichols and his wife, Priscilla. They also included future Bear Islanders Jesse Lovejoy and Nathaniel Dockham. The last two of the leading signers were Daniel Wiggin and his wife, Sally.[1] The entire group of petitioners came from only 12 different families. There were nine Nichols, seven Bickfords, and five Lovejoys amongst the 41 petitioners. Dolly Nichols' son, Robert, and his wife, Huldah, were two of the signers. Robert Bryant Jr.'s son, Abram, was also a signer, as was his wife, Mahala Bickford Bryant. The preponderance of individual petitioners—23 of the 41— at one time or another either lived on Bear Island or owned property on it. Seven of the 41 were living on the island permanently at the time of the petition, and another seven had lived on it previously.

The church was built fairly quickly, apparently completed by the end of 1839 thanks to the cooperative efforts of the people of the Neck and Bear Island. Its history thereafter is rather sketchy. One account indicates that in 1843, just four years after its founding, the church "was largely broken up." Perhaps not so coincidentally, the Meredith Village Free Will Church disbanded the following year.[2]

Very early Neck Meetinghouse

Meredith Neck Meetinghouse c. 1890s

No explanation for these break-ups has ever been offered, but the evangelical history of the period suggests a logical rationale. The early 1840s were the peak years of the ecclesiastical phenomenon known as Millerism, a religious movement that prophesied the second coming (Advent) of Christ during the Hebrew year ending March 21, 1844. The movement's founder was William Miller, a Vermont farmer turned preacher who studied the Bible for absolute truths. In *Daniel 8:14*, he found his truth about the second coming. Miller published a book about his prophecy and followed up with innumerable speaking engagements in New Hampshire and elsewhere in the Northeast. In 1843, he gained the adherence of a Boston Baptist pastor, Joshua Himes, who was taken by the strength and conviction of Miller's message. Himes embarked upon an almost fanatical advocacy of Miller's apocalyptic message, producing charts,

---

[1] They, of course, were the folks who took in Robert M. Nichols when he left his mother, Dolly, in the late 1820s.
[2] <u>History of Merrimack and Belknap Counties</u>, pp. 449-450.

buying the largest tent in the country for revival meetings, and publishing journals to widen the reach of the message. The movement known as Millerism was spawned as a result.[1]

Across the Northeast and especially in New England, thousands of Christians drifted from the tenets of their established faiths (led by Baptists and Methodists but encompassing all denominations) in anticipation of the fateful day. The Lakes Region was part and parcel of the frenzy. Nathaniel Davis hosted a revival meeting on Governors Island where Miller himself spoke.

The Advent never occurred as prophesied, of course. The fateful March 1844 day came and went, as did a revised date seven months later. But the movement did not die out. Various congregants around the region did not revert to their previous systems of belief. Quite apart from the anticipated Advent, they embraced a doctrine that emphasized the equality of all men (including slaves), equal roles for women within the church, and espoused principles of health reform that included temperance and abstention from tobacco. During the 1840s, a new denomination gradually evolved known as Adventism. The first such group was established in Washington, NH.

It appears that the congregants on Meredith Neck also made the decision to adopt Adventism. One strand of oral history tells us that the Neck meetinghouse became an Adventist church 1843, although the reason given was "due to dwindling attendance." It goes on to say that the revival meetings held there "proved to be a drawing card for the young men in the area, who gathered from miles around to watch the proceedings from the windows," enjoying "the stomping and shouting."[2] The timing is quite plausible given the frenzy around Miller's Advent prediction. [3] The Adventists continued to call the Neck home until an Advent church was established in Meredith Village towards the latter part of the century.[4]

By the early 1890s and presumably some years before, the Neck church fell into disuse. The "little abandoned church" became a natural draw to the Methodist ministers who established summer homes on Pine Island during the 1890s.[5] They began holding Sunday services there. For several years, the congregation included the families of Neck farmers.[6] It is not known how many summers these services took place, but the Pine Islanders eventually moved them to the Bear Island House, perhaps around 1910. The Neck church history in the immediate years thereafter is not known. It apparently again fell into disuse. Under the auspices of The Union

---

[1] Christianitytoday.com/history/people/denominationalfounders/williammiller.

[2] Transcript of a talk by Ruth Wakeley about the history of the Neck church. http://unionchurchmeredith.com/about.

[3] It is without question that the Neck meetinghouse became a Seventh Day Adventist church sometime before 1858. Advent cove had received its name by then. See Crocker's 1858 map of the lake. One possible flaw in this scenario is that a Free Baptist minister named Hugh Beede is said to have preached at the Neck Church during the 1848-1851 period. The native ministry of New Hampshire, Nathan Carter (1906), p. 706. However, in the fluidity of the times, the two were not mutually exclusive. The Neck church was not stricken from the Free Will Baptist church rolls until 1867 after years of not reporting. Free Baptist Cyclopaedia (1889), p. 464.

[4] The timing of the move to Meredith Village has proven to be elusive. By the 1870s, Adventism was very popular, and Alton was a favorite location for camp meetings. In 1875, for example, an enormous audience estimated to number 30,000 gathered at the Second Adventists camp grounds for their annual gathering. Lake Village Times, September 4, 1875, p. 3.

[5] See Chapter 37, Pine Island, regarding the Methodists who purchased Pine Island.

[6] Knight, "Pine Island," p. 5.

Church of Meredith Neck, summer services were eventually reinstituted. The building was rehabilitated in the 1950s and a bell from the original steamer, the *Mt. Washington*, was installed in the tower.[1] Once again people from the Neck and the islands were drawn to the meetinghouse on the hill. It remains a delightful sanctuary and an enduring link to those who first settled the Neck.

The Meredith Neck Meetinghouse, c. 2016.

---

[1] "Meredith Neck Union church," in <u>Reminiscences of Meredith</u>, p.32.

Chapter Twelve

Bear Island: The 1840s

In general, the 1840s were years of prosperity for Meredith and its farmers, including those on Bear. The regional economy was strong, and the population was growing. The sheep craze reached its high point during this decade, and at least a few of the island farmers on South Bear enjoyed the benefits that accompanied the craze.

Specifically on Bear, the 1840s witnessed the least amount of activity amongst property owners since the earliest years of settlement. However, there was one fundamental change that impacted North Bear for decades to come.

North Bear

The fundamental change on North Bear occurred in 1845 when the Gilford owner of Lots 1 and 2, John Blaisdell, leased his seasonal pastures to Waldo Meloon.[1] The transaction was the beginning of the almost 40 years' presence of the Meloons on the island. Waldo and his family became the first year-round farmers to live on North Bear.

Waldo's background is a little obscure. He was born in Gilford in 1806. In 1827, he married Abigail (Betsey) Dockham of Meredith, the only daughter of Theophilus Sr. and Abigail Dockham.[2] Initially, Waldo moved his bride to the north country of New Hampshire. Their first four children-- John, Stephen, Francis, and Melissa--were all born while they were living in the north. A fifth child, David, was born about 1838, although it is unclear where. By 1840, Waldo and his family were back living in Meredith. Waldo did not own any land, but the records show that he had a flock of nine sheep as well as five cows.[3]

Shortly after Waldo's lease of Lots 1 and 2, John Blaisdell Jr. sold the land back to his Stephen B. Dockham in 1846.[4] The change in landlords probably suited Waldo just fine since Stephen B. was his brother-in-law. Waldo built the first house on this part of the island since the days of Henry Jenness. This was the place that eventually became the Bear Island Hotel.

The two North Bear lots next to Waldo had already undergone some ownership changes during the 1840s. Lot 3 was sold after the death of Caleb Lovejoy in 1841.[5] It was initially

---

[1] Meredith Inventory and Tax Report, 1845, note next to John Blaisdell (MHS Archives). The precise basis of Waldo's occupation is not spelled out, but leasing of land was common practice in those days.
[2] Hanaford, p. 637. Abigail's brothers were, of course, Stephen B., Nathaniel, and Theophilus R. Dockham. The Dockham and Meloon family trees can be found in the Appendix.
[3] Meredith Inventory and Tax Records, 1841 (MHS Archives).
[4] BCRI, B/P 8008/281.
[5] Caleb's son, Herbert, took over ownership of Caleb's mainland property which was next to what is now the public parking lot at Shep Brown's. BCRI, B/P 28/274.

purchased from Caleb's estate by John Smith in 1842.[1] Smith was a Neck farmer who lived on Lot 41 near the current day intersection of Barnard Ridge and Pleasant Street and was interested in the island for seasonal pasturage.[2] Three years later, in 1845, Smith sold Lot 3 in undivided halves to the second of Caleb's sons, Jesse, and to Charles Bickford.[3] Jesse and Charles were neighbors on the Neck, owning different parts of Lot 78 facing Bear.[4] Within a few months of the purchase of Lot 3, Charles Bickford sold his half interest to his younger brother, Eleazer Jr. (now 23), who was still living with his parents on Lot 6S.[5]

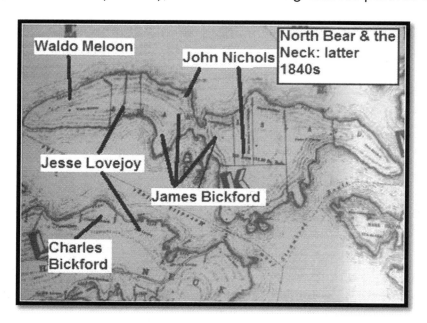

This purchase of Lot 3 was Jesse's first on the island, but of course, he was quite familiar with it from his childhood days. Moreover, Jesse was married to another island veteran, Eleanor Bickford, the youngest child of Jonathan Bickford Sr. and the sister of current Bear Island farmers James, Brackett, Jonathan Jr., and Priscilla Bickford Nichols. Jesse raised sheep like all of the other farmers who owned property on Bear, maintaining a flock that grew as large as 17 sheep in 1847.[6]

In 1850, Jesse bought out Eleazer Bickford Jr.'s share of Lot 3, giving Jesse ownership of all of it.[7] As a seasonal farmer, he did not lay down deep roots. There are no cellar holes or wells wells to be found nor are there any rock walls except for the two boundary walls that run from shore to shore along the north and south lines.

North Bear Lot 4 also underwent some major ownership changes during this period. In 1840, Brackett Bickford's son, Thomas, subdivided his 36 acre section of Lot 4 (the Nokomis parcel). He sold 15 acres to his uncle, John Nichols, the permanent farmer living on the interior half of Lot 6N.[8] Two years after that, in 1843, Thomas sold the remaining 21 acres to his uncle,

---

[1] BCRI, B/P 8003/127. David Lovejoy was the Executor of the will..

[2] The current address is 12 Meredith Neck Road. Earlier members of the Smith family were the ones who established the cemetery located next to the bridge on Meredith Neck Road, sometime before 1816. It was formerly called the Smith Cemetery but is referred to as the Meredith Neck cemetery most often now. The cemetery was built on the northwest corner of Lot 53.

[3] BCRI, B/P 22/428 and 8008/75. The sales were separate transactions.

[4] Jesse had purchased his mainland farm only a few years earlier, in 1841, from Jeremiah Jenness for $800. It encompassed what is now Camp Menotomy and its southern bound was Black Cove. BCRI, B/P 8007/510. Charles had purchased his in 1838.

[5] BCRI, B/P 8008/76.

[6] Meredith Inventory and Tax Records, 1847 (MHS Archives).

[7] BCRI, B/P 22/427. The previous year, Eleazer Jr. had embarked upon a new career as pilot of the brand new passenger ship, the *Lady of the Lake*. See below, 'Vignettes,' for more about Eleazer Jr.

[8] BCRI, B/P 8005/263. As a reminder, John Nichols was a son of the early Bear settler, Paul, and he was married to Thomas Bickford's aunt, Priscilla.

James Bickford, who already owned the Jerry Point section of Lot 4.[1] James permanent homestead farm was still on Lot 5, and he used Lot 4 for grazing and wood.

South Bear

While the lots on the northern end of the island were trading hands, South Bear experienced far less activity during the 1840s. Lots 5, 6S, 7, 8 and 9 were all retained by the owners who had purchased them in the 1820s and 1830s.[2] Only one lot, the interior half of Lot 6N, saw any change, but the change was noteworthy. In 1848, Theophilus R. Dockham purchased the 29 acre homestead farm on the interior half of Lot 6N and the 15 acre parcel on Lot 4 from John Nichols.[3] The youngest son of Theophilus Sr., Theophilus R. (32) and his wife, Mary (Wiggin), had two children and owned a farm on parts of lower Neck Lots 81 and 82 that they had purchased in the 1830s.[4] They sold it and moved permanently to Bear Island.[5] They were accompanied by Theophilus R.'s parents.[6]

Theophilus Dockham's Lot 6N cellar hole.

With Theophilus' arrival, there were now two Dockham children living on Bear Island year-round (his sister, Abigail Meloon was the other), along with their parents. A third child, Stephen B., owned the land occupied by Waldo and Abigail Meloon. The fourth child, Nathaniel, lived on the Neck next to the Meetinghouse Cemetery, and his farm ran down to the Winnipesaukee shoreline opposite Pine Island and included part of Kelley Cove.

[1] BCRI, B/P 8006/491.

[2] On a side note, Eleazer Bickford and other islanders petitioned the town to build a road from Jonathan Bickford's to "the Ferryway" and from the Ferryway landing on the Neck to the Neck road. (See Original Road Records 3218, May 15, 1844, State Archives.) The latter was handled by the town. (See Wyatt, Road Histories, p. 37.) There is no evidence that the town approved the road on Bear Island. There is little question that some kind of cart path existed on Bear covering the ground proposed, but it does not appear that the town credited the island farmers for their labor in developing it.

[3] BCRI, B/P 8012/40. Theophilus financed part of the purchase with a mortgage loan from his brother, Stephen B. See BCRI, B/P 18/68.

[4] B/P 8014/464; 18/29. Part of his Lot 81 holding was sold in 1839. BCRI, B/P 18/29.

[5] The 1848 deed of sale was not found.

[6] See 1850 Census, completed geographically, listing the parents next to Theophilus R.'s household.

Summary

All told, this was perhaps the most stable decade during the farming era on the island. There were now six year-round farmers living there. These included the newcomers, Waldo Meloon and Theophilus Dockham; together with three Bickford brothers: James, Brackett, and Jonathan Jr.; and their uncle, Eleazer Bickford Sr. Meanwhile, Lots 3, 4, 7, and 9 continued to be used for seasonal pasturage and wood lots.

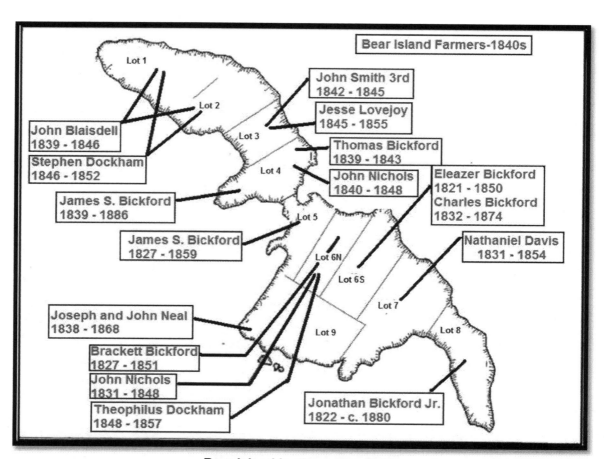

Bear Island Farmers-1840s

Lot 1
Lot 2
Lot 3
Lot 4
Lot 5
Lot 6N
Lot 6S
Lot 7
Lot 8
Lot 9

John Smith 3rd
1842 - 1845

Jesse Lovejoy
1845 - 1855

Thomas Bickford
1839 - 1843

John Nichols
1840 - 1848

Eleazer Bickford
1821 - 1850
Charles Bickford
1832 - 1874

Nathaniel Davis
1831 - 1854

John Blaisdell
1839 - 1846

Stephen Dockham
1846 - 1852

James S. Bickford
1839 - 1886

James S. Bickford
1827 - 1859

Joseph and John Neal
1838 - 1868

Brackett Bickford
1827 - 1851

John Nichols
1831 - 1848

Theophilus Dockham
1848 - 1857

Jonathan Bickford Jr.
1822 - c. 1880

Bear Island land owners, 1840s.

Chapter Thirteen

The Railroad and the Steamboat

The Railroad[1]

For Bear Island and the Lakes Region, the late 1840s bore witness to the arrival of the railroad, one of the most impactful inventions of the Industrial Revolution. In every sense of the word, the railroad revolutionized transportation. It was a gigantic leap forward in the evolution of travel, and it transformed the nature and extent of communication between central New Hampshire and the rest of the country.

In the earliest settler days, travel was very difficult. Inland travel by horseback was possible, but there were only paths wide enough for a horse, a cart perhaps, and not much more. In the latter 1700s, travel became modestly easier as cart paths evolved into passable wagon roads, the most important of which was the Province Road.

During the late 1700s and early 1800s, major improvements in travel came in the forms of turnpikes and canals. In the latter regard, the completion in 1802 of the Middlesex Canal between Charlestown Harbor, MA and the Merrimack River in Chelmsford, MA opened travel and commerce between Nashua, NH and Boston via the Merrimack River. Previously, transportation of a wide variety of goods and raw materials was too expensive; but the new water connection opened up the region in unimagined ways. By c. 1815, the Merrimack connections were expanded by canals around other falls further up the river, so that Concord became directly linked to the commercial markets in Boston.[2]

In an effort to retain its commercial significance, New Hampshire authorities located in Portsmouth tried in vain to develop alternative canal connections that would link the Lakes Region and western parts of the state to the Seacoast; but multiple canal companies that sought to develop a water route from Winnipesaukee to the Seacoast were unsuccessful. Among other things, they were unable to overcome the geographic impediments that the ice age had left in the way. More importantly, the potential economic benefits were too few to attract sufficient capital. The residents of interior New Hampshire were already quite satisfied with the commercial channels south to the population centers of Massachusetts. A connection to the Seacoast would only really benefit the merchants there who would then transship goods down the coast to Massachusetts and beyond.

Simultaneously with the canal era, travel by road improved quite a bit when the New Hampshire legislature chartered a number of companies to build turnpikes in the state.

---

[1] Most of this discussion is drawn from R. Stuart Wallace and Lisa Mausolf, "New Hampshire Railroads: Historic Context Statement," April 2001.
[2] Farmer and Moore, A Gazetteer of the State of New-Hampshire, 1823, p. 106.

These were toll roads built by for-profit, private companies. They were incorporated by the state, granted rights of eminent domain, and were given monopolies over specific routes. Ten turnpikes were completed by 1803. In the ensuing years, some 600 miles of these roads were added. The turnpikes enjoyed something of a golden era from 1820 to 1845, although few really had much of an impact on the Meredith region.

As the roads were being built, travel accommodations improved markedly with the development of the stage coach. Led by the invention of the famed Concord (NH) Coach by Abbott-Downing Company, travelers were afforded a means of relatively comfortable travel throughout the state. By the 1840s, at least 25 stages left Concord every day and returned every night.

Stage coach in front of the Old Country Store in Moultonborough.

This situation all changed with the development of the railroad. Railroad technology had evolved slowly during the first three decades of the 19th century. The first successful steam locomotive was built in the early 1800s by a British engineer, George Stephenson. It was not until 1815 that the first railroad charter was granted in the United States; and it was not until 1826 that the first tiny, impractical line was constructed in Massachusetts. Finally in 1830, steam powered engines were improved to the point that the Baltimore & Ohio Railroad successfully ran its American-built locomotive, the 'Tom Thumb', for the first time. This was the take-off point in the American railroad era.

New Hampshire officials did not initially embrace the railroad. There were substantial vested interests that were opposed to it, such as the turnpike owners, the stage coach owners, and the tavern/inn owners among others. It was not until 1835 that the first three railroad companies in the state were finally chartered by the legislature. In 1838, the Boston & Lowell Railroad reached Nashua, NH, and in 1842, the Concord Railroad completed laying track between Concord and Nashua, replacing the river connection that linked the economic heart line of New Hampshire (Concord, Manchester, and Nashua) to Boston. Yet there were still only 56 miles of track in the entire state. Distrustful politicians in Concord halted even this modest expansion of railroads altogether by passing laws that eliminated the railroad companies' critical rights to eminent domain and the limited liability of shareholders.

In 1844, this political 'Railroad War' in the New Hampshire legislature was finally resolved when changes came to Concord. More favorable laws were enacted, and the industry quickly expanded thereafter. Some 10 new railroad companies were chartered in 1844, and another 29 were incorporated between 1845 and 1850.[1] As these numbers suggest, the railroad companies were not large corporations. They were the equivalent of the turnpike companies, being granted monopoly privileges over very specific routes.

Among the 10 companies chartered in 1844 was the Boston, Concord, & Montreal Railroad (the BC&M).[2] Despite its ambitious name, the BC&M was a small 'up-country' line chartered to establish a rail connection from Concord through the Lakes Region and Plymouth to Wells River, VT, a distance of about 90 miles. The BC&M was thus a little, 'linking' railway that had to pay rent to use the tracks of other railroad companies from Concord south and eventually from the Vermont border north.

The leadership and financial support for the BC&M all came from people living north of Concord. The men behind the idea of the company were from Haverhill, NH. Its longtime President, Josiah Quincy, was from Plymouth, NH. As the BC&M annual report noted in 1848, "stockholders in our road are nearly all residents in the country" (i.e. rural residents).[3] An 1849 newspaper article said that "it is called a farmers' road, as it has been built without the aid of capitalists, and the farmers along the whole line own more or less (all of the) shares."[4] They all had a vested interest in having the line built, opening the area to improved commerce and tourism. Meredith was one of the parties quite interested in the new railroad. The town purchased $10,000.00 worth of company stock to ensure its place in company plans. Meredith (Bridge) men served at times as directors of the company as well, including Stephen C. Lyford, James Bell, and John T. Coffin.

The company began laying down tracks during 1847. In 1848, the tracks were extended to Sanbornton Bridge (now Tilton) in March, to Meredith Bridge in August, and finally to Lake Village (Lakeport) in October. The following year the Weirs and Meredith Village were connected. It was the connection to the Weirs that opened up Winnipesaukee to an entirely new era of summer travelers.

---

[1] By the end of the 19th century, over 260 separate railroads were incorporated or hosted in New Hampshire. Wallace, p. 11.
[2] For a detailed account of the BC&M, see: Edgar T. Mead, The Up-Country Line, (1975).
[3] Annual Report of the BC&M Railroad, 1848. In 1849, the Annual Report noted that "this corporation has had no aid from the monied interest of New England."
[4] Boston Semi-weekly Atlas, August 4, 1849, p. 2.

The Steamboat

The introduction of the railroad prompted the resurrection of the steamboat industry on Lake Winnipesaukee, an industry that had been largely dormant since the sinking of the *Belknap* in 1841. Lakes Region settlers were never in the forefront of invention when it came to commercial and passenger boating. In the earliest years of settlement there, merchants initially developed their own, homemade version of the so-called 'gundalow'.[1] This was a flat-bottomed scow or barge that first appeared in New Hampshire waters in the mid-1600s. An off-shoot of European (and probably Nile) river barges, it was used by the first colonists to transport goods up and down the coastal waterways where all of the earliest towns were established. It had an oar-sweep to provide steering and a sail to provide power. For early New Hampshire gundalows on the seacoast, however, the primary motive power was the tide. Shedules were timed to move up river as the tide came in and down river to the coast as the tide went out. Construction was not uniform, as every gundalow was the unique creation of its builder; but the basic design remained fairly consistent.

Gundalow (courtesy Historic New England)

The first gundalow to be built on Winnipesaukee took to the lake in the late 1770s in Moultonborough Bay.[2] Thereafter, this barge and others plied the waters primarily between Moultonborough, Wolfeboro, and Alton. During the early 1800s, routes gradually extended out to other parts of the lake as settlements increased in size. By the early 1820s, a Dover merchant, Joseph Smith, was advertising regular transport services across the lake "provided by a safe and commodious packet" between Meredith Village, Center Harbor, Alton Bay and the Seacoast. By "packet" Smith simply meant that his boats—almost certainly gundalows--followed regular schedules. Smith owned store houses in the three lake towns.[3] The gundalow dominated early commercial boating on the lake, but it was not well

---

[1] See: Wooden Boat, The Magazine for Wooden Boat Owners, Builders, and Designers, July/August 2013, #233, " Piscataqua: A new gundalow for New Hampshire," pp. 82-86.
[2] See, for example, Van Veghten, Meredith Bay, pp.9-15,
[3] Portsmouth Journal of Literature and Politics, June 21, 1823, p. 4.

suited for Winnipesaukee because without tides, its motive power—the oar sweep and sail—left it at the mercy of prevailing winds.

      Two developments eclipsed it in the 1830s. One was the horse boat, a barge powered typically by two horses walking on an onboard treadmill.[1] The origins of the

horse boat dated all the way back to the Romans. Like the gundalow, horse boats were in regular use on rivers and canals during the 1600s and 1700s. By the early 1800s, they were in regular use in various parts of the United States, including Lake Champlain, the Hudson River, and many locations further west where river, canal, and lake commerce was developing. The horse boat was finally introduced to Winnipesaukee in the mid-1830s.[2] The first one was built in Meredith, but others soon were found around the lake as they offered far more reliable motive power than the sail and sweep driven gundalows.

      The other key development in the 1830s, that eventually eclipsed both the gundalow and the horse boat, was the steamboat. The steamboat was also a relatively late introduction to Winnipesaukee. The first commercially successful steamboat in the world was developed by American, Robert Fulton, in 1807.[3] Fulton's steam-powered paddle boat, named the *Clermont*, proved itself by sailing 150 miles up the Hudson River from New York City to Albany, completing the journey in the then-astounding time of 32 hours.

      The following year, two brothers who had worked with Fulton, John and James Winan, moved to Burlington, Vermont. There, with the help of local businessmen, they launched their own steamboat, the *Vermont*, in 1809. The introduction of the *Vermont* on Lake Champlain altered the course of travel on that lake thereafter. Unlike New York, Vermont did not grant monopoly privileges to the steamship company. It left the competition open. As a result, over the next 20 years, several additional steamboat companies came into existence, competing for freight, passengers, and towing business.[4] The market was much more attractive than anything New Hampshire had to offer. Lake Champlain was an important link between Canada and growing downstate New York which were connected by the Hudson River and a canal system that was built between 1815 and 1825.

---

[1] Jim Kennard, "Horse Powered Ferry Boat discovered in Lake Champlain," July 2, 2005, www.shipwreckworld.com. Picture courtesy of the Laconia Historical Society.
[2] Talk of using horse boats on the lake came up as early as 1825 when Jonathan C. Everett petitioned the state legislature "for the exclusive right of navigating the Winnipiseogee by horse power boats." But his petition was apparently denied. Portsmouth Journal of Literature and Politics, June 18, 1825, p. 2.
[3] Fulton was granted a monopoly by the state legislature of New York, the same process used by New Hampshire to foster infrastructure development.
[4] See among others, "Full Steam Ahead: Steamboats on Lake Champlain," at www.plattscsd.org/GLOBAL/steam.

Following its success on Champlain, steam boating was introduced on Lake George in upstate New York in 1817. Somewhat like Winnipesaukee, the towns along the shores of the lake were small, and local business was not especially strong; but the Lake George region had become a Mecca for early tourists who travelled up the Hudson for vacation getaways. Nearby locations like Saratoga Springs were in the forefront of the tourist/vacation phenomenon that emerged with the Industrial Revolution.

The possibility of steam boating on Winnipesaukee finally reached New Hampshire in 1823. Similar to New York, the state retained control of the process. As it did with the turnpike operators before, the legislature gave a monopolistic charter to a group led by the Seacoast merchant, Joseph Smith. The charter gave him a 20 year monopoly on Winnipesaukee if he were successful in building a steamboat within an allotted time period.[1] But Smith's group suffered various setbacks over the next several years, and it was never successful.

Following Smith's failure, the legislature gave a monopoly in 1831 to a new group led by Stephen C. Lyford and Ichabod Bartlett. They built the first Winnipesaukee steamer, the *Belknap*, which was first launched in 1832 and began regular service in 1833.[2] Its captain was Winborn A. Sanborn. Initially at least, the *Belknap* was the proverbial bucket of bolts "furnished with a wretched worn out engine taken from a saw mill." When underway, it made an extreme racket that could be heard from miles away. This characterization of it has persisted down through the decades. A local correspondent, writing in the mid-1840s, wished there were still a steamboat on the lake but

"…not such a one however (like the *Belknap* that) in days of yore roared and hissed as it labored up and down the lake, frightening the fish in their solitudes, and the birds in the dark woods; …Never in the annals of steamboat building was such an anomaly as the "Belknap" created; the wreck of which even now moves the beholder with wonder and mirth."[3]

Despite its reputation, the *Belknap* was perhaps not such a monstrosity. Its engine was apparently replaced after the first season, with a new one cast by the well-known, south Boston munitions' firm of Alger & Company. During the 1833 season, it was called "a really elegant steamboat" by one passenger who said that people around the lake flocked to the wharves when it arrived in town.[4] An 1834 passenger called it a "fine steamer" and referred to his ride on it as "a delightful sail, never to be forgotten.[5]

---

[1] New Hampshire, like Massachusetts, was unwilling to raise the taxes of residents to pay for infrastructure development. State issued charters for companies building infrastructure all contained monopoly clauses to entice the investors to risk their capital.
[2] There is some disagreement about the year in which it started full time service on the lake. One fairly authoritative source, Paul Blaisdell, wrote that it did not begin regular passenger and freight service until 1834. Three Centuries, p. 24.
[3] Boston Evening Transcript, September 15, 1846, p. 2.
[4] Portsmouth Journal of Literature and Politics, July 20, 1833, p. 2.
[5] Saturday Morning Transcript, July 19, 1834, p. 183.

STEAMBOAT NOTICE.
Lake Winnipisseogee and the White Mountains.

The public are respectfully informed that the Steam Boat BELKNAP will perform her trips across Lake Winnipisseogee during the travelling season, commencing June 21, three times a week each way, and will leave Alton Bay on Tuesdays, Thursdays, and Saturdays, at 1 P M. and arrive at Centre Harbor at 4 P. M. Stages leave Dover at 7 A. M. to intersect with the boat. Stages leave Centre Harbor for the White Mountains, by way of Conway, on the following morning, at 6 A. M. and arrive, by way of Conway, at the White Mountains the same day. The boat leaves Centre Harbor on Mondays, Wednesdays and Fridays, at 10 A. M. or immediately after the arrival of the stages from Conway and Plymouth, and arrive at Alton Bay at 1 P. M. in season for the stages for Dover and Portsmouth. Horses and carriages conveniently transported in the boat.

june17   ep3m   **W. A. SANBORN, Capt.**

1836 advertisement in a Portsmouth, NH newspaper[1]

Nevertheless, the *Belknap* was still severely underpowered. It chugged up and down Winnipesaukee at a top speed of about five miles per hour, hauling freight, towing logs, and ferrying some passengers. It monopolized the lake for seven years before it finally sank in a storm in 1841 while towing a log boom near Steamboat Island. The heavy winds that day were just too strong for the *Belknap's* engine to overcome.[2]

After the *Belknap*, several other attempts to build steamers occurred, but they had little success.[3] The challenge was trying to adapt steam engines designed for saw mills to boating. In the 1840s, Langdon Thyng made a breakthrough when he purchased a small steam locomotive engine and installed it in a horse boat. Named the *Jenny Lind*, it was a modest step forward in lake travel, but it had no lasting impact.[4] Other small, rudimentary steamers followed, but their presence on the lake was marginal and local. This all changed in 1848.

---

[1] <u>Boston Post</u>, June 23, 1836, p. 4.
[2] Blaisdell, <u>Three Centuries</u>, p. 28; Blackstone, pp. 9-10. An 1881 version of the story holds that the Captain and Engineer of the Belknap left the boat anchored off the island and went to Alton Bay to pick up a supply of rum and molasses. Upon their return, they found the boat on the shoals. O.W. Goss, "Lake Village," in <u>The Granite Monthly</u>, Vol. iv No. 12, September 1881, p. 489.
[3] There is little information about the emergence of other steamboats on the lake during the 1840s.
[4] Blaisdell, p. 24; Blackstone, pp. 13-14. Presumably the state legislative monopoly provisions slowed the process as well. This area would benefit from deeper research.

The Winnipiseogee Steamboat Company and the *Lady of the Lake*[1]

The incorporation of the BC&M Railroad finally provided the impetus for a grand new approach to steam boating on Winnipesaukee. In 1848, about the time the BC&M was laying its first tracks north, a Concord resident named William Walker Jr. recognized the potential that the new railroad service represented. He conceived a very ambitious plan to bring passenger steam boating to Winnipesaukee.

The 38 year old Walker was uniquely suited to develop the plan thanks to his previous life experiences that touched on tourism, steam boats, railroads, and freight services. He was born in Chester, NH to the proprietor "of a famous old-time tavern." He became a stage coach driver, at various times handling freight and passengers. He was noted for his courtesy and strong business acumen. He also spent some time operating a steam boat service that ran between Haverhill, MA and Newburyport, MA. In 1835, the family moved to Concord, NH where his father became proprietor of the Eagle Hotel. William developed a horse-drawn, stagecoach express freight business that became quite successful. With the opening of the Concord Railroad in 1842, William contracted with it to handle some of its freight business.

With the knowledge gleaned from this background, Walker approached one of the leading businessmen in Lakeport, Benjamin Cole, with the idea of building a passenger steam boat for Winnipesaukee. Walker and Cole recruited a well rounded group of other interested businessmen. The group included some of the leading men of the BC&M railroad, such as James N. Elkins, who was the BC&M's Agent (i.e. Chief Operating Officer) and at least two of the railroad's directors, Meredith Bridge residents Stephen C. Lyford and John T. Coffin. Walker and Cole also recruited the two most important Lakes Region people tied to the hospitality industry, namely John Coe, owner of the Senter House in Center Harbor, and Daniel Pickering, the leading businessman in Wolfeboro who built the Pavilion Hotel there in 1849. They petitioned the legislature for incorporation as the Winnipiseogee Steamboat Company (WSC) in June 1848. The company raised $50,000.00, including some $5,000.00 in bonds sold to the BC&M. William Walker was the largest shareholder.

Colonial Hotel, fka the Senter House (Laconia Historical Society)

---

[1] Among other sources, see: New Hampshire Men: A Collection of Biographical Sketches, Concord (1893); Genealogical and Family History of the State of New Hampshire, E. Sterns editor New York (1908); The History of Wolfeborough; various newspaper articles in the Concord Independent Democrat and the Concord Congregational Journal.

Construction of the new boat began in January 1849, and it was launched in May. Initially it did not have a name, but fairly soon it was called the *Lady of the Lake*. A majestic creation for the time and place, the *Lady* was an immediate success, revolutionizing passenger travel on the lake. Capable of carrying 400 passengers, it was reputed to have a top speed of 16 mph. Walker served as its captain for many years. His first pilot was none other than Eleazer Bickford Jr. of Bear Island. The *Lady* was based at the Weirs. Its ports of call were Center Harbor (by far the most popular gateway to the White Mountains) and Wolfeboro.[1] A key leg of the *Lady's* route to Center Harbor was past the western side of Bear Island and between North Bear and Pine Island. This happy circumstance had a great deal to do with the island's future.

Lady of the Lake at the Weirs c. 1880s. (Laconia Historical Society)

The Winnipiseogee Steamboat Company remained in operation until 1896. Benjamin Cole served as its president for most of those years. Its business evolved to include a great deal more than operating the *Lady*. Indeed, in 1851, the company leased the *Lady* to the BC&M RR and later sold it to the same company.[2] It developed a service business for the budding steam boat industry, buying waterfront properties and building wharves and other facilities in Center Harbor (1851), Meredith Village (1866), and Wolfeboro (1869). It also purchased Blackcat Island in 1853 to provide wood for its fueling business in Center Harbor. More dramatically, the company bought Diamond Island in 1865 and built the first island hotel on the lake. The hotel became a year-round attraction for tourists and fishermen until it apparently succumbed to gambling interests in the latter 1870s.[3]

---

[1] The mutual interest among the WSC's shareholders is apparent in this route.
[2] The ownership history of the *Lady* is not entirely clear. The WSC leased the *Lady* to the BC&MRR in 1851, but William Walker continued to be its captain. In 1862, the company sold it to George Clough of Concord, NH. By 1871, it was back in the hands of the WSC. By 1893, it was on lease again to the Concord and Montreal RR. See Boston Herald, August 2, 1862, p. 1 and July 2, 1893, p. 23. This is a topic that requires more research.
[3] See Chapter 37 for more detail about Diamond Island and the hotel.

The overlapping of shareholders and operating officers of the WSC and the BC&M RR had a great deal to do with the success of the WSC. The two businesses routinely coordinated advertising and travel schedules among other synergies that benefitted the companies and the shareholders alike. The WSC was finally sold and absorbed into the Concord & Montreal Railroad in 1896 as part of the settlement of a lawsuit brought against its owners by the railroad company.[1]

The WSC and the *Lady* were not the only game in town during the latter half of the 19th century. After the *Lady's* successful debut, a BC&M rival, the Cocheco Railroad, which began carrying passengers from Dover NH to Alton Bay in 1851, determined that it needed a competing steamer. In 1852, it launched the *Dover* (later rebuilt and renamed the *Chocorua*). The primary route of this vessel was from Alton Bay to Wolfeboro to Center Harbor, but it also made trips to Meredith Village. Other, smaller steamers joined these two during the 1850s and 1860s, many of them built on Long Island. The most prominent was the *James Bell*.[2] In 1872, the venerable *Mount Washington* was built to replace the *Chocorua*. The *Mount* became the undisputed queen of the waterways after the *Lady* was retired in 1893. It too routinely passed by Bear Island and came to make frequent stops at North Bear.

Centre Harbor landing c.1890. The *Mount Washington* is at the wharf owned by the Winnipesaukee Steamboat Company. The carriages belonged to the Senter Hotel.

---

[1] See CCRI B/P 106/283. The BC&M had been merged into the Concord & Montreal in 1889.
[2] The two best general sources about the early steamboats are: Edward Blackstone, <u>Farewell Old Mount Washington</u> (1969) and Paul Blaisdell, <u>Three Centuries on Winnipesaukee</u> (1936).

Part III:

The Transition Period:

From
The Farming Era
to
The Summer Tourism Era

Chapter Fourteen

The Mid-Century Inflection Period: The 1850s

The decade of the 1850s was an inflection period in the history of Bear Island. All of the original permanent farmers departed the island for farms on the Neck or because of health problems. As a result of these developments, most of South Bear—the bastion of year-round farming on the island--became unfarmed land used predominantly for timbering and seasonal grazing (with Lot 5 a brief exception). On North Bear, however, a completely new reality came into being.

South Bear

The first original Bear farmer to leave the island was James Bickford, whose homestead was on Lot 5.[1] In 1852, he moved off the island after living permanently out there for 25 years. He bought the homestead farm of Elisha and Phebe Smith on Meredith Neck.[2] Located east of the 'old Neck road' (now Barnard Ridge Road), the 72 acre homestead consisted of half of original Lot 42 and parts of Lots 35 and 36.[3]

James retained his ownership of Lots 5 and 4 on Bear.[4] After his departure, his two oldest sons, Oliver and Alonzo (born in 1832 and 1836, respectively), began living permanently on Bear Lot 4 (Jerry Point).[5] Indeed, they probably dug the cellar holes that are still evident there today.[6] Oliver's place was located nearest the point, while Alonzo occupied the place in the rear.[7] They also had a garden and orchard on the property.

In 1859, James sold his original homestead on Bear Lot 5 to his sister, Mahala Bickford Bryant, after 32 years of ownership.[8] She was the wife of Abram Bryant, who was the son of Robert Bryant Jr. With this purchase, Mahala became the sixth child of Jonathan Bickford Sr. (out of 11) to own property on Bear Island.[9] Abram (29) and Mahala (27) had married around 1832. They both had likely grown up on Bear Island. In their early married years, they lived on

---

[1] Charles Bickford had moved off the island to a farm on the Neck in 1838; but even though he was the part owner of record of Lot 6S, he was a young man who had been living with his parents on Bear Island prior to the move. His parents and siblings continued to live full time on Bear after Charles moved.

[2] BCRI, B/P 28/35. See also mortgage deed, BCRI, B/P 20/57 and 20/58. This property was acquired by a Meredith conservation trust in 2017.

[3] BCRI, BP 28/35; 20/58; 20/57.

[4] In 1857, he purchased the only part of Lot 4 he did not own, a 15 acre piece by then in the hands of Theophilus R. Dockham. BCRI, B/P 30/142. Interestingly, the deed stipulated that Theophilus retained the timber rights on the parcel seemingly in perpetuity. These rights were sold in subsequent transactions. See for example, BCRI, B/P 42/16, when the timber rights were sold by Daniel Wiggin to Stephen Meloon in 1865. Wiggin had purchased the rights the previous year. These 15 acres comprise the core grounds of Camp Nokomis today.

[5] Oliver and Alonzo are listed in the 1860 Census among other known Bear Islanders. Moreover, Meredith school tax records for Bear Island list them among the Bear residents. "Memorandum Book", signed by Levi Towle, 1860-1861, School District Taxes, Meredith Historical Society.

[6] No one else had lived on Lot 4 permanently before. James Bickford's island home was on Lot 5.

[7] In 1856, James sold his island holdings to Oliver in one of the typical 'retirement' arrangements often made by settlers. A year later, however, Oliver sold them back to James for the same amount, apparently finding that it just would not work for him.

[8] B/P 33/76.

[9] Mahala, James S., Jonathan Jr., Brackett, Eleanor, and Priscilla.

the Neck and were among the 41 Neck/island settlers who petitioned to establish the Neck Meetinghouse in 1839. By the time they purchased Lot 5 on Bear, the couple had four children, including Lorenzo, Harriett, Arvilla, and Hosea. Bear Island became their year-round, homestead farm. The island schoolhouse was located on their land in the Carry, and thus it became their property.

A little further south on Lot 6N, the original ownership roles began to change in 1851 when the long-time owner of the eastern half, Brackett Bickford, passed away. The lot was purchased out of his estate by his son, Ebenezer.[1] But Ebenezer had no interest in owning island island property. He quickly sold the parcel to Theophilus R. Dockham, who had purchased the interior half of Lot 6N in 1848.[2]

But Theophilus' ownership was fraught with difficulties. Initially, he had seemingly flourished on Bear after moving to the island. When Dolly Nichol's departed for the last time in 1853, he took over responsibility for maintaining the Bear Island boat that was used to ferry people to the island from the Neck.[3] For a brief period, he was a member of the town's Prudential Prudential Committee, serving as the school representative for the island. But the fortunes of Theophilus and his wife, Mary, worsened severely beginning in 1855. Their oldest child, Martha, died that year at the age of 16. Then only a year or so later, their youngest son, Stephen, died at the age of seven. Compounding the difficulties, Theophilus himself became gravely ill in 1857. The family was forced to sell the Bear Island farm and move back to the Neck. They bought the homestead farm of Madison Chase on parts of Lots 75-76 on the lower Neck.[4]

To facilitate his move off of the island, Theophilus sold Lot 6N in 1857 to his brother-in-law, Waldo Meloon, and his brother, Nathaniel Dockham.[5] They were probably motivated simply to help him deal with the difficult times. Waldo had already been assisting the family for some time.[6] Theophilus died in 1858. He was buried in the Meetinghouse Cemetery where his two children were previously interred. He was survived by his wife, Mary, and their son, Luther.[7]

In contrast to Lot 6N, the situation on Lot 6S was one of the most stable on the island. During the early 1850s, it was in the year-round care of Eleazer Bickford Sr. and his family. The latter included his wife, Sarah, and his two youngest children, Eleazer Jr. and Almira. However,

---

[1] BCRI, B/P 18/93.
[2] BCRI, B/P 18/103. Theophilus borrowed $500 from his brother, Stephen B., to finance the purchase. See BCRI, B/P 28/488.
[3] Meredith Annual Report, Mar 1854. See Chapter 15 for more information about the Bear Island boat.
[4] BCRI, B/P 28/497. The purchase was again done with the financial help of his brother, Stephen. The new homestead was bounded on one side by the property of Theophilus other brother, Nathaniel, who lived next door to the Meetinghouse cemetery.
[5] BCRI, B/P 38/280.
[6] Meredith Annual Report, 1856-57. Waldo was paid $26.00 by the town for his assistance to Theophilus.
[7] Mary lived with Luther on the Neck at least into the latter 1870s. It does not appear that she remarried. Her final resting place is not known. Luther's travails did not end with the death of his father. He married a teenage girl named Emily c. 1860, but she died in December 1861 at the age of 19. She was buried in the Meetinghouse cemetery with Theophilus and Luther's two siblings. About the time of her death, Luther volunteered to fight in the Civil War. He remained in the war until it ended in 1865, one of the relatively few who fought in it from beginning to end. He returned to Meredith after the war. In 1877 he was serving on the Prudential Committee in charge of school district 17. (Meredith Selectmen Accounts, 1877, p. 74 [MHS Archives]). He died in 1892. His burial site is also unidentified.

by the end of the decade, they had all moved to the Neck, living with Eleazer Sr.'s oldest son, Charles, on his farm on Lot 76.[1] Lot 6S became their summer farm for years thereafter.

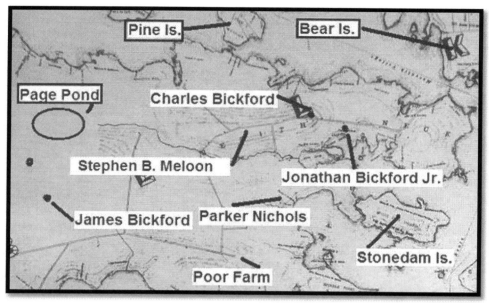
Location of former Bear Island farmers on the Neck.

Next door, Governors Island owner, Nathaniel Davis, finally sold Lot 7 to Parker P. Nichols in 1854 after 23 years of ownership.[2] Parker was one of Paul Nichols' sons and was another child of the island who had spent some of his early years on this very lot before 1820. Parker's purchase made him the second of Paul's sons, after John Nichols, to reestablish ties to the island. But Parker and his wife, Lydia,[3] had no plans to make Lot 7 their permanent home. Like Davis, they used it for seasonal grazing and timber. Their homestead farm was on Neck Lot 74, where they had lived with Paul since 1827.[4]

Meanwhile, the ownership transition on Lot 8 came to resemble that of Lots 5 and 6S. Jonathan Bickford Jr. bought a 50 acre farm on Neck Lot 79, across the Neck road from his cousin, Charles Bickford.[5] Jonathan continued to maintain the Bear property as a summer farm.

Meanwhile, Lot 9 was still in the hands of the Neal family which had bought it in 1838 for timber and seasonal usage. One of the two owners, Joseph Neal Jr., passed away in 1855. His half interest in the property was inherited by his son, Smith Lock Neal. Smith did not want to be involved, so he appointed Charles S. Prescott as trustee in charge of all of his assets.[6] The other other half ownership remained with Smith's uncle, John Neal.

---

[1] See 1860 Census in which they are all listed in the same household under Charles.
[2] BCRI, B/P 22/302.
[3] Lydia's lineage is not known. Given the propensity for intermarriage among the early island families, it would not be surprising if she were Lydia Bickford, the oldest child of Jonathan Bickford Sr., who was born a few years before Parker. If that were indeed so, she would have been the seventh of Jonathan Sr.'s children to own property on Bear. Parker and Lydia had no children of their own.
[4] Paul died not long after Parker's purchase of Lot 7 on Bear, at which time Parker took over complete ownership of the Neck lot. Paul's grave site has not been identified.
[5] B/P 23/272. Another neighbor of his was David Lovejoy.
[6] B/P 44/309. This included the family homestead in the First Division as well as Lot 9.

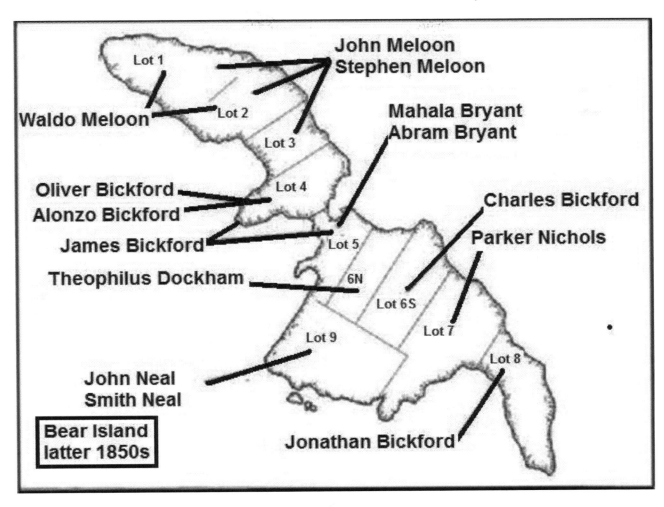

John Meloon
Stephen Meloon

Mahala Bryant
Abram Bryant

Lot 1

Waldo Meloon

Lot 2

Lot 3

Oliver Bickford
Alonzo Bickford

Lot 4

James Bickford

Charles Bickford

Parker Nichols

Theophilus Dockham

Lot 5

6N

Lot 6S

Lot 7

Lot 9

Lot 8

John Neal
Smith Neal

Jonathan Bickford

Bear Island
latter 1850s

North Bear

While the year-round farmers were gradually departing South Bear, the other end of the island moved in a radically different direction. Waldo Meloon had leased Lots 1 and 2 in 1845, establishing a year-round farm where only seasonal farmers had lived before. In 1852, he purchased the two lots from his brother-in-law, Stephen B. Dockham.[1] By this time, Waldo's two oldest boys, John and Stephen, were no longer residing with the family. Waldo and Abigail had Francis (20), Melissa (16), David (14), and George (5) living with them. Waldo's mother-in-law, Abigail (Alse or Else) Dockham, had moved in with them following the death of her husband, Theophilus Dockham Sr. circa 1851.[2]

In 1855, the family was rejoined by the oldest sons, John and Stephen, when they bought

---

[1] BCRI, B/P 19/438-439. Waldo gave Dockham a mortgage for $1050.00 to fund the purchase, with repayment terms of four years.
[2] 1850 Census. Theophilus Sr. died in 1851 or 1852. He was born c. 1768. His burial site was not identified. There is no grave site for him in the Meetinghouse cemetery, the most logical place.

an undivided half interest in the Meloon's Bear Island property.[1] A month after that, John and Stephen jointly purchased the adjoining 50 acre, Lot 3 from Jesse Lovejoy.[2] Unfortunately, it was less than two months after they bought their initial share of the island farm that tragedy struck John and his wife, Tamer. Their three year old daughter, Sarah, died in the all too familiar roll call that characterized life in the 1850s.[3]

During the decade, Waldo was quite active in a variety of affairs. After Theophilus R. Dockham left Bear in 1857, Waldo took charge of the ferry service to the mainland, and he eventually had a fleet of three boats, including a gundalow and a horseboat.[4] Waldo also remained involved in various town-related matters. From 1858 to 1864, for example, he was a member of the Prudential Committee of the School board in charge of the school district on Bear Island.[5]

The Meloons also adapted to the changing times in a way never before seen on Winnipesaukee. Waldo recognized the potential that arose from the rapidly increasing summer traffic on the lake that was created by the 1849 arrival of the BC&M railroad and the *Lady of the Lake*. The *Lady* cruised past Waldo's property on Bear every day on its primary route to Center Harbor, carrying hundreds of tourists who were awed by Winnipesaukee and its scenery. The BC&M and the Winnipiseogee Steamship Company had created special travel packages for tourists and promoted them widely. For several years, these simply involved cruises between the Weirs, Center Harbor, and Wolfeboro. There were no stops on the islands.

This all changed during the latter 1850s.[6] By 1858 at the latest, Waldo had seized upon the *Lady's* presence to create a hospitality business for large groups of summer day-trippers.[7] This was the beginning of the summer era on Bear Island. Waldo built a wharf and a boathouse on the northwest end of the island where the mail dock exists today. The location was a natural one, being the closest place where the *Lady* passed the island. It also enjoyed the easiest access to and from the center of North Bear where the Meloons' farmhouse was located. He also turned the northern tip of the island and its "beautiful grove of white maples" into a visitors' area where picnickers could enjoy the island and lake. Swings made of hemp ropes were hung from several trees. He either built a new building or converted a barn near the landing that was fitted up with a bowling alley. On occasion, he put up a "refreshment tent" in the grove. He and his family also provided meals at his farmhouse "up the hill." He acquired some rowboats that

---

[1] BCRI, B/P 35/599. Just prior to the purchase in 1855, Stephen (26) had married Sarah Richardson. The Meloon's son, Francis, had left home perhaps a few years earlier. By 1856, Francis was married to the widow, Elizabeth O. Watson, and living in the Lake Village section of Gilford. Thereafter Francis continued to move north (to Campton by 1870 and ultimately to Wentworth by 1895). He became the only child of Waldo and Abigail to have no active role on Bear Island. 1860 and 1870 Census and NH Death and Burial Records, 1654-1949; BCRI, B/P 26/324, 26/340, 29/467, 95/129.
[2] BCRI, B/P 22/279.
[3] BCRI, B/P 35/599; See "The Maloon Family," undated paper, Meredith Historical Society.
[4] E.H. Maloon, "Glancing Over Meredith's Past," *Meredith News*, November 8, 1922. It is most likely the remains of Waldo's gundalow that can still be found off the Bear Island mail dock.
[5] See Annual Town Reports for those years. For more on the Bear Island school, see Chapter 17, Vignettes: The 1860s.
[6] The exact timing has proven elusive, but it was no later than 1858.
[7] His bold step was either of his own volition or perhaps the persuasion of the owners of the *Lady* who were looking for more reasons to get travelers on board the boat.

tourists could use for fishing. And he also raised an American flag at the highest point on North Bear (now known as Sunset Rock) to which guests could hike and take in the majestic view to the north.[1]

Sunset Rock c. 1890s. (Thompson-Wright collection).

A clear indication of what he developed is apparent from the account of a Unitarian group of 350 men, women and children who made a day trip to the island in 1858.[2] The group caught the morning BC&M train in Concord, NH at 7:45 a.m., taking it to the Weirs. They then boarded the *Lady* for the half hour ride to Bear Island, reaching it by 11:00 a.m. Once on shore, the group engaged in different activities, some strolling in "the grove"; some enjoying the swings; a few walking around the island to do some "research;" and still others taking to the boats for rowing and fishing. Others hiked to the flag set amongst the "two gigantic boulders" where they found "the view (to be) one of great extent and quiet beauty." They could see great distances while also noting "listless groups of cows" near the beaches and hearing cowbells on the Neck.

The group reconvened for a "bounteous" lunch in the grove around noontime. They were entertained by various speakers, a choir, and the Belknap County band. Following all of these activities, the *Lady of the Lake* returned to pick them up, and they got back to the Weirs by 4:30 p.m. The group then boarded the train, arriving in Concord around 7:00 that evening.

The Meloon family was naturally heavily involved in providing for the guests. Most of the groups brought picnic lunches, but the Meloons supplemented their efforts. On one 1859 excursion, the visitors made special note "that they were greatly assisted by Mr. Waldo Meloon and wife, his son John and his wife Tamer; also, by Stephen B. and Melissa J. Meloon, and Laura Gilman."[3] The following year, it was noted that "many (in the party) visited the house on the hill, where they were met with great cordiality and good cheer at the 'very lowest prices in the market.'"[4] In 1862, members of one group went "to the house located a quarter of a mile from the the landing on a gradually rising eminence, and occupied by Mr. Walter Maloon (sic), whose kind and obliging wife served an excellent and substantial dinner to several who made her a call, and also pleased them much with her remarkable good humor."[5]

---

[1] "Picnic on Bear Island," Independent Democrat (Concord, NH), Thursday September 16, 1858, p. 3.
[2] "Picnic on Bear Island," Independent Democrat (Concord, NH), Thursday September 16, 1858, p. 3; "Picnic on Bear Island," New Hampshire Patriot and State Gazette (Concord, NH), Wednesday, September 15, 1858, p. 2.
[3] Boston Mirror and Farmer, August 27, 1859, p. 3. Laura Gilman has not been identified.
[4] Concord Independent Democrat, August 18, 1860, p. 1.
[5] Manchester Daily Mirror, August 1, 1862, p. 2.

As a result of the Meloon's efforts, Bear Island became one of the most widely known islands on the lake and among the handful of destinations trumpeted by the BC&M railroad and the *Lady*.[1] One group summarized its visit in 1862 this way: "Arriving at home without any accident, we voted Bear Island a big place to have a big time on. Go and see for yourself."[2] The 1858 group was characteristic of other groups that came. In 1859, there were several large "excursion" parties that specifically arranged to go to Bear Island from Concord and other towns. In 1860, there were eight large groups of excursionists who visited Bear.[3] One traveler noted that "more than three times as many persons have crossed the Lake this season as ever before…"[4] Another report referenced Bear as "the usual stopping place for excursions."[5] The groups routinely averaged in the several hundreds of visitors. A group from the Seacoast amounted to 600 people in 1862. They had purchased round trip tickets for $1.00 that covered a special train and passage on the *Lady* for the trip to Bear Island.[6] Another group from the Universalist Society Society in Manchester numbered about 500 people.[7]

The frequency of these visits was especially strong through the first half of the 1860s. Reports become very spotty thereafter. It is probable that the interest in visiting Bear dwindled after the Winnipesaukee Steamboat Company, the owners of the *Lady of the Lake,* built a hotel on Diamond Island in 1866. Naturally, the *Lady* began to advertise special excursions to Diamond thereafter, and it ascended to the position of most favored island destination.[8] During the late 1860s and very early 1870s, it appears that only smaller groups visited Bear. They were often transported on the smaller commercial steamers, with the *James Bell* doing much of the work.

---

[1] Long Island was similarly well known among the islands as many commercial steamers also stopped there.
[2] Manchester Daily Mirror, July 19, 1862, p. 2.
[3] Boston Mirror and Farmer, September 9, 1860, p. 1. Waldo subscribed to this newspaper.
[4] Boston Mirror and Farmer, August 25, 1860, p. 2.
[5] Concord Independent Democrat, August 16, 1860, p. 2.
[6] Manchester Daily Mirror, August 12, 1862, p. 2.
[7] Manchester Daily Mirror, August 1, 1862, p. 2.
[8] See Chapter 36, Diamond Island, for additional detail.

Chapter Fifteen

Vignettes: The 1850s

The Late 1850s Tax Revolt

During the later 1850s, Bear Islanders were experiencing a great deal of discontent over taxation by the town of Meredith. They felt that they were not receiving enough benefit from the town and apparently had stopped paying their taxes. There is no insight into the problem except for the following summary written by a visiting correspondent in 1858:

"(Bear Island) is at present a revolted province (of Meredith), and defies the tax gatherer. The residents, like the North American colonists in olden time, demand that if they pay tithes they have a voice in government, and the island receive some share of the public attention and improvement."[1]

This was probably not the first time these concerns arose, and it certainly was not the last.[2]

The 'Bear Island Boat'

Very little information exists regarding the means by which the 19th century farmers traveled to and from Bear Island during the non-winter seasons. Oral tradition has firmly established that Joseph and Dolly Nichols provided the first and likely only ferry service available during the first few decades of the 19th century. The service probably involved a small barge or raft that was hand-propelled across the channel between the landing on Neck Lot 82 (much later named Cattle Landing) and the tip of Lot 9 on Bear. After Joseph's death or departure, Dolly continued to provide the service. She apparently did so until the early 1850s when her health finally forced her to move to the Meredith Alms House.

The role of ferry master shifted to Theophilus R. Dockham after her departure. He was the logical person to take it on. His house on the western half of Lot 6N placed him in the closest proximity to the ferry site. By this time, the ferry was recognized by Meredith officials as something of a public utility for which the town had responsibility.[3] The town paid Theophilus $32.05 in 1854 for building a boat on Bear Island.[4]

Waldo Meloon took over responsibility for the ferry service after Theophilus left the island in 1857. It is unclear if or when he relocated the ferry service from Cattle Landing, but at least by

---

[1] "Picnic on Bear Island," Independent Democrat, September 16, 1858, p. 3.
[2] See Chapter 34, Vignettes, "The 1988 Tax Revolt."
[3] The boat seemed to fall within the same category as road repairs. The Town credited settlers every year for plowing and maintaining the roads.
[4] Meredith Annual Report, Mar 1854. James Bickford was also credited $2.00 for working on the boat. Meredith Annual Report, Mar 1853.

the 1850s he had built his own wharf and boathouse on his island property where the current mail dock is located.[1] Crocker's 1858 map of the lake indicates there were two ferry routes to the island by that time, with one going straight across from the Neck to Waldo's property. It is possible that he established a Neck landing spot in Kelley Cove where Lots 77 and 78 met. There was a range way between the two lots that ran up to the Neck road that would have provided far more convenient access to the islands for his family and others.

In the early 1870s, it appears that the island boat was overhauled on at least two occasions based upon the amounts credited to individuals. In 1871, Charles Bickford received $75.00 from the town, and Waldo's son, David, was paid $100.00 for the "ferry boat" in 1873.[2] By this time, the boat was probably a horseboat. Waldo apparently maintained responsibility for the ferry until he left the island in the early 1880s. Solomon Lovejoy took over from him when he bought out Waldo in 1883.[3] He acquired Waldo's fleet,[4] and at least by 1885, Solomon had his own steamboat.[5] The town continued to credit various people throughout these years who contributed either labor or materials to maintaining the Bear Island boat. These credits persisted into the latter 1890s.[6]

The town-subsidized boat was by no means the only way farmers could access the island. There were an increasing number of other boats plying the waters of Winnipesaukee every year, although there is very little information about individual boating prior to the 1900s. The first surge in boating most likely occurred after the Civil War ended in 1865. Some broader trends can be gleaned from scraps of information. In 1874, for example, the Meredith Town Clerk, Ebenezer Bickford, noted (for unknown reasons) at least six small boats owned by people with either Bear Island connections or proximity thereto, including Waldo Meloon, Stephen Meloon, Moses Bickford, Lucian Kelley, Herbert Lovejoy, and John B. Nichols.[7] Another Bear Islander, John Crane, owned a sailboat.

By 1888, the boating world on Winnipesaukee had changed dramatically. Small, private steamers were then appearing in increasing numbers as the vacation era took over the lake and Bear Island. There were at least six of these that were housed on or near Bear or on the Neck opposite Bear. They included the *Undine* (John Crane), *Idlewilde* (Ezra Lovejoy), *Checo* (C.C. Badlam), *Island Maiden* (Solomon Lovejoy), *Nonesuch* (H. Bickford), and *Charlotte* (C. Banfield).[8]

[1] See: "Picnic on Bear Island," <u>Independent Democrat</u>, September 16, 1858, p. 3; BPRI, B/P 35/597.
[2] Meredith Town Reports, 1871 and 1873. Other largish payments were made in 1882 and 1896.
[3] Meredith Town Report, 1887.
[4] BCRI, B/P 70/633.
[5] Hawkes, <u>Winnipesaukee and About There</u>, p. 58.
[6] In re credits given for the boat, see Meredith Town Reports, 1868, 1871, 1873, 1876, 1881, 1882, 1887, 1888, 1889, 1894, and 1896.
[7] Meredith Records and Orders, 1874 (MHSA)
[8] This information cannot be authenticated. It is contained in a loose leaf binder shelved in the history room at the Laconia Library. On the other hand, all of the individuals listed were active on that part of the lake in the late 1880s. There were surely many more small steamboats around by then.

Eleazer Bickford Jr.

Eleazer Bickford Jr. (1822-1904) was a child of the island. He was born on Bear, arriving just months after his parents purchased Lot 6S.[1] He grew up a farmer, but his interests gravitated towards the lake. At the age of 11, he got his first taste of real boating when he had the opportunity to watch (and hear) the lake's first steamer, the *Belknap*, make its way among the islands hauling logs, freight, and passengers. By his teens, Eleazer probably began working on the *Belknap* as a deck hand, becoming the first Bear Islander to do so.[2] In 1849, he was able to parlay his boating experience and his knowledge of the lake into earning the job as the first pilot on the *Lady of the Lake* which was launched that year.[3]

While preoccupied with boating, he also tended to the farming business of the family with whom he was still living on Bear. In 1851, Eleazer bought 12 acre Mink Island from Andrew Gray of Meredith.[4] Eleazer owned.Mink Island for nearly 12 years.[5] His interest in owning the little island presumably involved its grazing and wood potential.

Eleazer's priorities shifted somewhat in the early 1860s when he met and married Ann Blaisdell of Gilford. In 1861, he took over as Captain of the *Lady*, certainly resulting in an increase in pay.[6] He decided to move off of Bear Island. In 1863, he bought a 43 acre homestead farm in Gilford.[7] The introduction to his wife and the decision to move may have been influenced by his brother-in-law, Stephen B. Dockham, whose farm was in Gilford. Stephen's first wife, Charlotte, was another of the Gilford Blaisdells. After Charlotte died in 1861, he had married Eleazer's younger sister, Almira.[8]

Eleazer's fortunes were clearly on the rise. He spent perhaps 25 years operating Winnipesaukee steam boats.[9] He was well liked by all who met him. As one passenger on the *Lady* described him: "A more affable and gentlemanly skipper could not be desired."[10] Those years were apparently very good to him as he was among the relatively few who built up enough savings so he could actually loan money to the town of Meredith to support its annual operating budget.[11]

---

[1] See the Boston Traveler, August 11, 1857, p. 4 and the Independent Democrat, August 3, 1870, p. 2, in which the correspondent was told this by Eleazer.

[2] Numerous other Bear Islanders worked on the boats in the following decades, right into the present. Stephen and David Meloon were the next to follow Eleazer, taking jobs on the steamers by 1860. Today, Jim Morash, whose family has summered for over 100 years on the southern end of Bear, owns and operates the Mount Washington, the Sophie C, and the Doris E.

[3] The Boston Traveler, August 11, 1857, p. 4 In the 1850 census, he recorded his occupation as "boatman".

[4] B/P 105/244. See Chapter 37 for more detail about Mink Island's history.

[5] BCRI, B/P 40/121.

[6] The Boston Herald, August 2, 1862, p. 1.

[7] BCRI, B/P 38/527.

[8] This was Almira's third marriage. Previous to this one, she was married to her cousin, Ebenezer Bickford, who died in 1856.

[9] In 1870, Eleazer listed his occupation as "Capt. of a Lake Steamer" in the 1870 census. (1870 Census, p. 46.)

[10] The Boston Herald, August 2, 1862, p. 1.

[11] Meredith Selectmen Accounts, early 1870s (MHS Archives). The annual Meredith Inventory and Tax Reports also show that his cousin, Jonathan Jr., also built up savings accounts during these years.

In 1866, Eleazer and Ann moved to Meredith Village, buying a house on Lang Street (now #17).[1] By 1874, Eleazer had retired from the boating business and acquired a grocery store in Meredith.[2] In further keeping with his Bear Island heritage, Eleazer apparently purchased in the 1880s, one of the houses built on North Bear by either Waldo Meloon or Solomon Lovejoy and then had it hauled by oxen across the ice to Lang Street where it became an addition to his existing home.[3]

Eleazer was very active in town affairs during his later years. He represented Meredith for one term in the state legislature in 1876. He was a selectman of Meredith from 1878 to 1880, and he also served as an auditor of the town in 1889 and 1890. According to a contemporary, E. H. Maloon, Eleazer was known to the people of Meredith as "an extra fine man" and a man "held in high esteem."[4] He and Ann remained living at the Lang St. house until his death in 1904. Eleazer was buried in the Meetinghouse cemetery with other members of his family.

The Lakeport Dam

The first dam at Lakeport was built about 1781 by Abraham Folsom Jr. He was the son of Abraham Folsom Sr. of Epping who had become a 'second' Meredith township proprietor in c. 1765 when he purchased the original proprietor's right of Nathaniel Bartlett Jr. The location was Point Lot 14 in the First Division of the new town. It was one of the most strategic locations identified very early on by the first settlers, because it included the narrow channel between Long Bay (now Paugus Bay) and Little Bay (now Lake Opechee). As a result, it was a natural place to build a dam and establish mills utilizing the water power. The location became known as Folsom's Mills. Abraham Jr. and then his son, Abraham, owned and operated the mills until 1824.

Folsom's Mills were sold by the heirs of Abraham Folsom 3rd in 1827 to Nathan Batchelder (1787 – 1867), a wealthy businessman from Louden, NH.[5] Batchelder built a new loose boulder and rubble dam just below the Folsom dam in 1830 to improve the flow of the

---

[1] His next door neighbor on Lang St. for a few years was Dolly's son, Robert M. Nichols. Another Bear Island veteran, Thomas Nichols, lived less than a quarter of a mile away at the bottom of Winnipesaukee Street. Thomas was a son of Nathaniel Nichols, and his grandfather was the very early Bear Islander, Paul Nichols. Thomas was married to Climena Bickford, the daughter of Brackett Bickford and a second cousin of Eleazer Jr. Another Bear Islander, George Bickford, became Eleazer's neighbor on Lang St. in 1879 when he bought Robert Nichols' house following the death of first Robert and then his wife. George was the son of Brackett Bickford. He was probably born on Bear Island and spent his first 20 years of life living there. By 1880, he was working for the railroad. (1880 Census, p. 24.)

[2] The Lake Village Times, October 24, 1874, p. 3. 1880 Census, p. 24.

[3] Deduced from discussion with Steve Austin, the present owner of the house, and Dave Hamblet , the owner of Y Landing.

[4] Meredith News, Jan 31, 1923.

[5] Batchelder bought the one-third widow's dower from Abraham's wife, Mary, in May 1827. BCRI, B/P 9013/47. He purchased the mills and water privileges from Abraham's two oldest sons, George and Abraham, the next month. BCRI, B/P 9013/46. At the same time, he also purchased a neighboring 175 acre farm the deceased Abraham had left to his two young sons, Joseph and Charles. BCRI, B/P 9013/46. In total, Batchelder paid $6000.00, a huge amount in those days. Less than one-third went to Abraham's widow. For Abraham's will, see: NH Probate Records, Srafford County, Vol. 32, 1824-1825. See also, Recollections, by Major John Aldrich (1917), p. 50.

water through his mills.[1] The mills and dam changed hands again in 1833 when Batchelder sold them for $40,000.00 to the Winnipisiogee Lake Cotton & Woolen Manufacturing Company (the WLCWM Co., aka the Lake Company).[2]

The WLCWM Co. had been chartered by the state in 1831. Its primary stockholder was David Pingree, a Salem, MA merchant who had inherited a "vast fortune" from his maternal uncle, Thomas Perkins, in 1830.[3] Pingree used the inheritance to develop a large business empire that included a sizable fleet of ships that traded internationally as well as numerous business operations in Massachusetts and New Hampshire.[4] The Lake Village purchase was part of that business expansion. Pingree's board of directors included Batchelder along with other local business heavyweights such as Stephen Gale, Nathaniel Davis, and Joseph Thyng.[5]

The Lake Company remained a locally oriented operation until 1845 when it was sold to Abbott Lawrence of Boston.[6] Lawrence was a leading member of the so-called Boston Associates, an informal name for an amorphous group of Boston area businessmen who introduced the Industrial Revolution to Massachusetts and northern New England. The Boston Associates built the integrated textile mills that started in Waltham, MA in 1813 and then were developed in later years in Lowell, Nashua, and Manchester, NH.[7] In the mid-1840s, Lawrence chartered the Essex Company to develop another huge mill complex at what was to become Lawrence, MA. With the increasing demand on the Merrimack River for water power causing periodic supply shortages, Abbott Lawrence determined that he needed to control the ultimate source of the river, Lake Winnipesaukee. He purchased the Lake Company from Pingree to achieve that goal.

Lawrence's first step to improve the water flow from Lake Winnipesaukee was to dredge the channel at the Weirs. His Lake Company owned at least some of the shore frontage on either side of the channel, thanks to purchases originally made by Pingree. The dredging took place in 1845 and 1846. The impact of the dredging was apparently quite substantial. It was estimated that it allowed Lawrence to draw down the lake an additional four to six feet.[8] Lawrence's next step had an opposite but similar substantial impact on water levels in

[1] There is much disagreement about the timing of this dam, but 1830 appears to be the correct date. See: WLCWMCo. To Abbott Lawrence, Oct 1845, BCRI, B/P 8007/561. It is not clear how much impact the new dam had upon the level of Lake Winnipesaukee. In 1833, for example, the Weirs channel "was a shallow and rather violent stream." Dredging was necessary to create a new channel to allow the new steamer, *Belknap*, to pass through. Even with the dredging, the *Belknap* had to be lightened and buoyed by barrels and hogsheads to get through. Blackstone, *Farewell*, p. 10. It was during this dredging that Endicott Rock was discovered. On the other hand, it apparently led to the separation of Mink Island from Mark Island.
[2] BCRI, B/P 9014/169. The sale included various shops and 250 acres of land. It also included rights of flowage that Batchelder had acquired from local shorefront residents.
[3] In re Pingree's founding role, see BCRI, B/P 8007/561.
[4] See website for the Peabody Essex Museum, www.pem.org, "David Pingree (1795-1863), Shipping Merchant."
[5] Nathan Davis was the owner of Lots 7 and 9 on Bear Island and Governors Island at the time. Stephen Gale was heavily involved with the mills at Meredith Bridge. See, BCRI, B/P 9015/156 for a list of directors.
[6] BCRI, B/P 8007/561; 8007/565; 8007/567. The latter two deeds were from Pingree to Lawrence and included various pieces of property. The total payments made by Lawrence in the three transactions amounted to $60,000.00. For a contemporary news report, see *Exeter News-Letter and Rockingham Advertiser*, October 27, 1845, p. 3.
[7] *Enterprising Elite: The Boston Associates and the World They Made*, Robert Dalzell, Jr., New York, 1987; The Lawrence History Center website: www.lawrencehistorycenter.org.
[8] See Parker V. Winnipisiogee Lake Cotton & Woolen Company, 67 US 545 (1862), p. 4.

Winnipesaukee. In 1851, the Lake Company built a new stone dam at Lakeport. The new dam was much tighter and somewhat higher than the existing dam. As a result, seasonal water levels in the lake rose considerably, flooding large sections along the shores.

The impact of the new dam was quite noticeable in the vicinity of Bear Island. A new island was created when rising waters resulted in a channel being carved across the neck of what was then known only as Steamboat Island. The new island eventually came to be called Birch Island.[1] In one other case, Witch Island became the submerged Witch's Rocks as that area was inundated, its trees eventually rotting away.[2]

The rising waters also had the effect of raising the tempers of lakeside farmers who saw their fields flooded every spring.[3] In 1859, this led to a riot during which irate farmers tried to dismantle the Lakeport Dam. Their efforts were defeated, and the courts upheld the rights of the Lake Company.[4] The Lake Company augmented the 1851 dam with a newer wing dam in 1861, although this did not raise the level of the lake. The company then proceeded to purchase the right to 'flow' (i.e. flood) as much shore front around the lake as it could get its hands on. Nearly all the property owners on Bear Island and the surrounding islands willingly sold either a one rod (16.5') deep strip of shoreline or the rights to flow that land during the last decades of the 1800s.[5] 1800s.[5] The WLCWMCo. remained in the hands of two Boston-controlled entities (the Locks and and Canals Company of Lowell and the Essex Company of Lawrence) until 1889 when it was purchased by a consortium of Lake Village and Laconia businessmen.[6]

[1] Regarding Birch, Hersey's 1772 map shows Birch and Steamboat as one island.

[2] In 1850, Witch Island was sold along with the Forty Islands and all of the Masonians' unnumbered islands to four men from Gilford. BCRI, B/P 26/331. Coincidentally, the man representing the seller's estate was John Blaisdell Jr., the former owner of Lots 1 and 2 on North Bear.

[3] In an effort to facilitate a process by which it could establish its rights to flood the shoreline, the Lake Company commissioned a detailed survey by William Crocker of all shore front owners on Winnipesaukee in 1858. It is available at the NH State Archives in Concord. The map is highly detailed and by far the best early map of the lake.

[4] "Winnipesaukee Water Wars," New England Historical Society, www.newenglandhistoricalsociety.com.

[5] For a good example of this, see: Meloons to WLCWM Co., June 1861, BCRI, B/P 35/597. In re Neck Lot 74, see Mead to WLCWM Co., August 1868, BCRI, B/P 47/349.

[6] Boston Post, July 13, 1889, p. 4.

Chapter Sixteen

The 1860s

North Bear

Waldo Meloon's tourist business flourished during the first half of the decade, but change was in the air for his family. Waldo's sons (and joint owners of the farm), Stephen and David, decided to pursue other careers. Not surprisingly, those careers were associated with the growing steamboat business. Stephen took a job as a 'deckhand,' and his much younger brother, David, became a 'fireman on [a] boat'.[1]

Stephen's personal life also had suffered a severe blow at this time when his wife, Sarah, died in 1860.[2] With his life in flux, Stephen moved off of the island in 1865. He sold back his interest in Lots 1 and 2 to Waldo and bought a small farm on parts of Lots 75 and 76 on the Neck Road. He retained his half interest in Bear Lot 3, and in 1867, he purchased the other half from his brother, John, giving Stephen full ownership of the 50 acre parcel.[3]

While Stephen was moving to the Neck, John took a completely different path. In 1867, he decided that life on the island and in New Hampshire were not for him and his growing family. On the same day that he sold his half of Lot 3 to Stephen, John sold his share of the Meloon's island farm to his youngest brother, George W. (age 20). John and his wife, Tamer, along with their three children, left Meredith some time thereafter, eventually migrating west. By 1880, they were living in Elkhart, Indiana, where John worked as a carpenter.[4]

Just south of the Meloons, Bear Lot 4 continued under the ownership of James Bickford throughout the 1860s, but there was a fundamental change in its use. In the first couple of years, it was still occupied on a year-round basis by James' two oldest sons, Oliver and Alonzo. Both of the boys had recently married, not surprisingly staying within the Bear Island/lower Neck orbit of families. Oliver married Julia Nichols, the daughter of Nathaniel Nichols, and Alonzo married Phebe B. Dockham, the daughter of Nathaniel Dockham. The boys' situation changed dramatically in 1862 when Oliver enlisted in the 12th NH Volunteer Regiment and went off to fight in the Civil War.[5] Alonzo left the island around 1863. Initially, he purchased a half interest in the Neck farm of his father-in-law, Nathaniel Dockham.[6] By 1870, he and Phebe were living in Meredith Village where Alonzo had taken a job at a saw mill.[7] With the departures of Oliver and

---

[1] 1860 Census. They were likely working on the *Lady* with Eleazer Bickford.

[2] The timing and details of Sarah's demise are not known. Meloon Family, MHS. In 1861, Stephen remarried, this time to Betsey E. Thompson, another Meredith Neck resident.

[3] BCRI, BP 42/16; 46/411; 36/516. As part of the first purchase, Stephen also acquired the wood and timber rights to the 15 acre piece of Bear Island Lot 4 that Theophilus Dockham had originally reserved in the deed when he sold the land to James Bickford in 1857.

[4] 1880 Census for Elkhart, Indiana.

[5] For a more detailed summary of Oliver's Civil War experience, see below, Chapter 17.

[6] See Meredith Tax Records, 1863, (MHS Archives). This farm was located next to the Meetinghouse cemetery.

[7] The Lake Village Times, June 19, 1869, p. 2. See also, 1870 Census, p. 5. The saw mill was probably the Meredith Shook and Lumber Company. Alonzo died in 1903. He was buried in the Meredith Village Cemetery.

Alonzo, Bear Lot 4 saw the last of its year-round inhabitants leave for the mainland. It became a summer farm under the auspices of the family patriarch, James S. Bickford and his son, Moses.

South Bear

Far greater changes occurred on South Bear during the 1860s. In 1863, Mahala Bryant sold the family farm on Lot 5 after four years of year-round living there, and the family moved to the Neck. She initially bought a farm on Neck Lot 81 but then sold it soon after so she could purchase a 67 acre farm on Lot 43 next to her brother, James.[1] Their departure marked the end of an era in the island's history. Mahala and Abram were the last permanent farmers on South Bear and the last of the Bryants on the island.[2]

Mahala sold Lot 5 to Charles W. Neal.[3] He was the 24 year old son of Richard and Betsey Betsey Neal who lived on the upper Neck, just north and east of the intersection of Barnard Ridge Road and the Center Harbor road (now Rte 25). Charles owned Lot 5 for less than one year.[4] In December 1863, he sold it to his sister-in-law, Elisabeth K. Neal, who was the wife of Joseph S. Neal, the postmaster in Meredith Village.[5]

Not long thereafter, Lot 5 became unified with abutting Lot 6N. In 1863, Lot 6N was put on the market by Waldo Meloon and Nathaniel Dockham who had owned it since Theophilus R. Dockham's departure in 1857. They sold it to John M. Wiggin and Samuel H. Randall.[6] Two years later in 1865, Wiggin and Randall bought Lot 5 from Elizabeth Neal.[7]

John M. Wiggin was a carpenter whose permanent homestead was in the First Division of Meredith. His father, Richard R. Wiggin, had settled there in the very early 1800s. Their farm was on Meredith Bay where he was a near neighbor of John and Joseph Neal (who owned Lot 9 at this juncture).[8] John Wiggin was interested in Bear Island for its grazing and wood lot value.[9] Samuel H. Randall was a farmer whose home was on a 16 acre parcel on Meredith Neck Lot 40, near the intersection of Barnard Ridge and Pleasant Street. Among his neighbors around this time were Bear Island veterans John Nichols and James Bickford, along with the recent returnees from Bear, Mahala and Abram Bryant.

In 1866, John Wiggin sold his half interest in the Lots 5 and 6N to James Gilman, Gilman becoming the joint owner with Randall. The two men were friends, living within a mile of each

---

[1] BCRI, B/P 38/278. Mahala bought the new Neck farm from her brother, James, who lived on Lot 42. She was the sole owner of the real estate. Her husband, Abram, was not a party of record. The Lot 43 farm was located at the end of today's Snell Road.

[2] BCRI, B/P 39/325.

[3] Charles was the son of Elizabeth K. Neal who was a sister of Joseph Neal Jr. who owned Bear Lot 9.

[4] Later in his life, Charles served as a Selectman of Meredith from 1877 to 1880. He subsequently served as town auditor for at least five years.

[5] BCRI, B/P 38/278; 41/478. Elizabeth K. Neal was married to a son of Joseph "Red Oak" Neal.

[6] BCRI, B/P 38/280.

[7] BCRI, B/P 41/536.

[8] Wiggin's D1 farm was the same area once owned by the early Bear settlers, John Bickford and his son, Jonathan Sr.

[9] BCRI, B/P43/125; 12/121; 29/316; 15/544.

other on the Neck. This purchase was the introduction of the venerable Gilman family to the island.[1] In 1868, James' brother, David, bought out Randall's half ownership of Lots 5 and 6N; then on the same day, David sold half of his interest (or one quarter interest in the property) to John Smith, a Neck farmer who lived near both Gilman and Randall.[2] The three Neck farmers used Lots 5 and 6N for seasonal grazing and as a wood lot.

Further south, Lot 7 was also subject to substantial ownership change. Parker P. Nichols had held it since 1854. In 1860, the childless Parker (now 56) deeded the island property and his Neck homestead (on Lot 74) to his nephew, George W. Sanborn of Gilford, in a 'retirement' deed that had a reversion clause if George did not keep the terms of the deal.[3] But in 1864, another plan was hatched with George. Parker bought a two-thirds interest in George's Gilford farm and sold George the Nichols' Neck farm. As part of the deal, the island property reverted back to Parker who quickly sold it to his nephew, John B. Nichols, and Franklin Canney.[4] Parker moved to Gilford thereafter.

John B. Nichols (38) was the son of Parker's brother and Bear Island veteran, John Nichols. John B. had spent his formative years growing up on the island after his family established the permanent farm on the interior half of Lot 6N in 1830. In 1864, John B. owned a Neck farm on Lot 52 along Blueberry Hill Road where his neighbors included his father, James and David Gilman, and Sam Randall.[5] With this purchase, John B. became the third generation of Nichols to own Bear Lot 7. But his tenure lasted only three years. In 1867, he sold his interest to Franklin Canney.[6] The sale marked the end of the Nichols presence on the island.

Canney's purchase was a distinct change in the typical owners of Bear property. He was neither a farmer nor a Neck resident. He was one of five children of John and Abigail Canney who owned a farm in Center Harbor. But Franklin lived in Meredith Village. Real estate and timber investment figured prominently in his activities. Lot 7 on Bear Island fell into the latter category.

Meanwhile, the ownership of Lot 9 also experienced some changes. In 1860, it was owned jointly by Smith Neal's trustee, Charles S. Prescott, and John Neal. In 1863, John Neal passed away, and his ownership share was inherited by his son, John Mead Neal. In 1866, Prescott sold Smith Neal's half interest in the lot to William Neal, a relative and neighbor in the First Division. The following month, Prescott reentered the picture on his own behalf by acquiring the half interest owned by John M. Neal.[7]

---

[1] BCRI, B/P 43/126.
[2] BCRI, B/P 47/165 and 47/166. See Meredith tax records (MHS Archives) for the 1860s in re the Gilmans' flocks of sheep.
[3] BCRI, B/P 34/61.
[4] BCRI, B/P 39/437; 39/502; 39/520.
[5] BCRI, B/P 37/610.
[6] BCRI, B/P 46/94.
[7] BCRI, B/P 44/615; 44/613.

Charles S. Prescott was a wealthy shoemaker ('cordwainer' in 1860s parlance) in Meredith Village who was a very active investor in real estate all around the town. Among many other things, Charles and his brother, James M. Prescott, owned parcels on Pine Island and two of the smaller Beaver Islands. In 1870, Prescott also served as a selectman for Meredith.[1]

Both Charles Prescott and William Neal were solely interested in the wood on the island, not farming or pasturing. In April 1867, only five months after purchasing it, Prescott sold his share to Stephen Boardman Jr., but he reserved his wood rights.[2] Stephen Boardman Jr. was the son of the Stephen Boardman who had briefly owned Bear Lot 2 in 1822. Stephen Jr. was the Neck farmer who had donated part of his land in 1839 for the Meetinghouse. In 1868, Stephen Jr. bought out the other half of Lot 9 from William Neal.[3] In 1870, he bought the remaining one acre lot touching Deep Cove that Robert M. Nichols had sold to Charles Bickford in 1837.[4] Original Lot 9 was now reunified under a single owner.

In sharp contrast to all of the changes on Lots 7 and 9, the ownership of Lots 6S and 8 remained unchanged during the 1860s. The former had become a summer farm and wood lot for Charles Bickford, while Jonathan Bickford Jr. used the latter along the same lines.

Summary

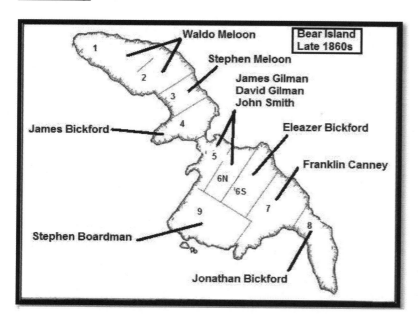

Thus, by the end of the 1860s, the ownership and usage patterns on Bear Island were fully redefined. On the northern end of the island, Waldo Meloon was the last permanent farmer on the island, although he spent more than a little of his time catering to the tourism business. To his south, his son, Stephen Meloon (Lot 3), and three members of the Bickford family (Lots 4, 6S, and 8) were using their island properties for summer farming and wood lots. The rest (Lots 5, 6N, 7 and 9) belonged to various people who used the land for seasonal pasturage and wood lots.

---

[1] BCRI, B/P9/429; 44/6150; 44/309.

[2] BCRI, B/P45/422. The deed of sale lists the grantee as Stephen 'Bowman', but subsequent deeds properly identify him as Stephen Boardman. Prescott's reservation read "all the wood and timber now on said land with the Privilage of taking the same off of said land any time within five years from this date." It is not clear how the reservation worked given Prescott owned an <u>undivided</u> half of Lot 9. He probably made a side agreement with William Neal.

[3] BCRI, B/P 48/287. Similar to Prescott, William Neal reserved the right to cut and remove half of the wood and timber at any time for five years.

[4] BCRI, B/P 52/31. The parcel is now part of the property owned by the St. John's on-the-Lake Chapel Association.

Chapter Seventeen

Vignettes: The 1860s

Oliver Bickford, Civil War 'Deserter'?

In August 1862, Oliver Bickford enlisted in Company I, 12th New Hampshire Volunteer Infantry when that Civil War regiment was first being organized in Meredith. He was paid a bounty of $25. The 12th was deployed to the Virginia theatre during the fall of 1862, not long after the battle of Antietam, the bloodiest battle of the war. In December, his unit was lightly engaged in the Battle of Fredericksburg, which proved to be a major loss for the Union forces. Then in the spring of 1863, Oliver's unit was heavily involved in the devastating battle at Chancellorsville. The 12th NH Regiment suffered severe losses with 41 killed, 213 wounded and 63 missing out of a total strength of 558 men. Ten Meredith men died on the battlefield or from wounds received during the fighting. Captain J.W. Lang, for whom Lang Street was named, was badly wounded. The reports of the losses "cast a pall over Meredith."[1]

Oliver Bickford was one of the missing. He was captured by the Confederate Army on May 3, 1863.[2] He was confined in Richmond until May 9th and then transferred to nearby City Point on the James River from where he was 'paroled' on May 15th. 'Parole' was a process by which the Union and the Confederacy exchanged prisoners with the agreement that the individuals would not reenter active combat. Two days later, Oliver was sent to the Union's 'Camp Parole' at Annapolis, Maryland.[3] The camp, established in 1862, was an overcrowded and increasingly squalid place where the parolees apparently did little more than busy work while trying to survive on meager rations.

Oliver deserted from Annapolis on July 21, 1863. It was rumored that he had returned to Meredith. On March 12, 1864 the Provost Marshall, Nathaniel Wiggin, wrote to the Meredith sheriff, Hanson Bedee, asking for his help in capturing Oliver. Wiggin's letter said that he understood that Oliver was hiding out on Bear Island. He asked Bedee to investigate and arrest him. Bedee followed up on the request without success. He reported back to Wiggin on March 18th that there was no trace of Oliver anywhere, including the surrounding towns. He said that the story of Oliver being out on Bear had been around for six months, but Bedee believed that Oliver had left the area the previous fall.[4]

Meredith lore holds that Oliver was hiding on Bear Island when Bedee supposedly went out across the ice to search for him there. The story goes that Oliver evaded Bedee by using a

---

[1] Van Veghten, "Chancellorsville and the Twelfth New Hampshire Volunteers," mhsweb.org. The 1864 Meredith Annual Report indicated that 45% of the 500 male voters in town served in the war. Some 122 of them served as officers and enlisted men, and another 105 entered as substitutes for others. Annual Town Report, 1865.
[2] Civil War records of Oliver L. Bickford. Muster Roll, May & June, 1863.
[3] Memorandum from Prisoner of War Records, No. 328
[4] Civil War records of Oliver L. Bickford.

hidden passageway between two of the cellar holes under the Bickford's houses on Lot 4. The story makes good telling, but there is no indication that Bedee even went out to the island to search for Oliver, much less was fooled by him. A viewing of the cellar holes makes the story seem highly unlikely. Rather, one has the suspicion that Bedee was not really interested in finding Oliver and never really pursued him.[1] In any case, Oliver was never caught and his whereabouts during this period are unknown.

Once the war was over, Oliver resumed his life in Meredith. There were no repercussions. His war records show that he was simply mustered out of the army in July 1863 (the month he deserted) with no negative references around his discharge. He again became a normal, active citizen in the town.[2] In 1868, he bought a farm on the Neck Road from former Bear Islander, Thomas Nichols, and his wife, Climena, who happened to be Oliver's cousin.[3] In 1871, he donated (or repaired) the Village watering trough; between 1870 and 1886, he was the Prudential (school) Committee representative in charge of a Neck school district on six different occasions; and in 1897, at age 65, he was selected to be a Fish and Game Warden.[4] He died in 1912 and was buried in the Meetinghouse cemetery.

Oliver's reputation in Meredith historical literature is that of a deserter; and he technically was a deserter. But he hardly warrants the negative implications associated with the term. Oliver was a man who served quite honorably in one of the most devastating battles of the Civil War, the same conflict during which Stonewall Jackson was mortally wounded. His desertion was not from duty but from the tedium and squalor of the parolee camp while he was prohibited from active duty in the army anyway. This was assuredly recognized by his subsequent welcome back to Meredith.

Oliver Bickford was one of three men who lived at some point on Bear Island and who served in the Civil War. The other two were Theophilus Dockham's son, Luther, and Nathaniel Nichols' son, Nathaniel. Luther served during the entire war and came home unscathed. Nathaniel became ill during his service and died in 1866. Several others were drafted but did not serve, cognizant as they certainly were of Oliver's experiences. Two of them, Alonzo and James E. Bickford, were Oliver's brothers and were drafted in 1864. They were able to provide substitutes to take their places. The same was true for Charles S. and Joseph L. Bickford, the two sons of Oliver's cousin, Charles Bickford. Three others connected to Bear, Jesse Lovejoy's

[1] Hanson Bedee served many years as deputy or sheriff of Meredith from the early 1850s. He had a reputation for being very fair with townspeople. See E.H. Wilcomb, "Sheriff Played Santa Claus," in Rambles About the Weirs, 2nd part, pp. 14-16. Wilcomb says that Bedee was exempt from Civil War duty because he was poor and had five kids. He died in 1903 at the age of 92. He was buried in the Meredith Village cemetery.
[2] Meredith tax records for 1866 and 1867 list him along with everyone else. In 1866, his only asset was a cow. In 1867 he had four cows and four sheep. Meredith Tax Records, 1866 and 1867, Meredith Historical Society archives.
[3] BCRI, B/P 47/457. The transaction was another family affair. Oliver's wife, Julia A., was the sister of Thomas and a daughter of Nathaniel Nichols. Thomas had taken over the family farm after Nathaniel was killed in the 1855 collapse of the new Meredith town meetinghouse. Climena was the daughter of Brackett Bickford. The current address for this farm is 206 Meredith Neck Road.
[4] Meredith Annual Reports, 1871, 1879, 1880, 1883, 1886, and 1897.

sons, Ezra and Solomon, and Stephen B. Meloon, also found substitutes.[1] Another member of the 12th NH Regiment was indirectly connected to the island. This was George Nichols, the son of Robert M. Nichols and the grandson of Aunt Dolly Nichols. George signed on in August 1862 when that regiment was first being established. His service, however, was extremely short. He fell ill within a matter of weeks, like so many others did during the war. He died of pneumonia in October.

The Bear Island School

In c. 1805, the state of New Hampshire mandated that school districts be established in every town to promote the schooling process. Meredith finally reached this goal in 1811.[2] The town established a so-called Prudential Committee consisting of local residents who were each given charge of a school district to ensure acceptable teachers were hired and paid and that the proper curriculum was followed.

The Bear Island school was established in 1846, if not a year or so earlier.[3] It was initially designated as District #21 by the town.[4] It was a much needed addition. There were an ample number of school age children on the island by then, and the alternatives for them were not attractive. The schoolhouse nearest the island was located on Boardman Hill, across from the Neck Meetinghouse. A school had existed there since the late 1830s.[5]

The small Bear schoolhouse was centrally located in the Carry on Lot 5. The lot was under the ownership of James Bickford at the time. The first teacher was Miss S.E. Morrell. She was paid $4.00 per month and a total of $15.08 for the year. The length of the school year was nine weeks, probably split between summer and winter terms as was common practice.[6] There were 14 students ("scholars") who attended the school in 1846, nine of whom were under the age of 14. All of the children would have been living on Lots 1, 5, 6, and 8. Most of the children were from the families of brothers James, Brackett and Jonathan Bickford. Others probably belonged to the Meloon family and John Nichols.[7] The school was probably quite viable into the early 1850s. The various Bickford, Nichols, Meloon, and Dockham families all had young children of school age.

---

[1] Meredith Annual Report, 1865. Substitution was a widespread, fully accepted practice during the Civil War which came to be called a "rich man's war but a poor man's fight."
[2] Meredith Annual Records, 1809 - 1811, (Meredith Town Hall).
[3] Report of Superintending School Committee of the town of Meredith for the year ending March 1847, loose leaf binder, (Meredith Historical Society).
[4] There were 23 school districts in Meredith by then.
[5] See BCRI, B/P 5/100. The September 1839 deed mentions the southerly corner of Lot 64 "whereon stands a school house." This reference did not appear in 1836, the previous time the parcel was sold. BCRI, B/P 15/600. For an 1854 reference to the same school, see BCRI, B/P 24/456.
[6] School Report, March 1846, in Report of the Selectmen, (Meredith Historical Society).
[7] Report of Superintending School Committee of the town of Meredith for the year ending March 1847, loose leaf binder, Meredith Historical Society. These families were the permanent farmers on the island during 1846. The other lots were owned by people who used them for wood and seasonal pasturage.

By 1854, however, there were only five students who attended school during the eight week summer session.[1] The district had begun to struggle as the younger children grew up and the permanent farmers began leaving the island. Waldo Meloon took the leadership for most of the period, serving as the district's representative on the Prudential committee for a number of years. The school received a modest boost in 1859 when Abram and Mahala Bryant bought Lot 5. Abram took a turn on the Prudential committee, and their daughter, Arvilla, took over teaching duties for at least a couple of years.[2]

Only a few bricks remain from the old school.

Nevertheless, the Bear Island school was losing its vitality. In 1859 and 1860, again only five students attended.[3] The town report concluded that it was "too small to create much interest or try the capacity of the teacher."[4] In 1863, only three boys attended the school which held classes taught by Arvilla for only five weeks during the winter.[5] The school's last year of operation was 1863. Whatever tenuous existence it had was lost with the departures from the island of not only Abram, Mahala, and Arvilla but also Oliver and Alonzo Bickford and their very young families.[6] Thereafter, the little schoolhouse in the Carry disintegrated from disuse.[7] Pieces of it remained evident well into the 1900s. All that remains today is a very rough footprint and a few red bricks.

The James Gilman Family

The extended Gilman family played a major role throughout colonial New Hampshire history. The town of Gilmanton, for example, was named after the family, and the original list of 177 township proprietors included 24 members of the Gilman family when it was incorporated in 1727. The Gilman branch that ultimately developed a connection to Bear Island traced its roots back to Moses Gilman who was born in Hingham, England about 1630. Moses immigrated to Massachusetts where the next two generations of the family, James (1) and Timothy, lived.

---

[1] School Report, March 1855, Meredith Historical Society. There was no winter term that year. The Bear Island District was now #23.
[2] See Annual School report section of each Meredith Annual Report of the Selectmen.
[3] School Register for District 23, for years 1859 and 1860 (MHS Archives). In 1859, the five children included two Meloons and an adopted son of Mahala and Abram named Hosea. The other two children, with a last name of Nicholson, probably belonged to parents employed by the Meloons on their farm. In 1860, there were four Meloon children along with Hosea Bryant.
[4] School Report, March 1861. The Bear Island district tax base in 1860 included only seven paying households totaling $20.05. Three of the taxpayers were Meloons (Waldo, Stephen and John), two of them Bickfords (Oliver and Alonzo), Abram Bryant, and Nathaniel Dockham. School taxes, 1860-1861, compiled by Levi Towle, "Memorandum Book", loose leaf binder, Meredith Historical Society. Nathaniel Dockham was taxed for his half ownership of Lot 6N. All of the others were permanent residents on the island.
[5] Annual school report, 1863. By then Bear was registered as District #1.
[6] By 1870 Arvilla was employed in Meredith Village as a "labourer in (a) hosiery mill." (1870 Census, p. 9).
[7] Interestingly, when Mahala Bickford sold Lot 5 in 1863, she specifically reserved out ownership of the schoolhouse. BCRI, B/P 38/278. But Mahala never came back for it.

During the first half of the 1700s, James (1) moved north to New Market, New Hampshire where another son named James (2) was born in 1750.

In 1789, James (2) moved to Meredith where his cousin, Bradbury Gilman, and several other Gilmans were already settled. Upon arrival, he purchased Lot 51 on Meredith Neck from Bradbury.[1] This purchase made James one of the earliest settlers on the lower Neck. The 95 acre lot was located on the northern side of the range way that is now known as Blueberry Hill Road. The following year, he purchased Neck Lot 57 at a sheriff's auction.[2] James built his homestead farm there. The farm stayed in the family for 123 years.[3] In subsequent years, James James expanded his holdings on the Neck. His core properties included lots 57 and 51 along with lots 50 and 60. At various times he owned additional land at various places on the Neck.

James (2) was also active in the budding Village of Meredith. In 1802, he joined with several Meredith men, including other Neck leading lights (William Mead, Joseph Neal and John Roberts) to buy the saw mill located in the village. James owned a one-eighth share.[4] He also served as a Selectman from 1805 through 1807 as well.[5]

James (2) was quite well to-do. A quick review of the 1829 Meredith tax report shows that the Gilman's wealth in land, pasturage, and animals far outstripped almost everyone else on the Neck.[6] James (2) and his wife, Deborah, had six children, including four sons and two daughters. daughters. Of the sons, Josiah died in 1791 at the age of four. Samuel (1779 – 1857) and James (3) (1777 – 1854) became successful farmers in Center Harbor thanks to their father's largesse.[7] largesse.[7] The fourth son, David Gilman (b. 1785) died at age 32, but not before fathering three children, including the Bear Island land owners, James (4) (1813-1887) and David (1816-1900), and Martha. After their father died, the children and their mother, Sally Clark Gilman, moved in with their grandfather, James (2).

In 1835, the aging James (2) sold the family homestead and other Neck parcels to his grandson, James (4), as part of a 'retirement' plan.[8] On the same day, James (4) sold half of it to his brother, David. James (4) was 22 years old at the time, and David was only 19. David

---

[1] BCRI, B/P 9002/169. Brad Gilman had a farm on the upper Neck.
[2] BCRI, B/P 9002/168. The lot was auctioned because the non-resident, proprietor-owner had not paid the annual taxes on it.
[3] This place, now 64 Meredith Neck Road, became the home of the famous 'Archie' comic book author, Bob Montana, in 1960.
[4] BCRI, B/P 9004/46; 9004/192; 9006/425; 9005/9; 9005/169; 9006/307; 9006/307. James and the other owners sold the mill in 1811 to John Bond Swasey and Daniel Avery, the men who developed the canal through the village in the years thereafter.
[5] Town Meeting Records, 1794 – 1804, bound volume located at the Meredith Town Hall.
[6] Meredith Tax Report, 1829. (Meredith Historical Society). Gilman had 35 acres of pasture, 13 mowing, two arable, and one orchard. He had six cows, four cattle, 2 oxen, and 1 horse. Near the other end of the spectrum were Paul and Parker Nichols who had two acres of pasture, one mowing, one-half arable, and one-eighth orchard. The vast majority of settlers on the Neck (and probably throughout the town) were a lot closer in wealth to the Nichols than to James Gilman.
[7] In 1803, James (2) gifted Samuel half of a 177 acre farm the family owned in Center Harbor. Sometime later James (3) had moved to Center Harbor where he was living on another large family farm. But James (3) was ailing of health or mind (or both) by 1827 such that James (2) sold the farm occupied by James (3) to Samuel with the agreement that Samuel would take care of his brother for the rest of his life. James (3) remained an active farmer and land owner, including owning part of Neck Lot 60.
[8] BCRI, B/P 9017/17; 9012/206; 9013/462. He leased the properties back for the rest of his and his wife's natural lives.

ultimately ended up occupying the original family home on Lot 57 after Grandpa James (2) died in 1838. Brother James (4) built a neighboring home just south of it on the Neck Road.[1]

In 1836, grandson James (4) married Susan Mead, a daughter of William Mead. They had eight children, including three boys and five girls. Two of the children died when they were very young; three eventually moved to California (James M., Granville and Ellen Lil); and the other three children, Mary, Martha, and David Frank remained in Meredith. James (4) died in 1887. His brother, David, died in 1900. David left the property to his nephew, David Frank. He died in 1912, and the family's estate on the Neck and Bear Island ultimately ended up in the hands of his sister, Ellen Lil, the last surviving child of James (4). She sold the Neck property in 1913, some 123 years after its original purchase by Grandpa James (2).[2]

Grandpa James Gilman (2)

---

[1] BCRI, B/P 15/17; 16/549. These houses are numbers 64 (David) and 76 (James) on Meredith Neck Road.
[2] BCRI, B/P 138/8. Among other things, she reserved out the Gilman cemetery that can be found near the Neck Road just south of the former family dwellings.

Chapter Eighteen

The 1870s

The decade of the 1870s witnessed the continued divergence of approaches to living on Bear that had first emerged in the 1850s. The tilt towards the evolving summer era became more pronounced on the North end, while the rest of the island remained well ensconced in the seasonal farming era.

North Bear

The decade of the 1870s brought some challenging times to the Meloon family on North Bear. Their youngest son, George, died of heart disease in January 1872 at the age of 25, leaving his wife, Pamelia, and two infant sons. When Pamelia sought to sell George's interest in the property to cover his debts, she ran into a problem. George's share had never been defined; it was simply an undivided quarter of the Meloon farm. The situation was taken up by the probate court which, as was normal practice, established a committee of local citizens to define George's property. Two specific parcels were carved out by the committee, amounting to 30 acres. One of the two was a six acre piece of land with 875' of shore front on the eastern side of the island facing the mountains. The other was a 24 acre parcel with buildings on the western side facing the Neck.[1]

In 1873, Pamelia sold George's interest in Bear Island to her brother-in-law, David S. Meloon (then 35), prompting his return to the island after a decade or so away. He came back with his wife, Susan C. Alexander, and a family of three young children.[2] David Meloon's life prior to his 1873 return had been quite different than most, reflecting the changing times. He was 14 when his parents bought the island farm in 1852. By 1860, he had become a 'fireman' on one of the steamers.[3] By 1864, he had saved enough money to buy a home in the Lake Village part of Gilford, next door to his older brother, Frances, who had left the island many years before.[4]

Sometime during this period, David gave up the boating business and became an engineer on the railroad. The change in careers apparently led him to move again, this time out of state. By 1871, David and his wife were living in Jersey City, NJ. It was around this time that David had a near death experience that changed his life. A train that he was operating plunged off the tracks into a river, and David nearly drowned. Thereafter, he lost his nerve for the business. He moved back to Lake Village in 1871, again buying property from his brother, Frances. Less than two years after his return to New Hampshire, David's brother, George, died.

---

[1] See B/P 57/209. Also <u>Lake Village Times</u>, October 4, 1873, p. 4. The buildings on the 24 acre piece perhaps included the house that is now #432 Bear Island.
[2] B/P 57/209.
[3] 1860 Census.
[4] Frances sold David the property. B/P 40/54 and 40/267.

David and Susan took the opportunity to buy George's share of his father's farm and return to Bear.[1]

A few months before David's arrival at the end of 1873, Waldo agreed to sell his 'picnic' business to a group of Lake Village businessmen led by John Crane. It is likely that they approached Waldo with an offer as they had developed extensive plans to make Bear Island "one of the most popular resorts on the lake."[2] The Boston Mirror and Farmer described the transaction thusly:

"A company of citizens from Lake Village and Laconia have purchased the wharf property, grove and bowling alley on Bear Island in Winnepisseoge Lake, and contemplate fitting up the grounds, erecting a hotel or boarding-house and leasing ground for building summer cottages."[3]

Waldo made the actual sale to John S. Crane individually. There is almost no information about who else might have been working with him.[4] The property included the wharf, a five and one-half acre parcel on the very end of the island, and the buildings thereon. Waldo reserved the right to use the roadway leading from the wharf to his house; to use the wharf itself; and to access and maintain his boathouse located next to the wharf. Crane reserved the right to cross the Meloon's property to 'the hill' (i.e. Sunset Rock).[5]

John Crane was a Springfield, MA native, born in 1834. He was a direct descendant of Governor Bradford of Massachusetts and a 32nd degree Mason. As a young man, after schooling in Berwick, ME, he sailed around the world on a schooner. Upon his return and looking for a vocation, he spent several years learning the knitting business in Salmon Falls, NH, Lawrence, MA, and Lowell, MA. Still seeking 'something else', he headed out West for a period, before returning to Manchester, NH and the knitting trade.

Crane moved to Lake Village in the 1850s where he initially went to work with William Pepper in the knitting industry. In 1859, Crane's business was the first in town to successfully manufacture a new type of spring knitting needle used in the rapidly evolving knitting machines that were starting to revolutionize the knitting business.[6] He went on to parlay his work experience into a series of partnerships that by the 1860s involved the manufacture of the knitting machines themselves. In 1870, he formed a joint venture with Benjamin Peaslee. They

---

[1] B/P 54/56. 1860 Census for Meredith; BCRI, B/P 40/54; 40/267. E.H.Maloon, Meredith News, November 18, 1922. Some of this story is inferred.

[2] The Boston Traveler, September 1, 1873, p. 2.

[3] The Boston Mirror and Farmer, September 6, 1873, p.3.

[4] One of the others was Samuel C. Clark, a prominent Lake Village attorney who clerked for Stephen C. Lyford and went on to play a major role in local politics. He also served as a representative in the state legislature on several occasions during the 1870s and was also Clerk of the House at least twice. He owned ¼ of the Bear Island property according to a petition filed by his wife after Samuel died in 1897. (B/P 100/31). We have found no other records dealing with this partial ownership or with any other shares. None of the Crane deeds makes any mention of partial interests.

[5] BCRI, B/P 70/163.

[6] Historical Sketches of Lakeport, "Corporations and Manufactures," (1915).

enjoyed substantial success and, in 1872, patented a machine for making shirts and underwear. In 1878, after Peaslee retired, Crane formed a new entity called the John S. Crane & Company in Lakeport. It became one of the largest employers in the Lakes Region. He also got involved in New Hampshire politics, first representing Laconia in the state legislature in 1875 and then Gilford in 1878.[1]

Not surprisingly, given his early adventures at sea, John Crane was an avid boat's man. In 1868, he built his own sailboat, named the *White Wing*, which was widely acknowledged for its beauty by the residents of Lake Village. The Lake Village Times called it "doubtless the finest sailing boat upon the lake" when it was launched.[2]

Crane and fellow Lake Village entrepreneurs never acted upon their plans for Bear. They continued to host 'excursions' on the island, but those visits were fewer than during Waldo's hay days of the early 1860s. They built a new wharf in 1875 in an apparent attempt to lure more steamboat traffic, but Bear became more of a haven for campers supplemented by sporadic, small group getaways made by local inhabitants.[3]

Meanwhile, in the absence of the proposed hotel, Waldo apparently decided to fill some of the void. He reportedly converted his island home into a boarding house sometime around the end of the decade. Waldo's daughter, Melissa (then 40), and her husband, Leonard Davis, joined Waldo to operate it.[4]

---

[1] The Illustrated Laconian, pp. 129-130. Among his other business activities, John Crane was an incorporator and shareholder in the Laconia and Lake Village Water Works in 1883, and in 1892, he was one of the incorporators of the National Bank of Lakeport. Historical Sketches of Lakeport, "Corporations and Manufactures," (1915).
[2] Lake Village Times, September 5, 1868, p. 3. See also, Historical Sketches of Lakeport (1915), Chapter VI. In 1869, Crane advertised renting it to "pleasure parties" to sail on Long Bay, "skipper furnished". Lake Village Times, June 19, 1869, p. 4. William Pepper was apparently a co-investor in the boat.
[3] In re the wharf, see the Boston Mirror and Farmer, April 10, 1875, p. 4. In re camping, see, for example, Lake Village Times, July 10, 1875, p. 3 and the Lowell Daily Citizen and News, July 15, 1879. In re small excursions, see Lake Village Times, July 15, 1876, p. 3 and the NH Patriot and Gazette, July 31, 1879, p. 2. There were no newspaper reports of visits by the *Lady of the Lake* or the *Mount Washington* which began service on the lake in 1872. The small excursion groups were carried by the *James Bell*.
[4] See, "The Bear Island House Burned To The Ground," Meredith News, Nov 1934. There is almost no information about the boarding house. This article is the only source that mentions it, and even then its very terse specifics are incorrect.

But in December 1879, tragedy again struck the Meloon family. Waldo's son, David, drowned when he fell through the ice just off of the Bear Island wharf while he was returning on ice skates from a trip to the mainland.[1] David's wife, Susan, decided of necessity to sell David's island properties. Waldo bought them back, but the transaction stretched his finances. He had to take a loan from James H. Plaisted, an active real estate lender in Meredith, to complete the deal.[2] By the end of the 1870s, the 73 year old Waldo was beginning to struggle on Bear Island.

The Rest of Bear

The decade of the 1870s was quite stable on the rest of Bear, with very few changes of note. Just down the shore from Waldo on Lot 4, life for James Bickford and his son, Moses, generally remained routine. They continued to use the Bear Island property as a summer farm. Similarly on combined Lots 5 and 6N next door, brothers, James and David Gilman, and their neighbor, John Smith, continued using the 112 acres for seasonal grazing and as a wood lot. Nearby on Lot 6S, there was only a modest change in ownership during the late 1870s. Charles Bickford sold the lot to his younger brother, Eleazer Jr., in 1879.[3] By then Eleazer Jr. was operating a grocery store in Meredith Village. He presumably used Bear as a seasonal farm, growing fruits and vegetables.[4] Meanwhile, Lot 8 remained the domain of Jonathan Bickford Jr. and his family, while Lot 9 continued under the ownership of Stephen Boardman Jr. In both cases, the properties were used as wood lots and for seasonal grazing throughout the decade.

On the other hand, Lot 7 underwent a bit more ownership change during the decade. First, Franklin Canney sold it to his brother-in-law, Rufus L. Coe of Center Harbor, in 1872.[5] Coe was one of six children of John and Lavinia Coe, the owners of the Coe House in Center Harbor.[6] But Rufus quickly flipped the lot, retaining the logging rights for three years. He sold it to to John A. Perkins and another brother-in-law, Charles H. Canney.[7] Perkins and Canney were both farmers who were next door neighbors in Center Harbor. Perkins had moved to Center Harbor from Boston back in 1854, while Charles Canney had been raised there and owned his own farm.

---

[1] Boston Journal, December 29, 1879, p. 4. David's son was with him but managed to get to shore. Boston Post, December 29, 1879, p. 2. Interestingly, ice skating was apparently a common mode of winter travel during this period. In December 1871, George Brown skated with his son from Long Island to Lake Village. "Long Island of the Past," presentation by Philip Parsons and Clark Myers, June 8, 1987, transcript at the Moultonborough Library.

[2] BCRI, 67/594; 67/632; 57/209; 68/37. Susan and her children moved back to Meredith Neck, probably to her parent's (Daniel and Fanny Alexander) farm off Blueberry Hill Road. In January 1881, some 13 months after David drowned, Susan remarried. Her second husband was David's brother, Stephen B. Meloon. Stephen was in the same circumstance as Susan. His second wife, Betsey, had died only four months before in September 1880. Stephen lived on the Neck on Lot 76, across the Neck road and just south of the Meetinghouse Cemetery.

[3] B/P 65/68; BP 51/350. By this time at age 70, Charles was getting tired, and it is likely that his wife, Augusta, was experiencing declining health. She passed away in 1881. Charles appears to have been planning for their senior years for some time. Some nine years earlier he had completed a 'retirement' deal with his oldest son, Charles H., by deeding the family farm on Neck Lot 78 to him. The deed required that Charles and Augusta have continued use of the farm for their natural lives, while Charles H. took care of the farm and related expenses. Charles died in 1893.

[4] Among other things, apple trees could be found on this lot well into the 1960s.

[5] BCRI, B/P 39/520.

[6] John and Lavinia had purchased the old Samuel Senter homestead farm and Senter Hotel overlooking the bay in 1855 (BCRI, B/P 24/471). They changed the name of the hotel to the Coe House. Interestingly, during the 1850s and 1860s, the Coe House was a stop on the underground railroad for former slaves travelling north to Canada. The house still stands; although it is currently for sale..

[7] BCRI, B/P 55/453. Like some of his predecessors in owning Lot 7, Coe reserved the right to take "all of the growth now standing on said lot, excepting the growth in the swamp on the upper end of the lot, and the right to cut and remove the same at any time within 3 years."

Summary

The decade of the 1870s came to a close with the north end of the island struggling with change. John Crane's summer business was limping along, and Waldo was dealing with family issues while trying to develop a boarding house. Everywhere else on the island, the ownership remained relatively stable and use of the property continued to follow the traditional patterns of seasonal usage for pasturage and access to wood and timber.

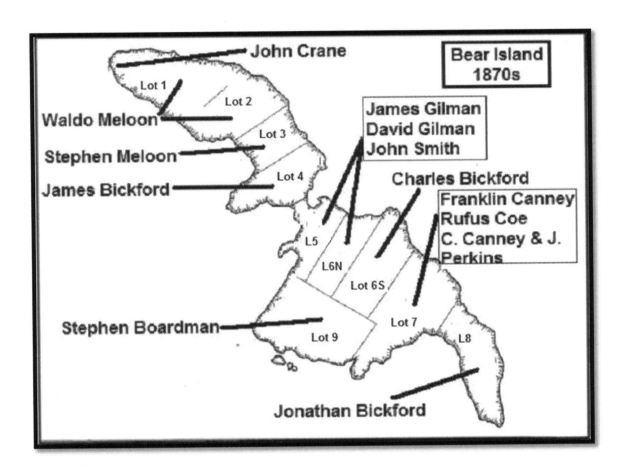

Part IV:

The

Summer Vacation Era

Reaches

Bear Island

Chapter Nineteen

Backdrop to Summer Vacationing[1]

The concept of a summer vacation did not exist during the first half of the 19th century. The vast majority of people were farmers whose livelihoods depended upon their constantly attending to the unrelenting chores of the farm. Only a fairly small number of people- occasional travelers or tourists- had the resources, the time, and the interest to visit the interior of New Hampshire. One man who fell into this category was Timothy Dwight, recognized as New Hampshire's first tourist. The president of Yale, he made annual pilgrimages north, primarily for the benefit of his health.[2] He and the few other visitors like him stayed overnight at taverns or farms. There were no hotels or inns dedicated to tourists in those days.

The situation began to change significantly when the road system was sharply upgraded. New Hampshire chartered numerous private companies to build toll roads all over the state, and these turnpikes enjoyed something of a golden era from 1820 to 1845. As a result, tourism went from a trickle to a torrent beginning in the 1820s. Improved travel was abetted by the development of the stage coach as the preferred means of travel.

During this period, the White Mountains became the prime tourist destination in the Northeast. Their proximity to Boston and New York made the Whites quite accessible. They were extolled nationally and internationally as the Switzerland of America. Mt. Washington was the particular favorite.

To accommodate the growing number of tourists, a hospitality industry emerged in New Hampshire, concentrated in the White Mountains. The Crawford House in the town of Hart's Location was the first hotel built in the region in 1828. It became the best known hotel in the state from the 1830s into the 1850s. On one occasion in 1833, for example, the Crawford House had 75 guests. Other hotels were fairly rapidly developed. By 1835, the largest hotel in the area was the Lafayette House in Franconia Notch. Other tourist 'houses' in that era included The Notch House, The Willey House and Morse Horn Tavern.

The Lakes Region and Winnipesaukee were not on any list of tourist destinations at this time. But some of the towns around the lake became active way stations on the trip to the Whites. Early on, the most important of these was Center Harbor which emerged as a key stop on the route to the mountains because of its strategic location. It was a crossroads for the stage coaches crossing the state from the east to reach the Franconia Notch area or from the west to get to the Conway area. The Senter Hotel became Winnipesaukee's largest and best hotel when it was built above the bay during the 1830s. Tourists often lingered there for a day or two to enjoy Red Hill, but Center Harbor was not a destination in and of itself.

---

[1] Much of this section is drawn from Cindy S. Aron: <u>Working at Play, A History of Vacations in the United States</u> (1999).
[2] Charles Lane, <u>New Hampshire's First Tourists</u>, Chapter 1.

Developments arising from the Industrial Revolution brought fundamental changes to the region, leading to far more visitors. Improvements in the transportation network were the most significant. Railroad lines reached the Weirs and Alton by mid-century, cutting travel times by 90% and improving comfort markedly.

The concomitant introduction of the steamboat to Winnipesaukee in 1849 led to the lake becoming a preferred leg on the journey to the Whites. Travel guides routinely recommended the steamer passage as the most pleasant route when traveling north.[1] The lake route was extolled for the beauty of the scenery. For those riding on the *Lady of the Lake* from the Weirs to Center Harbor, the most dramatic of views occurred when the boat passed between Bear Island and Pine Island, revealing the Whites framed between Red Hill and the Ossipees.

'The View' on the steamer route between Bear Is. and Pine Is. Mt. Chocorua is on the right of the most distant range.

This view and this route, for example, beguiled the eye of Edward Everett, a former U.S. Secretary of State, U.S. Senator, Massachusetts Governor, and president of Harvard. In an oft quoted summary of his ride on the *Lady*, Everett wrote in the latter 1850s:

"I have been something of a traveler in our own country … and in Europe have seen all that is most attractive, from the Highlands of Scotland to the Golden Horn of Constantinople, from the summit of Hertz Mountains to the Fountain of Vaucluse; but my eye has yet to rest on a lovelier scene than that which smiles around you as you sail from Weirs Landing to Centre Harbor."[2]

---

[1] See, for example, Charles Sweetser, Book of Summer Resorts (1868), p. 63.
[2] Quoted in John Bachelder, Popular Resorts and How to Reach Them (1875), p. 43-45. Of note, Everett was the speaker who preceded Abraham Lincoln' s Gettysburg Address in 1863.

Similar testimony was provided in 1859 by Thomas Starr King, a well known Universalist minister and poet from Boston whose views were widely respected:

"The most striking picture, perhaps, to be seen on the whole lake is a view which is given of the Sandwich range in going from Weir's to Centre Harbor, as the steamer shoots across a little bay, after passing Bear Island, about four miles from the latter village. The whole chain is seen several miles away, as you look up the bay, between Red Hill on the left, and the Ossipee mountains on the right. ... The quiet of the water and the sleep of the hills seem to have the quality of still ecstasy."[1]

With the popularity of the steamer route, Center Harbor's significance among Winnipesaukee towns grew markedly.[2] John Coe's Senter House gained an admirable reputation. One 1849 correspondent raved about it: "Here is one of the best if not the very best hotel in New Hampshire." The place was "crammed full" of people, arriving at an average of 60 a day going to or coming from the White Mountains.[3]

An 1872 visitor captured the Centre Harbor activity thusly:

"The village of Centre Harbor is small—a church, schoolhouse, a few stores and scattering farm houses, exclusive of the hotels and boarding houses, compose it. ... This becomes a lively place when passengers arrive or embark. ...Upon the arrival of the steamers, the spectator for a few minutes beholds the hurry and confusion of a miniature city. Disembarking from the steamers are representatives from almost every city—portly gentlemen just run down for a moment from the city with their wives and grown-up daughters, men of leisure, a full delegation of clerks out for a holiday, nondescripts who would puzzle Darwin, children crying, nurses ambitious to sooth them, invalids in quest of health, who hope by inhaling the invigorating breeze of the mountains to regain lost strength, all of these and many more, with trunks, hand-boxes and bundles, are the daily freight of the boats as they come streaming over the lake from Wolfeborough, Alton Bay and the Weirs. A past age is blended with the improvements of the present. While guests are enjoying their cigars or promenading the piazzas, the stage drawn by four horses drives gaily up, loaded to repletion with passengers from North Conway, West Ossipee and all the country round. And so on, day after day, this pleasing panorama is reenacted."[4]

---

[1] Thomas Starr King: White Hills, p. 54. King moved to San Francisco in 1860. During the Civil War, he was a strong proponent of the Union and received national acclaim for his oratory efforts on behalf the Union. He died of pneumonia in 1864, and his renown was such that over 20,000 people attended his funeral.
[2] The Weirs, Alton and Wolfeboro were also important way stations. They were the key departure points from which the steamers took passengers to Center Harbor.
[3] Boston Daily Bee, August 4, 1849, p. 1.
[4] Boston Daily Advertiser, July 11, 1872, p. 2.

The White Mountains remained virtually the only draw through much of the 1800s. Visitors were enthralled by the grandeur of the mountains. Mt. Washington continued to be the major focus. Its popularity was so great that a lodge, the Tip Top House, was built on the peak in 1853 to welcome climbers. The road to the top of the mountain was completed in 1861, just as the Civil War was breaking out. The cog railway was completed in 1866, and opened in 1869.

By the 1850s, traditional tourism was evolving into what became known as a vacation. The term 'vacation' itself gradually came into the vernacular as something other than its original definition as the break enjoyed from school by students and teachers. But there was a great deal of angst amongst the population about actually taking a vacation. There was a fear in those days about leisure and idleness. Activities such as card playing, dancing, theatre and the mixing of the sexes were frowned upon, if not forbidden, in many quarters. The concept of having a good 'work ethic' dominated the 19th century social and intellectual landscape. The country's Puritan roots, life on the farm, and the pervasiveness of religion all stamped society with the core belief that it was work and not play that was the key to success in life.

Offsetting the concerns about leisure, one of the earliest and strongest rationales for taking a vacation was its health benefits. Doctors increasingly recommended time off and time away as the best cure for whatever ailed people. A better climate, clean water, and fresh air were the prescription, especially for the growing urban populations. The pervasiveness of this rationale was apparent in the simple report of one 1853 vacationer:

"Two or three weeks passed in breathing the exhilarating atmosphere of the Mountains and Lakes of New Hampshire, tends most wonderfully to reinvigorate the whole system, and adds new life and energy to the spirits."[1]

Other acceptable reasons for vacationing took root with the passage of time. In addition to physical health, the benefits of mental and spiritual renewal were emphasized. Recreation became an acceptable end in itself, although many people were quick to distinguish the concept from 'amusement'. But there remained a constant concern about many large resorts that catered to the vacationing public. They were dubbed 'watering holes' where the moral integrity of the patrons was deemed to be at risk.[2] One of the earliest and most popular of these was Saratoga Springs in upstate New York.

Still, before the Civil War, the privilege of vacationing was limited to a relatively small subset of the population, i.e. people with enough wealth to afford it. The major exception to this rule arose in the form of the religious camp meetings that were adopted primarily by the

---

[1] Boston Daily Bee, July 26, 1853, p. 2.
[2] The Diamond Island House, while never a large hotel, gained a negative reputation for gambling in the 1870s and was shut down c. 1880. See Chapter 37. In 1849, one traveler noted that John Coe kept the Senter House "on strictly temperance principles." Boston Daily Bee, August 4, 1849, p. 1.

Methodists. These multi-day religious programs attracted thousands of people from the lower classes who could not afford or rationalize time off otherwise.[1]

An expanding vacation era got underway after the Civil War ended in 1865. It was then that the Industrial Revolution had a far more dramatic impact as the pace of technological change really increased. A burgeoning economy provided more and more Americans with both the time and resources to travel. Numerous hotels, spas, resorts, and camp grounds of every sort blossomed all over the country. They ranged in location from the seashore to the mountains.

The expanding reach of the railroad system contributed extensively to it, not only providing the means of travel but also actively promoting vacations to enhance ridership. By 1875, rail lines had more than doubled from before the war. In New Hampshire, one could easily travel by train to almost any popular location. At one time, for example, Crawford Notch had 57 trains arriving each day to handle the tourist demands. The railroads advertised vacation trips widely, and they built their travel schedules around vacationing. The whole process fed upon itself: more railroad track led to more resorts which led to more railroad track and so on.[2]

This time frame marked the full-blown emergence of the summer vacation era in the United States. The era saw an entirely different and far more populous group of travelers emerge. The acceleration of the Industrial Revolution created a whole new 'middle class' of people who felt entitled to time off from work for rest, relaxation, recuperation, and recreation. The group included salaried employees who were not wealthy, but they enjoyed a perceived distinction based upon their economic, social and cultural position. Their numbers grew constantly as new corporations hired more salaried workers; as government bureaucracies expanded; and as towns, schools and hospitals brought on more and more people. The class also included salespeople, managers, bookkeepers, school teachers, and on and on. These workers enjoyed designated vacation periods each year, though usually just a week. The ingredients for the vacation era became firmly established: a financially comfortable population with enough income to afford a vacation; work schedules that included vacation time; a wide range of vacationing alternatives to choose from up and down the scale of affordability; a transportation network catering to the vacation bound; and evolving societal norms that encouraged vacationing.

With prosperity, improved transportation, and blossoming hospitality alternatives, the idea of what constituted a summer vacation kept evolving. Among the biggest changes, families began spending entire summers at vacation spots. Many places were deemed safe enough for bread winners to leave family members. Religious camps, initially just multi-day affairs, developed into seasonal places where people could rent camp sites in 'safe' environments. Two prime examples were the Second Advent Christian camp at Alton Bay (opened in 1863) and the

---

[1] See Chapter 36 for a history of the Methodists
[2] The railroads even built their own resorts. For example, the BC&M rebuilt the Pemigewasset House in Plymouth after it burned in 1862.

Methodist camp at the Weirs (opened in 1873). In time, the practice of spending a summer away from home became established. Working fathers became weekend warriors, taking the train to a get-away on Friday and returning on Sunday night. Meanwhile, the spectrum of options from which to choose continued to widen. They ranged from the resort hotel, to a smaller hotel, to a boarding house, to a cottage, to a farm house, to a camp site. Other places, like Chautauqua, NY emerged to provide educational vacations for those who could not rationalize any other form.

New Hampshire welcomed these vacationers with open arms. By 1892, there were more than 200 large hotels in the state, although it is telling that almost all of them were located in the White Mountains. The Lakes Region did not have a single one that fell into that category. Still, as the vacationing population expanded, the Lakes Region slowly became a destination place for vacationers. The towns around Winnipesaukee were within easy reach of those who could not afford the big hotels. One rough measure of the relative popularity of NH towns with vacationers is found in a comparison of estimated summer vacation dollars generated in each for 1873.

Vacation Dollars by town in 1873[1]

Town	Dollars
Conway	160,000
Wolfeboro	125,000
Franconia	120,000
Center Harbor	50,000
Ossipee	25,000
Meredith	20,000
Alton	20,000
Gilford	10,000
Moultonborough	3,000
Tuftonborough	2,000

It was not until the 1880s that the Winnipesaukee islands started to become much more than simply a scenic leg on the way to the White Mountains. People from outside the local area began to discover the possibilities of vacationing on the lake. They had been preceded in many cases by local men who had started using the smallest islands as fishing headquarters at least as early as the 1850s.[2] The big, un-bridged islands like Bear had not attracted any vacationers because they were completely owned and occupied by farmers, and they were not easily accessible. This all began to change as the vacationing public slowly discovered the immense pleasures of summering on the lake.

---

[1] The Statistics and Gazetteer of New-Hampshire (1874). In it, information is found separately by town. These numbers are very raw estimates and are offered only to provide a proportional sense of the popularity of the towns with people who boarded in each during the summer
[2] See below, Chapter 37, *Early History of Other Islands*.

Chapter Twenty

The 1880s

The decade of the 1880s was a period of fundamental change on Bear Island. It bore witness to the passing of many of the island's most notable farmers, while welcoming the arrival of the summer vacation era in ways never seen before.

North Bear

By 1880, Waldo Meloon and his wife, Abigail, were struggling to make ends meet on the island. By 1883, they had had enough. They finally gave up the ghost in February, selling "all of our homestead farm" to Solomon Lovejoy.[1] Waldo's sale marked the end of year-round farming on Bear Island.[2] The purchase included all of Hugh Kelsea's original Lots 1 and 2, except for the five and a half acres owned by John Crane. In addition to the farm house itself, the Meloon property had at least two other houses along the shore; one (now likely part of #12 Bear Island) was located on the eastern side of the island, abutting John Crane's land, and the other (now likely #432) was on the western side, abutting the other end of John Crane's land.[3] Solomon also acquired Waldo's three boats,[4] his boathouse next to the wharf, and the same rights to use the steamboat wharf that Waldo had retained when he sold it to John Crane. Solomon had already purchased Bear Lot 3 from Stephen Meloon the previous year.[5]

With the arrival of Solomon Lovejoy, the vacation era entered a new phase on Bear Island. Solomon was 39 years old when he took this bold step. He had married Sarah 'Lizzie' Wiggin, some nine years before.[6] The couple did not yet have any children.[7] Solomon was perhaps the perfect person to recognize the potential of Bear Island. He was not a farmer by nature; he was an entrepreneur and "a true Yankee" as one 1885 visitor described him.[8] The island, of course, was in his blood. It is said that he was born there in 1844 to Jesse and Eleanor Bickford Lovejoy. He grew up on a 50 acre farm, just across from the island, on Neck Lot 78,

---

[1] BCRI, B/P 69/460.B/P 70/633.

[2] Waldo and Abigail moved to the Neck, perhaps living with Stephen. Abigail died in 1887 and Waldo in 1889. Both were buried at the Meetinghouse cemetery.

[3] The existence of these two houses is based in part upon the information in the 1873 deed from George Meloon's wife to David Meloon B/P 57/209. Further support derives from their presence at the time the properties were sold by Solomon in 1884 and 1886 (see below). A third house, #407, may also have been built by the Meloons as it is one of the oldest on the island. Current Meredith tax records indicate that it was built in 1887, but there is no information to substantiate that date either way. In general, the dates when many of the houses were built on this part of Bear are very difficult to pin down. Current Meredith tax information contains an estimated date of construction for every house on the island; but in the cases of most of the homes on this part of Bear, the information is purely 'ballpark'. Town officials developed it decades ago, and there is little data in any of the extant documents to support the estimates. Deed descriptions and town tax records provide almost the only insights, but the former are inconsistent and the latter are incomplete and occasionally inaccurate. The difficulty is compounded by the fact that a few of the earliest houses on Bear were later moved to other locations. It is also possible (perhaps likely) that a house or two was moved on to Bear as well.

[4] One of the three was a horseboat. A second was a gundalow.

[5] BCRI, B/P 69/460.

[6] Lizzie was the daughter of Daniel Wiggin, the Advent Cove farmer who had taken in Dolly's son, Robert M. Nichols, when he left Bear Island.

[7] Their son, Ralph M. Lovejoy, was born the following year. He later became a very successful business man in the automotive field. See below, Chapter 25.

[8] The Springfield Republican, July 13, 1886, p. 3. The anonymous writer was W.S. Hawkes who visited the island the previous summer.

bordering Black Cove.[1] His grandfathers were Caleb Lovejoy on one side and Jonathan Bickford Sr. on the other. During his youthful years on the island, he was surrounded by relatives who were year-round veterans of Bear Island, including uncles Jonathan Jr., James, and Brackett Bickford, and an aunt, Mahala Bickford Bryant.

Meloon farm late 1880s.

It is hard to say when Solomon decided to acquire the Meloon farm. He had purchased his first farm in 1875 on Neck Lot 76 from his cousin, George S. Bickford.[2] In 1878, 1878, he purchased a 30 acre parcel of land on the southern end of Lot 77, giving him shore frontage on Kelley cove where he built a boat house.[3] An inveterate entrepreneur, in 1880 he purchased a 100' by 44' parcel of land adjacent to the Meetinghouse Cemetery and began selling burial plots to local farmers.[4] By 1882, however, his his thoughts turned to Bear Island when he purchased

Bear Lot 3 from Stephen Meloon. This was his family's old summer sheep pasture.[5] The purchase of the Meloon farm next door was a logical next step.

Barn and shed on North Bear c. 1890 (courtesy of the Thompson family).

Whatever the efforts the Meloons had made to establish a boarding house, Solomon did not continue it. Moreover, he had no plans to develop a hotel at that time. In his first couple of years of ownership, Solomon focused upon the day-trip business while also planning to sell off

---

[1] B/P 7/510. The farm became Camp Menotomy, and it is a little north of Cattle Landing.
[2] B/P 59/38. George was the son of Brackett Bickford.
[3] B/P 64/113. This made him a neighbor of his uncle, Herbert Lovejoy, who had taken over the family farm of Caleb Lovejoy.
[4] Among his first customers were Stephen B. Meloon, Charles S. Bickford, and Eleazer Bickford Jr. B/P 66/84; 70/377; 68/89; and 112/214.
[5] B/P 69/460.

vacation lots along the shoreline of the island.[1] Based upon a visit in 1885, Winfield Hawkes described the situation thusly:

> "The new settlement springing up on the north end of Bear Island is known as Kunnaway, the Indian name for *bear*... Farmer Lovejoy proposes to occupy the 'White House' on the hill, and to be prepared to furnish all needed supplies to cottagers and campers; also to keep his steam-barge at Kunnaway Landing for the convenience of fishing, berrying or sailing parties, and for freighting purposes; small boats and fishing appliances may also be obtained."[2]

With regard to Sol's focus on selling shorefront lots, Hawkes had this to say:

> "A long street has been laid out south of the Landing, and several house-lots sold in the pine grove along the lake's margin. It is the plan of (Sol) to make the place attractive to clergymen and their friends who wish simple rustication in the vicinity of good fishing and in sight of most splendid natural scenery."[3]

An April 1887 article in the Boston Journal picked up on the same themes:

> "At Bear Island, on the route of the steamer *Lady of the Lake* to Centre Harbor, the old wharf is being renewed to meet the demands of the settlement which is springing up thereabout. The beautiful picnic grounds in the grove of great beeches, birches and maples which cover the north end of the island are to be prepared for excursion parties; and Solomon Lovejoy, who owns the one farm house on the island, is to occupy it the present season, enjoying its commanding situation, tilling the excellent farm, and supplying camping and cottage people with farm and other provisions, which will be a great convenience to that part of the lake. ...A summer Post Office is also one of the probabilities at this place; this, with the landing, known for so many years as Bear Island wharf, and the settlement springing up about it, will be named Kunnaway..."[4]

As Hawkes mentioned in his account, by the mid-1880s, Sol's fleet of boats included his own small steamboat, the *Island Maiden.* He built it himself and used it to transport visitors to and from the mainland as well as for excursions on the lake. The engine in the boat was "a unique affair, having three cylinders and a toggle in the propeller shaft, by which means the propeller fan may be made to steer the craft as a fish directs his motions with his tail."[5]

---

[1] W.S.Hawkes, Winnipesaukee and About There, (1887). This little book was written for the Boston & Lowell RR. Hawkes was a Congregational minister from South Hadley, MA. He and his wife bought one of Sol's lots in 1886, the year after Hawkes' field trip to the lake occurred. It is unclear what, if any arrangements, Sol made with John Crane regarding the wharf and day-trip business. Sol had the right by the Meloon deed to use the wharf. He also had ample land to host picnic groups. My sense is that Crane had probably given up the summer business by the early 1880s.

[2] Hawkes, Winnipesaukee, p. 54. 'Kunnaway' was the Algonquin word for 'bear'.

[3] Ibid. This 'road' later became known as "Lovers' Lane."

[4] "Granite Mountains in Winter," by Special Correspondent, Boston Journal, April 16, 1887, p.5. This article was datelined South Hadley Falls, MA, suggesting that it was also written by Winfield Hawkes.

[5] "Granite Mountains in Winter," by Special Correspondent, Boston Journal, April 16, 1887, p.5.

Sol used his steamer to establish better access to the island from Meredith Neck. This

naturally augmented the already established connections made via the passenger steamers— predominantly the *Lady* but also the *Mount Washington*-- that ran past the island. Upon his purchase of the Bear property, Solomon assumed responsibility from Waldo Meloon for operating the town subsidized 'Bear Island boat' that ferried people to and from the island. He changed the mainland departure point from the Ferry landing at the end of the Neck (i.e. Cattle Landing) to his place in Kelley cove.[1]

Sol's *Island Maiden*. William Puffer's *Wanderer* is tied up to it.

In 1886, Solomon took another major step to improve boating access from the Neck. He purchased a half acre of land and a small building on Neck Lot 78 from Charles Bickford, directly across from the former Meloon farm. This location became popularly known as 'Lovejoy's Sands' (or simply the 'Sands') as well as Lovejoy's Landing.[2] Sol built a road, with town financial support, from the range way between Neck Lots 77 and 78 across the property of his uncle, Herbert Lovejoy, to the new boat landing.[3]

Solomon may have purchased the Sands as an alternative landing spot for the passenger steamers because the Bear Island wharf was apparently in deteriorating condition. One correspondent noted in 1890: "At one time the steamers made regular stops (on Bear), but during the past few years passengers have been transferred to small boats (at the Sands) opposite the island."[4]

---

[1] Meredith Tax records, 1890. B/P 72/82. Solomon sold this Kelley Cove property to Stephen Meloon in October 1883 but reserved the right to use the boathouse and orchard.

[2] See, for example, B/P 129/169.

[3] B/P 75/452; 116/510. The Sands aka Lovejoy Landing later became Shep Brown's Boat Basin. At the time Solomon purchased it and until the early 1900s, mainland access to the landing was not the straight road that is now Lovejoy Sands Road. This was precluded because the land was still owned by Bickford. Rather, access was made via a road that started down the range way between Lots 77 and 78 (now likely Soley Lane) and then turned south a few hundred yards before reaching the shore, and then running east to the landing. This land was part of the original farm that Caleb Lovejoy purchased in 1813. Herbert Lovejoy had taken it over in 1842 after his father had passed away. See, for example, Meredith Selectmen Accounts, 1891, p. 210 (MHS Archives). In 1890, the town paid Herbert $12.00 to compensate him for damage done to his property during the widening of the road.

[4] "Centre Harbor," from our Regular Correspondent, <u>Boston Herald</u>, July 6, 1890, p. 8.

During the latter 1880s, tourist groups continued to make excursions to Bear, although the size and frequency of them are not known. In June 1885, for example, the Knights Templar of Concord took the *James Bell* to the island for an outing.[1] In August 1886, a group of 150 people from Conway took the *Lamprey* to Bear for a clambake.[2] Most interesting of all, in 1888, minor league baseball teams from Lake Village and Laconia played one of their games on Bear Island.[3] Meanwhile, small camping parties continued to come to the island for various lengths of stay.[4]

While continuing the day-trip business, Sol carved out at least a dozen vacation lots on the western side of the island, facing Meredith Neck.[5] He sold the first one in April 1884. Ironically, it was not within the subdivision; it was on the northeastern side of Bear, on the boundary line of John Crane. The appeal of the lot (now part of #12 Bear Island) was the presence of one of the houses built by the Meloons. The purchaser was a Lakeport, NH native, Andrew Gray. He was by no means new to the lake. At one time back in the 1860s, he owned Mink Island.[6] Gray quickly sold an undivided half interest in the house to a fellow-Lake Village resident, Henry Brown, later the same year.[7] Gray and Brown did not stay long. In 1886, Brown sold his share back to Gray who in turn sold the place back to Solomon later in the year.[8]

Solomon's first real burst in sales occurred in 1886 when he successfully sold off the first four lots within his subdivision on the western shore. These lots were located next to each other and adjacent to John Crane's land and the wharf. The lots were uniform in size, measuring eight rods (132') along the shore and running nine rods (148.5') deep. The first was sold to none other than Reverend Winfield Scott Hawkes of South Hadley Falls, MA (#432). The other three were sold to Edward Bosson (#431), Herbert Streeter (part of #430), and Mary F. Waters (part of #430).[9] The latter three were all from Chelsea, MA, and must have had some personal connection. The four buyers, of course, were the first of the innumerable Massachusetts vacationers that predominated among the summer population on the island in the years following.

Apart from being the author of the booklet about Bear Island, Winfield Scott Hawkes was a Congregational minister who was presumably named after the Union Civil War hero, Winfield Scott Hancock. Hawkes was the first of a multitude of clergymen to be drawn to the peace and beauty of the islands in Winnipesaukee. The lot purchased by Hawkes (#432) already had a house on it, most likely a legacy of the Meloons and one of the oldest houses still standing on

[1] Boston Journal, June 19, 1885, p.2.
[2] Boston Herald, August 22, 1886, p. 6.
[3] Boston Herald, August 12, 1888, p. 3. Only the line score is given but the location is stated: "At Bear Island, Lake Winnipiseogee." Lake Village won 9-8. Baseball became a huge national sport after the Civil War. Lake Village and Laconia had minor league teams at least as early as 1875. The Lake Villagers were known as the "Red Stockings" and Laconia as the "Clippers." Lake Village Times, June 5, 1875, p. 3.
[4] See, for example, Boston Herald, July 29, 1888, p. 5 and August 5, 1888, p. 5.
[5] The actual plan was not found but is referred to in various deeds.
[6] B/P 40/121.
[7] Gilford residents predominated among the first group of people to buy property on the small satellite islands around Bear. Their interests ranged from fishing to timber to real estate speculation. See Chapter 37, Other Islands.
[8] B/P 73/439; 73/422; 76/11; B/P 93/19. Gray and Brown made their purchase as a speculative investment. It is doubtful they had any intention of using it as a summer vacation home themselves. It was not until eight years later, in 1894, that Solomon was able to sell the lot again.
[9] B/P 76/196; 76/231; 124/348; 103/63. The lots sold to Streeter and Waters were eventually combined in 1919 and comprise #430.

the island.[1] Edward Bosson was a 32 year old dye manufacturer. He was single when he acquired the property on Bear Island, marrying some five years later.[2] Herbert Streeter was a young telegrapher. He did not build a house on the island. He sold his property back to Sol Lovejoy in 1900.[3] Mary Waters was still quite young (only 17) when she purchased her lot. She may have come to the island to work at the hotel. She married William Cardy in 1891.[4] They held held on to the island property until 1908 but also never built on it.

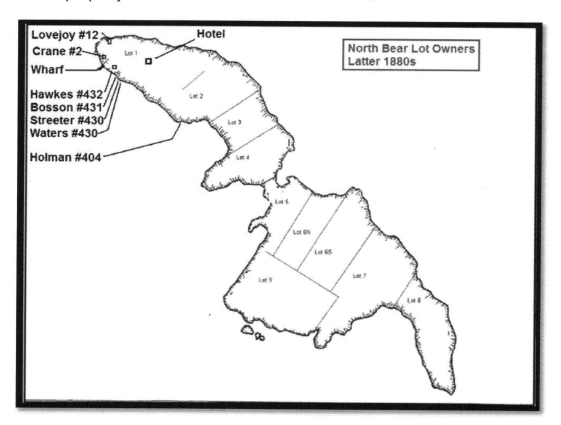

In 1888, Solomon sold his sixth lot (#404) to Silas W. Holman of Boston.[5] This place was located further down the western side of the island, well detached from the other vacationers. Holman was an MIT professor who initially established a tent platform for his camp and subsequently built a house in 1890 or so.[6] He had been a frequent visitor to the Lakes Region for many years before making this purchase.

Meanwhile, it was not until after the summer of 1886 that Sol decided to turn the former Meloon farmhouse into a hotel. Once he did, he apparently enjoyed a good deal of success. The

---

[1] B/P 188/377. The Bear Island property stayed in the Hawkes family for 42 years. Reverend Hawkes also purchased Hawk's Nest Island and Nabby Island, next to Three Mile Island, in late 1886. He built a small building or camp on Hawk's Nest. He sold the islands, now owned by the AMC, in 1892. B/P 76/529; 88/497. See Chapter 37.

[2] B/P 183/204. He owned his island summer place for 41 years, selling out in 1927. His extended family became regular visitors at the Bear Island House during the 1890s and beyond. They also bought property on the Neck along Lovejoy Lane, opposite Bear Island.

[3] B/P 103/63. The Streeters apparently preferred the amenities of the Bear hotel over cottage living as they continued to visit the island for summer vacationing. See <u>Boston Herald</u>, July 8, 1894, p. 4.

[4] B/P 124/502.

[5] B/P 82/183.

[6] Meredith Tax Records state he had a house in 1892. The records for 1891 suggest the house was built by then. (MHS Archives).

<u>Boston Herald</u> reported in July 1890: "The Bear Island Hotel accommodates about 25 people, and every season it is taxed to its utmost capacity."[1]

With the advent of the hotel, the northern end of Bear was firmly ensconced in the vacation era. It had begun to look more hospitable with the new houses going up on the shore line. There were six vacation places by then, where before there was only one. One Boston report summarized:

"Bear Island is fast becoming a popular summer resort, several houses being erected by Boston and New York people, who go there and remain during the season. This island is on the direct route of the steamers from Centre Harbor to the Weirs."[2]

During this decade of rapidly increasing summer activity, it does not appear that John Crane had much involvement with it. He and his fellow Lake Village investors apparently bowed out of the day-trip business prior to Solomon's arrival, leaving the hosting of campers and small excursions to Waldo.[3] There were, however, some changes evident on the property. By 1880, there was long since a stone wall around the property, separating it from the Meloons.[4] The house was also remodeled, at least to some extent. Crane may have converted the building with the bowling alley into a summer home (#2 Bear Island).[5] Yet later usage patterns suggest that the Crane family did not use the property as a summer vacation home until the latter 1890s.[6] By then Crane owned a steam launch, the *Undine*, that he used to access the island and enjoy the lake.[7]

The Rest of the Island

Next door to Solomon on Lot 4, the vacation era was still nowhere in sight. The lot was still owned by James Bickford, but James died in 1888.[8] The ownership was inherited by James' youngest son, Moses, who also inherited the family's homestead on the Neck.[9] Moses had a

[1] <u>Boston Herald</u>, July 6, 1890, p. 8.
[2] <u>Boston Herald</u>, July 6, 1890, p. 8.
[3] See, for example, the Farmington, NH Board of Education visited Bear in July 1882 for "an excursion and picnic."NH <u>Patriot and Gazette</u>, June 15, 1882, p. 5.
[4] The ends of the wall are located between current day lots #432 and #433 on the west side of the island and lots #10 and #12 on the northeast side.
[5] During a fairly recent remodeling of the house, the current owner came across a wall board showing that the place was renovated in 1881. The fragments of the names written on the board have not been identified. They were perhaps employees of Crane's business. It is possible that one of these employees carved '1873' and his initials (J.P.H.) in the 'mystery stone' found along the old hotel road not far from John Crane's house. No property owner on Bear had those initials. See <u>Bear Island Reflections</u>, p. 177.
[6] This conclusion is drawn from two data points. In 1894, Crane's son, Mazellah, and his family stayed at the Bear Island House. <u>Boston Herald</u>, July 15, 1894, p. 3. In 1897, they stayed at their island cottage. <u>Boston Herald</u>, July 4, 1897, p. 14. There are no references to John Crane and his wife, Clara, vacationing out there during these years.
[7] Blackstone, p. 83.
[8] James was buried in the Meetinghouse cemetery. His wife, Lucinda, had passed away years before in 1876 and was buried there as well.
[9] The deed trail for Moses taking ownership of Bear was not found in the on-line registry of Belknap deeds. In 1866, Moses acquired a half ownership in James Bickford's Neck farm. (B/P 44/87) His brother, James E., acquired a similar interest in 1867. (B/P 46/475) Moses and his own family lived with James until his death. Moses continued to live on the family farm on the Neck, while in 1894 James E. purchased the farm of Stephen Boardman on Neck Lot 64. (B/P 91/589)

family of five, including of his wife, Anna, and his three children, Gracie (b. 1871), Roy (b. 1876), and Myrtie (b. 1881).[1] Moses and Anna were island veterans, both probably born on Bear in the latter 1840s when the family was living there year-round. They continued to use their Bear property as a summer farm.

A little further south, Lots 5 and 6N had a somewhat similar transition in ownership during the decade. One of the key owners of these lots, James Gilman, also died in 1888. James' half interest in the two lots was inherited by his oldest son, Granville (then 51).[2] Granville then proceeded to bring the entire lot under his control. In 1889, he purchased his Uncle David's ¼ share in the two lots, and a year after that, he acquired the ¼ interest of John Smith, who had also passed away.[3] These transactions brought Lots 5 and 6N into one person's hands for the first time since before 1819.

Granville's interest in the Bear property was not motivated by any farming interest. He had moved to Oakland, California in the latter 1860s where he had become wealthy working in the spirits business. He probably unified the ownership because the opportunity presented itself with the aging of his uncle and the death of Smith, and he could easily afford to do so.

Meanwhile, nothing changed at all on neighboring Lot 6S. Eleazer Bickford Jr. continued to own it, presumably using it or leasing it as a summer farm and seasonal grazing area.

In contrast, Lot 7 experienced a kind of 'throwback' change in ownership during the decade. In 1881, Charles Canney and John Perkins sold Lot 7 to Lewis Eaton and David H. Clark.[4] Eaton was a descendant of one of the earliest Neck settlers, Jacob Eaton. Clark grew up on the Neck, and he owned a 54 acre farm on Blueberry Hill Road where his neighbors included James and David Gilman.[5] Like so many who bought property on Bear during the earlier decades, Eaton and Clark acquired Lot 7 primarily for seasonal grazing.

Similar to the situations on Lot 4 and Lot 5/6N, generational change also came to Lot 8. Jonathan Bickford Jr. died in 1880, and his wife, Priscilla, died in 1882. Lot 8 was inherited by their sons, Joseph L. and Charles S. (aged 45 and 40), who were still living on the family's Neck farm on Lot 79.[6] Neither had ever married nor left home. The two used the Bear property for seasonal pasture and timber.

The ownership of Lot 9 went through its own saga during the 1880s. Stephen Boardman

---

[1] Anna (aka Arianna) was the daughter of Moses' uncle, Charles and Augusta Bickford (Bear Lot 6S) and therefore Moses' second cousin.

[2] Granville also inherited the family homestead farm on Meredith Neck.

[3] BCRI, B/P 82/73; 83/180; 103/245; 103/245.

[4] BCRI, B/P 68/295.

[5] BCRI, B/P 70/282. He was the son of David Clark, a successful farmer who was born in Meredith and purchased several parcels on the Neck (49, 58 and 59) beginning in the 1840s and 1850s.

[6] Their home is now 341 Meredith Neck Road.

Jr., was decreed insane in 1884 at the age of 81.[1] His guardian, George Wiggin, sold the Bear property to long-time Meredith farmers, William Brown and his son, William H. Brown.[2] The Browns lived on the upper Neck (Lot 16, on Keyser Road) near the Center Harbor boundary line. As with previous owners, they were interested in the Bear property for timber and grazing purposes. In 1887, William H., who was a Meredith Selectman during the late 1880s, sold his share to his father.[3]

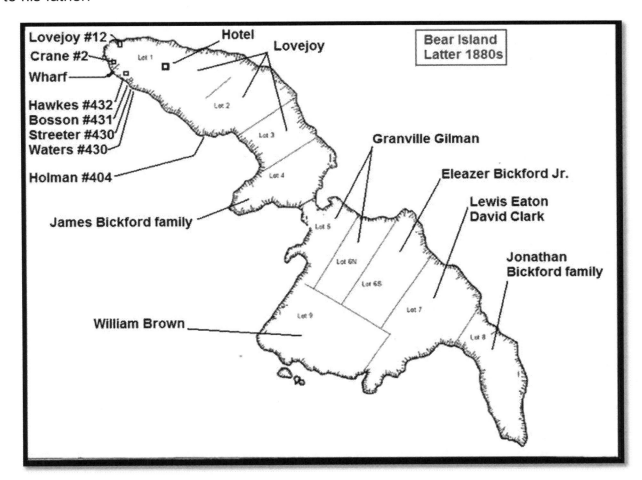

Summary

The 1880s represented a key transitional decade on Bear Island. There was a clear changing of the guard that occurred on almost every lot. It saw the demise of no fewer than five longtime island property owners: year-round farmers Jonathan Bickford Jr., James Bickford, and Waldo Meloon along with long-time seasonal farmers James Gilman and Stephen Boardman Jr. At the same time, the shift to the vacation era took an inexorable leap forward with Solomon Lovejoy's vacation lot sales and the opening of the hotel.

---

[1] He died two years later.
[2] BCRI, B/P 52/31; BP 73/74.
[3] BCRI, B/P 78/288.

Chapter Twenty-One

The 1890s: Solomon Expands the Vacation Business

During the 1890s, Solomon Lovejoy took several major steps to improve the vacation opportunity on North Bear. His first task was rebuilding the Bear Island Landing into the configuration that we know today. The motivation behind the rebuild probably arose when a severe tornado hit the Lakes Region in August of 1890. There was "a vast amount of damage" done around the lake and on the islands. At "Bear Island...the timber land was stripped, and several camps were destroyed." Elsewhere, the Long Island bridge was washed away, and the chimney of the Senter House in Center Harbor was "demolished". Moreover, nearly all of the telegraph poles between Center Harbor and Meredith were blown down.[1] The Bear Island wharf was almost certainly badly damaged as well in the process. Solomon rebuilt it shortly thereafter, making it a much better landing.[2]

Lady of the Lake **passing the wharf during its rebuilding c. 1891.**

---

[1] "Much Damage Done: Destruction Caused by the Tornado at Lake Winnipesaukee," *Boston Herald*, Saturday, August 2, 1890, p. 8. The article also notes that

[2] See below, Chapter 22, for additional history and pictures of the wharf.

In addition to improving the landing, Solomon took another step to improve logistics at his island hotel. He received government approval for a post office on the island in 1892. Sol became the first postmaster.[1] He also built a separate wharf further down the shore, directly across from Lovejoy's Landing.[2] This one was used exclusively by hotel personnel to handle the comings and goings of staff and supplies, among other things.

The hotel was apparently quite successful during the 1890s, a period in which the vacationing public was embracing the concept of an island getaway with greater and greater eagerness. As one indication of its popularity, an 1892 newspaper report indicated that the Bear Island House was "entertaining the usual number of guests" that summer.[3] The increasing success led Sol to begin expanding the capacity of the hotel in 1893, apparently carrying over construction into 1894. A Boston Herald article in July 1893 commented that "Solomon Lovejoy of Bear Island is erecting a large summer hotel." A visiting reporter noted in July 1894 that "this season (Sol) made an elaborate addition to his hotel to meet the demands of the people who wish to visit the island."[4] Even with the expansion, the Boston Herald noted that the "accommodations are (still) not equal to the demands of the people who wish to come here."[5]

Bear Island House after its first expansion in the 1890s.

[1] The Boston Herald, July 10, 1892, p. 13. This was not the first island post office. One was already established at the Long Island Hotel owned and operated by the Brown family.

[2] It was located between current lots #418 and #421 Bear Island. A well defined roadway leading to the hotel site, with stone walls on either side of it, can be easily found up on the island behind this former wharf area.

[3] "Meredith," Boston Herald, Sunday, August 7, 1892, p. 13. Among the visitors were Flora Randall (N. Grafton, MA), Lucy Young (N. Grafton, MA), Charles Badlam, and Mrs. Wright (Concord, NH). Members of the Streeter family (Chelsea, MA) also stayed at the hotel, although they owned a nearby vacant lot.

[4] Boston Herald, July 2, 1893, p. 23 and July 8, 1894, p. 4. It is not clear how much of an addition was made in 1893-94, but it was not the last addition. Regarding the higher capacity, Sol's tax base increased in 1895, but it appears that it was not until 1901 that the Meredith Inventory and Tax Recapitulation specifically noted his "Addition to hotel" as part of his real estate, along with the four cottages and the former Meloon farm. Solomon's total real estate tax basis rose from $2200.00 in 1900 to $3600.00 in 1901. The four cottages were valued at $1000; the farm at $2200; and the hotel addition at $400.

[5] Boston Herald, July 15, 1894, p. 3.

View from Pine Island. The *Maid of the Isles* is parked at the wharf. The Bear Island House is visible up on the hill. John Crane's house is to the left of the wharf.

After expanding the hotel, Solomon undertook yet another major step in the latter 1890s when he constructed three houses along the western shore of Bear. These were used for guests and staff.[1] The houses were located at current island addresses #421, #422, and #428. The three shared access to a well that is still to be found behind lot #424 next to the so-called 'Lover's Lane' pathway.[2]

While these improvements were being undertaken, six more families ventured to buy vacation property on the island. All of the properties except one were located on the western side of the island south of the Bear Island wharf. The first of these sales (#427) was made in 1891 and located just down the western shore from the first vacation purchasers. The property had only half of the shore frontage (4 rods or 66') of the lots Solomon had sold to its north. The purchase was made by a group of five men from Lake Village, NH led by Frank Bailey and Edwin Goldsmith.[3] They were young (23 and 21, respectively) and still single.[4] Like so many others, they probably made the purchase to use as a base for fishing vacations. The next year, 1892, three more land sales took place somewhat further down the shore towards the Gulf. The buyers included Lucy Young of Worcester, MA, who bought almost 200' of frontage (now #s 409, 410,

---

[1] One of the 'cottages' was built in 1897. <u>Boston Herald</u>, June 27, 1897, p. 28. Meredith Inventory and Tax Recapitulation, 1901 (MHS Archives). The entry for Solomon specifically references for the first time '4 cottages on Bear'. The fourth was probably #407. The timing of the entry does not necessarily indicate when the houses were built. Meredith tax assessors were only beginning to collect timely data about islanders then.

[2] See B/P 57/209; 67/632. This shorefront area was part of the 24 acre parcel that was set aside for the widow of George Meloon in 1873 and sold to David Meloon.

[3] B/P 85/379. Current Meredith tax records indicate that the house at #427 was built in 1880, but the deed of sale suggests pretty clearly that the men just bought land. It refers to the land as "being house lot No. 9 in a tier of lots staked out by me (Lovejoy)." Meredith tax records show that a 'cottage' was present there by April 1892.

[4] B/P 242/270. After marriages in 1892 and 1897, respectively, Frank and Edwin eventually bought out the other three men. They retained the property until 1939.

and 412); Ellen Tucker of Hampden, MA (#425); and John Salter of New York City (#424).[1] Salter was the first out-of-state buyer on the island who was not from Massachusetts.[2] The other lot sold by Solomon in 1892 was on the other side of the island. The buyer was William Wilkinson, a mason from Boston.[3] It contained 90' of frontage, but its exact location is not clear. It eventually ended up back in the hands of Solomon, still undeveloped.[4] The growth in vacationers did not go unnoticed in the press. A <u>Boston Herald</u> reporter noted in August 1892 that "several fine cottages have been erected on (the island's) shores, and they are occupied every (summer) season by their owners with few exceptions."[5]

The sixth sale did not occur until 1895 when William Wright of Nutley, New Jersey bought a lot (#396) in the Gulf south of Silas Holman. The 35 year old Wright was a professor at the New Jersey State Normal School. He had been introduced to the lake around 1890 as a result of family connections. In 1887, Wright had married Fannie Bailey, the daughter of a Presbyterian minister also from New Jersey. Fannie's younger sister, Anna Bailey, had married William Puffer in 1889. Puffer was an MIT graduate who studied under the Bear Island vacationer, Silas Holman, there. Holman invited Puffer up to his place (#404) on the lake. William and Fannie Wright joined them.[6] They camped in front of Holman's house for several years. This led the Wrights to purchase their own place just down the shore from Holman.[7] Thereafter, the Wrights and the Puffers vacationed together every year until William Puffer bought his own island place in 1912.

William Wright   **Fannie Wright**

With the purchase by the Wrights in 1895, the vacationing population had grown to a dozen summer places on the northern end of Bear Island, with all but one located on the northwestern side of the island facing Meredith Neck. While the majority continued to come from

---

[1] B/P 88/524; 89/593; 89/249.
[2] We have not found the backgrounds of these vacationers. It is possible that all three worked at the hotel. None built a house on the island.
[3] B/P 87/593.
[4] Edward Bosson bought it from Wilkinson in 1899 (B/P 102/251) but then resold it to Lovejoy in 1905 (B/P 116/152). The lot was later part of the lands that Solomon sold to George Collins in 1909. See below.
[5] "Meredith," <u>Boston Herald</u>, Sunday, August 7, 1892, p. 13.
[6] See, <u>Boston Herald</u>, July 15, 1894, p. 3. On this occasion, there were five Wrights and four Puffers staying with the Holmans.
[7] The Wright family still owns the place on the island and has the distinction of being the longest tenured family in the same place on the island at 123 years and counting. The Puffer line also still owns its Bear Island property (106 years and counting).

Massachusetts and New Hampshire, the Wrights were the first of a relative flood that eventually came from New Jersey.

Wright's and Puffer's camping tents, 1890s.

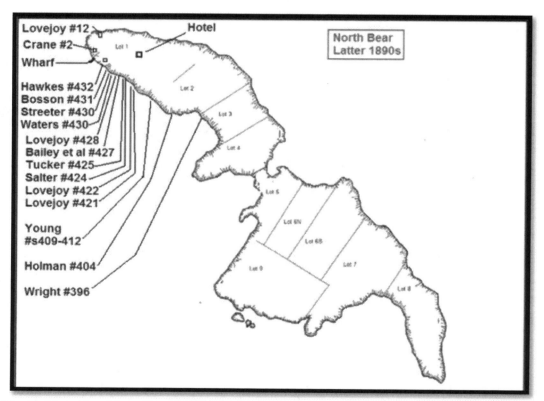

The <u>**Boston Herald**</u>, noting the obvious, reported in 1899 that "each year Bear Island is growing in popular favor as a summer home."[1]

---

[1] <u>Boston Herald</u>, August 13, 1899, p. 27.

Chapter Twenty-Two

The Bear Island Wharf

The original Bear Island landing was constructed by Waldo Meloon. It was built at least by 1858 and was probably built several years earlier.[1] Waldo built a boathouse there as well. His 1873 deed of sale to John Crane contained a reservation allowing Waldo (and his successors) to use the wharf and maintain the boathouse.[2] John Crane rebuilt the wharf in 1875. In the latter 1880s, Solomon Lovejoy shifted the commercial steamboat traffic away from the wharf to his new landing at Lovejoy Sands, presumably because of deterioration of the island docking facility.[3] He reversed that approach when he decided to build the hotel. By the early 1890s, he had established some sort of understanding with John Crane that Solomon could rebuild the landing. After the rebuild, the commercial steamboat traffic permanently shifted back to Bear.

Mt. Washington **passing Bear Island c. 1891.**   *Maid of the Isles* **at the new wharf c. 1892.**
(Courtesy of the Thompson and Wright families.)

Nevertheless, John Crane continued to own the wharf. In October 1906, when Crane sold a parcel of land just south of the wharf (now #434 and #433), he reserved the right to "replace, repair and forever maintain a wharf or steamboat landing where the same now is, and to extend the same out into the lake, so far as my heirs or assigns may choose and to extend the wharf in a northerly direction … provided that said wharf shall not be extended in a southerly direction" in front of the property just sold.[4]

---

[1] "Picnic on Bear Island," *Independent Democrat* (Concord, NH), September 16, 1858, p. 3. The article about a group of tourists states that the *Lady of the Lake* landed "on the north-easterly point of the island, near a beautiful grove of white maples…"
[2] B/P 70/163.
[3] Boston Herald, July 6, 1890, p. 8, "Centre Harbor."
[4] B/P 119/346. The buyer was George Merrill, about whom more can be found in Chapter 23.

Crane and his successors continued to own the wharf for many years thereafter. Finally, in May 1934, Ingeborg Townsend, by then the owner of Crane's property, agreed to sell the landing and a small strip of land 23' deep and 38' in to Frank R. Prescott, a Meredith manufacturer of wheelbarrows and boxes who was also involved in town government.[1] The next year, in April 1935, Prescott sold the wharf and property to the Town of Meredith which has maintained ownership ever since. The address of the wharf property is #1 Bear Island.[2]

The canopy shown above was added to the Bear Island wharf in c. 1893. According to the Boston Herald, it originally served as the railroad station canopy at the Weirs. "(T)he old awning that has adorned the pier (for) several years has been taken to Bear Island for the accommodation of passengers at that place."[3]

---

[1] For more background on Frank Prescott, see Heyduk, Stories in the History, pp. 272-273.
[2] B/P 212/423 and B/P 217/40.
[3] Boston Herald, July 15, 1894, p. 3.

Other early 1900s postcard scenes of the North Bear steam boat wharf.

Chapter Twenty-Three

The 1890s: The Rest of Bear

Badlam's beach (Thompson-Wright)

While a dozen vacationers had purchased lots on North Bear by 1892, there were none to be found anywhere else on the island. The first change in this pattern occurred in 1894 on South Bear's Lot 5. It was an anomaly. In 1894, Charles Badlam of Boston apparently leased the beautiful beach-front section of the lot facing the Ossipees from Granville Gilman.[1] Badlam perhaps discovered the pleasures of island living during a stay at the Bear Island House.[2] He was a traveling salesman who was related to General Stephen Badlam of Revolutionary fame. Charles and his wife built a small cottage (left) on the beach which became known as Badlam's beach for years thereafter. An experienced boat's man, he was able to reach his new vacation place on his own steamer, the *Checo*.[3] But Badlam was alone on this part of Bear. Granville made no other arrangements with vacationers. In 1899, he sold Lots 5 and 6N, along with the original Gilman family homestead on the Neck, to his younger brother, David Frank, who was living in the family's old Neck house.[4]

The second section of Bear to enter the vacation era was Lot 7 on the southern end of the island. In 1897, Neck farmers, Lewis Eaton and David Clark, sold it to a businessman, James Aiken, of Franklin, NH.[5] The lot encompassed about 89 acres and had shorefront on both the southern end of the island as well as on the eastern side facing Dollar Island. But the initial phase of the vacation era occurred only on the southern end across from Mark Island.

Aiken had previously invested in vacation property near the Weirs, buying lots in the huge vacation development called 'Interlaken' which was developed in the early 1890s on the Gilford side of the Weirs channel. But he found Bear more to his liking. James built his house (now

---

[1] Boston Herald, July 8, 1894. Leases were not always recorded so we have no way of knowing how many others may have vacationed on the island in this manner. Leasing was a very viable alternative. W.S.Hawkes, writing about the vacationing opportunities on the lake in 1887, noted: "If one does not wish to buy, he can get ground rent very cheaply, some good spots being leased (for) ten years for $10.00, while good comfortable cottages can be built at small cost..." Hawkes, Winnipesaukee and About There (1887).
[2] He was a frequent visitor at the hotel every year from the early 1890s through at least 1909, the last year for which there are records. Bear Island House Registers, 1894-1898 and 1899-1908, Meredith Historical Society Archives. See also, Boston Herald, July 8, 1894.
[3] Badlam never bought any property in Meredith or Belknap County that we can find. He shows up on Meredith tax rolls in 1901 with a cottage on Bear Island. (Meredith Tax Rolls, 1901. Meredith Historical Society.) A handwritten listing of steamers indicates that he owned the *Checo* as early as 1888. (Untitled binder, Laconia Library History Room).
[4] BCRI, B/P 103/218; 103/245. The Gilman house on the Neck is now #64 Meredith Neck Road,
[5] B/P 99/174. As part of the sale Clark reserved the right "to pasture six cattle on the premises during the season" for two years free of charge.

#259) on a sandy beach in a small cove facing Mark Island.[1] It became known locally as Aiken cove.

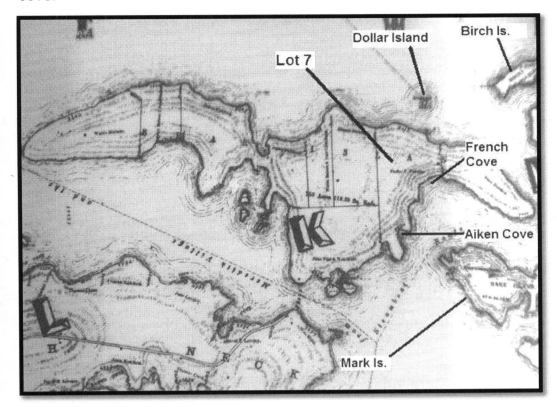

James Aiken had something of a similar background to the much older John Crane whom he undoubtedly knew through industry and family ties. James was the son of Walter Aiken, an influential and accomplished inventor who owned a large knitting company in Franklin.[2] James was active in the business community, serving, for example, on the board of the local telephone company. Unlike Solomon Lovejoy, James bought the property primarily for his own use. He was a businessman interested in vacationing. At the same time, he was not averse to making some money from his investment when the opportunities arose.

And arise they did in the name of the Gokey family of Allston, Massachusetts. Very shortly after acquiring Lot 7 in September 1897, Aiken sold two lots to members of that family. The sales began a remarkable era on the southern end of Bear Island that is still going strong. With only the exception of the Wright family, the extended Gokey family enjoys the longest tenure of any still owning property on the island.[3]

---

[1] The cottage was built at least before 1900. The first reference to it in the Meredith tax records is in April 1900.

[2] Walter Aiken was an interesting figure in his own right. He was born in Dracut, Massachusetts, but the family moved to Franklin where Walter and his brother, Jonas, cut their teeth in their father's machine shop. Walter married Susan Colby of Warner in 1853, and their first child, James, was born in 1854. Walter and Jonas were leaders in the invention and manufacture of knitting machines. Franklin was an ideal location for them because the large manufacturing mills had been operating there on the Winnipesaukee River since the railroad came to town in 1846. The large Franklin Mills Corporation was built along the river in 1852. By 1863, there were several large mills in town focused upon the hosiery business. After the Civil War, in which Walter fought, he and his brother built a large machine shop to manufacture knitting machines for the hosiery business. Aiken's machines and tools became 'celebrated' throughout the industry. Walter's interests ran much further afield than simply great success in the knitting business. Among his noteworthy achievements, he built the house on top of Mount Washington in the late 1860s, retaining a half ownership interest. He also assisted in building the cog railway up the mountain, and he designed the locomotive for the cog. He then served as the general manager for the railway. Among his many other achievements, he was a 33rd degree Mason, and he served in the state legislature for four years. See Hurd: The History of Merrimack and Belknap Counties (1885), p. 326.

[3] The extended Gokey family has owned property on the island for 120 years. The longest tenure among the original island farmers was the 118 years of the Jonathan Bickford Sr. family on Lot 8(1801-1919).

James Aiken's original house (photo taken in the 1940s)

Aiken sold the first lot to Paul N. Goodrich and the second to his brother, Philip Gokey (#237 and #238, respectively).[1] The lots were located in the large cove adjoining the boundary wall with old Lot 8, a good distance east of Aiken's smaller cove. Both men built cottages shortly after acquiring the properties.[2] The area became known as French Cove.

Paul Goodrich and Philip Gokey were sons of Albert Norbert Gauthier (b. c. 1824) and his wife, Madeline Cartier, who immigrated to Springfield, Massachusetts from Nova Scotia probably in the 1840s. Albert was a horse trainer by trade. After arriving in the United States, he changed the family surname from Gauthier to Gokey, believing that his French Canadian surname was disadvantageous. The Gokey's had a very large family, totaling 13 children.[3] Among some of the family's many pleasures was fishing, and Lake Winnipesaukee became their favorite fishing grounds in the 1890s. It was in pursuit of this pleasure that they found Bear Island. In the early 1890s, they rented row boats at the Weirs, and they camped, fished, swam, and picnicked in the uninhabited cove area of Lot 7. A favorite site was the western facing beach on Lot 8 that they dubbed 'Lake Shore Park'.[4] It apparently attracted many visitors during the 1890s.

Paul Goodrich

Paul Goodrich (b. 1864) was the Gokey's fifth child. He was originally named Paul Napoleon Gokey, but he was not enamored with his name. He changed it to Paul N. Goodrich, his choice inspired by a chance encounter on a train with B. F. Goodrich of automobile tire

---

[1] B/P 99/386; 99/395.
[2] Meredith Tax Records, April 1900 (MHS Archives). Meredith officials did not list Paul and Philip until 1900.
[3] See Reflections, p. 137.
[4] See, for example, BCRI, B/P 107/438, James Aiken to Albert Gokey, December 1901. The beach is now part of Camp Lawrence and known as West Beach.

fame.[1] Paul was an inventor and an avid bicyclist. In 1901, he patented an adjustable bicycle seat, and a few years later he invented adjustable handlebars. In 1907, he and Philip started their own company, the Ideal Plating Company, to manufacture bicycle handle bars and seat posts, among other things. Paul's inventions were so well received in the industry that the company was purchased by Iver Johnson, a Fitchburg, Massachusetts company that was among the most popular bicycle brands in the early 1900s. Paul was also an avid boat's man. In 1904, he owned a 28 foot 'speed launch' named the *Comet* capable of going 15 mph.[2]

Within a year or so after the Gokey brothers' purchases, Aiken sold a third lot. The buyer was unique. It was Fred A. Bickford, a fourth generation descendant of two of the original Bear Island founding families. He was a son of the Civil War veteran, Oliver Bickford, and his wife, Julia Nichols.[3] Fred was born in 1858, very possibly on the island.[4] He was the only direct relative of an early Bear Island family to purchase a property on the island solely for vacation purposes. A carpenter, he and his wife, Henrietta, were living in Laconia by the late 1890s. They built a house on what is now Bear lot #249.[5]

The Gokey children c. 1892. **Top Row:** Horace, Joe, Minnie, Annie (Duquette), Albert, Homer, Harvey.
Front Row: Eddie, Phil, Mira, Paul (Goodrich), Laura.
  Annie, Albert, Harvey, Phil and Paul all came to own summer homes on Bear Island. *(Photo courtesy of Roger Dolan.)*

  Not far from Aiken Cove, Lot 9 changed hands one last time before the vacation era began there. In 1892,

---

[1] Bear Island Reflections, pp. 137- 143.

[2] "The Rudder," 1904, p. 226.

[3] His grandfathers were James Bickford and Nathaniel Nichols.

[4] On a side note, Fred's brother, Frank, was also very likely born on the island in 1861. He too became a carpenter, but he remained living in Meredith. During the winter of 1906-1907, Frank built the first motor boat to be owned by any vacationer on Birch Island. It was a 25 footer with a 'torpedo stern' and a McDuff engine. (Bradford, Birch History, p. 25).

[5] B/P 104/588. The date of the sale is unknown because the original deed was lost. A replacement deed was completed in August 1900. By then Fred Bickford had built a house on the property. The lot consisted of all of current lot #249 and pieces of lot #248 to the east and the unnumbered lot to the west (now owned by the town).

William Brown's heirs sold it to Arthur E. Leavitt. Arthur E. was the grandson of the renowned Dudley Leavitt, and he lived on the family farm off of Quarry Road on Neck Lot 45.[1] Arthur was a prominent member of the Meredith community, serving as a Meredith selectman on at least eight occasions between 1877 and 1896.[2] He owned Bear Lot 9 for six years, using it for seasonal grazing, although very early on, he sold an undivided half of the 89 acre parcel to the Meredith Shook and Lumber Company for $500.[3]

Meredith Shook & Lumber Co. located in Meredith Bay (now Church Landing)

The vacation era came to Lot 9 in 1898 when Ellery Channing Mansfield bought out the interests of Arthur Leavitt and the Meredith Shook. These sales brought to a close the farming era on the section of the island where the very first settler had made his home.[4] The parcel, of course, had not had any year-round residents living on it since the departure of Dolly in the early 1850s.[5]

Ellery Channing Mansfield (1849 – 1937) was a self-made man. Born in Barton, Vermont in 1849, his family moved to Massachusetts when he was a boy. His father was in the dry goods business, so Ellery followed down that path. During the 1870s, he worked as a traveling salesman for a Boston dry goods business. In 1878, he moved to Meredith to establish his own dry goods retail business.[6] He lived in a local boarding house when he first arrived and then

---

[1] The Moulton Farm is located on part of this property now.
[2] BCRI, B/P 78/288; 87/376. Arthur E. inherited the family farm from his father, Isaac (1798-1881), who was Dudley's oldest son.
[3] BCRI, B/P 87/311. The Meredith Shook and Lumber Company began operations in 1886. Among other places, it bought part of Stonedam Island and the timber rights to Jerry Point on Bear.
[4] BCRI, B/P 100/444; 100/457.
[5] The land still bore the footprints of Aunt Dolly. The broken down frame of Dolly's house was said to be visible into the 1930s. Her nearby well was also quite evident. The Nichols-Bryant cemetery, as now, was located just north of the point. Moreover, in 1898 the access road from the ferry's landing to the interior was still well defined; Leavitt's deed to Mansfield reserved the right of the public to use the "road, driveway or passway" across the property.
[6] Mansfield's store advertised "Dry and Fancy Goods, Wrappers and Shirt Waists, Clothing Boots and Shoes, Men's Furnishings, Trunks, Carpets, Hats and Caps, Furniture, Etc. International Tailoring Co. Ladies' Home Journal."

bought a house on High Street in 1883.[1] He established his store on Main Street (now #48) in the Village center. Meredith tax valuations show that Mansfield was quite well off by 1884.

E.C.Mansfield's store on Main St. in Meredith Village c. 1900 (Meredith Historical Society)

Mansfield was a lover of the outdoors and the lake. Shortly after his arrival in town in 1878, the youthful Mansfield embarked on a rowboat tour of the entire 186 mile Winnipesaukee shoreline, something he apparently did almost every year until 1923.[2] It was his first tour that exposed him to Bear Island. In time, he acquired his own sailboat, the *Ripple*.[3] As his personal fortunes improved, Mansfield was able to purchase Bear Lot 9 in 1898 where he built a summer house. He built it on the point (#310) across from Cattle Landing and very close to where Dolly had lived. Within a couple of years, he had built two more homes for family members and guests on the northwestern side of his property (#313 near the point and #321 deeper in the cove to the north). But he did not subdivide his property or sell off any shorefront lots.

Right after buying the Bear property in 1898, Mansfield had an observation tower built on the highest point of his land.[4] He wrote many years later that it was built "as an inducement for the public to visit it, and get a complete view of the 'Switzerland of America'."[5] He and his guests could enjoy spectacular views in virtually all directions from the tower. He maintained a register of visitors who came from all over the country and from many foreign countries. Mansfield's idea

---

[1] 1880 Census; B/P 71/343
[2] Meredith News, April 23, 1936.
[3] Van Veghten, Meredith Bay, p. 34.
[4] This is the spot where the St. John's Chapel now stands and was probably the spot where Robert Bryant made his home nearly 100 years before. The tower was built by James P. Leighton of Center Harbor. Leighton also built the Chapel in 1927.
[5] Meredith News, April 23, 1936.

of a tower was not unique in that period. Observation towers were built in numerous places as people everywhere enjoyed the panoramic views they could see from them. The nearest example of a tower, and one that Mansfield undoubtedly visited as a youth, was located (aptly) on Tower Hill behind the Weirs docks. It was erected in 1881 but burned to the ground in 1885. In another example, the Appalachian Mountain Club built an observation tower on Three Mile Island in 1902. It doubled as a water storage facility.[1]

Mansfield formally named the southeastern half of his property, with its tower, the 'White Mountain Park'.[2] It is said that Mansfield's wife objected to the name because she was afraid people would assume it was a park open to the public. Indeed, one story goes that a boat pulled up to the Mansfield dock one day, and the operator asked to be guided up to the tower. Upon returning to the boat, the operator paid Mansfield for his services without ever knowing with whom he was dealing.

In addition to his ownership on Bear, Mansfield bought half of Timber Island in 1903. He also bought Shepherd Island in the Carry Cove 1905.[3] He held onto Timber for the rest of his life, selling only one lot on the entire island during that period. In his later years, Mansfield played a prominent role in trying to protect the lake. He was a founder and the chairman of the Winnipesaukee Protective and Improvement Association which was formed in 1910. In 1911, he led an organizational petition drive to get the state Legislature to take control of the lake level which was being unpredictably drawn down by the mills that controlled the Lakeport dam. There was wide concern that this would "interfere with navigation, and the prospect was that boathouses would be left on dry land."[4] Legislation was enacted that year to establish state control over the dam.

In sharp contrast to the arrival of the newcomers on Lots 7 and 9, the vacation era did not reach Lots 4, 6S, and 8 during the 1890s. Lot 4 was owned by James Bickford's youngest son, Moses, who had inherited ownership of it in 1888 after James died. Moses and his family continued to use the island property as a summer farm during the 1890s. Just down the island

---

[1] Meredith News, May 13, 1936. The Three Mile tower was also built by J. Leighton. A History of Three Mile Island Camp, p. 30.

[2] The naming of properties and individual estates had become a widespread practice during the vacation age. The name can be found on the maps of the lake from that period. Mansfield's choice to publicize his park was perhaps inspired by the 'Ossipee Mountain Park', a 500 acre estate established across the lake in the Ossipee Mountains by Benjamin Franklin Shaw in 1879. Shaw's park included the land now occupied by the Castle in the Clouds. Similar to John Crane and the Aikens, Shaw's wealth came from the hosiery business, with Shaw's located in Lowell, MA.

[3] B/P 148/210. See Chapter 37 for more detail about Timber Island and Shepherd Island.

[4] Meredith News, May 20, 1936.

on Lot 6S, the only change that occurred came when Eleazer Bickford Jr. leased his summer farm to one Josiah Morrison. Morrison built a small house not far from the original Eleazer Bickford cellar hole.[1] Morrison's particulars are not known, but he was apparently a local farmer who had no interest in the water front. Similar to Lot 4, nothing changed on old Lot 8 during the 1890s. Jonathan Bickford's two sons used the island property for summer pasturage and timber, just as it had been used for decades.

Summary

The 1890s witnessed the first island-wide arrival of vacationers on Bear Island. The

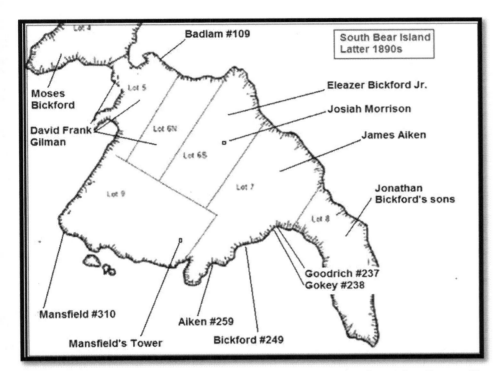

number of vacation places more than tripled from six to 19 during the decade. The total included 13 on North Bear, four in French Cove, one on East Bear, and one on Dolly's Point (Lot 9). The preponderance of vacationers was from Massachusetts, but two families had arrived from New Jersey and New York. The three largest land holding vacationers were successful, local businessmen from Laconia and Meredith. At this point, they were primarily interested in the island for their own pleasure and not for its profit-making potential.

By way of context, the arrival of these vacationers on Bear was not unique by any means. Many of the small, satellite islands near Bear were occupied during the 1880s and 1890s.[2] All four of the Dolly Islands (Dolly, South Dolly, Little Dolly, and Penny), three of the four Carry Islands (Shepherd, Rock, and Palmer), Loon, Three Mile, Hawk's Nest (aka Little Three Mile), three of the four Beaver Islands (Big Beaver, Middle Beaver, and Beaver), Pine Island, Birch Island, and Jolly Island had all become home to vacationers. However, the background of these new islanders was markedly different. The owners of the smaller islands were almost all New Hampshire folks who built summer fishing camps on them. It seems that they gravitated to the

---

[1] BCRI, B/P 111/206. The dilapidated structure of the Morrison house was still very much in evidence into the 1960s. Today, one can still see a bedspring, a piece or two of an old stove, and an old Worchester Buckeye mower there. The outline of an old well is also easily recognizable near the remnants of the house, and not far to the south one can find a dug well.

[2] See Part VI, Chapter 37, *Early History of Other Islands*, for historical detail about these islands and others.

smaller islands because they were readily available to them. Many were from Gilford and Lake Village where they knew the owner, George W. Sanders, of Gilford. While he was more interested in the timber on those islands, he was apparently happy to sell them when asked. In a very different trend, Pine, Birch, Jolly, and Steamboat were all acquired by Methodists whose affinity for a natural setting led them to acquire those modest sized islands where they could establish communities of like minded people. Altogether, the number of summer places on these islands was more than double the number on Bear. The closest of them, the Dolly and Carry islands, together had half as many summer places as Bear did at the time.

Chapter Twenty-Four

1900 – 1910: More Changes on North Bear

The first decade of the 20th century was highlighted by two very different developments. First, beginning in 1900, the pace of vacation era growth on Bear Island accelerated rapidly compared to the previous two decades. The number of summer places on the island more than doubled from 18 in 1900 to 41 by the end of 1910. North Bear experienced a little of the growth, but other sections of the island enjoyed most of it. Second, the prime mover of the vacation era, Solomon Lovejoy, decided to take his leave.

During the early 1900s, the Bear Island House welcomed a constant flow of summer visitors. By this time, the hotel had been expanded from 25 rooms to 55 rooms.[1] Solomon also added some amenities to enhance its appeal, including a piano in 1906 to accompany the existing organ for the benefit of dancers.[2] He also built tennis courts.[3] 'Roads' leading to two beautiful beaches—one on each side of the island--were built behind the shorefront lots and down the center of the island.[4]

Postcard of the expanded Bear Island House. (MHS)

While overall activity on the island increased markedly during the 1900-1910 period, Solomon Lovejoy did not play as big role in it as one might expect. In fact, he only sold three more lots from his large land holdings during the decade. His first lot sale occurred in 1900 when

---

[1] Boston Herald, April 21, 1907, p. 37.
[2] Boston Herald, August 26, 1906, p. 47.
[3] The exact timing of these improvements is not known.
[4] One beach was located at the base of The Gulf and the other was on the eastern side of the island (later known to residents as Alvord Beach).

Nellie and Harris Nye of Cliftondale, MA, bought one of the smaller lots originally subdivided by Solomon (later part of #420). This lot had frontage of only four rods (66'); but it included one of the houses Solomon had built.[1] Harris Nye was a bookkeeper. The Bear Island property remained in the family until 1923 when it was sold after Harris passed away.

The second sale occurred in 1901 when Caroline and Charles Maudant, also of Cliftondale, MA, purchased a similarly small sized lot (also now part of #420) next to Nye.[2] The purchase is curious because they already owned a lakefront lot on the Neck right next to "Lovejoy's Sands".[3] The Maudants had purchased their Neck lot from Charles H. Bickford in 1897.[4] The third sale by Solomon occurred in 1903 when Walter and Jennie Chaloner of Boston bought lot #426. This too was a smaller lot (4 rods of frontage). The Chaloners built a "picturesque studio" called "Rymlake" there a couple of years later.[5] Walter Chaloner was a renowned water color artist whose prints are still of great value. One summer, he rented the houseboat, *Iris*, for two weeks and traveled about the lake teaching water-color sketching to a small group of women vacationers.[6] He was "a great admirer of Lake Winnipiseogee, and his views ...attracted wide attention."[7] He was also a founding subscriber of the AMC purchase of Three Mile Island.

John Crane also made a contribution to the growth of the vacation community.[8] He sold a piece of his land with 274' of frontage adjacent to the Bear Island wharf to George and Mary Merrill of Laconia in 1906.[9] Within a year, the Merrills built a cottage (#434) next to the mail dock dock for their large, extended family.[10] The Merrills were from Laconia and had decided to develop a service business among the rapidly growing summer population. They were handymen and carpenters who became almost legendary among vacationers for all of the houses they built on the island and all of the services (food, milk, ice, and taxi) they provided. Before 1910, the Merrills removed Sol Lovejoy's old boathouse that stood in front of their lot and built a new one.[11] They subsequently built a store and an icehouse from which they provided for the varying needs of the islanders.[12]

---

[1] B/P 105/97.

[2] B/P 107/31. Maudant sold the lot to Nye in 1904. B/P 113/149.

[3] B/P 101/554. For the reference to Lovejoy's Sands, see, for example, C. Maudant to W. Sweetser in 1910, B/P 129/169.

[4] B/P 113/149.

[5] *Boston Herald*, August 7, 1904, p. 35. B/P 121/183. In re the timing of the house, see Meredith Tax Records, 1906 (MHS Archives).

[6] Blackstone, p. 71. See also, Springfield Republican, October 21, 1902, p. 5.

[7] *Boston Herald*, July 1, 1906, p. 30.

[8] John Crane also adopted the idea of subdividing his five and one-half acre island getaway into saleable lots. In keeping with the times, he called his 1908 subdivision 'Bear Island Park'.[8] But Crane died in 1910 having only sold one lot.

[9] B/P 119/346.

[10] The cottage was built in 1907 (Meredith Tax Records, 1908, MHS Archives). In 1906, the extended Merrill family included Arthur, Edith, Fred, David, and Edgar along with Hattie Merrill Fay whose husband, Park Fay, and child, Wilbur, were also living with them on the island and in Laconia. See: US Census for 1900 and 1910.

[11] B/P 131/52.

[12] The store and icehouse were completed before 1912. (Meredith Tax Records 1912, MHS Archives). See Reflections, pp. 33 – 38. B/P 131/52. In 1923, the Merrills also purchased a mainland lot with 85' of shorefront opposite Pine Island where they built a wharf. B/P 167/341. This was their access point from which they went to and from Bear Island. This is now the location of the Y Landing Marina.

Not long after the arrival of the Merrills, the Chaloners decided to enter the real estate game themselves. They bought the large, unimproved property that Lucy Young had purchased from Solomon in 1892.[1] They subdivided it into three parcels and sold all three in July 1907. One One (#409) was sold to Park Fay, the Lakeport carpenter and handyman who was married to Hattie Merrill; the second (#410) was sold to Arthur Merrill, Hattie's brother; and the third lot (#412) was sold to Mary Worden, also from Lakeport.[2] The following year, 1908, Solomon made his final lot sale when he resold a small parcel (now part of #430), originally purchased by Herbert Streeter, to William Huntington of Concord, NH.[3] Huntington was a 37 year old bank clerk.

The Huntington transaction was Sol's last lot sale on Bear Island. Perhaps having grown weary of the business, Sol (then 64) had decided to sell the hotel and his Bear Island property. He hired a Laconia real estate agent, J.H. Gingras, to market them in early 1907.[4] Gingras began publicizing the sale widely, and his pitch appeared in the <u>Boston Herald</u> throughout the winter and spring:

> "Lake Winnipesaukee's most beautiful spot, white sand beaches and general healthfulness; equally desirable for summer school or sanitarium; has always been a big paying proposition as a hotel; property consists of 55-room hotel, 4 shore cottages, 200 acres of land, having 10,000 ft. of lake frontage, worth at least $2 per front foot; a proposition with unlimited commercial possibilities; price $22,000."[5]

Sol found his buyer in 1909. He sold all of his island holdings to George A. Collins of Laconia, NH in a series of transactions that were closed over the course of the year.[6] Collins (1868 – 1941) was a Laconia businessman who decided to become an hotelier and real estate speculator. He was born in Manchester, NH and moved to the Laconia area in the latter 1800s. By the early 1890s at least, he lived in Lakeport[7] on Union Avenue and owned an 'apothecary' on Elm Street. His business was called G. A. Collins & Co. It sold drugs, stationary, and fishing tackle. He was married to Georgia Cheney, and the couple had two children, George P. and Dorothy. George sold his business just prior to purchasing the Bear Island assets of Solomon.

Collins adopted a dual approach for marketing the island shorefront. Within a few months of his 1909 purchase, he enjoyed some success on both sides of the island. On the eastern side of Bear, rather than personally selling individual lots, in 1909 he sold an 1100 foot stretch to

---

[1] B/P 121/55.
[2] B/P 121/55; 121/143; 121/159; 121/1420.
[3] B/P 458/123. Sol had originally sold this lot to Herbert Streeter in 1886 but had repurchased it in 1900.
[4] For more on Gingras, see <u>The Illustrated Laconian</u>, p. 68. In the late 1890s, Gingras owned a shoe store in Laconia.
[5] "Bear Island Hotel," <u>Boston Herald</u>, April 24, 1907, p. 37.
[6] B/P 125/25 was the primary sales transaction.
[7] The town of Lake Village changed its name to Lakeport in 1891 to reflect its size and stature that had resulted from its industrial growth over the previous decades.

another Laconia businessman, George D. Mayo. The parcel began at the hotel beach (on old Lot 3) and ran north from there (from approximately #52 Bear to #36 Bear).[1]

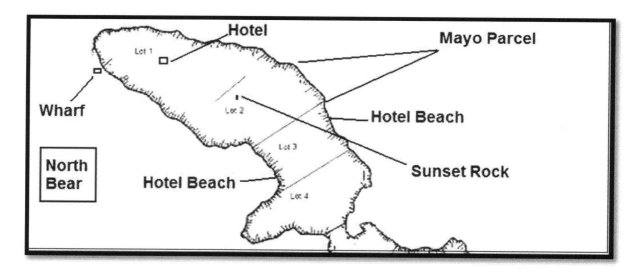

On the densely populated western side, Collins quickly sold two lots (#400 and 413) to fellow Lakeport resident, Dr. George Saltmarsh. Saltmarsh, the original mail boat overseer, executed the purchases as trustee for his son, Robert C. Saltmarsh, who was still a minor.[2] Collins also sold a third lot (#407) to Edward C. Mansfield, the postmaster of Boston. The lot adjoined Silas Holman's place. It included a house that was probably built by Sol Lovejoy in the 1880s.[3]

While these additions further built out the western shoreline of North Bear, it was further south on the island that most of the growth took place.

---

[1] B/P 125/562; 276/197.
[2] B/P 126/351; 127/278.
[3] B/P 126/74. He was unrelated to Ellery C. Mansfield who owned Lot 9.

Chapter Twenty-Five

1900 - 1910: The Rest of Bear

The accelerating pace at which vacationers were buying property on North Bear carried over to the rest of the island during the first decade of the 20th century. The number of new homes more than doubled on the island during this period, most where no one had lived before.

The Carry Coves: 1901 – 1907

The coves on either side of the Carry welcomed the arrival of vacationers just after the turn of the century. The area included parts of old Lots 4 and 5. The first summer presence in this area occurred in 1901 on the northeast side of the island on part of Lot 4. A camp site (now part of Camp Nokomis) was sold by Moses Bickford to Willis M. Rand, a Meredith blacksmith. Also in 1901, Moses sold another small lot next to the Rand camp but farther into the cove (part of #90) to L. D. Fogg and E. W. Holtham, both of Plymouth, NH.[1]

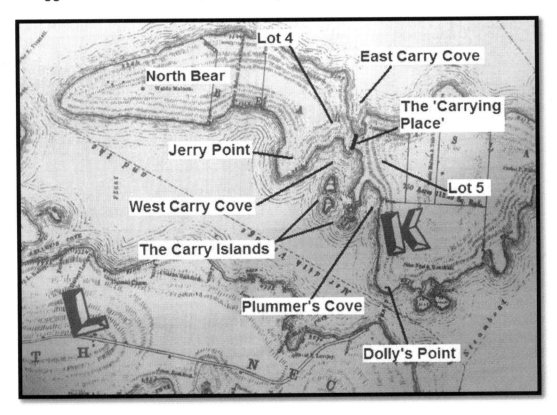

A few years later, vacation interest focused upon the coves on the western side of the Carry facing Meredith Neck. In 1904, David Frank Gilman put all of old Lot 5 and Lot 6N on the market. He placed ads in the Boston papers reading:

---

[1] The Rand deed was not found, The Rand camp is referenced in B/P 110/23 and 114/465. See also B/P 107/444; B/P 126/315; 128/199; B/P 126/315. Eight years later, in 1909, Moses sold another 30' of frontage to Fogg who, by this time, had bought out Holtham.

Lake Winnipesaukee.

Bear Island property. 115 acres: 6000 feet water frontage: about equally divided between the east and west sides: fine mountain view: many shade trees on shore and high grounds: several good springs: on mail route between The Weirs and Centre Harbor: price $6000. D.F.Gilman, Meredith, N.H.[1]

But he attracted no takers for it over the next few years. Finally in 1907, he found an interested party for a piece of it. James L. Little purchased 265' of shore frontage at the base of Plummer Cove.[2] This was an add-on property for Little who had purchased some abutting land on Lot 9 from E. C. Mansfield the year before. In 1908, Little purchased an additional 100' of frontage from Gilman, extending his property across virtually the entire base of the cove.[3]

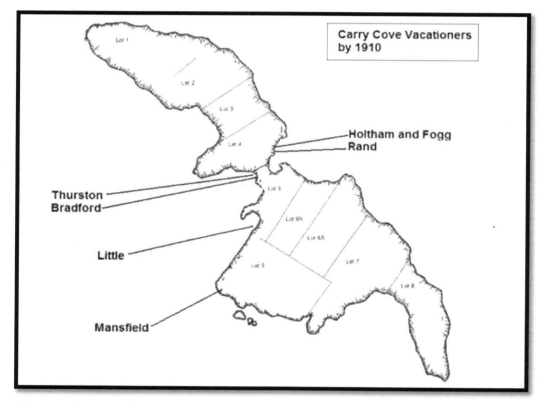

Carry Cove Vacationers by 1910

Holtham and Fogg
Rand

Thurston
Bradford

Little

Mansfield

A little further north in the neighboring smaller cove where the Carrying Place was located, two more summer vacationers purchased parcels from Gilman. In 1908, George H. Thurston of Meredith bought a lot (#352) with 100' of frontage. The lot was 114' deep, and it abutted the old road that ran through the Carry into Moses Bickford's land on old Lot 4.

The northern side boundary line of Thurston's lot was established 50' south of the stone wall that divided old Lot 4 from old Lot 5. The set-off of this strip formalized what Gilman labeled the 'Carrying Place'.[4] Thurston got a new neighbor in 1909 when Gilman sold an adjoining 100' of

---

[1] Boston Herald, April 17, 1904, p. 39.

[2] 'We have adopted the name 'Plummer cove' for ease of identification. It was the name given the area in the deed of the 1908 sale to Little. B/P 123/555. The origin of the name is unknown. We found no one named Plummer playing a role anywhere on the island. The name was never perpetuated, and the cove has no official name.

[3] B/P 121/449; 123/555. The properties extended 150' inland and abutted "a road reserved by the grantor". This was the island road that began at Dolly's Point and ran through the Carry into old Lot 4. Little never built on the land in the cove, and the land is still one of the few pieces of island shore front that is unimproved (and unnumbered) today.

[4] B/P 124/418. This was the first and only time the 'Carrying Place' was ever formally defined. 'Carrying Place' was a generic term used by New Englanders for any place where they could carry canoes between two bodies of water (or around dams). This part of Bear was also often referred to as the 'Narrows'. In 1909, Thurston bought an additional 100' of frontage to his south, giving the entire property 200' of frontage. B/P 126/465.

frontage to Thomas and Harriett Bradford of Phoenix, R.I. (#352).[1] Bradford was the first Ocean Stater to buy property on Bear.

Thus by 1909, there were two vacation places located in the base of the Carry Cove on the western side of the island facing the Neck. Their nearest neighbors to the north were the Bickfords on Jerry Point; to the south there was a peninsula and extensive, uninhabited shoreline before one reached James Little's large land holdings and his house in Plummer Cove at the base of Dolly Point.

Steamer Mt. Washington passing the west side of the Carry Cove, c. 1934.

Old Lot 4 Inches Towards the Vacation Era: 1901 – 1908

During the first few years of the 1900s, Moses Bickford's sale of the camp sites on the eastern side of the Carry were the only direct steps he took with regard to selling the shore frontage of old Lot 4.[2] In 1908, however, a bigger step was taken that set the stage for the eventual subdivision of the lot. Moses and his two daughters reached an agreement with Moses' son, Roy, to divide up the property. In exchange for releasing his ownership interest in the rest of Lot 4, Roy was given sole ownership of a long stretch of shorefront on the northwest side of the property in what is today known as The Gulf. It included 1100 feet of frontage and encompassed the land from #377 to the stone wall that separated old Lot 4 from Solomon Lovejoy's Lot 3 between #382 and #384 Bear Island.[3]

---

[1] B/P 126/466.
[2] In 1905, Moses did strike a deal with the Meredith Shook and Lumber Company to sell it all of the hemlock, poplar and pine trees (with some exceptions) on Jerry Point for $1000. B/P 116/357.
[3] B/P 124/265; 124/359.

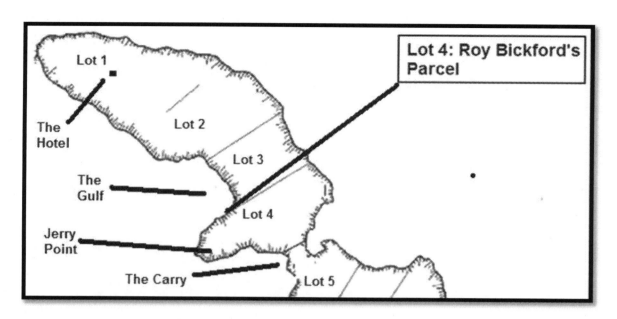

The East Bear Island Colony on Old Lot 6S: 1903 – 1909

The largest increase in new vacation places occurred on the eastern side of South Bear during the early 1900s. At the time, the only vacationer in the area was Charles Badlam who was leasing the beach area on old Lot 5. In 1903, Eleazer Bickford Jr. decided to sell Lot 6S which had been in his family since the very early 1800s. He sold it to an enterprising local man named George Washington Greene who sought to take advantage of the booming summer trend.[1] A man of many talents, Greene was from Center Harbor, where he was a farmer, a carpenter, and even the sheriff for awhile. He saw an opportunity in the emerging demand for summer lakefront property and the need for island services it created.[2]

Greene subdivided Lot 6S and sold 22 1/2 acres along the eastern shore to Edward Luce, a Birch Island resident from Niantic, CT.[3] Luce had grown up in a fairly wealthy family. He was a fishing boat captain in his early years and came to own a manufacturing plant in Connecticut later on. In 1894, he had purchased a summer place on Birch Island in conjunction with several other Methodists.[4] His entrepreneurial spirit and Methodist connections led to Luce's purchase of Bear Island.

Luce subdivided the shorefront of his property on Bear into eight lots and proceeded to market them.[5] The first purchase was made in January 1905 by Reverend John H. Newland of Willimantic, Connecticut. He was a Methodist Episcopal minister and a member of the New England Southern Conference of Methodist Episcopalians. The latter organization, as well as

---

[1] B/P 111/206.
[2] See Chapter 26, *Vignettes: Early 1900s,* for more information about George Greene.
[3] B/P 114/53. George Greene retained 36 acres of backland as well as a shore front lot (#140) that bordered James Aiken's land (old Lot 7) to its south.
[4] See Chapter 36 regarding the Methodists on the lake, and Chapter 37 for a brief history of Birch Island.
[5] Luce Plan of 1905, 18–1317.

annual Methodist camp sessions, undoubtedly brought Newland into direct contact with Luce and the other Methodist ministers who had settled on Birch and Jolly islands beginning in 1892. Newland bought lots two and three in the Luce plan, amounting to 275' of frontage (today this covers four lots, #135 through #138).[1]

In January 1906, Luce sold two more of his lots (#127) on the northern end of the subdivision to 67 year old James W. Pearsall (1839 – 1918) of Ridgewood, New Jersey.[2] The link that connected Pearsall and Luce also probably arose from their extensive involvement in the Methodist Episcopal Church. Pearsall was very active in the Methodist church, among other things superintending the Sunday school program in Ridgewood. He also became a trustee and later

The Pearsall's Rockwood.

Treasurer of the Methodist-founded Drew University in Madison, NJ. Pearsall developed one of the most elaborate 'estates' built on the entire island at the time. It consisted of a large house, an ice house, a 30' water tower, and a gazebo. He called it *Rockwood*. The water tower eventually served several nearby houses on either side of Pearsall. He owned a small steam boat that was named *She's a Daisy*.[3]

Pearsall earned his wealth through the success of the New Idea Pattern Company which he founded in New York City in 1894. The company developed new clothing patterns (in those days, it was common for people to make their own clothes). It also developed a highly innovative, direct marketing approach for the business. Pearsall's success was such that "he had a palatial Georgian-style home with horse-drawn carriages and a staff of servants" in Ridgewood.[4]

---

[1] B/P 114/218.

[2] B/P 117/57; 117/39.

[3] B/P 117/30; In re the Pearsalls and Rockwood, see "The Bear News," May 1986, Stan Patten Editor; Bear Island Reflections, pp. 63 – 65.

[4] Genealogical History Of Hudson And Bergen Counties New Jersey: James W. Pearsall, Originally published in 1900, Cornelius Burnham Harvey, Editor. Pearsall's success is often associated with the Butterick pattern business, but it was not until after his death that his New Idea Company was acquired by Butterick.

Pearsall had six children with his first wife, Hannah, including daughters Ella, Laura, and Lina, and sons William, Edward, and Silas. After Hannah died in 1899, Pearsall married the widow, Sarah Cleary Rhodes (1851 – 1934), of Providence, R.I. Sarah had one child by her first marriage, Fannie Pearl Rhodes, who married Charles H. Patten in 1906. Most of this large extended family enjoyed vacationing on Bear Island and several of them came to own property on it.

The Pearsall family on Bear Island: <u>Front row</u>: Horace Patten; Ruth Earp; Beatrice Patten; Muriel Patten; Mae O'Neill. <u>2nd Row</u>: Luella O'Neill with Evelyn; Annie Pearsall; Ella O'Neill; James W. Pearsall; Sarah Pearsall; James Earp. <u>3rd Row</u>: Wainwright Pearsall; Albert O'Neill; Edwin Lee Earp; Ethel Pearsall; Charles Patten; Pearl Patten; Ray Pearsall; Lina Earp; Addison O'Neill.

Also in January 1906, Luce sold a lot (#129) abutting Pearsall to William Halcrow, a highly respected builder from Providence, Rhode Island. Halcrow was yet another Methodist Episcopalian who was very actively involved in the church. Perhaps an acquaintance of Sarah Pearsall through the church, Halcrow was hired by James Pearsall to build the latter's home on the island. Halcrow then built his own, almost identical, house next door.[1]

Later in 1906, Luce sold another lot located at the southern end of the new colony to Robert C. Bacheller of Newport, RI.[2] It was lot 1 in the Luce subdivision (now #139), located next to the shorefront parcel retained by George Greene. At the time, the 50 year old Bacheller owned a carriage painting company.

At the end of 1906, the nascent East Bear colony therefore consisted of four summer places along with Greene's parcel. It also had another important feature. Beginning in the fall of 1905, Luce undertook construction of a community wharf that he had promised to his lot purchasers.[3] The dock was very similar to those in existence on Birch Island and Jolly Island,

[1] BCRI, B/P 117/30B/P 118/275; Both Pearsall's and Halcrow's houses are still in use on the island. It is also likely that Halcrow built Newlands house which was very similar in style. Newland's house no longer exists. It was torn down in the 1970s.
[2] BCRI, B/P 117/30B/P 118/278.
[3] BCRI, B/P 117/30.

not to mention North Bear. Luce, of course, was a Birch Islander himself, so he had a perfect example of what the dock should look like. It was 'L' shaped to permit easy landing and departure by the mail boat and any other large boats.

The Original East Bear wharf c. 1920. Rev. Newland's house is visible in the background.

Luce built the dock between lots three and four of his subdivision where he carved out a 40' wide strip of land that ran to some backland that he had retained. The strip included a small beach. All of the deeds to summer land owners included rights of way and rights to utilize the dock and beach. Lot owners became owners of the wharf and were responsible, proportional to their land holdings, for maintenance and repairs. There were 12 shares or lots, with Luce's backland counting as five shares. The mail dock quickly became the focal point of the colony, much like the other mail docks on the islands. The mailing address was originally called Pearsall's Landing, a phrase that remained in use into the 1940s.

The next expansion of the East Bear colony occurred in 1908, but it did not have anything to do with Luce and his land. James Pearsall was interested in making the island a retreat for his family. With expansion to his immediate south blocked by Halcrow's lot, he sought to acquire the contiguous property to his north. This shorefront was part of Lot 6N and was owned by David Frank Gilman. Pearsall negotiated the purchase of three adjoining lots from Gilman in the names of three of his children, Ella Pearsall O'Neill (#125), Laura Pearsall (#124), and Silas

Pearsall (#122).[1] Houses were quickly built on both of the daughters' lots, while Silas and his wife, Anne, built a tent platform on their property.[2]

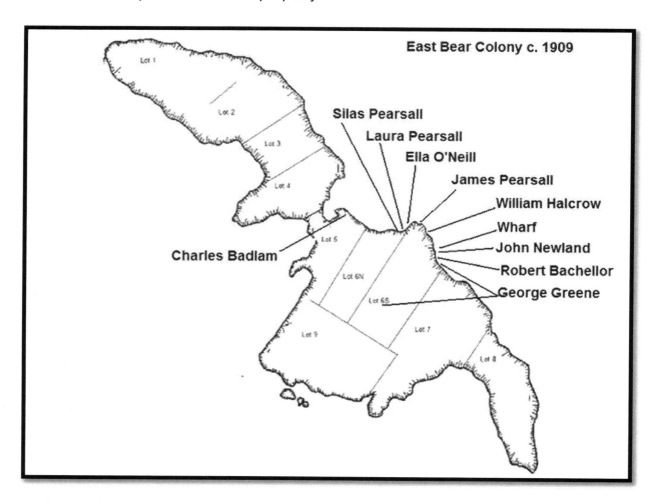

James Aiken and the southern end of Bear

At the turn of the century, the southern end of Bear (old Lot 7) consisted of only four vacationers, including two members of the Gokey family, Fred Bickford, and James Aiken. In 1901, James Aiken sold another lot (#232 and 233 combined) to a third Gokey brother, Albert R., the oldest of the boys.[3] This parcel adjoined the boundary of Lot 8. There were no further lot sales by Aiken during the first decade of the 20th century. But one other transaction was noteworthy. In 1906, Annie Gokey Duquette purchased Fred Bickford's place. Annie was the sister of the three Gokey boys and the second oldest child in the family.

---

[1] B/P 123/587; 123/588; 124/58.
[2] The two daughters' houses were also likely built by Halcrow and were quite similar in style to Pearsall's house. In 1909, Laura Pearsall sold her home to her daughter, Lina Earp. She was married to Edwin L. Earp, a professor first at Syracuse University and then at Drew where he taught Christian Sociology. The ownership of the house subsequently passed to Lina's daughter, Ruth Earp Douglass. The home remained in the family until it was sold in 2015: a total of 107 years. James Pearsall's line still has a continuous presence on Bear Island. James' great, great, great grandson, Chris Lord, has his own home further down the shore on East Bear (#153).
[3] B/P 107/438.

Thus by 1910, the character of the fledgling colony was established. It now had five vacation places, four members of the Gokey family lived in French Cove bordering old Lot 8, and James Aiken's house was somewhat west in Aiken Cove. French Cove was also noteworthy at the time for having "without doubt the fastest motor boat on Lake Winnipiseogee." Paul Goodrich had built or acquired a new 33' boat powered by a 36 horse, six cylinder engine capable of going 27 miles per hour.[1]

Mansfield and Old Lot 9

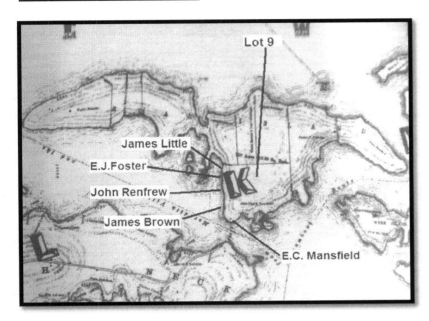

Meanwhile, on old Lot 9, E.C. Mansfield decided to subdivide the most attractive portion of his shorefront on the northwest side of Dolly's Point. He created a 10 lot subdivision with each of the lots having 100' of frontage.[2] Mansfield had immediate success in attracting summer vacationers. In 1906, he sold seven of the lots in the subdivision to four separate buyers.[3] The first sold was his lot # 5 (now #323) which was bought by John Renfrew, a retail clothier from Plymouth, NH. Three weeks later, he sold his lots 6 and 7 (#325 and 327) to E.J. Foster who owned a peg mill in Plymouth, NH. Days later, he sold his lot #1 with the house thereon (now #321) to Dr. James S. Brown, a medical physician from Manchester, NH. Finally in the fall of 1906, Mansfield sold his lots 8, 9 and 10 (now #329) to the aforementioned James L. Little of Brookline, MA. Little was by then an independently wealthy, former dry goods merchant who first came to Meredith for his summer pleasure in 1901. In 1903, he had purchased extensive shore frontage on the Neck along what became Lovejoy Lane. In another purchase, he acquired what became the public beach and parking lot at Lovejoy Sands.[4]

Thus by 1910, old Lot 9, known as Dolly's Point, was home to five vacation places, running from the point directly across from Cattle Landing down into Plummer Cove.

---

[1] Boston Herald, July 7, 1907, p. 14.
[2] The plan is not in the Belknap Registry but is clearly identifiable in the deeds (e.g. B/P 119/297 and 121/8). The subdivision included one of the houses he had built around 1900.
[3] B/P 118/279; B/P 120/404; B/P 119/13; 119/297; B/P 121/8.
[4] B/P 113/493; 110/50. The public parking lot and beach were close to the parcel purchased by Sol Lovejoy's grandfather, Caleb Lovejoy, in 1813. That 37 acre property had remained in the Lovejoy family until 1903 when it was sold by Herbert Lovejoy's widow, Fannie, to P.H. Downes (B/P 109/531). Downes quickly cleaved off the waterfront piece to Little.

Summary: Bear as of 1910

The first decade of the 20th century witnessed a very sharp increase in the numbers of vacationers who chose to summer on Bear Island. In 1900, there were 18 summer places on the island with the majority (12) on the western side of North Bear. By 1910, the number of vacation lots had more than doubled to 41. Most of this increase occurred during the five year period from 1906 through 1910 when some 17 of the 22 new places were sold. The western side of North Bear continued to account for a fair amount of the growth with five new vacation places. But the opening of newly available land on East Bear accounted for eight places, while Mansfield's subdivision on Dolly's Point led to four more.

Also by 1910, another characteristic of these new lot buyers was that they were beginning to come from further away. While nearly 80% of first time buyers were from Massachusetts and New Hampshire (almost evenly split), the southern New England states of Rhode Island (3) and Connecticut (1) were now represented as were New Jersey (5) and New York (1).[1]

Nevertheless, large swaths of shoreline still remained unoccupied, especially on the eastern sides of both North and South Bear. Some of the land was simply not available for sale, while in other parts, the unsurpassed views were not enough to offset its relative inaccessibility; its often steep shoreline; and its exposure to the northwest winds that regularly chopped up the lake on that side of the island.

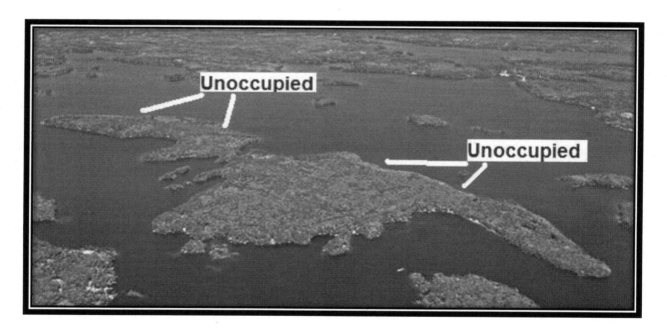

---

[1] The analysis is rather limited in measuring the states of origin of vacationers. It only picks up the first-time buyers. No attempt was made to capture the data on re-sale buyers. There were 11 re-sales during the 1901-1910 period.

Chapter Twenty-Six

Vignettes: Early 1900s

The Island Services Business

The island services business began shortly after Robert Bryant and the earliest farming families settled on the island. It was predominantly a summertime issue when access to the mainland was the most difficult. During the winter months, the islanders had it far easier as they could walk, skate, or sled across the ice quite easily.

As discussed previously, Dolly Nichols and her husband, Joseph, were the first service providers, establishing the ferry business between the island and the lower end of Meredith Neck. In subsequent years, Dolly augmented that service by selling supplies she obtained at the Weirs. The ferry service remained in place after Dolly left the island in the early 1850s. After her departure, the task of ferry operator was taken over by Theophilus Dockham, then Waldo Meloon, and finally Solomon Lovejoy. The arrival of the *Lady of the Lake* in 1849 added a new dimension as she regularly brought supplies and provided transportation services during the summer. These services were augmented by the increasing number of smaller steamers beginning in the 1850s.

Solomon's arrival on the island in 1883 led to major changes in the provision of services

to islanders. In 1886, his purchase and development of the landing at 'the Sands' provided a new mainland base from which to access the island. The need for services was amplified, of course, by Sol's development of the hotel and the sale of lots.

Sol's Sands house, early 1900s.

By this time too, boating was becoming more popular, and several people owned small steamers. Among others, Sol built his own steamer, while his Neck neighbors, Charles 'Henry' Bickford[1] and a partner, Willie D. Brown, also owned a steamer. They not only provided boating services to lake visitors, they also provided provisions. After the

---

[1] Charles H. Bickford (1846-1916) was the son of Charles Bickford and the grandson of Eleazer Bickford Sr. In 1893, he inherited the Neck farm on Lot 78, across from Bear Island. The Lovejoy Sands lot was originally part of this farm. Current day Lovejoy Lane is on this property.

AMC purchased Three Mile Island, the two men filled a major role for the campers. As the island director reported to the AMC in October 1900:

> (T)here are neighbors upon Meredith Neck, Bickford & Brown, who run a steam launch, the *Fawn*, during the season, supplying campers with the necessities of life,-- meats, vegetables, milk, ice, etc. By ordering a day in advance one can obtain anything that can be found in the stores at Meredith."[1]

During this early period, the island services business was dominated by 'tinkerers', i.e. mechanically oriented individuals who 'could fix anything'. Some of the earliest vacationers fit well in this milieu. William Puffer and Paul Goodrich, for example, were engineers. Most vacationers were also amateur handymen who did some of their own construction. They were complemented by professional carpenters who came out to the islands for specific projects. One of the most sought after in this regard was James P. Leighton of Center Harbor. He built Mansfield's tower in 1898, and he built all of the larger buildings on Three Mile Island in the early 1900s.

But as the vacationing population really began to take off in the early 1900s, a new type of island service provider emerged. These people bought island property and became island residents.

George Washington 'Spinach' Greene

The first person to take this step on Bear Island was George Washington Greene (1872 – c.1935) whose hard work, multiple skills, and typically good humor were warmly remembered by vacationers. Greene had a lean build and a scraggly beard that earned him the nickname of 'Spinach' after the curled stringiness of it. He was from Center Harbor where he was a carpenter and also served as sheriff, at least for a little while.

Greene established himself as an indispensable handyman not only for island dwellers on East Bear but also on Birch, Jolly, and Welch islands as well.[2] He maintained Eleazer Bickford's seasonal farm on the backland (old Lot 6S) where he also had a small orchard. In addition to fruit vegetables, and other supplies, he provided ice to islanders and ran a taxi-service for them. By 1911, he had established a store near the East Bear maildock.[3]

---

[1] Three Mile Island Camp, p. 8. There were others, of course, including Benjamin 'Frank' Brown who operated his steamer out of Blackey's Cove near Center Harbor.

[2] See Gunstock Parish, pp. 238-239; Bradford, "Birch Island," p. 20; Forbes, "Gone But Not Forgotten...Ernest Abbott." Mary Donsker, Welch, pp. 26-27; Carvell, Far Echo Cove, p. 5.

[3] See Elliot Burwell's 1911 map of Winnipesaukee. Greene also apparently developed a road from the mail dock up to his farm, and the "broad road" continued on to Mansfield's observation tower. Rev. Kenneth Forbes to Islanders, July 1927.

In c. 1903, he also took on the contract to maintain three of the newly installed light buoys that the state had set up around the lake for navigation purposes.[1] These were powered by kerosene, and every two days he would ride out in the evenings to refill the lamps. One of the most enjoyable activities for islanders—especially kids-- was to take a 'lighting trip' with Spinach. These evening cruises always included treats, songs, and stories.[2]

Spinach became part of the fabric of island life for vacationers in the early 1900s. Kenneth Carvell recalled of his days renting on Birch: "Buying from (George Greene) was part of the day's entertainment. He knew all the local gossip, and was eager to pass it on. He seemed happier to see the islanders than to make money."[3] The experience on Welch Island had a similar ring to it:

"He provided cheerful taxi service, and if one wanted to go mountain climbing he'd come back and pick you up, take you to the mountain and guide you to the top. Then he would deliver you safely back to camp. It must have been a special experience with him as a guide, especially since Spinach was very 'well read' being able to talk about everything from how to repel skunks to current events."[4]

George Greene on the left at Welch Island c. 1910. (Mary Donsker photo).

Greene's barn on Lot 6S c. 1938 (Roger Dolan).

---

[1] The buoys were located off Sandy Island, the Barber's Pole between Tuftonborough Neck and Cow Island, and off Melvin Island. Jolly Island: One Hundred Years, 1893 – 1993, p. 51.
[2] Ibid. Greene gave the lanterns to the Newland family on East Bear when the light buoys became electrified. The Newlands donated them to the Gilford Historical Society Museum.
[3] Carvell, Far Echo Cove, p. 5.
[4] Donsker, Welch, p. 27.

Greene was also an entrepreneur who hoped to use real estate to make his fortune. Aside from the East Bear parcel he sold to Luce, he also attempted a large vacation-oriented subdivision on Meredith Neck. He bought the 95 acre Neck Lot 80 facing Stonedam Island to the south in 1910.[1] The development was not successful, and he sold it in 1913 to Charles Hubbard.[2] Greene also apparently gave up his islands' business in 1913,[3] although he held on to his property on Bear Island until 1928. In that year, he sold his shorefront lot,[4] and he transferred ownership of the backland to his son, Frank. He moved to Gilmanton where he lived for many years thereafter working in the real estate business.

The Merrills of North Bear and the Fays of East Bear

On North Bear, George Merrill and his family expanded the services business a great deal more. They arrived in 1906, buying the property next to the wharf. They were entrepreneurs and became local legends for the full range of services that they provided to islanders.[5] These services included carpentry (they built quite a few houses around the islands), an ice delivery business, and a store. In later years, they also tried their hand unsuccessfully at real estate development on Pine Island and the Neck's Fairhaven development across from Loon Island.[6]

The Merrills island business eventually spawned another one, that of Wilbur Fay. Wilbur (1904 – 1958) was the son of Park and Hattie Merrill Fay. He spent his early summers learning the trades from his grandfather, George Merrill, and his father on North Bear. At the age of 14, he began working the non-summer seasons for the W. J. McDuff Machine Company in Lakeport. In his mid-teens, he worked summers at Camp Passaconaway, driving their boats and picking up campers, mail, and supplies. He also served as a handyman for the Appalachian Mountain Club on Three Mile Island.

In 1928, Wilbur married Hazel Cleary. He moved to East Bear (#140) three years later to establish his own summer business. Like others before him, he delivered ice and groceries, and provided hauling services, carpentry, and plumbing to anyone who needed it on East Bear, Birch, Jolly, and Steamboat among other islands. In 1944, he started his own marina on Varney Point in Gilford. His son, Merrill, was born in 1936, and by the end of the 1940s, he was playing an active part in his dad's businesses from their home at the end of the colony. By the latter 1940s, Wilbur and Hazel had moved to Rochester, NH, for the off-season where he was the hockey coach for Spaulding High School. His son, Merrill, graduated from Spaulding in 1954, spent one year at Phillips Exeter Prep school, and then attended the University of Michigan. Merrill's matriculation was cut short in 1958 by the death of his father. Merrill returned to New

---

[1] B/P 136/498; 136/492.
[2] B/P 136/501. Old Hubbard Rd. was named after Charles.
[3] Much of Greene's island services business was picked up by Ernest Abbott who came to Winnipesaukee in 1913. See Forbes, "Gone But Not Forgotten...Ernest Abbott."
[4] B/P 190/13.
[5] Bear Island Reflections, pp. 33-39.
[6] In 1922, they bought several lots on Pine Island that were eventually foreclosed upon the following year. B/P 163/263; 168/289.

Hampshire and took over the family business. He became something of a legend around the lake in his own right, a worthy successor to all of the unique lake men who preceded him.

The Mail Boat Service: 1902, not 1892

Since the 1960s or so, lake histories have consistently dated the beginning of the mail boat service on Winnipesaukee as 1892. However, the first mail boat service on Lake Winnipesaukee was not awarded until 1902. The confusion arose from mixing up the date of the first post office on Bear Island (1892) with the first mail boat service.[1]

The mail boat service was a product of the Rural Free Delivery program which was first introduced experimentally by the U.S. Postal Service in West Virginia in 1896.[2] It was immediately welcomed by the largely rural population of the country. After a few years of experimentation, a process was established by which RFD routes were awarded upon receipt of a petition with at least 100 signatures. Rural Free Delivery became a permanent service when it was finally fully authorized by the U.S. Congress in 1902. By then, the Post Office had received more than 10,000 petitions. The Winnipesaukee mail boat was one of 24 new RFD routes opened that year in New Hampshire.

Winnipesaukee was the first water route established in the country. At the time, there were two post offices on the lake, one at the Bear Island House and the other at the Long Island House. The idea of the mail boat was recognized as a real boon for islanders, promoted by some as benefiting perhaps 1000 people. It enhanced the attractiveness of the islands, allowing vacationers to keep in touch with their regular affairs. As one contemporary observer phrased it, with the new mail boat "this becomes a desirable spot for a summer vacation."[3]

Dr. George Saltmarsh of Lakeport was appointed 'carrier' when the mail contract was first awarded in June 1902, but it was understood that the work would be handled "under his direction by a sub-carrier."[4] Saltmarsh was an avid steam boater when not fulfilling his first love of providing medical care to the citizens of Lakeport.[5] The sub-carrier was Archie L. Lewis of Lakeport. The contract was awarded with the understanding that a new steamboat, specifically being built for the mail service, would be ready to carry the mail beginning in July 1902. In the interim, the first craft to carry the mail was Saltmarsh's small steam boat, the *Robert and Arthur*.[6]

---

[1] It is difficult to pin down how the confusion began. It may have resulted from a little book by Ronald Gallup, Lake Winnipesaukee, written in 1969, that used the 1892 date. See p. 20. Among recent publications to pick up this date, see, for example: Sophie C website, *CruiseNH.com; "Special Delivery, @Boston.com, July 31, 2011*; Bruce Heald, Meredith, p. 81; Bear Island Reflections, p. 42.
[2] There are various histories of RFD on the internet. See, for example, "The History of Rural Free Delivery," *www.grit.com*.
[3] The Boston Herald, May 25, 1902 and July 6, 1902.
[4] The Boston Herald, May 25, 1902, p. 10.
[5] See, Blackstone, Farwell Old Mount, 88-89. Saltmarsh started practicing medicine in Laconia in 1884 after graduating from Dartmouth College. He was also active in politics, serving one term as a representative in the state legislature in the mid-1890s. In 1909, well after his mail boating days had ended, Saltmarsh purchased vacation property on the western shore of North Bear Island.

Arthur.[1] The new steamer, the *Dolphin*, was built "by a local syndicate" of Lakeport men and went into service in 1903.[2] As demand picked up from the increase in the summer population, a still larger boat became a necessity. In 1907, the iconic *Uncle Sam* took over the mail delivery services under Lewis. Archie Lewis went on to operate the mail service on the lake for 30 years.[3]

The *Uncle Sam*

In later years, he took most of the credit for getting the mail service for the lake.

> "I thought up the scheme of rural delivery by water. I went down to Washington and talked with Congressmen and the Postmaster General. They told me if I could get the names of 100 families on the lake they'd recommend the plan to committee. My goodness, I had to stir around to get 100 families in those days. We took in shacks and everything."[4]

The mail boat ran two trips a day from Monday through Saturday during July and August, and one trip each day during the shoulder months of summer. In addition to mail, the boat carried newspapers, supplies, telegrams, and baggage. Initially, however, the use of the mail boat was slow to catch on. Lewis recalled: "I didn't need any assistance at first, I could carry all the mail in my pocket."[5]

Based at Lakeport, the first route established by the Post Office included 17 stops.[6]

---

[1] Lewis took over the mail contract from Saltmarsh in 1903, after Dr. Saltmarsh resigned. Blaisdell wrote that the mail service did not actually begin until 1903 due to problems with the boat. Three Centuries, p. 61. I have not found any definitive information either way; however, one newspaper report in July 1902 clearly suggests that the service was up and running then: "...the daily double service (i.e. two trips per day) of free mail delivery ... went into effect July 1..." The Boston Herald, July 6, 1902, p. 33.

[2] The Boston Herald, May 25, 1902, p. 10.

[3] Archie's brother, Orrin H. Lewis, was the mail carrier on RFD#1 in Lakeport in 1902. Orrin later became the manager of the Bear Island House. Bear Island Reflections, p. 42; Farewell Old Mount, p. 89.

[4] The New York Herald Tribune, July 12, 1936. Blackstone's history gives Saltmarsh credit for the idea. Blackstone, Farewell Old Mount, p. 89.

[5] Ibid.

[6] Historical Sketches of Lakeport (1915), "The Post Office." This list differed from the May 1902 announcement carried in the papers.

Outward bound Leg	Return Trip
The Weirs	Long Island wharf
Eagle Island	Camp Island
Tuttle's Landing (near Horse Island)	Timber Island
Bear Island wharf	Round Island
Pine Island (southern end)	Pitchwood Island
Three Mile Island	Lakeport
Five Mile Island	
Quinby's Island (i.e. Dollar Island)	
Jolly Island	
Birch Island	
Sandy Island	
Cow Island (Camp Idlewild)	

Various other stops were added in the years following. East Bear Island was added permanently in 1906. At one time or another, other stops on Bear Island included Mansfield's White Mountain Park (old Lot 9), Goodrich's Landing (French Cove), and Camp Passaconaway (now Nokomis). Other nearby stops included Lovejoy's Landing, Loon Island, and the Gypsy Camp on Meredith Neck (Black Cove).

Telephone Service

Telephone service was extended to Bear Island in 1903. The phone company ran the wires from Meredith Neck across Goose Island to Pine and then over to Bear .[1] The wires to Pine were above ground.[2] An underwater cable was run across to Bear. The connection with the latter was celebrated by island residents at an evening event that included concerts and remarks by Congressman Samuel Powers of Newton, MA.[3] The demand for phone services was probably led by Sol Lovejoy for the Bear Island House and the Speare family on Pine. The Speares also owned extensive shorefront on the Neck in the vicinity of Pine.

Solomon Lovejoy's Son, Ralph

Ralph Lovejoy was born in 1884, just a year after Sol and Lizzie acquired the Bear Island property of Waldo Meloon. Ralph was an apple that did not fall far from the tree when it came to mechanical genius. Ralph grew up during the automobile age. His focus rested upon the quality of the ride offered by new cars. Among other things, Ralph began experimenting with shock

---

[1] The mainland take-off point was then owned by Ohio Barber.Iit is now The Oliver Lodge. Goose Island was owned by the Pine Island Outing Club.

[2] See B/P 119/323.

[3] *Boston Herald*, August 23, 1903, p. 28. On a side note, Powers donated the land for what is now Powers Road, the side road off of the Neck Road that provides access to the shorefront facing Pine Island, Goose Island, and part of Kelley Cove. In the early days, those places were only accessible by boat.

absorbers, and in 1919, he invented a lever-armed hydraulic damper that was designed to cushion the ride significantly. The hydraulic feature was a major improvement over the dry friction snubbers that were traditionally used. In 1921, he incorporated the Lovejoy Manufacturing Company in Brookline, MA to manufacture his shock absorbers, and he trade-marked the product. It became very popular. In 1922, a former salesman of his established a distributorship in Los Angeles exclusively to market the Lovejoy hydraulic shock absorber. Ralph improved the product thereafter, getting his last patent in 1926.

Sol, Ralph, and Lizzie c. 1892 (Thompson-Wright)

By the latter 1920s, the General Motors Company began knocking off Ralph's shock absorbers without paying him. It was a wild and wooly era in the auto industry, and GM was pushing hard at the head of the pack. Originally formed in 1908, GM had grown rapidly through acquisition in the 1920s. Its modus operandi was generally to ignore legal niceties and use muscle to get its way. Ralph would have none of it. He sued GM for patent and trade-mark infringement. In 1927, the court found in Ralph's favor. GM was forced to buy Ralph's company, paying him something like $800,000.[1]

Ralph moved to St. Petersburg Beach, Florida, sometime thereafter. He built a number of beach cottages that he named the 'Wiggin Cottages' after his mother's maiden name. Ralph managed the operation until his death in 1953.[2]

Jerry Point and The Gulf: From where did these names come?

Jerry Point and The Gulf are among the very few places on Bear Island that were given 'names' around the turn of the 20th century. Neither of these names derived from the early history of the island. The 19th century farmers were not concerned with names for places. In the early days, place names arose from some immediate logic, typically based upon the last name of an owner of a property or some descriptive term. Life was simple, however hard it might be. There just were not that many places that required names during the era when there were few people, travel was fairly limited, and there was no mail to be delivered. In the latter part of the 19th

---

[1] This was a huge sum of money in those days, the equivalent of many millions today. GM consolidated the business into its Delco Products operations in Ohio. "The Changing U.S. Auto Industry: A Geographical Analysis," James M. Rubenstein, NY, 1992.
[2] Based upon information provided by Ralph's step-son, written in the Winnipesaukee.com general forum by 'dockrat8', May 24, 2013.

century and into the 20th century, place names began to proliferate. In most cases, they were simply 'thought up' or 'manufactured'. In the Lakes Region, perhaps the two most obvious names that fell into this category were invented in 1871 when Long Bay was changed to Lake Paugus and Round Bay was changed to Lake Opechee by Professor J. Warren Thyng, and by his associate, Martin Hayne, the editor of the Lake Village News.[1] The original names had been given by James Hersey on his map of the lake in 1772.

There were no place names on the early maps of Bear Island. The most detailed and accurate map of the lake was William Crocker's chart completed for the Lake Company in 1858. It showed only a few place names and descriptions around the lake. Near Bear, the only label he inserted was the 'Ferry' landing that is now Cattle Landing. In a few other places, he used names of unknown origins. For example, on the western side of the Neck facing Stonedam Island, he named Tommy's Cove, Flag Cove, and Fish Cove. He also labeled Kelley Cove and Advent Cove. But on Bear, there was no Gulf and no Jerry Point.

With the coming of the vacation era, more and more attention began to be paid to the lake. It was a period in time during which the fashion was to 'name' places, much like they did in old Europe. The era began in the early 1880s on Bear. Sol Lovejoy, for example, named his property Kunnaway (Abenaki for 'bear'). Other vacationers also adopted the practice.

In the case of 'The Gulf', the term came into use before the mid-1880s. Winfield Hawkes picked it up in 1885 when researching his booklet about the lake for the railroad.[2] Interestingly, he understood it to reference the Carry Cove and its west-side islands. Wrote Hawkes:

> "About half-way down the west shore (of Bear) is 'The Gulf,' where the bear was shot which gave the island its name; in this gulf are some pretty islands, and about its shores several nice sandy beaches."[3]

In 1903, the Winnipesaukee Yacht Club was established in Gilford by summer residents from Boston. Among other things, this group was greatly concerned with navigation on the lake. Elliot Burwell of Boston was its first secretary-treasurer. An ocean man, Burwell was an avid sailor and ship designer among other things. In 1907, he took up the task of producing the first detailed navigational map of Winnipesaukee.[4] 'The Gulf' and 'Jerry Point' were two of the Bear Island 'names' enshrined on it along with Aunt Dolly's Point.

Burwell placed 'The Gulf' in the location described by Hawkes on his first map in 1907. However, when his map was reprinted four years later, 'The Gulf' label was moved to the northern side of the point. It has been used to name that area ever since. Regardless, the choice

---

[1] See Heyduk, Stories in the History, pp. 149-150.
[2] For context suggesting its then common usage, see Hawkes, p. 35.
[3] Hawkes, p. 45. See also: Springfield Republican (MA), October 1, 1887, p. 8.
[4] For some background, see "Boating Magazine," April 1907, pp. 27-28. Burwell was a life member of the Appalachian Mountain Club which built its camp on Pine Island in 1900.

of the term 'Gulf' is still a mystery. Its use is almost unprecedented on inland waterways. It is an ocean term and certainly not a term or name that any of the old farmers, like the Bickfords, would have used. Speculatively, the name perhaps arose from people associated with the commercial steamers that carried passengers daily along those shores. Maybe something about the cove and its islands reminded them of a previous experience, or maybe they simply wanted a different term than the historical descriptions of Carrying Place and Carrying Place islands.

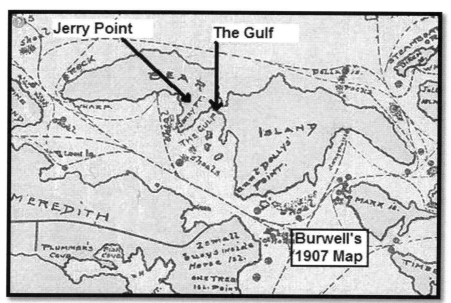

Elliot Burwell's 1907 map of Bear Island[1]

The origin of the name 'Jerry Point' eludes any determination. It was not referenced anywhere by Winfield Hawkes. It is widely assumed by islanders that the name somehow derived from James Bickford, the long time owner of the point. As logical as that seems, there is nothing in the historical records to hint at the possibility. James Bickford was always simply referred to as 'James' in the historical documents. E.H. Maloon, a Meredith businessman who knew James Bickford, referred to him in 1936 newspaper articles as "Uncle Jimmie Bickford" and "Uncle Jim Bickford".[2]

Furthermore, the Bickford family did not use the name to refer to the property. As late as 1905, James Bickford's son, Moses, explicitly referred to the area simply as the 'Point' in a deed in which he sold timbering rights to the Meredith Shook and Lumber Company. The pertinent language in the deed was "excepting and reserving a clump of trees near a sandy beach ...and another clump southerly of the above on 'the point', so called..."[3]

---

[1] Mistakes could easily happen, especially in those days. Note on the map segment above that Burwell misplaced Fish Cove to what was then known as Round Cove, and he used the name of Plummer Cove for what was then Fish Cove. The names Fish Cove, Round Cove, Flag Cove, and Tommy's Cove were all established in 1858 on Crocker's map. The use of Plummer's Cove catches one's attention because that is the name used by James Little for the otherwise unnamed cove northwest of Dolly Point.
[2] Meredith News, "Glancing Over Meredith's Past," November 15, 1922 and Nov 18, 1922. Maloon was related to Waldo Meloon.
[3] B/P 116/357.

Nevertheless, 'Jerry Point' entered the lexicon in the early 1900s. Its first 'official' appearance was on Burwell's 1907 map of the lake. How or from whom he picked it up remains anyone's guess.   One possibility is the name was given to it by the Meredith Shook and Lumber Company to identify its operations there.

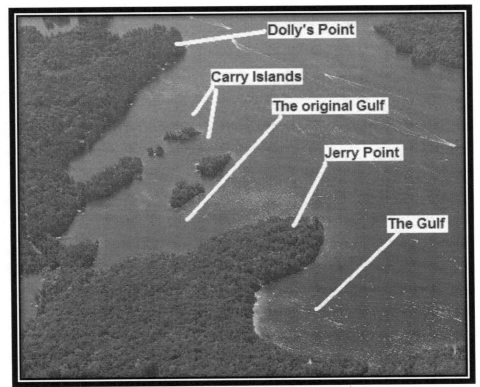

'The Gulf' and other place names.[1]

---

[1] Deep cove is another 'place name' on Bear Island, although it did not appear on any of the lake maps. Interestingly, the name—"deep cove so called"-- appeared in the deeds as early as 1837 when Mac Lovejoy sold old Lot 9 to John Batchelder. See B/P 9016/207. There is no mystery to its origins. It is a descriptive name typical of the 19th century. The water in the cove is very deep. It was not until the vacation era that people began inventing names for places. The name Deep Cove was widely used in the 1920s after the Chapel was built on the island. See, for example, correspondence of Rev. Kenneth Forbes, April 13, 1927, in which he references "the church's landing in Deep Cove." Occasionally people refer to it as Church Cove.

Chapter Twenty-Seven

The Summer Era on Bear: circa 1910 to 1920

The pace of change on Bear Island slowed considerably during the decade from 1910 to 1920 as a result of World War I. The number of newly purchased vacation places dropped dramatically from 21 during the previous decade to only six. The most noteworthy feature of the period was another changing of the guard that took place on all sections of North Bear (old Lots 1-4) and part of South Bear (old Lots 5 and 6N). The changes entailed the final departure of all the ownership ties to the Meredith families whose presence had informed Bear for decades.

North Bear

Crane's Point

John Crane, in some ways the island's first vacationer, died in January 1910. Crane's death halted the subdivision of that piece of the island into more vacation homes. His 1908 plan for 'Bear Island Park' was not pursued by his heirs. His property passed to his wife, Clara, and their two granddaughters, Bertha Coleman and Winnifred Tetley. In 1913, Clara and Winnifred transferred their interests to Bertha. Ownership of the property remained in Bertha's family into the 1920s.[1]

The Hotel

There is almost no information available about the hotel operations following George Collins' 1909 acquisition of it. He did make "a substantial addition...to the landing facilities" during the summer of 1909, but that is all we know.[2] It likely prospered under Collins until the outbreak of World War I.

[1] B/P 128/506; 138/118. Winnifred and Bertha were the daughters of John and Clara Crane's only child, Mazellah. The mother of the two was his first wife, Georgia. By 1913, Bertha was married to Adam Iovine.
[2] Boston Herald, May 30, 1909, p. 20.

Collins owned the Bear Island House for 14 years.

Lot Sales: George Mayo and the Eastern Shore of North Bear

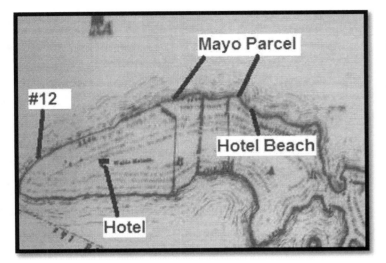

George D. Mayo had purchased a large swath of shorefront on the eastern side of North Bear from George Collins in 1909. He created a 12 lot subdivision for the parcel running from present-day #36 through #52. It bordered a strip of some 100 feet of the beach (later known as Alvord Beach) used by hotel guests.

Mayo (1850 – 1920) was the son of William Mayo who, like Walter Aiken, was an inventor and builder of knitting machines. William Mayo had moved his family from West Lynn, MA to Franklin, NH in the late 1880s to expand his involvement in the knitting industry. George D. Mayo followed in his father's footsteps and developed further inventions related to the knitting machine. In 1903, he established his own company, The George D. Mayo Machine Company, in Lakeport, where the Mayo Knitting Machine was manufactured. Similar to

the Aiken family, the knitting machines focused upon seamless hosiery. In 1911, Mayo merged his company with Scott & Williams which became a leading employer in the area for many years thereafter.[1]

But Mayo's business success did not translate into real estate success on Bear Island. He was unable to sell a single lot in his subdivision. The eastern side of the island was the least attractive at the time, and the outbreak of World War I in 1914 further curtailed vacation interest. George died in 1920, and the property passed to his widow and son.

Lot Sales: George Collins Activities on North Bear

George Collins also had virtually no success selling lots on the other parts of the eastern side of North Bear during this period. His parcels comprised two large sections of shorefront on either side of the Mayo parcel. To the north of Mayo's subdivision, there were eventually 12 lots that emerged (#14 through #34). To the south of Mayo and running to the wall bordering old Lot

---

[1] Fibre & Fabric,: The American Textile Trade Review, January 7, 1911, p. 13.

4, there eventually emerged another nine lots (#53 through #62, plus an unnumbered lot next to the wall).

In all of this stretch, only a single lot was sold before the 1920s. John H. Murphy of Boston bought a parcel (#58), not far from the Lot 4 wall, in 1917.[1] Murphy never built on it. The entire eastern side of North Bear remained uninhabited from the former Meloon house (#12) next to Crane's Point all the way down to old Lot 4.

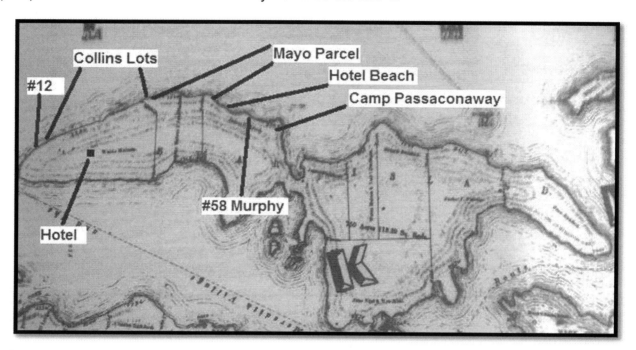

It was a similar story on the western side of North Bear. Collins developed his own 12 lot subdivision on the vacant land located amongst the lots previously sold by Sol Lovejoy. But Collins made his only sale in 1914 when Carl Sanborn, a young postal clerk from Laconia, bought a lot (#393) located just south of William Wright in The Gulf.[2] With the Sanborn purchase, the western shore colony on North Bear grew from 17 to 18 separate places, stretching from Sanborn's (#393) around Crane's Point to former Meloon house (#12) by then owned by the Merriam family.

The Bickfords Depart from Old Lot 4

At the beginning of 1910, old Lot 4 was still almost entirely owned by Moses Bickford and his children. Only three small lots had been previously sold by Moses in the Carry Cove on the

---

[1] B/P 170/164. This became the Marselis lot in 1923.

[2] B/P 140/430. George Collins was involved in some other major real estate ventures during this period as well. In 1910, just after buying the Bear Island property from Solomon, he bought a large swath of land on the end of the Neck facing Stonedam Island from George 'Spinach' Greene. The land was part of original Lot 80. Collins developed a comprehensive subdivision plan for the property that laid out 19 building lots, but he had only modest success in selling them. Collins also purchased various other properties on the Neck, including shorefront opposite Pine Island and down towards Center Harbor (pieces of original Lots 62 and 77). He was not successful in selling many lots in these areas either. These had to be trying times for Collins as he had taken on extensive mortgage debt to finance his many ventures.

eastern side of the island. These lots were now consolidated under L. D Fogg. In 1910, the Bickfords sold Fogg an additional 170' of frontage, increasing his total shorefront in the cove to 240'.[1]

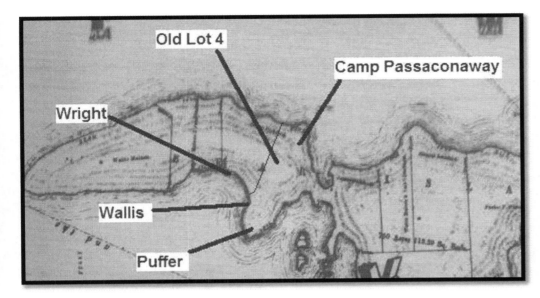

The first big step in the transition to the summer era occurred later in 1910 when Moses' son, Roy Bickford, sold his entire 1100' shoreline parcel (running from #377 to #384) to L. Theodore Wallis of Brookline, Massachusetts.[2] Wallis was a 1905 graduate of Dartmouth and was teaching at the Browne and Nichols School in Cambridge, MA in 1910. He bought the property on Bear with the idea of establishing a boys' camp on the island, something that never came to fruition.[3] In 1912, Wallis bought Treasure Island (known as Red Head Island back then), near Rattlesnake Island, where he started a boys' camp called Mishe Mokwa that operated for 25 years.[4] Nevertheless, Wallis held on to the Bear Island property until after World War I.

These sales were but a precursor of the future. By 1911, Moses (66) was not in good health and nearing the end of his life.[5] In 1912, he and his daughters sold all of the family's remaining island property in two separate transactions, bringing to an end the Bickford era on Lot 4.

The first transaction was the sale of the western half of Lot 4--Jerry Point-- to William Puffer in January.[6] Puffer was an 1884 graduate of MIT where he had finished first in his class. He was hired that year by MIT to teach physics and head a newly established dynamo-electrical department. He moved up the professorial ranks at MIT until he resigned in 1907 and established his own electrical engineering company that provided expert consulting services.

---

[1] B/P 128/199.

[2] B/P 129/368. The property included the Bickford's icehouse (now part of #380 Bear) that was built sometime before the turn of the century. Current Meredith Tax information suggests that the house at #380 was built in 1895, presumably reflecting the long standing presence of the ice house before Wallis bought the property. There is no way to determine when it was actually built.

[3] B/P 129/368; 136/429.

[4] B/P 137/296. See Chapter 37.

[5] Moses died in 1913 and was laid to rest in the Meetinghouse Cemetery. His son, Roy, continued to live on the family farm on the Neck for years thereafter. Roy later became a town Selectman.

[6] BCRI, B/P 133/115.

By 1912, Puffer had already spent nearly than two and a half decades summering on

Bear Island. William and his four brothers were quite adventuresome. In 1886, they spent more than a month rowing around the entire lake, similar to the sojourns of E. Channing Mansfield.[1] Beginning in the late 1880s, the families of Puffer and his brother-in-law, William Wright, spent a few summers camping on the island property (#404) of Puffer's MIT Professor, Silas Holman. After Wright bought his own place in 1895, the two families spent their

William Puffer at the Wright's place c. 1895.

summers there. During this time, Puffer also acquired a couple of steamboats, called the *Wanderer* and *Wanderer II*, and built a boathouse for them.

William Puffer's *Wanderer* and boathouse at Wright's place c. 1895.

Within days of the sale to Puffer, the Bickfords sold the land on the eastern 'half' of old Lot 4 to Wallace Richmond and Alfred Dickinson, two highly respected Newton, Massachusetts high school teachers.[2] The former taught physics and natural history and the latter mathematics and athletics. They proceeded to establish the first summer camp on Bear Island. It catered to boys aged nine to 15 and focused upon sports and good citizenship. They called it

Camp Passaconaway in honor of the 17th century Penacook chief who had lived in harmony with the early colonial settlers. Richmond and Dickinson quickly developed Passaconaway into a

---

[1] The Puffer boys kept a diary of the trip which they entitled "The Logbook of the Homeless Wanderers". The diary is still held on Jerry Point by William Puffer's granddaughter, Ellee Thompson.
[2] B/P 133/141.

very successful camp. They built a main lodge, various sheds, a directors' cabin, tent platforms, a baseball field, and tennis courts for the campers. Passaconaway flourished despite World War I. The number of boys grew from about 30 initially to 80 (plus 20 counselors) by 1918.[1]

South Bear

Carry Cove Sales and Generational Change on Old Lots 5 and 6N

The western side of the Carry coves, facing the Neck, contained only the two homes of George Thurston and Harriett Bradford in 1910. In 1911, a third lot (#351) was sold by David Frank Gilman to J. Willis and Lizzie S. Mead whose permanent home was on Meredith Neck.[2] The lot was tiny, a trapezoid with only 25' of frontage. It was located south of and adjacent to the lot Gilman had sold to Bradford. Willis Mead was the son of Neck resident, Joseph R. Mead II, who was a direct descendant of the 1760s Meredith settler, William Mead.

The sale to Mead was the last made by David Frank Gilman who passed away in 1912.[3] His death ended the seasonal farming era on this part of Bear for all practical purposes. He left the island properties to his younger sister, Ellen Lil Prescott (60). She had long since moved to Oakland, California. Her husband was Frederick S. Prescott, a former Meredith Neck farmer whose family lived across the Neck road from the James Gilman farm where she grew up. Fred owned a sewing machine business in Oakland. The couple had one biological son and three adopted children.

---

[1] See Bear Island Reflections, pp.97 – 105.
[2] B/P 135/310.
[3] He was buried in the family's Gilman Cemetery on Meredith Neck just south of the home originally built by James Gilman in 1790.

Ellen Lil undertook an aggressive marketing effort to sell the property on Bear Island as well as the extensive Gilman land on the Neck.[1] As part of the marketing effort, she commissioned George W. Bartlett of Meredith to complete a subdivision of the island property in 1914. Bartlett's plan divided Lots 5 and 6N into 40 shore lots.[2]

But like George Mayo and George Collins on North Bear, Ellen Lil had little luck in selling the lots. Her only land sales occurred in the Carry coves where western-facing, existing vacationers modestly expanded their properties across the Carry isthmus to the base of the cove on the east side of the island.[3] These small sales were the only ones made by Ellen Lil over a ten year period.

The East Bear Island colony: 1910 - 1920

The East Bear colony enjoyed the addition of one new place during the decade. In 1911, Joe Pickford, a Boston businessman, purchased a large lot (#131 and 133 combined) just north of the mail dock. With his arrival, the East Bear colony consisted of ten families, and it spanned the entire shoreline of old Lot 6S and spilled a little way north along the shore of old Lot 6N.[4] It was about this time that George Greene gave up his island services business, although he retained his shorefront lot and summer farm on Bear.

Lot 7: Aiken's Property

The status quo remained unchanged on James Aiken's old Lot 7 and French Cove. Aiken made no additional land sales between 1910 and 1920. The little colony consisted of five houses. James was located in Aiken Cove, separated by a good distance from French Cove where Paul Goodrich, Phil Gokey, Albert Gokey, and their sister, Annie Duquette had purchased lots.

Multiple Generational Change and the Final Departure of the Bickfords on Old Lot 8

In 1910, old Lot 8 (the future Camp Lawrence) continued to be owned by the sons of Jonathan Bickford Jr. But Joseph L. Bickford died in 1914, and his brother, Charles S., passed away two years later, in 1916. The Bear Island property was then inherited by eight extended family members, including Hezekiah Bickford, Charles H. Bickford, Solomon Lovejoy, and Ezra Lovejoy.[5] In January 1918, Hezekiah Bickford bought out the other heirs.[6] He had grown up on the Neck, but his home by this time was in Lakeport where he owned a machine shop and

---

[1] She inherited large holdings (#64 Meredith Neck Rd.) from David Frank, and in 1912, she purchased the 100 acre James Gilman homestead next door (#76) and the 80 acre Mead lot from her brother, Granville. The land included Pinnacle Hill. B/P 135/127.
[2] Bartlett's Plan was not recorded.
[3] BCRI, B/P 140/371; 142/405; 138/151; 126/465.
[4] This total includes George Greene and Badlam's place that was located well down the shore on Lot 5.
[5] All eight were cousins of the deceased. Brothers Hezekiah and Charles were sons of Charles Bickford, the former owner of Bear Lot 6S . Brothers Ezra and Solomon Lovejoy were sons of Eleanor Bickford Lovejoy, an aunt of the deceased.
[6] B/P 150/493.

manufacturing company called Sun Tools.[1] But in September 1918, Hezekiah passed away. Ownership of Lot 8 then passed to his three children-- Harry Bickford, Nellie Sanborn, and Gustavia Wilkinson. The three had no interest in retaining the property. They sold it in 1919 to lumber dealers, Harry Kendrick and Charles Gilbert, of Hudson, NH.[2] The sale marked the departure from Bear Island of the last property owners with direct ties to the original Bear Island settlers. Lot 8 had been occupied by the Jonathan Bickford Sr. family since at least 1805 (over 114 years).

A Little Change on Dolly's Point

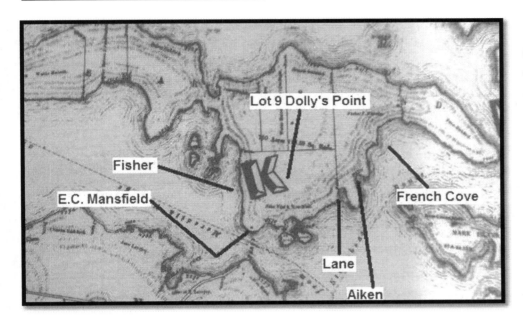

Dolly's Point enjoyed some modest growth during this period. Two additional lots were sold by E. Channing Mansfield. The first (now part of #323) was purchased in 1911 by Fred W. Fisher, a department store buyer from Manchester, NH.[3] It was located on the northwest side of Dolly's Point, slotted between the lots sold to Dr. Brown and John Renfrew in 1906. The other lot sale (#282) was noteworthy because it was well outside of Mansfield's subdivision. It was located at the entrance to Deep Cove, well to the south of Mansfield's place and the rest of the colony. The lot was purchased by Frank W. Lane in 1918. He preferred that location because it put him in closer proximity to French Cove. He was related to the Gokey clan through marriage. From Newton Center, MA, Lane at one time owned a shoe company, and he had spent time on the lake since the 1890s. He developed a passion for boats which he raced for years at the Weirs.[4]

---

[1] His machine shop was located on the spot where the steamer, *Lady of the Lake*, was originally constructed in 1849. Blaisdell, <u>Three Centuries</u>, p. 29. He had spent some of his adult life establishing his career in Cincinnati before moving back to Lake Village.
[2] BCRI, B/P 154/257; 154/330; and 155/201. Kendrick and Gilbert were not strangers to the property. They had previously purchased the timber rights on the parcel from Hezekiah Bickford in 1918 in what had become a bit of a tangled mess. Before selling the property to Hezekiah Bickford in 1918, the heirs sold the timber rights to Eugene Stowell of Ashland, NH. Stowell was supposed to only sell logs, and his end buyer was the company owned by Kendrick and Gilbert. Seven months later, Hezekiah abrogated the deal with Stowell, reselling the rights to Harry Kendrick and Charles Gilbert of Hudson, NH. He claimed that Stowell had violated the terms of his contract by cutting the logs into boards before selling them. B/P 151/26; B/P 130/374.
[3] B/P 130/374.
[4] B/P 151/480; <u>Bear Island Reflections</u>, pp. 140-141. Frank's son, Charles, was the founder of the Old Print Barn on Winona Road in New Hampton.

Chapter Twenty-Eight

The Vacation Era Takes Flight Again: The 1920s

The decade of the 1920s was a period of rapid growth on Bear Island. Coming out of World War I, the economy was expanding as was the country's population. The number of vacationers grew with them, reflecting the buoyancy of the Roaring Twenties. In 1920, there were 45 summer places, one hotel, and one boy's camp on Bear Island. By 1930, the number of summer places had increased to 64, and there were two camps and one church on the island.

North Bear

The Hotel

One of the most noteworthy changes on North Bear was another sale of the Bear Island House in 1923. George Collins sold the hotel and its grounds to J. Coleman Blair Jr. of Laconia for $10,200.[1] Collins retained ownership of all of the shorefront except the bathing beach on the east side of the island and a 25' wide strip on the west side where the hotel had a pump house and maintained a wharf.[2] Blair received the benefit of the same reservations that Waldo Meloon had insisted upon in 1873, allowing unfettered access to the steam boat wharf. Collins also reserved the right of his guests or tenants to utilize the road from the steam boat wharf to the hotel and to utilize the 'path' south of the hotel to access his land.[3]

Coleman Blair had worked in the summer hotel industry for more than twenty years before the purchase of the Bear Island House. As early as 1896, he was the manager of the Asquam House in Holderness. In 1907, he was touted as "one of the best known of the younger hotel men in the state."[4] Under Blair, the hotel enjoyed good success during the 1920s. By the mid-1920s, the hotel could accommodate 65 guests per night. Blair promoted the hotel effusively:

> "Our guests are as one large family; some have been coming for the past twenty-five years, and everyone joins hands and makes the social life one of our most attractive features. There is whist in the living room and dancing in the parlor. Musicales and other similar functions are of frequent occurrence. We have one of the best tennis courts. Many prefer to spend the evenings out of doors, and retire early; we will say that we always insist upon the termination of all gaiety at a reasonable hour. A lawn golf course of nine holes is adjacent to the house. On the

---

[1] B/P 169/195; 169/349. Blair financed most of the transaction by borrowing $3000 from the Meredith Village Savings Bank and by giving Collins a mortgage for $4200. The lower price than Collins had paid Sol Lovejoy presumably reflected the much smaller real estate footprint that Blair purchased.

[2] Now part of #420.

[3] B/P 168/339.

[4] Boston Herald, June23, 1907, p. 31. This was at a time when he was named the first manager of the Winnipiseogee Inn at Roxmont (Moultonborough Neck).

mainland, seven minutes ride by motor boat, saddle horses may be hired, also canoes and motor boats may be rented."[1]

Hotel from Sunset Rock c. 1925.   **Hotel from the south side.**

Among the attractions, Blair noted:

> -Perfect drainage and bath system with modern, sanitary plumbing.
> -A large island location with pure air, fine spring water, and a delightful panorama.
> -Although situated on an island, we have long distance telephone connections and excellent mail service.
> -We raise our own vegetables.

Rates for the summer were $2.50 per day and $12.00 to $15.00 per week, including meals.

Blair's hotel brochure went on to praise Winnipesaukee as "The Switzerland of America". It noted that "many travelers are emphatic in their belief that the delightful trips winding in and out

---

[1] "The Bear Island House," a four page brochure published by the hotel c. 1925. (Original copy provided by Jocelyn and Bill Wuester.)

among the islands surpass in scenery the views of the Swiss Lakes." The brochure was also perhaps the source of a new tidbit of historical lore, the apocryphal Bear Island's 'Deserted Village'. As part of its description of the island, the brochure included the following passage about the Jerry Point area:

"A favorite walk of three miles is to the 'Deserted Village' where one hundred years ago, a colony of sturdy pioneers held forth in their little cottages. The old cellars, an occasional fireplace, a dying orchard, the unmarked graves, and the rock pulpit of the little church, all testify to the passing of the brave colony."[1]

The success of the hotel was evidenced by Blair's ability to reduce his debt on it from $7200 to $5000 in 1928.[2] A few years later, the Meredith News observed that the hotel had become "the Mecca for many summer visitors…beautifully located…(and) one of the landmarks of that section. … They built up such a name for genuine hospitality that the place became well known and many famous people were sheltered there."[3]

Cleared top of North Bear with the hotel seen back left.

With its success, the hotel continued to be a feeder for island vacationers who purchased their own places after staying at the hotel. A classic example was that of Dr. Chester and Mary Brown of Arlington, New Jersey. They honeymooned at the hotel in 1923. They enjoyed the

---

[1] The 'Deserted Village' story was repeated almost verbatim in 1927 by the captain of the mailboat in his travelogue as he passed Bear Island. See: Mailboat brochure, 1927. The mailboat's travelogue also referenced the schoolhouse in the Carry, although it added another 100 years to the historical time frame.
[2] B/P 187/301; 187/303. He refinanced his mortgages in September 1928 by increasing his first mortgage from the Meredith Village Savings Bank to $4500 and paying down his mortgage with Collins to $500.
[3] Meredith News, November 15, 1934

island so much that they purchased the former Holman place (#404) the following year.[1] In an oft repeated pattern among island vacationers, they invited friends and colleagues to spend time with them on Bear. Another New Jersey medical doctor, Edward Willan and his wife, Mildred, were among them. The Willans were so enamored of the island, they purchased their own summer cottage just up the shore (#431).[2]

The Shorefront: The Western Colony on North Bear

As noted, George Collins retained almost all shore frontage that he originally purchased from Sol Lovejoy. During the 1920s, he had additional success in selling off five of the remaining six lots he owned on the western side of Bear to: Myra Fletcher of Newton, MA (#415, 1923); Edward Matz of Bradford, PA (#428, 1923); Clara Roberts of Somerville, MA (#421-422, 1927); Edith Bulkley of Arlington, NJ (#416, 1928); and Walter Jacques of Laconia (#385, 1929).[3] On this most vibrant stretch of the island from the steam boat wharf south into the Gulf, these sales brought the total number of vacation places to 23, including the two houses (Iovine and Merrill) on John Crane's land.

The Shorefront: Eastern Side of North Bear

The eastern side of North Bear also continued to belong to George A. Collins. Inhabited only by the Merriam family (#12) next to Crane's Point, Collins continued to struggle to find buyers. It was not until 1928 that he finally sold his first lot. R.J. Titherington, a chemist from Philadelphia, PA, bought a lot (#14) with 50' of frontage next door to Merriam.[4] Collins had no other success during the 1920s.

Further south on the Mayo parcel, there was even less success. Following the death of George D. Mayo in 1920, his son George inherited the property. But he apparently was preoccupied with other matters. No lots were sold. As a result, the long northeastern shorefront of North Bear remained vacant from the Titherington lot all of the way down to the hotel beach.

North Bear 'Beach Colony' Takes Shape

A far different pattern emerged further south of the hotel beach on old Lot 3. A new colony emerged next to Camp Passaconaway during the 1920s. It was largely beach front and somewhat sheltered from the northwest winds that can play havoc with that side of the island. At the outset of the 1920s, there were no houses, but one shore front lot (#58) was in the hands of John Murphy who bought it in 1917. The rest was still owned by George Collins. In 1923,

---

[1] B/P 171/318. The house is still in the family. In 1944, the Browns purchased #407 Bear which is also still in the family. B/P 270/53.

[2] B/P 183/204. The seller was Edward Bosson, who had purchased the lot in 1886 and built the house that still stands there. Dr. Willan's grandson summered on the island for years, and he and his wife, whom he met on the island, now live year-round just across the lake near Shep Brown's.

[3] B/P 174/231; 170/326;182/489; 187/106; and 192/202. Matz was the first Bear vacationer from the state of Pennsylvania.

[4] B/P 187/237.

Murphy sold his lot (#58) to John Marselis, a medical doctor from East Orange, NJ.[1] He had learned about the pleasures of the island while working summers at Camp Passaconaway during his medical school years. Over the next six years, Collins sold three lots adjoining Marselis. The first (#61) was bought by Octavia and Gardner Chapin of Medford, MA in 1926.[2] In 1928, Ray Farnsworth of Ashland, MA bought the lot (#59) between Chapin and Marselis.[3] Lastly in 1929, Bert Wadley of Laconia bought a lot south of Chapin (# 63).[4] Thus by the end of the 1920s, a new colony of four vacation places had emerged along the beach front.

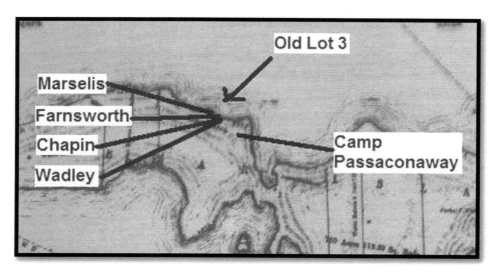

Crane's Point

On the point of North Bear, the five acres or so of land were still in the hands of John Crane's daughter, Bertha Iodine, at the beginning of the decade. But in 1923, she sold it all to Ingeborg V. and Henry Townsend of Acton, ME, ending the 50 year stay of the family of Bear Island's first vacationer.[5] Henry Townsend was the owner of a blanket mill in Maine.

Jerry Point

There were no additional vacationers on Jerry Point during the 1920s. William Puffer and his family maintained ownership of the bulk of it. However, the 1100' of frontage (#377 - #384) originally sold to Theodore Wallis in 1910 was now in the hands of Edward and Florence F. Sharp of Brookline, MA, who had purchased it in 1919.[6]

---

[1] B/P 170/164 . The Marselis family still owns it. See Bear Island Reflections, p. 104.
[2] B/P 179/408.
[3] B/P 187/123.
[4] B/P 166/381.
[5] B/P 166/381; see also 213/181.
[6] B/P 155/175.

Camp Passaconaway

By 1920, Wallace Richmond and Alfred Dickinson Jr. had developed a thriving boy's camp on the eastern side of old Lot 4. In 1923, the two men purchased a farm on the Neck to provide fresh vegetables for the growing camp.[1] Serendipitously, the same farm (206 Meredith Neck Road) was once owned by Oliver Bickford, who, of course, grew up on old Lot 4 and was an older brother of Moses Bickford who had sold the Bear Island property to Richmond and Dickinson.

But Passaconaway foundered in 1928 when Dickinson, its driving force, passed away.[2] After enduring a partial foreclosure by the Newton Trust Company, the camp was sold to Arthur and Mary Carlson of Brookline, MA. The Carlsons mortgaged the property with the Newton Trust Company in the amount of $28,500. The camp became their livelihood. Both were 33 years old when they bought the camp, and they had only been married for a year. Little did they know that the Great Depression was just around the corner.[3]

South Bear

Lot 5 and 6N

Major changes occurred on old Lots 5 and 6N during the 1920s. The owner at the start of the decade, Ellen Lil Prescott, passed away in 1920. The Bear Island property was inherited by her children, Frank, Leo, and Margaret. They decided to take a more aggressive approach in marketing it. They hired the Edward T. Harrington Co., a real estate brokerage firm based in Boston, to sell the property. Harrington produced a several page advertising brochure entitled "Bear Island, Lake Winnipiseogee" to attract potential buyers.[4]

The brochure began by hailing the area as the 'Switzerland of America'. It laid out the legend of how the lake got its name. Then it described the island thusly:

"The beauties and attractions of Bear Island are so many and varied that we can only mention them in a casual way. To properly appreciate or get even a fair idea of them, one must visit the island, wander through the wooded glens, or, from the hills, view one of the grandest panoramas of scenic beauty in the world, while a Bear Island sunset is unapproachably beautiful."

The parcel was estimated at 108 acres and included nearly 5000' of shorefront. It was subdivided (at least on paper) into six parcels that were each given a 'name'. Drawing upon the

---

[1] B/P 170/202.
[2] Dickinson was highly respected as an athletic coach and leader. In 1930, the Newton (MA) High School named its new football stadium after him. About the same time, a stained glass window honoring Dickinson was also donated to the St. John's chapel on the island.
[3] B/P 186/390; B/P 186/393; B/P 186/395.
[4] A copy of the brochure can be found at the New Hampshire Historical Society and the Lake Winnipesaukee Museum.

Prescott's California roots, the names were Alcatraz Point, El Dorado, Linda Vista, Sandy Beach Grove, Oakland Heights, and Vista Del Ray. The Carry cove on the western side of the island facing the Neck (the original 'Gulf') was dubbed Carmel Bay, while the eastern side was called Half Moon Bay.

In touting a 36 acre inland parcel, the brochure observed that the previously cultivated land "could easily be converted into golf links." It also claimed that there were eight springs on the island. Six of them were to be found on this parcel, and that "some of these springs are said to possess water of great medicinal value."[1]

View from ridge on E. Bear looking north c. 1921.

View from old Lot 6S looking east c. 1921.

Badlam's Beach c. 1921.

'Road' or path into the interior c. 1921.

Despite the grandiosity, the brochure had no impact. Not a single one of the six large lots was sold.

Finally in 1926, the Prescotts sold the entire property in one small and one very big step. First, they sold a lot (now #119 and #121) adjoining the East Bear colony to William Gilbert, a professor and Methodist theologian from Drew University in Madison, New Jersey. Gilbert had learned about Lake Winnipesaukee and Bear Island from his Drew colleague, Edwin Earp, whose wife, Lina, was the daughter of James Pearsall and summered just two places down the

---

[1] Only two springs are known to exist on the parcel, one of which is still functioning. The other was capped in the 1990s.

shoreline.[1] Shortly after the Gilbert transaction, the Prescotts sold all of the remaining land of old Lots 5 and 6N to the owners of a girls camp called Camp Kuwiyan.[2] The buyers of record were Stuart M. Link of Roland Park, MD and Bernard Hoban of Newport, R.I. The sale was something of a watershed event. It ended the last direct familial connection to any of the early 19th century Meredith families that owned property on Bear Island.

Camp Kuwiyan ("little women") was originally founded by Elizabeth Embler of Stamford, CT, and had opened in Alton, NH, in 1910. In its early years, it was quite small.[3] Stuart Link joined the camp as a councilor in 1916 after his junior year at Princeton. Stuart's goal in life was to be a teacher, and the wildly popular children's summer camping scene drew him in.[4] After graduating from Princeton in 1917, Stuart became a teacher at the Gilman School in Maryland. But he also returned to Kuwiyan during the summer, having just married Helen Hammer. They met Bernard Hoban and his wife, Barbara, who had also joined the staff at the Gilman School in 1917. Among other things Bernard was the school's football coach.

In 1918, Stuart was pulled away by World War I, leaving behind his pregnant wife. Stuart's first child, Helen S., was born while he was serving in the medical corps in France. Stuart's wife and daughter spent their summers at Kuwiyan in his absence. Upon his return from the war, Stuart resumed his career at the Gilman School, and he took over the majority ownership of Kuwiyan in the early 1920s. Hoban and Embler remained as minority owners and continued to work at the camp as well. As the camp grew, it was moved to a couple of different, leased sites in Wolfeboro, but each time these proved to be inadequate. Finally, by the mid-1920s, with enrollment approaching 50 girls, Stuart began searching for a permanent home. After toying with a site on Chocorua Lake, he learned about the property for sale on Bear Island. He decided to move Kuwiyan there in 1926.

---

[1] B/P 179/311.
[2] B/P 180/149.
[3] "Twenty-Five Years of Kuwiyan: A History as Told at the Last Council Ring of 1934, " Meredith Historical Society Archives.
[4] His precise connection to Kuwiyan is not clear, but apparently a relative, Lillian Link, was one of the first councilors to work with Elizabeth Embler.

While he was negotiating the purchase of the Bear property, Stuart came across another

property on Meredith Neck. It was the former Caleb Lovejoy farm on old Lot 78, abutting Lovejoy Sands and the recently established marina owned by Shep Brown.[1] Stuart bought the Neck property jointly with Elizabeth Embler in July 1926.[2] Deciding that the Bear Island property would be a perfect complement, Link and Hoban closed on it three months later.[3] In short order, Kuwiyan built a new lodge with a large wharf on the Neck property. [4] They also developed various facilities around the 40 or so acres of the old farm.

Stuart Link, far right; Bernard Hoban, far left; Helen Link top row, second from the left c. 1939.

With the vast majority of activities centered at the Neck camp grounds, the campers used Bear Island intermittently for field trips and overnights. No facilities were ever constructed by Kuwiyan on Bear.[5] The usually deserted beach area was often used for swimming and picnic outings by other lake vacationers who also routinely got water from the spring located just back of and south of the beach.[6]

Kuwiyan campers at Bear Island *(Courtesy of the Meredith Historical Society)*

---

[1] Shep started the boat yard in 1924. See the Vignette at the end of this chapter.

[2] B/P 178/575.

[3] 180/149. Link, Hoban, and Embler took out four mortgages in 1926 to help finance their island and mainland purchases. See: B/P 178/577; 178/579; 180/153; and 180/409. Stuart Link may also have had some family money. His father was an oil broker from Manhattan, New York where Stuart grew up.

[4] Now presumably #9 Tall Pines Way.

[5] Badlam's little cottage was apparently removed at this time.

[6] The spring was called the "Fever-Bush Spring" by the campers. It was almost assuredly dug in the early 1800s by either Eleazer Bickford Sr. or James Bickford.

East Bear colony

Some 1000' down the shore from the beach, the East Bear colony underwent some

Joe Pickford. Behind him are the boathouses of Ham and Halcrow.

modest change during the 1920s, ultimately leading to a net increase of one vacation place in the colony. In 1921, Joe Pickford (#131-132) subdivided his land and sold the northern parcel (#131) to Robert and Hazel Ham of Dorchester, MA. Robert was a 28 year old public accountant. The addition was offset the next year, 1922, when the Hams bought out their neighbor, William Halcrow (#129), consolidating the two properties.[1] In 1926, as detailed previously, the colony grew to the north when Gilbert purchased 400' from the Prescotts and built a one room camp there. In 1928, another vacationer joined the colony when George Greene sold his shorefront lot (#140) to Gerda and Murray Worden of Cambridge, MA.[2] Greene retained ownership of his summer farm up back, but the farm lapsed into disuse.

Lot 7: French Cove Colony

After 15 years of no new vacationers in the French Cove, this closely knit colony experienced a wave of change during the 1920s. In 1921, James Aiken sold a vacation lot (#235) to another member of the extended Gokey clan, Ivan Patnode of Allston, MA. About this time, Aiken also sold a small parcel adjoining Annie Duquette (#246) to two of Annie's daughters, Jessie Day and Hazel Barry.[3] Also in 1921, Annie Gokey Duquette purchased adjoining lots on either side of her property from James Aiken, adding 175' of frontage to the existing 125' she already had. The property encompassed what are now Bear Island properties #247 through #249 and the unnumbered property owned by the town west of #249. Her house was on #249.[4]

---

[1] B/P 161/120; B/P 161/460; B/P 165/508.
[2] B/P 190/13.
[3] B/P 161/186; See B/P 182/408. In 1922, in keeping with the tradition of the times, Aiken also sold rights to all of the soft wood timber on Lot 7 to the Hill Lumber Company, granting it permission to set up a mill and harvest the timber over four years. B/P 166/267.
[4] B/P 161/195.

In 1922, Annie Duquette subdivided her land into five lots. In June 1923, she sold the entire property to her daughter, Otelah Morash, and her husband, Harvey. Just two days later, Otelah sold lot 5 of the subdivision (#247) to her sister, Edith M. Dolan, and her husband, Thomas.[1] Otelah and Harvey retained ownership of lot 4 of the subdivision (#248) where their descendants continue to live today. The next year, 1924, Otelah sold her mother's house on lot 3 of the subdivision (#249) to her sisters, Jessie Day and Hazel Barry, who already owned what became lot #246. Otelah also sold lots 1 and 2 of the subdivision (now unnumbered) to Noble and Mabel Butt of Buffalo, NY.[2] The Butts were the first vacationers in French Cove not related to the Gokeys since Fred Bickford left the island in 1906. In 1927, Annie Duquette's remaining daughter, Leah, joined the family in French Cove. She and her husband, George W. Rich, purchased the small lot with a house (#246) just east of Edith Duquette from her sisters, Hazel Barry and Jessie Day.[3]

While the Morash girls were dividing up Annie's lands, James Aiken made two more sales in French Cove in 1925 and 1926, both to members of the Gokey clan. He sold a vacant lot to the early vacationer, Paul Goodrich, (#234) and a larger parcel (#243 and 244) to yet another Gokey brother, Harvey.[4]

So by 1927, the French Cove colony had grown from four summer places to 10. Nine of the ten were owned by members of the Gokey family: Paul Goodrich and his brothers Albert R., Philip, and Harvey Gokey; Ivan Patnode; Leah Rich; and the five daughters of Annie Gokey Duquette: Otelah Morash, Edith Dolan, Jessie Day/ Hazel Barry. The tenth place was owned by the Butts. To the west of French Cove, James Aiken provided a somewhat isolated, western bookend to the colony in Aiken Cove.[5]

Lot 8: Camp Lawrence Comes to Bear Island

In the early 1920s, the owners of old Lot 8 were Hudson, NH-based lumber dealers, Harry Kendrick and Charles Gilbert. They were systematically clearing all of the timber on the southern end of Bear. They had built a saw mill on the end of the island opposite Mink Island to facilitate the cutting of the logs into boards. By 1921, they had stripped the area of most of its marketable timber. In their wake, they left a mess of downed trees and slash.[6]

Meanwhile, the Lawrence, MA, YMCA was looking for a new location for its summer boys' camp. At the time, it was located in Alton, NH, but the program had outgrown the space after 14 years in existence. Winnipesaukee was the focal point of their interest, and members of the

---

[1] B/P 174/353.
[2] This property is unnumbered today (it would be #250). It is owned by the town of Meredith as a result of a tax default in 1989.
[3] B/P 182/408. The purchase date of this lot by Hazel and Jessie is unclear.
[4] B/P 195/492; 192/29.
[5] His house was #259, and the land he still owned included the frontage that encompassed what became #251 through #271. Frank Lane was another Gokey relative, but his summer place (#282) was over on Lot 9.
[6] See the Lawrence YMCA' 75th Anniversary Book and Bear Island Reflections, pp.121 -135.

search committee undertook a tour the lake. After visiting Cow Island, they boated over to Bear where they inspected old Lot 8 which was then on the market. The committee was favorably impressed.[1] The Lawrence Y bought old Lot 8 for $6700 in June 1921.[2] The boys' camp moved to Bear Island that summer, and it became known as Camp Lawrence for Boys.

Camp Lawrence thrived in its new environment. There were 75 attendees in the first year. Initially everyone slept in tents while the arduous work of basic clean-up was undertaken. It took years to remove the mess left behind by Kendrick and Gilbert. In 1923, a large dining hall/lodge was built. In 1924, an elaborate development plan was established to upgrade the water supply and sanitary conditions; build an infirmary and other facilities like tennis courts; upgrade the tenting equipment; and add canoes and other boats for the boys. Throughout these years, the camp filled up every summer.

Lot 9: Dolly's Point

While other sections of the island expanded rapidly in the 1920s, old Lot 9 added only one additional place. It occurred in 1926 when E. C. Mansfield sold a parcel (likely #309) next to his house lot to Edward Herrick of Mahwah, New Jersey.[3] Herrick was a stain glass window artist.

A little later that year, one of the most important transactions in island history took place, although it did not involve a vacation place. Mansfield agreed to sell his observation tower to the

---

[1] The committee's views were reinforced by one of the Y's most influential board members, George Hamblet. He was familiar with that section of the island from an 1894 visit. In that year he and his future wife, Kate, had taken the train from Boston to the Weirs, rented a boat and rowed out to 'Lake Shore Park' (now called West Beach) for a delightful afternoon of swimming. George had a tremendous influence on the camp. Its main lodge is named after him. His grandson, David, owns the Y Landing marina on Meredith Neck.
[2] B/P 159/394.
[3] B/P 349/24.

New Hampshire Episcopal Diocese so a summer chapel could be built on this island.[1] The purchase included a strip of land down to the lake in Deep Cove. The strip ran along the stone wall that formed the original boundary between old Lot 9 and old Lot 7.

Summary

The decade of the 1920s witnessed another period of rapid increase among the vacationing population. The total number of new summer places increased by 19, from 45 in 1920 to 64 in 1930. Some two-thirds of the growth occurred in the already well settled areas on northwest Bear and French Cove. But the decade also saw the emergence of the first small colony on the east side of North Bear as well as the arrival of a second boys' camp. Nevertheless, there were still long swaths of vacant shorefront on both ends of the island.

Vignette

Shep Brown's Boat Basin

Entering the 1900s, the pleasure boating industry was in its infancy. There weren't any marinas on the lake, and repairs and maintenance had to be managed by individual boat owners

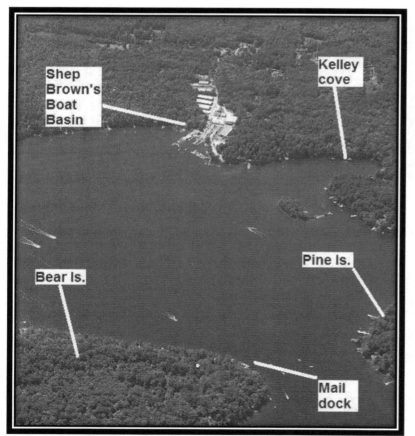

in most cases. Docking was another issue. In the 1880s and 1890s, most of the vacationing boat traffic on this part of the lake originated out of Lakeport and the Weirs. Islanders such as John Crane and James Aiken purchased landings in the Weirs channel or in Paugus Bay. As the vacationing and boating population grew, the demand for more boating services and facilities rose with it.

The first boat livery or rental place was established at the Weirs by the Blackstone family in 1899. Public docking at Glendale became available around the same time, providing parking for vacationers who hired small steamers to take them to the islands. The first 'marina' on the lake was perhaps the forerunner of Goodhue

---

[1] B/P 186/89. See below, Chapter 35 for a history of the Chapel on Bear Island.

Hawkins in Wolfeboro, established in 1903. Nothing similar to it emerged on the western side of the lake until 1919 when Jim Irwin developed a marina at the Weirs.

Shep Brown, c. 1950s (MHS)

With the rapid increase in the summer population during the 1920s, the need for boating services presented a big opportunity. It was seized by Shepherd and Adelaide Brown of Malden, MA. The two were no strangers to this part of the lake. Adelaide (called "Addie" as a child) had been coming up to the Bear Island House since at least 1894 when she was only 11 years old. Her parents, George and Henrietta Murray, were annual summer visitors for many, many years.[1] Shep Brown was also from Malden, MA and was an avid fisherman. Addie undoubtedly introduced him to the lake during their courtship years. He and Addie married in 1909, both age 26. Eleven years later, they were still struggling to find their place in the world. They were living with Addie's parents in Malden in 1920, and Shep was employed as a manager in a thread factory.[2]

Presumably still visiting the Bear Island House after the conclusion of World War I, they

House at Lovejoy Sands, pre-1920s. William Puffer's *Wanderer* **is parked at the wharf.**

witnessed the growth in summer boating around Winnipesaukee in general and Bear in particular. In 1924, they decided to establish Shep Brown's Boat Basin. They purchased the house and wharf at Lovejoy Sands that were then still owned by Sol Lovejoy.[3]

Shep and Adelaide also bought a house in the heart of Meredith Village on Highland Street in the early 1930s. About the same time, they leased and operated a service station at the base of Meredith Bay.[4] Brown's was without competition in the marina market in the area of Bear Island for three decades thereafter. In 1958,

---

[1] Bear Island House Registers, 1894-1898, 1899-1908. Meredith Historical Society Archives. George Murray was the Superintendent of the Post Office in Malden for most of his life. He also worked for a railroad company prior to that.

[2] U.S. Census, 1920.

[3] B/P 171/247.

[4] Shep and Adelaide also purchased a lot (#32) on the northeastern side of North Bear in August 1940, but they sold it at the end of the year. (B/P 249/23 and 249/333.

some competition emerged when Babe Hennen established Hennen's Marine on the mainland opposite Pine Island. Babe had acquired the land in the 1940s when he bought out the Merrill's house and store on Bear Island. Hennen's is now known as the Y Landing and is operated by David Hamblet.

Parking along Lovejoy Sands Rd. 1930s

Gordon Nelson (right) and Jeff Hopper (left) at Shep's c. 1951.

Chapter Twenty-Nine

The 1930s

The decade of the 1930s was a troublesome time in the United States. The Great Depression made life very difficult for nearly everyone, and it naturally effected the vacationing population. On Bear Island, the rather vibrant expansion of the 1920s was muted dramatically. The number of new summer places dropped to less than half of the total during the 1920s. Moreover, the iconic island hotel disappeared for good, sharply altering the milieu on North Bear.

North Bear

The Demise of the Bear Island House

The grand saga of the Bear Island House came to a sad end during the 1930s. Its ongoing viability was undoubtedly negatively impacted in the early part of the decade by the Depression, and it was also probably suffering some from the changing inclinations of vacationers that arose with the automobile age. Disaster struck in the fall of 1934. The Bear Island House burned to the ground just as the owner, J. Coleman Blair, (perhaps not so coincidentally) was on the water, leaving for the season. The hotel was a total loss, but the barn was saved by the fire department. The loss was estimated at $30,000, partially covered by insurance.[1]

The Bear Island House cellar hole.

Blair made no attempt to rebuild the hotel. In February 1935, presumably after settling with his insurance company, he paid off the mortgage debt he owed to the Meredith Village Savings Bank and George Collins. Two months afterwards, Blair sold the island property to his wife, Ina.[2] The property then lay dormant for three years. In September 1938, it was finally sold to Hazel and Jacob Mark of Cambridge, MA.[3] The Marks were research executives with Dewey & Almy, a Cambridge based sealant business. They apparently made the acquisition with the idea that the hotel could be revived. As part of the purchase agreement, they obtained the right to use the name, the 'Bear Island House'. Perhaps they felt that the time might be right to resurrect the hotel with the Depression winding down. Any such dreams, of course, did not come to fruition. The Marks were welcomed to Bear Island that fall by the catastrophic hurricane of 1938 which had a devastating

---

[1] "The Bear Island House Burned to the Ground," <u>Meredith News</u>, November 15, 1934.
[2] B/P 216/315. It is not clear why this sale was made. Blair continued living in Laconia thereafter. He died in 1942 at the age of 72.
[3] B/P 235/407.

impact on the entire island. As one islander later observed, it "felled the tall pines like jack straws down the center of the island, practically eliminating the many nature trails."[1]

The Eastern Shore of North Bear

Entering the 1930s, George A. Collins had high hopes of selling vacation lots on the eastern side of North Bear where he still owned a great deal of vacant shorefront. He got off to a modest start in 1931 when Dr. R.J. Titherington, who had purchased a lot (#14) in 1928, bought an additional 100' of frontage (#16) next door. Titherington quickly subdivided the small lot and sold it to a Pennsylvania colleague and friend, Avenir Proskouriakoff, a Russian national and chemist.[2]

The Titherington sale was the last made by George A. Collins. He died in 1934. Control of his island properties passed to his son, George P. Collins. He did his best to promote activity on Bear Island, advertising widely.

"**Bear Island Park**. Tenting or cottages in the pines. Sand beach. Great view of lake and mountains. Cold springs. Boating. Fishing. Bathing. Fireplace in the open. 150 acres of pine groves with trails. Quiet and healthful recreation. Garage and land Meredith Neck."[3]

Around the same time, George A. Collins' daughter, Dorothy Talbot, also became involved in the Bear Island real estate market. Not long after her father's death, she repurchased the still, fully intact 1100' section (#36 through #52) of northeastern Bear that her father had sold to George D. Mayo back in 1909.[4] Only a small camp (#38) existed on the property that the Mayo family had built before 1920.

With George P. Collins now in charge, some incremental progress was made despite the gloom of the Depression. He sold two lots in the 1930s, providing further definition to a nascent summer colony on that stretch. The first (#24) was sold in 1937 to Royal S. Bounty of Stamford, CT.[5] The following year, 1938, another lot (#22) was sold to Carlisle Boger of Freeport, Long Island.[6]

Northeast Bear Beach Colony

Well south of the lots sold to Bounty and Boger, the little beach colony near Camp Passaconaway also enjoyed a touch of growth in the 1930s. George P. Collins sold one lot

---

[1] Mildred Willan, "Bear Island, New Hampshire in the Twenties," unpublished family reminiscences (1982).
[2] B/P 202/74.
[3] Boston Herald, June 24, 1934, p. 29.
[4] B/P 214/223.
[5] B/P 227/453.
[6] B/P 233/391. This was the Boger family that purchased Shep Brown's Boat Basin in 1960.

(#56), located north of the Marselis family, to Julia Collins of Concord, NH in 1936.[1]

The Western Side of North Bear

On the heavily populated, western side of North Bear, George P. Collins had inherited only two vacant lots from his father. He made no progress in selling either until one of them (#389) was finally purchased in 1939 by Rose Dickinson of Chicago, IL.[2] The sale left Collins with only one lot (#418) on the market, a lot that was handicapped by major drainage issues.

By mid-1939, George P. Collins was ready to throw in the towel on Bear Island. He put the island property on the market to settle his father's estate. One ad read:

Lake Winnepesaukee, N.H.
Bear Island
For Sale – To Settle Estate
125 acres, wooded, 4000 feet shore
Frontage, 2 fine bathing beaches, high
Elevation, beautiful scenic spot. Ideal
For development, commercial purposes
or single estate, Post Office, telephone
connection, 2 large steamers daily,
1 mile from public wharf and town
Highway.[3]

Jerry Point: Modest Growth

Entering the 1930s, there were still only two vacation places controlling Jerry Point. After holding most of it for almost 20 years, William Puffer agreed to part with some of its prime shorefront. In August 1930, he sold a sizeable lot (#369) with 250' of frontage on the southern side of the point to Andrew and Lucie Bennett of Newton, MA. Andrew was a corporate lawyer.[4] This was the last land sale made by William.[5]

Two years later, in 1932, there was also activity on the 1100' of frontage owned by the Sharp family (#377-384). They subdivided their property, selling their house and 290' of frontage (#382 and #384), located on the beach nearest the base of The Gulf, to Walter and Edith Harrington of East Orange, NJ. Walter was yet another medical doctor.[6] Then, five years later, in

---

[1] B/P 223/435. Julia was not related to George P. Collins.
[2] B/P 242/461.
[3] Boston Herald, June 18, 1939, p. 58.
[4] B/P 196/122. The following year Puffer sold an additional 150' of frontage to the Bennetts. B/P 200/434.
[5] In 1937, the widowed William Puffer (c. 77) deeded the Jerry Point property to his daughters, Dorothy Puffer Ernst and Frances Puffer, reserving a life estate for himself. B/P 227/482.
[6] B/P 155/175; B/P 204/271.

in 1937, the Sharps sold the rest of their land (#377 and #380) to William Puffer's daughter, Dorothy, and her husband, Clayton Ernst. This parcel had approximately 810' of frontage.[1] Clayton and Dorothy Ernst were from Wellesley, MA. Clayton was a publisher and editor. He was one of the founders of The Torbell Company of Boston, the company that created and published a magazine called *The Open Road for Boys* from 1919 into the 1950s. Clayton was editor-in-chief of the magazine. He was also an author, writing a mystery called *The Mark of the Knife* (1920).

Camp Passaconaway: Times of Trouble

The Depression did no favors to Arthur and Mary Carlson. After borrowing heavily to finance their acquisition of the camp in 1928, they quickly ran into financial trouble. In desperation, they doubled down. In 1930, they added a second mortgage of $10,000 from a private investor, and the following year, they got yet another $10,000 mortgage loan from a relative.[2] It was all to no avail. At the close of the summer season in September 1932, the Carlsons still owed the bank all of the principal amount of their original loan ($28,500) plus unpaid interest of $9379.50. Also unpaid was the $20,000 they owed to the other mortgage holders. The Newton (MA) Trust Company foreclosed.[3]

The bank ended up owning the property for three years until they were finally able to sell it in 1935. The buyers were the former co-owners Wallace Richmond, Ethel Dickinson, and Alfred Dickinson Jr.[4] However, their second attempt to operate the camp was short lived. With the depression still casting a pall over everything, they were forced to close it after the 1936 summer season. In January 1937, they leased the property to one Lowie Grundy for one year. Then in October 1937, they sold it to Ernest B. Dane of Brookline, MA.[5]

Dane had no interest in trying to reinvigorate the camp. He bought the property for personal reasons. Dane was one of the more remarkable men who left his mark on the Lakes Region during the early 20th century. Quite wealthy by inheritance, he graduated from Harvard in 1892. He served as a director and later president of the Brookline Trust Company. Dane was as much a philanthropist as he was a businessman and real estate investor. He is credited with 'saving' the town of Center Harbor during the difficult times of World War I when he bought up a large number of failing farms and continued to employ the staff that worked on them. He bred Guernseys at his Longwood farm located along the shore of Winnipesaukee.[6] He bought another another farm, now the Waukewan Golf Club, for his Belgian work horses. He was also responsible for building the fire tower on Red Hill in 1927, donating the land and contributing to its construction. In the same year, he donated nearly half of the monies for the construction of

---

[1] B/P 229/396; B/P235/67. The following year, the Ernsts sold 150' of this frontage (#380) to their neighbor, Walter Harrington.
[2] B/P 196/389; B/P 199/235.
[3] B/P 205/341.
[4] B/P 216/261.
[5] B/P 230/301.
[6] The farm included the entire area where the Canoe Restaurant now sits.

the Bear Island Chapel. Dane Road in Center Harbor is named for him. Interestingly, he apparently rarely summered in the Lakes Region, preferring Maine's Seal Harbor in Acadia National Park where he had built a huge mansion called Glengariff in 1911. By 1937, when he bought the Passaconaway property, he probably viewed it as an opportunity to invest in the real estate and help some people along the way.

Carry Cove: Eastern Side

At the base of the Carry Cove, not far from Dane's property, George Thurston owned both sides of the Carry, and he had built houses on both sides at the outset of the 1930s. In 1933, he subdivided the property, selling the small cottage he built on the eastern side to Alvin and Roxie Brainard of Campton, NH.[1] Alvin was a yard foreman for a railroad. There were now two families in the cove on the eastern side.[2]

East Bear Colony: No Growth

Fay's icehouse c. 1950s (George Mayo)

No new vacation places were added to the East Bear colony during the 1930s but the decade did not pass without some important changes. Perhaps the most noteworthy, Gerda Worden sold her home (#140) at the southern end of the colony to Wilbur and Hazel Fay in 1931.[3] The Fays moved to East Bear to establish their own summer business. Wilbur delivered ice and groceries while also providing hauling services, carpentry, and plumbing to anyone who needed it on East Bear, Birch, Jolly, and Steamboat among other islands.

While Wilbur was developing his business on East Bear, some of his new neighbors were struggling with the Depression. Two lost their island homes. Pearl Patten, the owner of James Pearsall's *Rockwood* place, died in 1935. Her estate executor turned over the deed to the bank in lieu of foreclosure.[4] In 1936, the neighboring Hams were divorced and also forced to sell out. Their properties were purchased by the mortgagee, the Summit Thread Company of Boston.[5]

---

[1] B/P 210/151.
[2] The other place was #90 Bear which bordered the Passaconaway property. In 1936, this place was sold to Dr. Ezra Jones
[3] B/P 199/442. The Wordens moved to Pine Island.
[4] B/P 221/311.
[5] B/P 224/7-9. Summit Thread employed Robert Ham. Less than three months after Summit took ownership, the island abutter, Joe Pickford, reacquired the property from Summit. B/P 224/11. Pickford held on to the property for a couple of years before selling it in 1939 to Harry L. Densberger Jr. of Milton, MA. B/P 239/175.

French Cove Colony

Like most of the island, there was very little activity in French Cove during the decade. Only one new place was created when Harvey Gokey and his wife, Katherine, subdivided their property (combined #243-244) and sold the western parcel (#244) to their daughter, Madeline Daunt, in 1930.[1]

The decade was also noteworthy because the first vacationer on this part of the island, James Aiken, died in 1933. His island estate, including the backland, was inherited by his wife, Myra, his children Frank, Bertha, and Shirley Woodman Dresser. They continued to enjoy the lake property for many years thereafter.

The Southeastern Side of South Bear

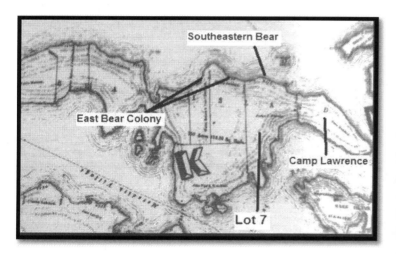

Entering the 1930s, the southeastern side of South Bear between the East Bear colony and Camp Lawrence was uninhabited. It was part of old Lot 7 and owned by James Aiken. That entire stretch of shorefront contained only a small house on the beach near Camp Lawrence built by Aiken for his own enjoyment. Shortly after James died, his heirs sold this house in December 1933 to Carl Fisher of Laconia. It was a small lot with only 50' of frontage (#162). Fisher held on to the lot for less than a year before selling it to Ethel Dow of Laconia.[2]

Camp Lawrence

In spite of the Depression, Camp Lawrence continued to operate without interruption during the 1930s. A large, permanent wharf was built for the camp launches in 1938. That same year the camp was hammered first by a tornado that cleared a 200' swath across the camp and then by the '38 hurricane that leveled most of the trees on the parcel. The impact of the storm remained apparent for years afterwards.

---

[1] B/P 196/352. A number of homes change hands among French Cove residents, almost entirely due to generational change. In nearly every case the properties remained within the family.
[2] B/P 210/319; 215/71.

Dolly's Point Colony

The effect of the Depression was evident on Dolly's Point as well. Only two new vacation lots were opened up during the decade. The first was in 1930 when E.C. Mansfield sold a lot near his own residence on the point to Alfred and Margaret Steinberger of Long Island, NY.[1] Alfred was a salesman for an electronics company. The second new place arose from back to back transactions in late 1932. In November, Edwin Foster bought 200' of frontage (two vacant lots, now #325) next to his existing place. In December, he sold the 200' to John and Adeline Outhouse of Shelburne, MA. John, a naturalized citizen from Canada, was a medical doctor.[2] Those were the only new lot sales.[3]

On a sour note, Frank Lane lost his home (#282) at the head of Deep Cove to the Laconia Savings Bank in 1938. As an indication of how dire his situation had become, the Superior Court of New Hampshire ordered the sheriff of Meredith to arrest Frank and his wife, Jean, and hold them until they paid past due costs and fees of $17.20 or until the bank agreed to their release.[4]

E. C. Mansfield was not around to witness the Lane's difficulties. He died in 1937 at the age of 88. His property on Dolly Point was inherited by his wife, Abiah. She died less than two years later in March 1939 at the age of 82. She died intestate, so the Mansfield estate went into probate.

Summary

The vacation era on Bear Island was much subdued during the 1930s as a result of the Great Depression. Only nine new lots were established on the island, less than half of the previous decade. Bearing further witness to the tribulations of the Depression, at least three islanders lost their homes to foreclosure during the decade. As a result, there were some 70 summer vacation places on Bear Island entering the 1940s.

Quite apart from that, the island also suffered the loss of two of its very first vacationing pioneers, James Aikens and E. C. Mansfield, who had brought the summer era to the lands originally settled by Robert Bryant and Paul Nichols.

---

[1] B/P 196/335.

[2] B/P 206/253; B/P 206/254.

[3] The challenging times associated with the Depression led to turnover among some of the existing vacationers. Perhaps the most noteworthy occurred in 1938 when the lot (part of # 321) originally sold to Dr. Brown in 1906 was sold for the third time, on this occasion to Archey D. Ball, a highly respected Methodist minister from Hackensack, NJ.[3] Reverend Ball's oldest son was Robert M. Ball (1914 – 2008) who rose to prominence as the commissioner of the Social Security Administration from 1962 to 1973. In 1986, a *Washington Post* article noted that for the previous 15 to 20 years, Robert Ball was "probably the nation's most influential Democrat—and possibly the most influential person of any party—in shaping the fate of the giant Social Security program..." After his death in 2008, the Social Security Administration building was renamed the Robert M. Ball building in honor of his decades of work.

[4] B/P 233/416;. In 1941 Alfred Steinberger lost his Dolly's Point home (#313) to foreclosure by the Meredith Village Savings Bank. B/P 253/441.

Chapter Thirty

The 1940s

The decade of the 1940s began on a positive note for would-be vacationers interested in Bear Island. Electricity was brought to the island in the fall of 1941. The wires were laid underwater, crossing the lake from near Shep Brown's. But within months, the country was shocked by the attack on Pearl Harbor and our entry into World War II. As a result, vacation interest during the first half of the 1940s was even worse than the Depression ridden decade of the 1930s. The War brought almost a complete halt to the arrival of new vacationers. But the end of the war in 1945 triggered a strong resurgence in new summer camps on the island.

North Bear

The Eastern-side Colony Grows

At the end of the 1930s, the eastern side of North Bear was home to only five vacation places,[1] three of which were located next to each other and abutting Crane's Point. The other

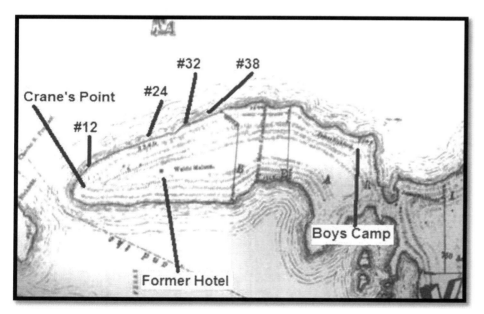

two were some ways down the shoreline. This all changed during the 1940s. Seven new vacation lots were established there during the decade, stretching the colony much further south. The first three of these new camps were established somewhat down the shoreline from Crane's Point. The first of them occurred before the war started when marina owners, Shep and Adelaide Brown, purchased 175' of frontage (#32) from George P. Collins in August 1940.[2] A nice piece of land, it was well separated from its nearest neighbor to the north (Bounty/#24). In 1944, Leroy and Julia Bagley of Laconia purchased a lot (#35) a little further south of the Browns, abutting the still-unoccupied former Mayo parcel.[3] This was one of only two new places purchased on the entire island while the war was underway. The third purchase

---

[1] The three only covered about half of the footprint of current lots #12, #14, and #16.
[2] B/P 249/23. The Browns owned it for only a few months, selling it to Hubert Jones in December 1940.
[3] B/P 272/257.

occurred in 1945 when the 'Mayo camp' (#38) was sold by Dorothy Talbot to William and Marie Nelson of Laconia in 1945.[1]

The end of the war triggered a great deal more interest near Crane's Point. There were already three places next to the point, including Ramsdell (#12), Titherington (#14), and Proskouriakoff (#16). In 1945 and 1946 four new, adjoining lots were purchased adjacent to Proskouriakoff. The first of these was sold by George P. Collins to J. Elmer Boynton of Laconia and Leslie Smith of New Hampton.[2] It had 200' of frontage. Another 200' parcel next to it was sold to Etta Cox of Laconia at the same time.[3] A few months later, the next lot south (#20) was sold to Lloyd and Dewey Cail of Waltham, MA.[4] Before the dust had settled on these purchases, Cox subdivided her parcel in two, selling the northern half (100') to Winnie Greenleaf and Winnie Boynton and the southern portion (also 100') to Eva Dodge.[5] All told, these sales created a tightly packed colony of nine houses adjacent to Crane's Point, running from Ramsdells (#12) down to Bountys (#24).

To the south of this cluster, there was over 1500' of shorefront (including the Mayo parcel) that extended to the former hotel beach. The entire stretch contained only the three camps owned by the Browns (#32), the Bagleys (#35), and the Nelsons (#38). The Nelson place was the only parcel sold in the 1100' of shorefront that comprised the Mayo property originally subdivided in 1909.[6]

Northeast Beach Colony

The small Beach colony south of the Mayo parcel also enjoyed some growth after the war ended. In 1945, a lot (#62) located between the Wadley and Chapin places, was sold to William and Marie Nelson, the same couple who had purchased the 'Mayo camp' (#38) from Dorothy Talbot the same day.[7] A second sale occurred in 1947 when the still-unnumbered lot on the southern end of the Beach colony, next to the former Camp Passaconaway, was sold to Ralph W. Theal Jr. of Laconia. Theal apparently only used it as a campsite.[8]

The George Collins Family Departs the Island

George P. Collins passed away in January 1948. Early the following year, his wife, Leona, as estate administrator, sold her husband's remaining Bear Island properties to John

---

[1] B/P 276/197.
[2] B/P 274/299. Within two months, Smith sold his share to Boynton. (B/P 275/27). The following year, Boynton sold a half interest to Glennes Weeks. (B/P 281/351).
[3] B/P 274/300.
[4] B/P 278/113.
[5] B/P 274/296; 287/290.
[6] In 1946, Dorothy Talbot sold a half interest in the parcel to her brother, George P. Collins, presumably to limit her exposure.
[7] B/P 276/199.
[8] B/P 296/315; 296/316. The boundary between Theal's property and Camp Passaconaway was the wall that separated old Lots 3 and 4 on Bear. The lot remains unnumbered. It is owned today by the Winnipesaukee Yacht Club and used by members for camping. There is no house on the property.

and Thomas McIntyre of Laconia. Dorothy Talbot sold her island interests to them at the same time. The Collins era on Bear Island was over after 39 challenging years.[1]

The McIntyre brothers were real estate professionals whose offices were in Laconia. They delved widely in the Lakes Region real estate market, buying and selling all types of properties. Bear Island was another—albeit different--kind of opportunity for them compared to their other activities.

The Merrills Leave North Bear

Next door and just south of the mail dock, another era on the island came to an end. In 1946, the last of the Merrill family left the island. Their property (#434 and 433) was originally purchased by George Merrill in 1906. It was passed down to George's sons, David and Fred in the 1920s. In the 1930s, David and his wife moved back to Laconia, apparently aghast that Fred married a former Ziegfeld Follies showgirl named Dottie Almende. Fred and Dottie prospered on the island for years thereafter. They continued to operate the Merrill's store, and Dottie became the postmistress for a number of years as well.[2] In the mid-1940s, she and Fred decided it was time to move on. In 1946, the Merrill home and the store were sold to Jerome ('Babe') and Edith Hennen of Canton, MA.[3] The Hennens continued to operate the store for several years.

Northwest Bear and Jerry Point

There was no expansion in the vacation community on either Northwest Bear or Jerry Point during the 1940s. The latter did, however, endure the impact of generational change during the decade. William Puffer passed away in the early 1940s, and the family home on the point was inherited by his two daughters, Dorothy and Frances. Dorothy and her husband, Clayton Ernst, already owned their own place on the point; but when Clayton died in 1945, Dorothy sold their place to William and Janet Wuester of Hillside, NJ (now #377).[4] William Wuester was a medical doctor from New Jersey, like his Jerry Point neighbor, Walter Harrington.

Another Attempt at a Boys' Camp on old Lot 4: Camp Seneca

On the opposite side of the island from Jerry Point, changes were afoot as well. Ernest B. Dane passed away in 1946 after owning the acreage for a decade. In 1947, his son, Edward, sold the former Camp Passaconaway property to William Ellis II of Cambridge, MA.[5] The 33 year year old Ellis had recently served in World War II as a member of the US Air Force. He purchased the property intent on reestablishing a boys' camp there. He named it Camp Seneca.[6]

---

[1] B/P 362/444; 310/63.
[2] Bear Island Reflections, pp. 33-38. Dottie succeeded Shep Brown's wife, Adelaide, as postmistress.
[3] B/P 286/219.
[4] B/P 297/450. Dorothy Ernst retained about 150' of frontage from the original parcel that she and her husband had purchased in 1937.
[5] B/P 294/489.

Seneca.[1] He gave a mortgage to the Meredith Village Savings Bank for a loan of $12,500 to help finance the purchase.[2]

South Bear

East Bear Colony Turnover but No New Places

Like much of the rest of the island, the East Bear colony did not grow at all during the 1940s. Among its 10 vacation places, several changed hands in the familiar drum beat that accompanied the passage of time.

French Cove Colony Grows By One

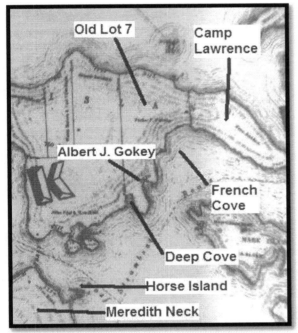

French Cove enjoyed a bit of growth the early 1940s. In 1942, James Aiken's heirs sold the next to last vacant lot in French Cove (now #245) to Leah Rich and her son, George Jr. This was the second of only two lots sold to new vacationers while the war was underway.[3]

But a more impactful change took place on this part of Bear during the 1940s as well. In 1944, Frank Aiken and his relatives sold their house in Aiken Cove (#259) and all of the remaining Aiken land on old Lot 7 to Albert J. Gokey, a third generation member of the Gokey family.[4] Albert J. was the son of Joseph A. Gokey and the grandson of the family progenitor, Albert R. Gokey. The property acquired by Albert J. not only included a dozen future lots on either side of his new home, but the property also included a huge swath of shoreline on the eastern side of the island running from the Camp Lawrence boundary north to Wilbur Fay's camp (#140) at the southern end of the East Bear colony.

Albert J. was interested in selling off shore lots, but none of his property changed hands until the end of the decade. In 1949, Hazel Duquette Barry bought the only remaining, unoccupied parcel (#240) within the settled area of the French Cove colony, next to her camp

---

[1] The name was presumably derived from the Seneca Nation, the western-most of the six Iroquois nations that controlled upstate New York prior to the colonial era.

[2] B/P 294/527.

[3] In 1943, another of Leah's sons, Arthur Rich, purchased the Disciullo's property next door (#244), bringing it back within the Gokey lineage. On the other hand, another non-Gokey related family entered the picture in French Cove about this time. In 1944, Madeline Daunt sold her property (#232-233) to Edward G. Morris of Quincy, MA. The Morris family was only the third in the history of French Cove without direct familial ties to the original Gokey line since the colony was originally established in 1897. B/P 260/95; 267/152.

[4] B/P 272/71.

(#238). The same year, however, the French Cove colony began to expand westward towards Albert J.'s new home (#259) when Edith Duquette Dolan bought a large parcel (#251-253) next to Mabel Butt (unnumbered).[1]

But not all of the expansion was in French Cove. Also in 1949, Albert J. opened up a brand new section of old Lot 7. The heretofore uninhabited 'point' or 'peninsula' that separated the former Aiken cove from Deep Cove was sold to Steve Chicola, of Arlington Heights, MA.[2]

Dolly's Point: The Colony Expands

Dolly's Point experienced a great deal of change during the 1940s. The estate of E.C. Mansfield's wife, Abiah, initially got mired in the legal world following her death in the l930s. It was not until August 1944 that the court authorized Daniel Eaton, a Meredith attorney, to sell Mansfield's property. Eaton commissioned a subdivision plan that delineated 18 separate lots, including the original Mansfield home (#310) on the end of Dolly's Point.[3] The family home was the first to be sold. It was purchased, appropriately enough, by the Mansfield's granddaughter, Mary Plancon, and her husband, C. K. Plancon in October 1945.[4] Mary was the daughter of the Mansfield's only child, Edwin C. Mansfield.

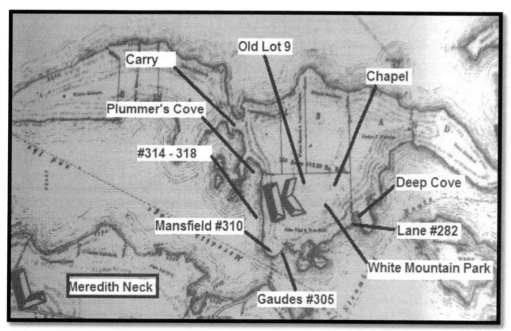

After this, Eaton turned his attention to selling the other lots. In 1946, the first new vacation lot in 14 years was opened up when Eaton sold a parcel with 400' of frontage (#314, #315, and #316) to Stanley T. and Ruth Stoothoff from New Jersey.[5] He was an engineer. Then in 1948, Eaton sold another new vacation lot (later #317-318) with 100' of

---

[1] B/P 779/208; B/P 384/128.
[2] B/P 315/454. The point consisted of some three acres. In 1955, Chicola purchased the point lot on Meredith Neck opposite Horse Island (part of old Neck Lot 82). (B/P 368/265). He developed the Golden Horseshoe pizza restaurant there. The restaurant was accessible by boat as well as by car. It closed c. 1970. At one time, its advertisements along the Neck Road read "Pizza on Earth and Goodwill to Men."
[3] This plan was not found in the Registry, but it was mirrored by a plan done for Ed Mansfield in 1950 which is found in the Registry.
[4] B/P 285/433. The parcel had 575' of frontage. In 1949, the Plancons were living in Warrenton, NC, where C.K. was an auto salesman and painter.
[5] B/P 291/6.

frontage to Ruth Hahn and the families of her two children, all of Middletown, CT.[1] Ruth was married to Edwin Hahn, a store clerk in Middletown. With these two sales, the entire northwestern shore of Dolly's Point was now in the hands of summer vacationers.

The following year, 1949, Eaton sold a lot with 100' of frontage (#305) to Walter Gaudes.[2] This was only the second lot sold in the area that E.C. Mansfield had called 'White Mountain Park'. The first had occurred 31 years earlier when Frank Lane bought the lot (#282) on Deep Cove. In November, Eaton sold the rights to all of the merchantable timber in White Mountain Park to R.S. Yeaton Inc., a lumber company in Plymouth, NH.[3]

In his last official act, Eaton sold the remainder of the Mansfield estate to Mansfield's son, Edwin C. Mansfield in December 1949. The purchase included the interior acreage (estimated at 85 acres) and all of the unsold shoreline on the south side of Dolly's Point around into Deep Cove.[4] Edwin Mansfield was 72 years old when he bought the property. Born in 1876, he had married Helen Pynn in 1907. They lived in Meredith where they had one child, Mary (b. 1910). During the early 1900s, Edwin worked as a salesman in his father's dry goods business in Meredith Village. He was very active in the Meredith town government, serving as Town Clerk, Health Officer, Selectman, and Secretary of the Board of Education at various times. By 1930, he was a successful accountant living on Vittum Lane (later Red Gate Lane) in Meredith where his parents had also lived towards the end of their lives.

Summary

By the end of the 1940s, vacation activity on Bear Island had rebounded pretty well after the near standstill caused by World War II. The summer population on the island had grown from 70 vacation places to 89. All but two of the increase occurred after the war drew to a close. About two-thirds of the increase occurred on old Lots 7 and 9. Together with other fill-in purchases, by the end of the 1940s, there was an almost uninterrupted string of houses from #24 on the eastern side of North Bear, around Crane's Point, down the entire shoreline of the western side of North Bear, into the Carry Cove. The string was interrupted by Plummer's Cove, but it picked up again on the northwestern side of Dolly's Point. It was interrupted again by large vacant stretches on Mansfield's former White Mountain Park but then began again at Chicola's point and ran through French Cove to the Camp Lawrence boundary wall.

This fairly dense occupation pattern stood in stark contrast to the northeastern and eastern sides of the island. Other than a few isolated places here and there, the only two areas

---

[1] B/P 310/374. The other buyers of record were Jeanette Hahn, married to Ruth's son, Edwin Russell Hahn, and Priscilla Hill who was Ruth's daughter.
[2] B/P 588/405.
[3] See B/P 329/232.
[4] B/P 317/404. Only the Gaudes and the former Lane properties could be found on this extensive stretch of the island that, for the most part, faced the Dolly Islands.

with fairly dense settlement were the East Bear colony and the Beach colony. There were also two boys' camps.

PART V:

The Post-War Vacation Boom:

1950 - Present

Chapter Thirty-One

The 1950s

Backdrop

The influx of new vacationers during the latter half of the 1940s did not carry over into the first few years of the 1950s. The country's economy was in recession, experiencing inflation as prices rose and the dollar weakened. On top of that, McCarthy's 'Red Scare' politics and the Korean War cast a pall over things. But by 1954, new vacationing activity on Bear Island began to take off again as the economic environment improved. The growth of summer vacationers on Bear continued largely unabated for the next 25 years, a period during which the seasonal island population more than doubled.

The foundation underneath this rapid increase in island vacationers was the multi-decade combination of rapid population growth, strong economic expansion, and increasing prosperity among a wide cross-section of the American populace. Between 1950 and 1980, the population of the country increased 48% from 152 million to 227 million people. The Northeast grew at a slower, but still robust, pace of 28% (from about 28 million to nearly 36 million people). Much of the increase resulted from the sharp rise in the birth rate known as the 'baby boom' generation.

Over the same 30 year period, the Real Gross Domestic Product of the United States increased almost 300% from $2.2 trillion to $6.5 trillion. The work force was buoyant as new industries emerged (e.g. aero-space) and old industries expanded (e.g. automotive). The economic benefits were shared broadly. During the 1950s and 1960s, the highest increases in Mean Family Income were found among the lowest 80% of the population (indeed the highest increases were gained by the lowest 20%).[1] The impact was quite evident in calculations of mean income that increased from $20,332 in 1950 to $40,999 in 1980.[2]

Vast improvements in transportation also played a big part in the rapid increase in island vacationers after 1950. The most important was the proliferation of automobiles which made getting there far easier. Nearly 58 million cars and trucks were sold during the 1950s, approximating one new car for every two adults in the country by the end of the decade.[3]

A second aspect of the transportation improvement was the evolution of the leisure boating industry. The invention of fiberglass (glass reinforced plastic-GRP) revolutionized boat building and allowed it to become a commodity business.[4] At the same time, rapid improvements in outboard motor technology led to increasing reliability. Both of the above made

---

[1] Pew Research Center, Social and Democratic Trends: "The Lost Decade of the Middle Class," August 22, 2012, p. 59.
[2] U.S. Census Bureau, Statistical Abstract of the United States: 1999, p. 877.
[3] There were far fewer cars before the war, and new car production stopped in 1942 when auto factories were reoriented towards the manufacture of war materiel. Moreover, gas rationing during the war precluded a great deal of automobile travel.
[4] George Marsh, "50 Years of reinforced plastic boats," <u>Materials Today</u>, 8 October 2006.

boating much more affordable for everyone interested. As a result, from the latter 1950s, the islands and the lake became far more accessible to the average family.[1] By 1960, nearly every island property owner had his or her own transportation to and from the mainland.

All of these things contributed to a decade of growth on Bear Island previously equaled only by the first decade of the 20th century.

North Bear

The McIntyres, the Wildlife Sanctuary, and Other Lot Sales

Entering the 1950s, the unsold shore front previously owned by the George Collins family was now in the hands of real estate professionals, John and Thomas McIntyre, of Laconia. Their holdings included what today are 10 shorefront lots on the eastern side of North Bear originally marketed by Mayo; five shore front lots north of the Mayo parcel; one beach front lot (#62) near Camp Seneca (now Nokomis), and one lot (#418) on the western side of the island. They also owned some of the interior lands that were not part of the old hotel property.

But like their predecessors, the McIntyres were not successful in selling any property at all on Bear during the first six years of their ownership. Discouraged, in June 1955, they adopted an exit plan. Most significantly, they reached an agreement to sell all of their interior lands as well as a 500' strip of frontage (current lots #26, 27, 28, and 30) on the eastern side of the island to the Mary Mitchell Humane Fund of Boston, MA.[2]

The Mary Mitchell Humane Fund was established in 1955 as a non-profit advocacy group whose mission it was to preserve wildlife in its natural habitat; prevent cruelty to animals; and provide care for animals. It was a sister non-profit of the Massachusetts Society for the Prevention of Cruelty to Animals (MSPCA). The purchase was only the first part of its plan to create a wildlife sanctuary on Bear Island. A month later, the group also bought the interior property that comprised the Bear Island House from Hazel and Jacob Mark in 1955.[3] The Mary Mitchell Humane Fund now controlled most of the interior of North Bear that once comprised old Lots 1, 2 and 3 in Hugh Kelsea's original 1819 plan.

Following these two purchases, the Mary Mitchell Humane Fund endowed the American Humane Educational Society, which became the legal owner of the property on Bear. The Society in turn established the Alvord Wildlife Sanctuary to manage its property on the island. Alvord's mission was to preserve the land for nature and for people to enjoy. It was under the direction of Robert Frey, a Plymouth State (NH) College biologist. Alvord developed a camp for

---

[1] Previously, vacationers accessed the islands either by commercial steamer, taxi boat, or personal steamers which only the wealthier could afford. Otherwise, one was left to manage with a canoe or a row boat (perhaps powered by a very low horsepower, very unreliable outboard).

[2] B/P 363/85.

[3] B/P 364/225.

children ages nine through 14. Its focal point was on the eastern side of the island where it put up various buildings on its 500' strip of shorefront (now lots #26 through #30). These included sleeping cabins, a lodge, a library, a 'mess' hall and a kitchen. In 1958, the Society purchased the former Merrill property next to the mail dock from the Hennens.[1] It converted the store into a museum.

The McIntyres Dispose of the Rest

After the sale to the Mary Mitchell Humane Society, the McIntyres made a concerted effort to liquidate their remaining shorefront holdings. They still owned the mostly unoccupied Mayo parcel (only one lot #38 had previously been sold); a couple of other lots to the north of it; and a single lot (#62) in the Beach colony near Camp Seneca. In 1955, they sold the Beach colony lot (#62) to the abutters, Seth Keller and James Stamps, who jointly owned #63. The next year, they sold a lot (now #41) within the Mayo parcel to Palmer and Dorie Smith of Darien, CT.[2] The Smiths were not newcomers to the island by any means. They were introduced to Bear by the Bounty family years before and had spent many summers camping on the island.

In 1957, the McIntyres began devoting additional attention to the old Mayo parcel. They developed a 12 lot subdivision plan for it.[3] But the effort barely bore fruit. They sold only one large lot (#51) with 225' of frontage to Charles and Arlene Rogers of Laconia.[4] The parcel was located next to the old hotel beach (what the McIntyres called the "Community Beach Lot").[5] The story was similar north of the old Mayo parcel. The McIntyres sold only a 50' add-on parcel to the Cails (#20).[6]

The McIntyres lack of success led them to finally give up on their involvement on the island. In 1958, they made their exit entirely by selling all of their remaining land to the Mary Mitchell Humane Fund.[7]

Crane's Point

The 1950s also marked an inflection point for the land originally purchased by John Crane in 1873. In 1954, the property was sold to Cornelius and Doris Maguire of Cochituate, MA.[8] Cornelius, a contractor, saw opportunity in the parcel. In 1955, he developed a subdivision plan for its 1055' of shore frontage. The plan called for the creation of 10 lots with 100' of frontage each (except the first lot where his house, the original Crane home, was located). The Maguires were able to sell two of their lots. The first (now part of #4) was bought in 1956 by James and

---

[1] B/P 389/480; 389;482.
[2] B/P 381/105.
[3] Their plan was very similar to the one that Mayo had originally devised in 1909.
[4] B/P 384/487.
[5] The purchase was apparently speculative in nature. They already owned property on Governors Island.
[6] B/P 373/342.
[7] B/P 385/395.
[8] B/P 358/129.

Elsie Yates of the Panama Canal Zone. The other was purchased in 1957 by Doris' parents, Stanley and Adma Currier of Littleton, NH (now #6).[1] Neither of the new owners built a house.

Meanwhile, two changes occurred on the former Crane property located south of the mail dock. Babe and Edith Hennen subdivided this former Merrill property in 1957 and sold a small lot (now #433) and an icehouse to Wesley and Mary Winters of Randolph, MA.[2] Soon after, the Hennens sold their main house (#434) and the store next to the mail dock to the Mary Mitchell Humane Fund.[3] With the improvements in boating, the previously indispensable island store had had finally become unnecessary after some 50 years of treasured service to the islanders.[4]

The Western Side Colony

Down the shoreline from the Hennens, the crowded western side colony of North Bear experienced very little change. The shorefront was already almost entirely built out. There was only one vacant lot (#418) remaining. It was sold to the Mary Mitchell Humane Fund as part of the 1958 purchase from the McIntyres.

Jerry Point

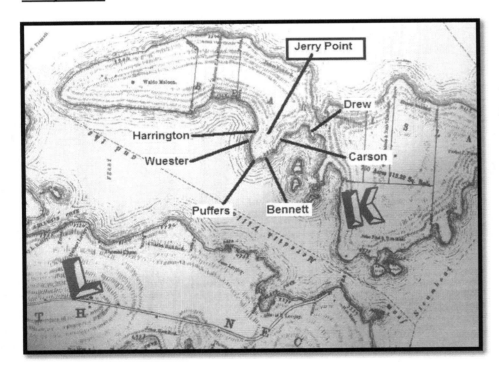

Jerry Point experienced only a bit of change in the 1950s. Entering the decade, there were four families living on the point. William Puffer's daughters, Dorothy Ernst and Frances Puffer, owned most of it, including the interior. The Bennetts were on the south side of the point in the Carry Cove; the Wuesters were to the north in The Gulf; and the Harringtons were next to the Wuesters, near the base of The Gulf.

---

[1] B/P 369/281; 373/24.
[2] B/P 370/429.
[3] B/P 389/482.
[4] The Hennens moved to the mainland opposite Pine Island where they established a marina for the growing population of summer boaters. The marina is now called the Y Landing and is owned by David Hamblet. B/P 286/281.

In 1950, two additional summer vacationers acquired lots from William Puffer's daughters. The first lot (#354) was sold to William and Louise Drew of Belmar, NJ.[1] It was located at the base of the Carry cove, bounding on the stone wall that separated old Lot 4 from old Lot 5. The original 'Carrying Place' ran along this stone wall to the south of it on old Lot 5. Most of the Drew property consisted of a small point of land that jutted out into the cove, giving the property some 550' of frontage. The lot also incorporated about 15' of beach front as well, with the rest of the beach retained by the Puffer daughters.

The second lot (#365) was sold to Joseph and Margaret Carson of West Hartford, CT in October 1950.[2] The lot was located next to the Bennetts but deeper into the Carry Cove. It had 400' of frontage. There was still some 600' of frontage between the lots sold to the Carsons and the Drews that remained in the hands of the Puffer daughters.

Camp Nokomis Replaces Camp Seneca

On the opposite side of the island from Jerry Point, Camp Seneca had been established by William Ellis in 1947 on the site of the former Camp Passaconaway. But Ellis ran into trouble very quickly in his new endeavor. The period after World War II was a difficult one in many areas of the country. The Northeast was hit hard by unemployment before the country's manufacturing base shifted from war footings to peace time operations. The year 1949 was particularly tough as camp enrollments plummeted in general followed by a viral epidemic that swept through them that summer.

Ellis became financially strapped. He had funded his purchase with a bank loan of $12,500 at the outset. He apparently took another loan of $3000 from the same bank to help him make it through the first couple of years. But Ellis was unable to make the camp viable. In July 1950, the New Hampshire Savings Bank foreclosed on its mortgage and took ownership of the property.[3]

Barely more than a year later, in September 1951, the bank found a buyer for the property. It was sold to Barbara 'Jinx' Metcalf (b. 1908) of Melrose, MA and Lawrence Palmer (b. 1909) of Winchester, MA.[4] The two were business partners with a mutual interest in establishing a girls' camp on the island. Jinx, divorced or widowed by this time, was a Winnipesaukee veteran. Her parents, William and Lucy Buck, had purchased a place on Birch Island back in 1917 when she was nine years old. That place was passed along to Jinx and her two older sisters in 1947 after their father died. Jinx was also a registered nurse and an executive director

[1] B/P 321/339
[2] B/P 327/71
[3] B/P 322/323-325.
[4] B/P 333/367; see also Bear Island Reflections, pp.107-119 for an excellent history of Camp Nokomis.

of the Girl Scouts. Lawrence Palmer had attended Boston University before becoming a salesman. He had a particular interest in swimming and aquatics.[1]

They selected the name 'Nokomis' for their camp, drawn from Henry Wadsworth Longfellow's epic poem, *The Song of Hiawatha*. Prior to opening the camp in 1952, Jinx met Frank McDonald while on a cruise in the Caribbean. Frank had grown up in the south and was a Baptist Sunday school teacher among other things. The two connected instantly, and they were married shortly thereafter. Frank embraced Nokomis as if it were his own, and he took a leading role in directing it from the outset. Before the start of the second season in 1953, Jinx and Frank bought out the ownership interest of Lawrence Palmer.[2]

The McDonalds enjoyed hard earned success during their early years operating Nokomis. As an unaffiliated, private camp, it faced many challenges, not the least of which were its many competitors. The existing facilities were refurbished and expanded. They developed a relationship with Shep Brown's Boat Basin to ferry campers and supplies to the island. Nokomis drew most of its campers from the Winchester, MA area, beginning with a modest total of 18 girls and six staff in 1952. Enrollment slowly grew during the 1950s, approaching 60 or so by the end of the decade. The facilities grew with the enrollment, but it was always a struggle to make ends meet in the camp business. In 1959, one straw almost broke the camel's back: the dining hall and program office burned to the ground that spring. They were rebuilt, but the cost placed an increasing burden on the owners as they prepared to forge ahead in the 1960s.

South Bear

The Carry Cove (Eastern Side)

Entering the 1950s, there were two houses on the eastern side of the Carry cove. One (#90) abutted Camp Nokomis. The other was a small house at the base of the cove, owned by Alfred Brainard. He had acquired the property in 1933, and he had held on to it through the Depression years and World War II. But in the summer of 1954, the house caught on fire and burned to the ground. Brainard did nothing to rebuild it; nor did he bother to pay his Meredith real estate taxes. In 1955, the town took the property at a Tax sale.[3] Two years later, in 1957, the town sold the lot with its 100' of frontage for $125 to Roland Smith and Rudolph Smith, who had acquired the Thurston place (#352) on the western side of the Carry in 1946.[4] The remains of the house were disposed of, and the land has remained vacant ever since then.

---

[1] Bear Island Reflections, p. 107.
[2] B/P 344/445.
[3] B/P 382/86.
[4] B/P 394/339.

Camp Kuwiyan Closes and Departs the Island

While the fate of the Brainard place played out, ownership of old Lot 5 and old Lot 6N experienced a fair amount of change in the 1950s. Entering the decade, this 108 acre tract was owned by Stuart Link and Bernard Hoban of Camp Kuwiyan who had bought it in 1926. In 1953, Link, acting as trustee for his daughter, Helen S.L. Graham,[1] purchased Hoban's half interest. The following year, Stuart gifted his half interest in the property to his daughter, making her the sole owner of it.[2]

The buyout of Hoban came with a minor catch. Hoban was given a five year lease apparently on the eastern half of the property (including the beach). He subsequently assigned the lease to one Thomas Tongue II. The lease did not preclude Kuwiyan from using the beach area for a few more years nor did it preclude Helen Graham from making sales on the western half of the property.

Camp Kuwiyan closed for good after the 1956 season,[3] and Helen put the Bear Island property on the market. She sold a large portion of it in November 1957, completing four transactions in which she sold all of the remaining shoreline and a large chunk of the backland around the western side of the Carry Cove.

The buyers consisted of three families, two of whom already had summer homes on the western side of the Carry. One of the families was that of Roland and Barbara Smith of New Brunswick, NJ, who had come to the island in 1946. The second was that of William and Louise Drew of Durham, NH, who came in 1950. The third was that of Ralph and Aubrey Mosher from Schenectady, NY. They had not previously owned any island property until they joined with the Smiths and the Drews in these transactions with Helen Graham. The three families had come together and developed a plan to buy a large portion of her land.

In the first transaction, the three families jointly purchased a 50 acre tract of backland with the ownership divided amongst them 43% (Moshers), 35% (Drews), and 22% (Smiths). In a second transaction, the Moshers bought the end of the large point that divides Plummer Cove from the Carry Cove where they established their summer home (#342). The lot consisted of some 1000' of shore frontage. Third, the Smiths bought 600' of shorefront on the northern side of the same point, running from now- #351 to the Mosher's boundary. And lastly, the Drews purchased two other tracts. Tract one was a parcel with 210' of frontage on the north facing side

---

[1] Helen (who was known as 'Bobby') graduated cum laude in 1940 from Bryn Mawr where she was captain of the swim team. She taught at the Brearly School in New York City before marrying John Warren Graham, a distinguished geologist.

[2] B/P 350/254; 356/29. Helen had provided the financing that allowed her dad to buy out Hoban's share. By this time Stuart Link had retired from his private school career and was living in Meredith. He had served as Dean of the Gilman School in Maryland from 1919 to 1929. In 1929, he became the headmaster of the private Sewickley Academy near Pittsburgh, PA, a position he held through 1949. Bernard Hoban had retired to New London, NH. He was a NH native, having been born in Claremont, NH, in 1918.

[3] Stuart Link continued to live on Kuwiyan's Neck property next to Shep Brown's. In 1958, he sold most of the Neck parcel to Shep Brown's. B/P 388/331. He retained a house on Turtle Lane, next to the parcel sold Brown. Stuart died in 1962, his wife having predeceased him by several years. His son, John D. and his wife, Ruth, continued to use the family home during the summer until 2008.

of the point between the parcels bought by Mosher and Smith. The second tract was a parcel with 100' of frontage in Plummer cove, adjoining the frontage the Drews already owned in the cove.[1] The Drews had already acquired the abutting property owned by the heirs of James L. Little. It included some 700' of frontage at the base of Plummer cove and the buildings (#329) located on Dolly's Point.[2] The Drews also acquired the last adjacent parcel near the base of Plummer Cove (#331) from Mansfield, connecting the former Little tract with the vacant land at the base of Plummer cove which they purchased in 1956 from Helen Graham.[3]

As a result of these transactions, a substantial portion of old Lot 5 and some of old Lot 6N was finally sold after decades of marketing. There was still quite a bit of shorefront and some 60 acres of backland on the eastern side of the island on the market. That property lay largely unused. The beautiful beach area remained vacant, periodically enjoyed by island residents and occasional Girl Scout encampments. By the latter 1950s, however, the bay and beach area began drawing as many as 60 weekend visitors who enjoyed 'rafting' their 'cruisers' there for the weekend.

Dolly's Point: Rapid Vacation Expansion

Unlike everywhere else on the island, the 1950s was a decade of very extensive growth

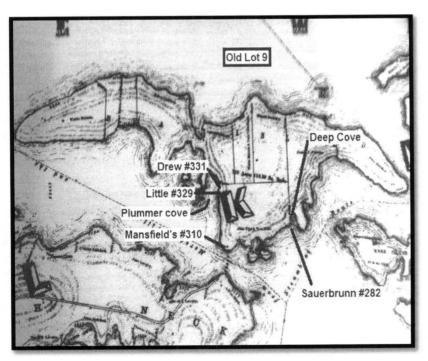

on Dolly's Point. More than half of all new vacation places purchased on Bear were on Dolly's Point. The Mansfield's son, Edwin, had purchased Dolly's Point after his mother passed away in 1949. He commissioned T. J. Collard to develop a subdivision plan for the uninhabited shoreline. Some 27 lots were laid out from the Church Dock in Deep Cove (#278) all of the way around to the Mansfield's original place (#310) on the point. The only occupied lots on this entire stretch were the Herrick lot near the beach (#306), the Gaudes lot (#305), and the former Lane place (#282).[4]

Almost all of this unoccupied shorefront was sold to summer vacationers over the course of the 1950s, first by Edwin Mansfield and then by his daughter, Mary Plancon. Edwin sold two

---

[1] B/P 384/177; B/P 384/178; B/P 384/175; B/P 384/173.
[2] B/P 377/11.
[3] B/P 384/173.
[4] B/P 285/375.

lots in 1950.[1] No lots were sold in either 1951 or 1952, and only one was sold in 1953.[2] Four more vacationers made purchases in 1954. All of the lots involved were contiguous.[3] In 1955, two more vacationers joined the fray when Edwin sold another lot (#303), and Mary Plancon subdivided her parcel (#310) and sold a piece (#308).[4] Edwin made his last sale (#302) in 1956.[5] He died in late 1956. Edwin's estate was inherited by his daughter, Mary Plancon. She continued selling off the subdivided vacation lots. She made six sales in 1957 and three more in 1958.[6] While all of this was going on, other vacationers on Dolly's Point were doing their own subdivisions. Two new vacation places were created when the Marcionette family sold portions of their large parcel (#313-316) and left the island during the latter 1950s.[7] Also in 1959, another separate place was created when the Hahns subdivided their 100' lot amongst themselves.[8]

Lot 7: French Cove Colony

In striking contrast to Dolly's Point, there were no new summer places added to the already heavily occupied French Cove during the 1950s. What change there was involved the ownership of existing lots moving either between existing lot holders or passed along to the next generation. Of note, however, Paul Goodrich died in Boston in 1956. His pioneering efforts, and those of his brothers, had spawned the establishment of a remarkable family colony on Bear Island.

Lot 7: Southeastern Shore Colony

Meanwhile, the very sparsely occupied eastern shore of old Lot 7 saw four new summer places purchased near Camp Lawrence, resulting in the emergence of another small colony. The first two sales occurred simultaneously in April 1954. Albert J. Gokey sold two small 50 foot lots (#163 and #164) to branches of the Sinotte family. The lots were next to the only occupied lot on that side of the island which had been purchased by their father, Eli Sinotte, in 1949. Eli also

---

[1] One (#298) was purchased by Ralph and Rosalie Conte of Needham, MA. The second (#304) was acquired by John and Lorene Rosborough of Lisbon, NH. B/P 340/328; B/P 326/429;

[2] This lot (#287) was sold to Kenneth and Helen Volk of Weymouth, MA. B/P 349/536.

[3] Two lots in Deep Cove were sold to Bertram and Kathleen Sauerbrunn of Hillside, NJ who had purchased the old Lane place (#282) in 1951. Three more of Edwin's lots (#285) were sold to James and Anna Whetton of Newton, MA. Two more lots next to the Whetton's place were sold to John and Susan Harrer, also of Newton, MA. Lastly the next lot over (#290) was sold to Arthur and Marion Rivers of Millis, MA. B/P 357/479; B/P 357/479; B/P 358/447; B/P 357/214; B/P 356/428.

[4] To Raymond and Rosa Weed of Wakefield, MA, B/P 370/353 and to William and June Fuller of Hudson, NH. B/P 372/116.

[5] To William, Arial and Donald Cruwys of Arlington, MA. B/P 363/424.

[6] The sales included #292 to Ann Herrick of Metuchen, NJ; part of lot #294 to Charles and Dorothy Cassasa of Somerville, MA and another part of now lot #294 to David and Ruth Harding of Billerica, MA; an add-on parcel was sold to Ralph and Rosalie Conte (became #299); another lot (#300) was sold to Virginia Weed and Lillian Ward of Reading, MA; Prescott and Eloise Smith of Concord, MA bought another (#301); in 1958, an add-on lot was sold to Arthur and Marion Rivers (#292) as was another add-on lot to the Contes (became #297); and finally a lot (#296) was sold to John and Gertrude Nichols. B/P 378/367; 379/195; 608/474; 608/476; 379/161; 385/373; 382/515; 401/174; 390/369; 390/529.

[7] In 1953, the Stoothoffs sold their large parcel to Henry and Marcia Marcionette of Winchester, MA, who had purchased the place next door (#313) in 1948. In 1955, the Marcionettes sold their initial home (#313) to the Sayce family (including their daughter, Dorothy Falk) of Charlestown, NH. They also sold part of the land acquired from the Stoothoffs (#316) to Stanley and Winifred Swanton of Andover, MA. Then in 1959, the Marcionettes subdivided their remaining parcel in two, selling one part (#315) to David and Daphne Higgins of Concord, NH, and the other (#314) to Scott and Kathleen Taylor of Gilford, NH. The net result was an increase of two more summer vacation homes on Dolly's Point. B/P 365/539; 366/34; B/P 397/275; 400/74.

[8] Ruth and Edwin Hahn took ownership a 65' piece (#318), and their son, E. Russell, and his wife, Jeanette, took ownership of a 35' piece (#317).B/P 401/507; 401/510.

expanded his property to the north, buying another 50' of frontage from Gokey. Then in 1955, Gokey sold another sizable lot with about 230 feet of frontage (#159 - #160) just north of Eli Sinotte to Joseph Golab of Cambridge, MA. Finally in 1958 Gokey sold an even larger lot with 300 feet of frontage (#165) adjoining the boy's camp to Madeline and James Kane. The Kane purchase resonated with the history of French cove. Madeline was the daughter of Albert R. Gokey, a French cove vacationer since 1901.[1] Thus by the end of the decade, the eastern side of old Lot 7 had a colony of five families living where there was only one before, traversing some 800 feet or so of shoreline.

East Bear Colony

Emily Brown's dock next to the ice-damaged mail dock.

In 1950, there were still 10 families owning places on East Bear, the same number as in 1926. The colony grew by two more during the decade, both the result of subdivisions created by departing vacationers. The first new lot (part of #133) was created in 1951 by Joe Pickford, who was one of the earlier vacationers on East Bear (1911). Between age and ailing health, the widowed Joe had decided that it was time for him to forsake the island. In January 1951, he divided his 176' of frontage and sold 50' of it to Mrs. Emily Brown of Dorchester, MA. She was Joe's long-time housekeeper. She had been living in a small trailer on this lot for years and had a dock extending out from the small beach next to the East Bear mail dock. Joe then sold the larger part of the lot, including his house and boat house, to his daughter and son-in-law, Marion and Harry T. MacKinnon of Dorchester, MA.[2]

Next door to the Pickford place, the colony grew by one more family in 1955 when Virginia Graf divided her property and sold the southerly parcel (#131) to George and Eleanor Holsten of Metuchen, NJ. The following year, Graf sold her place (#129) to Dr. Francis B. and Evelyn Nelson of Westfield, NJ.[3]

---

[1] B/P 354/182; 354/ 183; B/P 323/263; B/P 354/181; B/P 379/372; B/P 390/225.

[2] B/P 326/515; 326/ 516.

[3] B/P 360/176; B/P 369/242. The latter place was the original Halcrow house built c. 1907. Both the Holstens and the Nelsons were introduced to the lake by the Wuesters who bought property on Jerry Point in 1947. Eleanor Holsten was the sister of William Wuester while Bud Nelson practiced medicine with Dr. Wuester in New Jersey. Interestingly, as a result of these two sales, one third of the East Bear Colony made their permanent homes in New Jersey.

In contrast to this expansion, the southern end of the colony was becoming increasingly neglected. The original Bacheller place (#139) had fallen into disrepair, although the Crowther family brought back some life to the old, broken down house when they purchased it in 1954. Next door, the Newland home (#135-#138) was also showing the effects of disuse, and it remained largely unoccupied throughout the decade. Only the Fay's place (#140) at the very end of the colony was thriving.

Summary

The decade of the 1950s was the most vibrant in the island's history since 1910. Some 23 new summer places were purchased on Bear between 1951 and 1960, with the bulk of it occurring during the latter part of the decade. More than half of the growth occurred on Dolly's Point where the shorefront of the Mansfield estate was largely sold off. The rest of the growth was spread widely among various other locations around the island.

Chapter Thirty-Two

The Vacation Era: The 1960s

The decade of the 1960s witnessed a further acceleration in the growth of the summer population on Bear Island. The number of new vacation places increased by 27 during the decade, the highest ten-year total thus far. Almost all of it occurred on South Bear where there was more vacant land available. On North Bear, the expansion was quite modest, but islanders on that end were faced with the daunting prospect of large-scale real estate development on the former Alvord property.

North Bear

Neither the western shorefront (including Jerry Point) nor the eastern side of North Bear experienced any additional summer expansion during the 1960s. The western side was already heavily settled, and the undeveloped shorefront on the eastern side was tied up in the Alvord situation.

Crane's Point Lots Sold

Crane's Point at the tip of the island was an exception. Four new summer places were added there. At the beginning of the 1960s, the parcel contained only the original Crane house (#2), now owned by the Maguire family, and two vacant lots that had been sold in the 1950s. There was still 600' of unsold shorefront in the subdivision plan completed by the Maguires in the mid-1950s. All of this land was sold during the first half of the decade.[1] The subdivision and sale of John Crane's property closed the last remaining gap in the increasingly dense summer population that occupied the shoreline from the peninsula dividing the Carry cove from Plummer cove all the way around Crane's Point and then part way down the eastern side of Bear. This extended colony spanned current day addresses #342 through #24, amounting to some 49 separate houses.[2]

---

[1] The Maguire's first sale occurred in February 1961 when the director of Alvord, Robert Frey of Plymouth, NH purchased a large parcel (now #8 Bear).B/P 412/361. Frey did not build on the land. He sold the lots to Evelyn Hamilton in 1964. B/P 442/244. The Hamiltons built a house there in 1970. In March 1961, the Maguires sold a larger parcel (now #10 Bear) to Richard and Nancy Bounty of Darien, CT. B/P 413/302. The purchase was speculative. They already owned a house (#24) just down the shore. Bounty sold this land to Russell Hoyt in 1963. B/P 431/132. Shortly thereafter, the Maguires sold their last lot (now part of #4) to Arthur and Virginia Herald of Watertown, MA, who built a house not long thereafter. B/P 412/539. A few months later, the changes on Crane's Point were completed when the Maguire's in-laws sold the lot (#6) that they had purchased in 1956 to Charles Sweetser who built a house there soon after. B/P 416/306. The changes did not end there, however. Cornelius Maguire died in 1962. Two years later his wife, Doris, sold the original John Crane home to two families, including Roland and Marion St. Laurent and Lawrence and Corinne Landers of Nashua, NH.

[2] One vacant 100' lot from the Maguire subdivision remained on Crane Point at the end of the 1960s. This was the lot previously sold to James Yates in 1956. He sold it to Bruce Lund in 1961. Lund did not build on it. He retained it until 2007 when he sold it to Richard Laronde who incorporated it into Bear #4 which he purchased in 1994. B/P 2422/462.

A Crisis Emerges: Alvord Sells to a Development Group

Although the Alvord Wildlife Sanctuary had seemingly flourished on the island since the mid-1950s, the interests of its benefactors changed in the mid-1960s. They decided to sell almost all of the wildlife preserve and use the proceeds elsewhere. In July 1969, Alvord's controlling entity, the American Humane Education Society, sold the island holdings to an entity called Whortleberry, Inc. of Tuftonboro, NH. Whortleberry was originally established in Plymouth, NH in 1964 by none other than Robert Frey, the director of the Alvord. The purchase price was $80,000. The deal called for the transfer of all of Alvord's lands except a 17.5 acre parcel located in the center of North Bear.[1] The sale raised the specter that the deserted interior of the island would be developed, setting off alarm bells among Bear Islanders and touching off a challenging process that played out during the early 1970s.

Camp Nokomis Changes Hands

Much further down the shore on North Bear, the McDonalds were struggling by the early 1960s with the mounting costs of managing Camp Nokomis. They decided to sell it if they could find an appropriate buyer who would respect their pride and joy. They found such a buyer in 1962 in the name of the Lawrence YMCA, which owned Camp Lawrence on South Bear. The sale was closed in August. Frank and Jinx McDonald were retained to run the camp. The impact of the sale was quite positive. During the 1963 summer season, enrollment at the camp almost doubled, reaching 120 girls. Nokomis has thrived ever since.[2]

The McDonalds' Carry Cove Land

Frank and Barbara McDonald excluded from the sale to Lawrence a 440' tract of undeveloped frontage on the northern side of the Carry Cove. In 1967, they subdivided the property into three pieces. They sold one parcel (part of #93) in September to Ervin and Joanne Leavitt of Laconia, NH, creating a new vacation home there.[3] The following year, 1968, they sold another portion to the Jones family that already owned the house (#90) abutting Camp Nokomis.[4] They held onto the remaining parcel that was near the base of the cove.

South Bear

East Bear Colony

In sharp contrast to North Bear, there was extensive expansion on the southern half of the island. The East Bear colony experienced the most change of any part of the island during the

---

[1] B/P 523/319; 523/327.
[2] B/P 426/247; See also <u>Bear Island Reflections</u>, p. 133.
[3] B/P 481/47.
[4] B/P 507/434.

1960s. The biggest impact was felt on old Lots 5 and 6N, on the vacant land between the Carry cove and the end of the East Bear colony (#119). Helen Graham sold her remaining holdings--64 acres--in 1961 to the Bear Island Realty Corporation (BIRC), an entity established by Duane Keeler of Pembroke, NH.[1] Duane was a former insurance executive (among other things). The Keelers had previously spent several years boating on the lake and occasionally rafting off of the Kuwiyan beach. Duane recruited a number of relatives and friends to join him in the venture.

As a first step, the BIRC established a camp ground in the prime beach area. It then subdivided the shorefront on either side of the beach and began the sales process to pay off the mortgage used to buy the land.[2] The effort to sell shorefront lots bore fruit immediately. In 1962, the BIRC sold ten of the 15 lots laid out from the Carry Cove to the beginning of the original East Bear colony.[3] Four more shorefront lots were sold before the decade ended.[4]

Meanwhile, the original East Bear colony expanded by a net of three new places due to subdivision. One new summer lot was created in 1960 when the Hoppers subdivided their original lot (#119) and sold the southern half (#121) to Clifford and Mildred Sawtelle of Westfield, MA.[5] Further expansion occurred in 1966 after Nelson Page acquired the original property of the 1905 vacationer, John Newland, located south of the mail dock.[6] Page subdivided it, creating four lots, two of which he quickly sold.[7] The addition of these three new places was offset by one one when Mrs. Emily Brown sold her small lot next to the mail dock to Robert Stoller of Newburgh, NY in 1968. He had purchased the former Pickford place in 1965.[8]

While this was going on, there was one other noteworthy departure from the island. After 34 years, the Fays sold their place (#140) to George Mayo of Lexington, MA in 1965.[9] Interestingly, Mayo was the grandson of George D. Mayo, the Laconia businessman who had purchased the 1100' strip on the eastern shore of North Bear in 1909.

Thus, the 1960s was a period of dramatic change on East Bear. The colony more than doubled in size. Lot sales on old Lots 5 and 6N added 14 new places, while subdivision within

---

[1] B/P 420/45.

[2] The property was on the market for $12,000.

[3] One lot near the point of the cove (#101) was sold to Elmer and Dori Shirley of Goffstown, NH. A lot on the point of the cove (#102) was sold to Robert of Berlin, NH and Roger Garland of Newburyport, MA. The next two lots (#103 and #104) were purchased by Francis Covill and Roger Soley of Stoneham, MA and Newburyport, MA. Lloyd and Leah Creighton of Bradford, MA purchased lot #106, and Duane and Norma Keeler bought the large beach lot (#109). William Kneath of Andover, MA bought a small lot on the southern end of the beach (#110). The next three lots south were sold to Lena Wells of Epsom, NH (#111), Cedric Dustin of Bow, NH (#112), and Gerald Elwell of Suncook, NH (#113). The last lot (#117) sold in this first wave was purchased by Stanley and Helen Hopper who owned the northern most place (#119) in the original East Bear colony. B/P 432/459; 510/100; 428/102; 485/492; 793/301; 529/161; 520/331; 506/253; 504/334; 490/72; 435/440.

[4] One (#115) was sold to William Stafford of Laconia, NH in 1966. Two more (#105 and #114) were sold in 1967 to Harold Cady of Manchester, NH and Gerald Kelley of Belmont, NH, respectively. The last sale, also in 1967, was a lot (#97) near the base of the Carry Cove that was sold to Frank and Sieger Canney of Wilmington, MA. B/P 470/189; 489/318; 471/113; 660/356.

[5] B/P 407/384.

[6] B/P 473/100. Reverend John Newland was the first person to buy land in the East Bear Colony from Edward Luce back in 1905. Long since deceased, his large property had fallen into neglect.

[7] He sold one to John Tappan of Framingham, MA in 1967 and another to Richard Cole of Boscawen, NH in 1968. B/P 407/384; B/P 490/430; 506/323.

[8] B/P 456/85; 452/259; B/P 499/19; B/P 456/85.

[9] B/P 452/259.

the original footprint created a net of two more. And the changes went even further: within the original colony itself, seven of the 12 owners at the beginning of the decade sold out.

Old Lot 7: Deep Cove and French cove

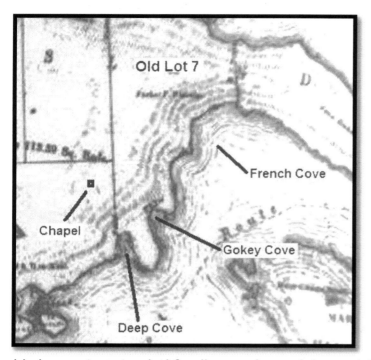

During the 1960s, there were modest additions on various parts of old Lot 7. Two new summer places were added in Deep Cove. Entering the decade, the only presence there was the Sauerbrunn house (#282) on the north shore point of the cove and the St. John's Chapel dock toward the base of the cove. In 1963, Albert Gokey sold a lot (#277) next to the church dock to Leo and Dorothea Tremblay. The next year, he sold an adjacent lot nearer the base of the cove (#276) to Herman and Barbara Story.[1]

Gokey also sold two new vacation parcels on the shore front between Gokey cove (#259) and the well settled French Cove colony. In 1967, he sold the lot (#256) next to his house to extended family members, John and Claire Burke, of Nashua. The following year, he sold the next lot over (#255) to Donna Frampton of Rowley, MA.[2] When the dust settled, there there remained only one unoccupied lot (#254) on the entire shoreline between the Deep Cove peninsula and Camp Lawrence.

Southeastern Bear Colony

While no new summer places were sold on the southeastern shoreline of old Lot 7 during the 1960s, Albert Gokey did make three shorefront sales, all basically speculative in nature. The first occurred in 1967 when George W. Mayo Jr., who owned the home (#140) on the end of the East Bear colony, purchased 260' of frontage (eventually #143 and #145) adjoining his property.[3] property.[3] The next year, Gokey sold a nearby parcel (#150) to Bud and Millie Sawtelle who already owned a place on East Bear (#121).[4] In 1968, Gokey sold the frontage between Sawtelle Sawtelle and Mayo to Robert E. Barrett who had a summer place on Governor's Island.[5]

---

[1] B/P 448/270; B/P 450/119.
[2] B/P 497/106; B/P 504/57.
[3] B/P 495/198.
[4] B/P 444/88.
[5] B/P 497/245. Barrett had owned the original Pearsall place on East Bear (#127) for 14 years before selling it in 1967.

Dolly's Point Colony

During the 1960s, no additional vacation parcels were sold on old Lot 9, but there was a noteworthy change. E.C. Mansfield's granddaughter, Mary Plancon, departed the island, selling the original Mansfield home to Norman and Grace Baker of Hingham, MA in 1962.[1] This transaction marked the end of the Mansfield era on Bear Island after 64 years.

Summary

Like the decade before it, the 1960s brought a good deal of change to the island. Some 29 new summer places were established on the island, raising the total number of vacation homes from 112 to 141. More than half of the increase took place on East Bear following the sale of the former Camp Kuwiyan property. Albert Gokey's sales on different parts of old Lot 7 accounted for another handful. Meanwhile, North Bear was confronted with the unwanted possibility of development of the interior of the island.

Vignette

The History of Cattle Landing

The public wharf on Meredith Neck known as Cattle Landing was acquired by the town of Meredith in 1960.[2] It was the town's third public access point on Winnipesaukee associated with Bear Island. The first was the Bear Island mail dock (1934), and the second was the public lot and docks at Lovejoy Sands (1948).

Cattle Landing was originally known simply as the 'Ferry Landing'. It was located on the shore of original Neck Lot 82. When Robert Bryant settled on Bear Island in the very early 1800s, it was the primary location by which people accessed the island because it was the closest point to it. The spot had a natural slope toward the water, still evident just south of the present location of the public dock.[3]

Lot 82 was unoccupied when the ferry landing was established.[4] The ferry was in use years before the first Meredith farmer bought the far end of Lot 82. It was not until 1817 that the southern-most 60 acres of it, including where the ferry landed, were acquired by the Mead family.[5] But the Meads had no problem with the ferry landing. They only used the lot for seasonal

---

[1] B/P 426/278.
[2] B/P 405/205.
[3] This lot is now #62 Cattle Landing Road.
[4] It was owned by Ebenezer Smith, Meredith's patron who lived near Lake Opechee.
[5] B/P9008/164. The acreage was sold to William and John Mead by John Mooney, Ebenezer Smith's son-in-law. John Mead sold his half to William in 1832. (B/P 9014/97). William sold the 60 acres to William S. Mead in 1861. (B/P 47/146). William S. Mead sold it to Smith Paine in 1895. (B/P 95/573). The ferry landing is not referenced in any of these deeds.

seasonal grazing and for wood.[1] Moreover, the ferry did not really infringe upon the land, other than having very small herds of stock driven across it to the departure point. Further, during the 1800s, Meredith farmers had little or no interest in shoreline property anyway. In the case of the Meads, this was made clear in 1868 when William Mead sold a one rod (16.5') deep strip of the shoreline to the Winnipesaukee Lake Cotton and Woolen Manufacturing Co.[2]

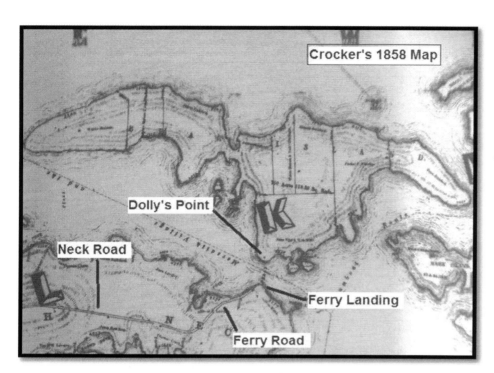

Joseph and Dolly Nichols established their ferry service about 1813. During these early years, there was no real roadway to the landing. Presumably, a cow path of some sort evolved off of the end of the Neck road, turning east toward the lakeshore where the modern day Cattle Landing Road starts. As demand for a better road to the landing arose in the 1840s, the town developed its first layout for it in 1844.[3]

Dolly operated the ferry service until the early 1850s when she left the island for the Poor House. Theophilus Dockham briefly ran the ferry during the middle 1850s, and then Waldo Meloon became the ferry operator. Waldo introduced a second departure point from the Neck, across from his farm on North Bear.[4] He also ferried people across from Dolly's landing until the early 1880s, when Solomon Lovejoy replaced him in 1883.[5] Neck farmers including the Gilmans, John Smith, Sam Randall, David Clark, and Lewis Eaton, all had stock transported to Bear Island for summer grazing. When David Clark and Lewis Eaton sold old Lot 7 to James Aiken in 1897, Clark reserved the right "to pasture six cattle" on the island for two more years.[6] By this time, there were numerous private steamers that were used to tow barges across the channel to Bear for the seasonal farmers. This activity continued into the early 1900s. There was enough traffic, for example, that still in 1898, a well-defined road was evident on Bear Island that began on Dolly's

[1] The 35 acres that the Meads did not own were purchased by various others including Theophilus Dockham, David Lovejoy and Thomas Clark.
[2] B/P 47/349.
[3] Wyatt, Road Histories, p. 37.
[4] His landing spot on the Neck is not known, but the logical place was the same that became Lovejoy Sands. It was owned by Charles Bickford, the former owner of Lot 6S. Charles had developed that spot before Solomon bought it, at least building a house there.
[5] Beginning in 1886, Solomon Lovejoy operated his own ferry service from Lovejoy Sands. He may have also handled ferry services for the Neck farmers, although most of his boating activity was related to the hotel.
[6] B/P 99/174.

Point.[1] The era was over, however, by the 1920s. By then, almost all of the Neck farmers that used Bear had sold their island properties. As Neck resident, Mary Hibbard, reminisced in 1925, "not even a single cow is kept on the island, although a few years ago they might be seen in the fall returning to the main land on a flat boat towed by steamer or motor boat."[2]

With the expansion of the vacation era and individual boating, the ferry service lapsed into disuse. Around this time, the landing (really, just the wharf) somehow came into the possession of Raymond Ramsdell, a Plymouth, NH native who bought a vacation place (#321) on Dolly's Point in 1912. He wanted it, naturally, to provide docking on the mainland. There is no record showing when or from whom Ramsdell acquired it. Indeed, it is an open question about who would have owned the wharf. There was no land (no parking lot) associated with it. Between 1897 and 1922, this portion of Lot 82 was owned by George K. Webster, a Rhode Islander who oversaw a highly successful jewelry business.[3]

Aside from the mysteries of when and from whom he obtained the wharf, Ramsdell took ownership of it, and it became his private dock. Sometime before his death c. 1930, he sold half interests in it to his island neighbors, Edwin Foster (#327) and John Renfrew (#323).[4] Foster held held on to his ownership share in the landing until 1949. John Renfrew's half, on the other hand, passed through a number of hands. In 1930, he sold his half in undivided quarter shares to Elmer Huckins individually and to Edward Brogan and J. E. Maynard jointly.[5] At the same time, John Renfrew sold undivided quarter shares in his Dolly Point fishing camp to each of them.[6] John Renfrew kept the remaining one-fourth share of the camp, but he no longer owned any part of the wharf. That ownership stayed in place until 1935 when Huckins sold his quarter share of "the old ferry" and the camp to Harl Pease who immediately sold them to Earle Renfrew.[7] Two years later, in 1937, the line-up changed again when Maynard and Brogan sold their joint quarter share in the wharf and their individual quarter shares in the cottage to Bertha Hughes of Plymouth.[8] The ownership structure changed yet again in 1938 when John Renfrew sold his remaining quarter share in the camp to Frances M. Chase, and Earle Renfrew sold his quarter share of both the wharf and the camp to Chase as well.[9] The Dolly Point camp was now owned in undivided halves by Frances Chase and Bertha Hughes. They also owned half of the mainland wharf. Edwin Foster, their next door neighbor on Bear, continued to own the other half.

Throughout this entire period, the owners of the wharf had no ownership interest in any of the land to which the landing was attached. It was simply accepted by anyone who cared that the

---

[1] B/P 100/444.
[2] Old Meredith and Vicinity, p. 93.
[3] By 1922, Webster had built a small house nearby. B/P 2/143. In re Webster, see also Chapter 37, Mark Island.
[4] See B/P 359/108 re Foster. Foster and Renfrew were also from Plymouth, NH. On a separate note, after Raymond Ramsdell passed away c. 1930, his family donated a stain glass window to the St. John's Chapel in his honor. His family continued to summer on Dolly Point until Ray's wife, Sybil, sold it in 1938.
[5] See B/P 220/470.
[6] B/P 220/20; 238/428; 238/429.
[7] B/P 220/470.
[8] B/P 238/420; 238/430; and 238/431.
[9] B/P 236/154; 236/155. We did not find a specific deed selling Earle Renfrew's share of the wharf but a later sale by Chase confirmed he had purchased it from Earle.

wharf was owned by the islanders, and their right of access to it derived from the town road.[1] This ownership of the wharf stayed unchanged until 1949. In June of that year, C.K. Plancon (#310) made them an offer they apparently could not refuse. He acquired complete ownership of the wharf, which for the first time in the deeds was referred to as "the Old Cattle Landing" as well as "the Old Ferry."[2] Plancon owned Cattle Landing for the next 11 years. It was not until May 1960 that the town of Meredith acquired the wharf from C.K.'s wife, Mary, and began development of Cattle Landing as we know it today.[3] In 1960, the town took possession of some some nearby land to construct the parking lot. Moreover, Cattle Landing Road was improved for the first time since 1947.[4]

---

[1] This was another case in which 'adverse possession' applied. By this time, the landing and the access to it had been in place for more than 140 years. The location was still quite remote. The 1844 road to the landing was hardly well defined. According to Harold Wyatt: "Until the summer of 1947, the only work on this road had been to cut the trees wide enough for one-way traffic." Wyatt, Road Histories, p. 37.

[2] B/P 358/107; 358/108. Smith Paine, who sold the property in 1897, had labeled the shoreline area "Cattle Rock Point". See B/P 98/216 and B/P 888/165. The first deed, from 1897, is very difficult to read. The second is a 1984 affidavit from Paine's daughter referencing Cattle Rock Point. Intervening deeds call the place Castle Rock, perhaps because of the illegibility of the first deed.

[3] B/P 359/107; 359/108; 405/205. The town had relocated and widened Cattle Landing Road in 1959, moving it to its current location. See Plan B/P 24/1835.

[4] For detail about the town's involvement, see Wyatt, Road Histories, copy of a letter located between pages 38-39.

Chapter Thirty-Three

The Vacation Era: The 1970s

During the 1970s, the increase in the number of summer homes on Bear Island reached a crescendo when 39 additional lots were sold on the island. The decade total amounted to more than 20% of all the places on the island today. The surge was experienced on almost all parts of Bear, but most of it occurred on the two previously neglected strips of shorefront on the eastern side of North Bear and the southeastern side of South Bear. Meanwhile, the decade was also noteworthy for the fight to keep the interior of North Bear from being developed.

North Bear

The Alvord Situation

Entering the 1970s, the extensive acreage and shoreline of the Alvord Wildlife Sanctuary were in the hands of Robert Frey and Whortleberry. They had no plans to hold onto their acquisition. Just seven months after acquiring it, they flipped the Bear Island property to an entity named White Water Trust B for something in the range of $165,000.[1] White Water, formed only a few months earlier in September 1969, was the creation of five Massachusetts real estate professionals who established it for the future benefit of their children.

Island residents were upset with Frey, the putative environmentalist. He turned his back on their overtures to buy the land and instead sold it to pure real estate speculators. The possibility of outsiders divvying up the remaining shorefront and perhaps developing the interior of North Bear roused island residents to fight the prospect.

Control over the former Alvord property dominated events on the northern end of Bear for most of the early 1970s.[2] Led by the yeoman efforts of Charlie Jobes and several others, North Bear residents took a number of steps to prevent White Water from developing the island. Working with the town, a special island zoning board was created in 1970 to regulate future plans for island development. Significantly, the board consisted of three members from Bear Island. They also began negotiations with White Water to purchase the property. The islanders created the Bear Island Taxpayers Association in 1972 with the express purpose of making the acquisition. In 1973, they reached an agreement to buy the property for $180,000. A new legal entity, the Bear Island Wildlife and Forest Preserve, was incorporated to make the purchase. Some $64,000 was raised from islanders to fund the down payment, supported by the personal guarantees of five of the islanders. The deal closed in December 1973.

---

[1] B/P 535/342; 525/490; B/P 535/350
[2] This section is drawn from <u>Bear Island Reflections</u>, pp. 145-149, which provides an excellent account of the situation.

The Bear Island Forest and Wildlife Preserve then adopted a plan to sell some of the lands it acquired to retire the debt owed to White Water. The plan had two broad facets. First, small, interior lots adjoining shore front properties would be sold to current residents so septic fields could be moved further away from the shoreline. This process was well received, and the sales of backland moved fairly swiftly.

The second facet entailed selling the unoccupied shore front on the eastern side of the island. The North Bear organization also enjoyed success in this endeavor. Some 15 new vacation places were carved out over the course of the decade. The roughly 500' strip north of the old Mayo parcel was subdivided into five lots (#26 through #30), all of which were sold to separate buyers in 1974.[1] Another lot (#34) was sold in 1976.[2] Within the old Mayo parcel (#36 through #54), five lots were sold in 1974, and the remaining four were sold over the next three years.[3]

The North Bear organization also had acquired two properties on the thickly settled western side of North Bear. One was the original Merrill place (#434) located next to the mail dock that included the Alvord museum. It was sold in 1974 to St. Laurent Realty whose principals, Roland and Marion St. Laurent, were joint owners of the former Crane house next door (#2).[4] Further down the shore, the last remaining vacant lot (#418) was also finally sold in 1974.[5]

While the sales efforts were underway, in 1975 the North Bear islanders created a new charitable trust, the Bear Island Conservation Association (BICA), to take ownership of and manage the more than 80 acres of backland it had acquired.

Meanwhile on Jerry Point

While the Alvord saga was playing out, one new vacation place was added on Jerry Point during the 1970s. John and Katharine Foster purchased the large property (#380-#384) on The Gulf from the Harrington family in 1972.[6] In 1976, the Fosters subdivided the lot and sold a parcel (#380-#382) to Joseph and Ann Divine of Milford, NH.[7]

---

[1] #26 to B. and B. Olmsted, B/P 641/154; #27 to J. and G. Stewart, B/P 642/26; #28 to J. and L. Milne, B/P 633/296; #29 to L. Ritchie, B/P 633/299; and #30 to H. and P. Koch, B/P 643/139.

[2] Sold to A. Merrill, B/P 688/317.

[3] #36 sold in 1977 to S. Heath of Center Harbor, B/P 711/330; #39 sold in 1976 to A. Cail and S. Fennell, both from MA, B/P 688/121; #44 sold in 1975 to L and M. Chen of New York City, B/P 665/12; #45 sold in 1976 to C. and J. Dougan of Ipswich, MA, B/P 671/246; #47 sold in 1974 to G. and L. Pedersen of Meredith, B/P 639/431; #48 sold in 1974 to P. and B. Ylvisaker of Cambridge, MA, B/P 631/251; #52 sold in 1974 to H. and B. Wilson of Williamstown, MA, B/P 633/265; #53 sold in 1974 to K. and M. Wieneke of Williamstown, MA, B/P 627/305; and #54 sold in 1974 to the Bertram Blaisdell Agency of Meredith, B/P 633/117. Lots #52 - #54 encompassed the well known hotel (later Alvord) beach area.

[4] B/P 626/389.

[5] B/P 657/21. To Lauren and Beverley Stevens of Williamstown, MA. This lot was first put on the market by Solomon Lovejoy c. 1886. It passed through the hands of every party that owned all or parts of the old hotel property including George Collins, the McIntyres, and the Mary Mitchell Humane Society.

[6] B/P 584/100.

[7] B/P 674/447.

Opposite Jerry Point, on the eastern side of the Carry cove, a potential summer place was taken off the market in 1976 when Jinx and Frank McDonald sold their 200' of undeveloped frontage to the adjoining Leavitt family (#93).[1]

South Bear

South Bear experienced its own share of growth along with some drama during the 1970s.

East Bear Colony

Entering the decade, the East Bear Colony consisted of an almost uninterrupted string of houses stretching from the Carry Cove (#93) to the Mayo place (#140). Nevertheless, four more vacation places were added during the 1970s. The first new vacation home was added in 1970 when George Mayo built a new place (#143) on the land next door that he had acquired a few years before.[2] He sold his existing place (#140) to David Erickson.[3] Then, two new vacation places were carved out within the bounds of the original East Bear colony. The first was in 1971 when Nelson Page sold part of his property (#136) very near the old mail dock to Jack and Eleanor McGee of Nashua.[4] The next year, in 1972, Page sold his remaining unoccupied lot (#137) to Philip and Anne Ackerman of Lexington, MA.[5]

Southeastern Shore Colony Grows Dramatically

South of the East Bear Colony, the southeastern shore was still largely uninhabited. There was a small colony of five places at the end next to Camp Lawrence. Most of the vacant shorefront was owned by Albert Gokey. This shoreline stretch was among the last places on the island to be acquired by summer residents due to its steep and rocky nature in most places. Modern technology (i.e. septic pumps) and perspicacity overcame the hesitations of those who had previously passed on the opportunity to build there. In 1971 and again in 1973, Gokey developed subdivision plans for it, carving out seven lots covering almost 900 feet of shorefront (#151 through #158). He sold three of them (#151, #153, and #155) in 1971 and 1972.[6] Another lot was sold in 1973 to his mother-in-law, Gladys Leigh, of Brighton, MA.[7] Three more lots (#152, (#152, #154, and #158) were sold to Phyllis Haffenreffer Stetson as part of a larger sale by

---

[1] B/P 699/199; 733/407.
[2] This lot extended the East Bear Colony into old Lot 7.
[3] B/P 547/407. He kept a vacant lot between the two with deed restrictions against any future house being built on it.
[4] B/P 567/323.
[5] B/P 574/305. This sale was unusual, because the property had only 15' of shore frontage. The cottage was built well back from the shore where the lot widened out. Fortunately, this type of subdivision is no longer permitted on the island.
[6] To J. and D. Lydon of Quincy, MA, B/P 601/308; to W. and A. Toth of Bolton, MA, 592/431; to N. and D. Page of Gilford, NH, 571/128. Page sold his lot to H. Gray who built on it in 1973. B/P 622/219.
[7] B/P 605/299. It already had a house on it, apparently built around 1960 by Gokey. The timing of the house is based upon information contained in the Meredith Tax Assessment card.

Gokey that included frontage on Deep Cove and all of his backland (64 acres in total).[1] Stetson in turn sold all of them over the next three years.[2]

In addition to all of these sales, the adjoining vacant land abutting the original East Bear Colony was also built out during the same time period. George Mayo had a hand in most of it. As noted above, in 1970, he built a home (#143) on a piece of the land he had acquired from Gokey in 1967. In 1972, Mayo bought the lot adjoining his new place from Barrett. Combining it with his own land, he created a six-lot subdivision. He ended up selling the land to three new vacationers.[3] Not to miss out on the market, Bud Sawtelle sold his parcel of vacant land (#150) to Sandor and Brooke Farkas of Youngstown, OH, in 1973.[4]

Thus, within a matter of five years, the southeastern shoreline of Bear was filled out with summer vacation homes. Indeed, the entire shoreline from the Carry Cove to Camp Lawrence was now one continuous string of summer places.

Deep Cove and the Backland of Old Lot 7

While subdividing the southeastern shore, Albert Gokey also worked to sell the last of his vacant shoreline in Deep Cove as well as the large tract of backland that he owned. In 1973, he struck a deal with Phyllis Haffenreffer to acquire almost all of it.[5] Phyllis was the daughter of John John M. Haffenreffer, who was a third-generation member of the Haffenreffer family that established the Haffenreffer Brewery in Boston in the 1870s. As part of the sale, Gokey required that the backland be protected from development. In keeping with this requirement, Phyllis entered into an agreement with the Meredith Conservation Commission in 1974 that prohibited any subdivision and anything more than one house on the back 56 acres of old Lot 7.[6]

A 15 acre parcel, with 165 feet of frontage at the base of Deep Cove, was not included in the conservation area. Haffenreffer developed a plan later in 1974 to subdivide this parcel into three interior building lots with access to the lake via an adjoining a strip of 'common land'. The subdivision plan raised a great deal of concern among the conservation minded. Similar to the fears raised on North Bear, they worried that any interior subdivision would not only over-burden the land but set a precedent for the potential development of other interior tracts of land that had limited or no direct ownership of shore frontage. Coming on the heels of the Alvord issues, Meredith planners established new zoning laws restricting this kind of subdivision on the island, although the Haffenreffer plan was not prohibited completely. With their plans meeting such opposition, the Haffenreffers decided that Bear Island was not the place for them after all. In

---

[1] B/P 605/276.
[2] #154 to U. Sonnerup of Hanover, NH, B/P 614/137; #158 to W. and M. Burdette of Colt's Neck, NJ, B/P 665/473; and #152 to J. Haffenreffer of Boston, B/P 665/268 and then to R. and M. May of N. Adams, MA, 701/298.
[3] Late that year he sold one lot (#147) to C. Richard Irving of Laconia. B/P 600/348. In 1973, he sold another lot (#145) to Peter and Mary Sutcliffe of Trenton, NJ, and a third one (#149) to Donald Benjamin of Doylestown, PA. B/P 602/36; B/P 621/262.
[4] B/P 618/165.
[5] B/P 605/276.
[6] B/P 631/70.

1977, they sold their island holdings to George Mayo who had served as Gokey's realtor and had found the Haffenreffers in the first place.[1] A year later, Mayo sold the lots in the 15 acre parcel to Helen Hamill.[2] Two houses were built on the landlocked parcels (#274 and #275) with overlapping ownership of the unnumbered 'common land' that included the shorefront.

French Cove Colony: The Last New Lot is Sold

Not to be left out, the last unoccupied parcel (#254) in French Cove was also finally sold by Albert Gokey in 1972 to Walter Trojan of Nashua.[3] It had taken 75 years, but the entire southern facing shore of old Lot 7 was now filled with vacation places.

Dolly's Point

The vacation population on Dolly's Point also expanded during the 1970s. Two additional summer homes were established. The first (#309) came about in 1972 when Mary Plancon, who had sold her main house (#310) back in 1962, sold 200' of vacant land next door to her old place to William and June Fuller of Hudson, NH.[4] The second lot was added in 1977 when Ralph and Rosalie Conte subdivided their property (#297-299) as part of a plan to leave the island. They sold one vacant lot (#299) to John Beerman, and they sold the remainder (#297-298) to Charles and Lillian Cullum of Quincy, MA.[5]

Apart from these two new vacationers, another 'new' place (#329) was developed on Dolly's Point when Jules Olitski purchased the lot adjacent to his island home (#327) located towards the base of Plummer cove.[6] He built an artist's studio on the new property. Olitski had made Bear his summer home in 1972. He was a world renowned American painter who enjoyed enormous acclaim in the 1960s and 1970s.[7]

Summary

The decade of the 1970s witnessed the greatest increase in new summer places Bear Islanders had ever seen. Some 39 new vacation places were carved out along the island's shores. As a result of this activity, the once detached summer colonies merged together in long

---

[1] B/P 733/231.

[2] B/P 740/12; 740/14.

[3] B/P 600/339.

[4] B/P 590/393.

[5] B/P 726/112. B/P 724/254. Sadly, Charles died the following year. Shortly thereafter, Lillian sold the island property to Lois B. M. Reed. B/P 761/253.

[6] B/P 631/423. This lot was acquired from the Drew family which had purchased it and other property in the 1950s from the heirs of James Little.

[7] B/P 610/439. Ukrainian-born, he was instrumental in the development of the so-called Color Field school of art. His abstract "spray paintings" of the 1960s are still considered landmark works of this movement. He was among a fairly small group of artists who brought this subset of Abstract Expressionist painting to prominence. For example, in 1966 he represented the United States at the Venice Biennale, and in 1969 he was the first living American artist to be given a solo exhibition at the Metropolitan Museum of Art in New York. Jules died in 2007, but the properties continue to be owned by his family.

strings of vacation homes. Only a few vacant lots remained interspersed here and there around the island.

Vignette

The East Bear Mail Dock

Until the late 1960s, the East Bear mail dock, located between lots #133 and #135, was the focal point for the colony's vacationers ever since it was first completed in 1906. Families and children would gather at the dock to meet the mail boat in the morning, just like the families did on North Bear. They would remain for a swim, make plans for the day, and return home for lunch. The pattern would more or less repeat itself in the afternoon when the mail boat made its second visit of the day.

The Uncle Sam arriving at East Bear wharf c. 1950s.

Once a year the children, usually unchaperoned, would buy tickets on the mail boat and ride it to the Weirs for an afternoon of fun in the arcades. They would then catch it on its return trip, making it back to the island by 3:30 or so. This was a highlight of every summer.

But the dock was subject to Mother Nature's annual abuse during ice out season. Tired of the constant repair costs, the East Bear Island Association voted to eliminate the mail dock after the 1971 season. The mail boat stop—now only a 'drop'--was moved to the private dock next door (#133) that was made available by the Stoller family in 1972. The mail boat still makes its daily 'drops' there, courtesy of the current owners, the Robinson family. But the elimination of the mail dock was a big loss for the colony. It was the embodiment of the sense of community that had enriched the lives of East Bear islanders for decades.[1]

East Bear mail dock c. 1930s

East Bear mail dock after a tough ice out, c. 1961

Morning swim c. 1945

East Bear swimmers c. 1945

[1] Communal mail docks on North Bear, Birch and Jolly still provide this crucial nexus for islanders in those places.

Chapter Thirty-Four

The Last 38 Years

By the 1980s, there were very few unoccupied parcels left on Bear Island. Indeed, over the entire 38 year period from 1980 to the present, there were only seven new vacation places built on the island, and four of these were built in the Carry cove.

The first new place was built in on the eastern side of the Carry cove (part of old Lot 4) in 1983. Michael Kelley of Westford, MA, bought a subdivided lot (#92) from the Leavitt family (#93).[1] The second of the seven was established near the Carry Cove on the western side of the island, facing Meredith Neck. The Smith family subdivided a parcel (#347) from its extensive land holdings and sold it in 1996 to Robert P. Higley of Flemington, NJ.[2] The same year, another new summer place was established on the peninsula forming the south side of Deep Cove. The Chicola family had purchased the entire peninsula in 1949. In 1985, they had developed a subdivision plan for it, but never followed through. After their deaths, their estate administrator revisited the subdivision, and in 1996, a three acre parcel (#271) was sold to Karen Philpot of Gilmanton, NH.[3] The fourth new vacation lot was added on Dolly's Point in 2004. Lois B. McAllister Reed subdivided her property (#298) and sold a parcel (#297) to Michael Robinson and Mary-Ellen Biggs of Haddonfield, N.J.[4]

The last three additions all occurred in 2001 on property that had once belonged to Camp Kuwiyan (part of old Lot 5). Duane and Norma Keeler sold lots on the south shore of the Carry cove to two of their sons, Craig (#98) and Jody (#99).[5] A third son, Eric, acquired the prime beach lot (#107).[6]

The Status Today

There are some 188 separate residences on Bear Island today, ringing virtually the entire island. The large unoccupied stretches between 'colonies' simply no longer exist. The last sizeable, undeveloped parcel (4.25 acres and more than 500' of frontage) was sold in September 2017.[7] It is located at the base of Plummer Cove, bounded to the south by Dolly's Point. This parcel has never been occupied. It was part of old Lot 5, and over the past century, it enjoyed the stewardship first of the James Little family and then the Drew family. Apart from that parcel, the most extensive, unoccupied sections of shore front belong to Camp Nokomis and Camp Lawrence. Here and there a handful of small, potential building lots can be found. All are privately owned except one small parcel held by the town of Meredith in French cove.

---

[1] B/P 845/38. The southern boundary of the Leavitt place was the stone wall that divided old Lot 4 from old Lot 5.
[2] B/P 1396/434.
[3] B/P 1364/757.
[4] B/P 2097/110.
[5] B/P 1654/148; 1654/149.
[6] B/P 793/301; 841/229; 841/329. With this purchase, members of the Keeler family owned five houses and one other lot on east Bear.
[7] B/P 3130/57.

The Backlands

One of the most striking characteristics of Bear Island history is the stark contrast in value different generations of islanders placed upon the interior lands versus the shorefront. During the farming era of the 1800s, the interior was everything, while the shorefront was willingly deeded away to the WLCWM Co. which owned the Lakeport dam. This flip flopped, of course, with the emergence of the vacation era. The shorefront became everything. During the transition years, the Bear Island House straddled the two.

In the early 1970s, the White Water Trust had designs of exploiting the interior of North Bear. Around the same time, the Haffenreffers also had modest plans to build inland summer homes with only very limited shore front. At other times, there were real estate oriented vacationers who also contemplated ways to exploit the interior for personal gain.

Fortunately for the conservation minded, none of these plans came to fruition. Town zoning laws were modified in the 1970s to create an island district which required that any residential building must have 150' of shore frontage. This would seem to preclude any sort of major development in the interior. The large acreage of the two camps, Lawrence and Nokomis, could potentially pose a threat to the status quo, but both camps appear to be thriving. Nevertheless, the rising value of island real estate might someday tempt the trustees of the Lawrence, MA, YMCA to tap into that value for use elsewhere.

There are eight land holders who control most of the interior of the island right now as detailed below:

The Largest Interior Island Land Owners

Rank	NAME	ACREAGE	TAX MAP	OLD LOT #
1	Society for the Protection of NH Forests	161	I07/2 (63.2) I09/9 (98.2)	Lot 7 Lot 6N & 6s
2	Lawrence YMCA	109	I11/1 (72.5) I04/8 (35.6)	Lot 8 Lot 4
3	Bear Island Conservation Association	80	I03/30 (63.7) I02/33 (16.3)	Lots 1-3
4	Falk	55	I06/7C	Lot 9
5	Keeler	33	I08/1C	Lot 5 & 6N
6	Jerry Point LLC	30	I04/5	Lot 4
7	Mayo	12	I10/8B	Lot 6S
8	DeGroot	11	I08/4	Lot 6N

North Bear Backland

Ownership of most of the backlands on North Bear is in the good hands of the Bear Island Conservation Association. The history of how the land ended up with this group was laid out in the preceding chapters as the interior was passed along from hotel owner to hotel owner and ultimately to Alvord before being acquired by BICA in 1973.

The only parts of North Bear backland not in the hands of BICA are on old Lot 4, just north of the Carry. As also detailed in the preceding chapters, two parties own that acreage. One is Jerry Point LLC, a legal entity that continues to be owned by lineal members of the Puffer family that bought Jerry Point in 1912. The other owner is now the Lawrence YMCA, which purchased Camp Nokomis from the McDonalds in 1962.

South Bear Backland

On South Bear, the situation is a little more complicated due to its greater size and varied ownership history. The pre-vacation era history was laid out in earlier chapters. With the transition to the vacation era, some parts of South Bear passed through a number of hands, while the ownership of other parts was quite straightforward.

The backland on Dolly's Point was acquired by E. C. Mansfield in 1898. It remained in the hands of his heirs until 1971. That year, Mansfield's grand-daughter, Mary Plancon, sold the back acreage to Scott and Kathleen Taylor.[1] The Taylors had a summer home (#315) near the point, which they had acquired in 1959. In 1986, the Taylors sold all of their holdings on the island. The backland was purchased by Craig and Dorothy Falk who lived two doors down (#313) from the Taylor place.[2] As part of the sale, the Taylors included a number of provisions prohibiting development or camping on it. The backland has remained in the Falk family ever since, and the prohibitions continue in effect.[3]

The backland of Lot 7 was acquired by James Aiken in 1897. His heirs sold it to Albert J. Gokey in 1944. In 1973, the backland was sold to Phyllis Haffenreffer. Gokey insisted that no development be undertaken on the majority of it. As a result, in 1974 Haffenreffer executed a Conservation Restriction Deed in favor of the Meredith Conservation Commission.[4] In 1977, Haffenreffer sold the property to George Mayo as part of a larger sale. In 1990 and 1991, Mayo gave the land to the Society for the Protection of New Hampshire Forests.[5]

However, not all of old Lot 7's interior is part of this conservation land. A separate 12 acre parcel that includes some of old Lot 6S is owned separately by Mayo's heirs. The property has

---

[1] B/P 585/442.
[2] B/P 960/176.
[3] Ownership was transferred to the Falk's sons, Holton and Bradford, in 2001. B/P1701/751.
[4] B/P 631/70.
[5] B/P 1158/83; 1165/639.

two narrow access strips to the waterfront on East Bear. There is the potential for development on it as it is grandfathered and not subject to the revised island zoning laws.[1]

Ownership of the interior lands of old Lots 5 and 6N went through a fairly straightforward process. They passed from the Gilman family heirs to the owners of Camp Kuwiyan in 1926. In the 1950s, the western 'half' was sold to three Carry Cove families—Smith, Moser and Drew-- who in 1995 donated the 60 or so acres to the Society for the Protection of New Hampshire Forests.[2]

Ownership of the eastern half of old lots 5 and 6N took different turns. Way back in 1910, an 11 acre piece of Lot 6N was sold by David Gilman to Lina Pearsall Earp behind her shorefront place (#124).[3] This parcel abutted the back of Lina's property (#124) and incorporated the natural spring that is still in use by islanders today. The backland property continues to be owned by Lina's heirs, although the family's waterfront property was sold in 2013. The remainder of old Lot 5 and most of Lot 6N are currently owned by Duane and Norma Keeler. The 34 acre parcel is part of their shorefront property (#109). They acquired the lands from the Bear Island Realty Corporation, the entity they formed in 1961 to acquire the former beach and interior lands from Helen Graham.

Old Lot 6S

Old Lot 6S had a number of owners over the years. The entire parcel was acquired by George Greene in 1903. He quickly sold 22 acres, including most of the shore front to Edward Luce, who proceeded to develop the East Bear colony. Greene retained some 35 acres of backland on which he maintained a summer farm for many years.[4] Greene transferred the interior lands to his son, Frank, in 1928. But Frank eventually stopped paying the town taxes on it. Finally, in 1946, the assessor took the land in lieu of taxes. In 1956, the tax office transferred it by deed to the town of Meredith.[5] In 1969, the town sold the land to the East Bear Island Association, a group comprised of the owners of the vacation homes that comprised the original East Bear Colony.[6] In 1990, the EBIA donated the land to the Society for the Protection of New Hampshire Forests.[7]

In the case of Lot 8, this land belongs to the Lawrence YMCA.

---

[1] B/P 2560/171. Two of the access strips to the lake are 18' and 23' wide.
[2] B/P 1361/122.
[3] B/P 129/356.
[4] He also retained a 240' shore lot (now #140 and adjacent land). He sold the shore frontage in 1913.
[5] B/P 377/38.
[6] B/P 529/96.
[7] B/P 1158/87.

Summary

As it sits today, the vast majority of the interior lands on the island are in the hands of good stewards who value Bear Island for its natural beauty and not for its potential monetary value. The future, of course, is unknown. One can only hope that all the interior remains in its undeveloped condition to protect its fragile ecology as well as preserving its natural beauty that is so appealing to everyone who has the pleasure of walking there.

Vignette

The 1988 Tax Revolt

Some 130 years after Waldo Meloon and other Bear Islanders staged a revolt against paying taxes to Meredith,[1] the island's residents 'revolted' again when tax rates increased steeply. An island-wide group was formed and funded in an effort to secede from the town of Meredith. The group hired legal representation to forward its case in the state legislature but met with insurmountable political obstacles. Meanwhile, the group also undertook a careful study of tax rates in Meredith. It found a gross inequity between the rates applied to mainland properties (80% of value) compared with island properties (117% of value). After appeals to the town officials fell on deaf ears, they took the case to the State Board of Land and Tax Appeals. The Board ruled in favor of the islanders, and a reassessment was ordered. The reassessment resulted in far more equitable treatment of island properties. Indeed, the total assessment of Bear Island and Pine Island was reduced by more than $5 million.[2]

---

[1] See, Chapter 15, Vignettes: "The 1850s Tax Revolt," p. 100.
[2] Bear Island Reflections, pp. 150-151.

Part VI:

***

The Bear Island Chapel

*****

The Methodists and the Camp Meeting

Chapter Thirty-Five

The Bear Island Chapel

The Bear Island Chapel is an iconic part of the unique essence that is Bear Island. It has stood for more than 90 years on the highest point of South Bear where the island's first settler, Robert Bryant, established his farm c. 1801. Elegant in its simplicity amongst the trees, the Chapel has become the 'true North' for generations of islanders.[1]

The idea of building a chapel on Bear Island was conceived by Bishop Edward Melville Parker of the Protestant Episcopal Diocese of New Hampshire about 1915. E.C. Mansfield's observation tower on the heights of Dolly's Point had caught his attention as a perfect location for such a chapel. Mansfield's tower stood 60 feet high and commanded a 360 degree view of the lake. It was deemed in those days to be the finest on-lake observation point open to the public. Over the years, it had attracted thousands of visitors from all over the United States, Canada, and Europe.

Serendipitously, in 1922 the Episcopal Reverend Kenneth Ripley Forbes purchased a summer home on Birch Island. Forbes was from Roxbury, MA where he was the rector of the St. James Church. Forbes' presence on the lake was wholeheartedly welcomed by Bishop Parker. The two men seized upon the happy coincidence of their interests to pursue the goal of an Episcopal chapel on Winnipesaukee.

In 1925, Parker obtained an option from Mansfield to buy his observation tower and a three acre parcel providing access to it from Deep Cove. Bishop Parker, however, died in October 1925 before he could complete the purchase and develop plans for the building. His successor, Bishop John Dallas, closed on the property the following year.[2]

Bishop Dallas appointed Reverend Forbes priest-in-charge of the new chapel. He was given complete responsibility for the design, funding, and building of it. Forbes embraced the opportunity. He quickly developed a design that envisioned the construction of a field stone sanctuary attached to the tower. Reverend Forbes began the effort to raise funding for the Chapel in the spring of 1927. His efforts went well as Ernest Dane contributed almost half of the needed monies, and numerous other vacationers, including some 15 Bear Islanders, donated the rest.

With donations in hand, ground breaking occurred in May 1927. The sanctuary was constructed in just three months by J. P. Leighton of Center Harbor.[3] The Chapel, called St.

---

[1] For a more thorough treatment of the history of the Chapel, see John A. Hopper, <u>The Bear Island Chapel</u> (2017).
[2] B/P 186/89.
[3] Leighton was a good choice. He had built Mansfield's tower in 1898.

John's -on-the-Lake, was open for use by the end of July, with Bishop Dallas leading the first service. It was a remarkable accomplishment that has stood the test of time quite well.

St. John's enjoyed immediate success that lasted through the 1930s. As priest-in-charge, Reverend Forbes provided strong leadership and disciplined adherence to the Episcopalian form of worship. Joined by other Episcopalian clergy, Reverend Forbes maintained a schedule of services on eight or nine Sundays each summer from 1928 through 1938.

But there were very different results in 1939. No services were held during the first half of the summer because the Chapel had been made inaccessible by the 1938 hurricane that ravaged New England. It was not until July that the Diocese persuaded the US Forest Service to send in a team of loggers to clear the trail. The Chapel finally was opened on August 6th with Reverend Forbes in charge.

After 1939, the viability of the Chapel changed dramatically. Reverend Forbes resigned as priest-in-charge at the end of that season when he relocated to Philadelphia. The Diocese of New Hampshire did not appoint a replacement. With Reverend Forbes' departure, the Chapel lost its driving force. In 1940, only two services were held, and there are no records of any organized services at the church during the years of World War II.

After the war, the activities at the Chapel began to pick up modestly. In 1947, another Episcopal clergyman, Reverend Richard Martin, began coming to the lake for three weeks of summer vacation. From Monroe, Connecticut, Martin stayed at the home of his brother-in-law on East Bear. He was naturally drawn to the Chapel and began to hold sporadic services there. This continued every year during the late 1940s and into the early 1950s.

In addition, at least a few non-Episcopalian services were also held after the war. Two of Reverend Martin's island neighbors on East Bear were Methodist ministers, Reverend William Wallace and Reverend Stanley Hopper. Both had purchased their summer camps in the mid-1940s, and the serene and usually empty sanctuary beckoned them. Throughout all of these years, the Episcopal Diocese made no attempt to resurrect the Chapel organization, especially after Bishop Dallas died in 1948.

The random use of the Chapel began to change in 1952. Reverend Martin was joined by a new group of vacationers who had recently made Winnipesaukee their summer getaway. The group consisted of several medical doctors who had become close friends at Elizabeth General Hospital in New Jersey. They were introduced to Lake Winnipesaukee by Dr. William Wuester of Hillside, NJ, a highly acclaimed cancer specialist whose summer place was on Jerry Point. The first to join them on Bear Island in 1951 was the Bert and Kay Sauerbrunn family who bought a place (#282) on the point on Deep Cove, near the church property shorefront. The arrival of the Sauerbrunns proved a happy occurrence for St. John's.

Within short order, they began holding 'family services' at the Chapel. During this period the Sauerbrunns made the acquaintance of and became good friends with Reverend Martin. Between the Sauerbrunns, Reverend Martin, and another Wuester compatriot, Robert Crane, several services were held each summer during 1952 and 1953. The services typically followed the Episcopal order of worship, but with the exception of Reverend Martin, the leaders were all laymen. Martin commented later that the "informal worship" style of these laity services held great appeal to the islanders who attended them. He observed that there were many Episcopalians in attendance "but more Methodists and Presbyterians, with various others included."

Apparently unaware of these Chapel services, in early 1954 the Diocese decided to turn over control of the Bear Island Chapel to the growing Trinity Episcopal Church in Meredith so it could be sold. Trinity owned only an unheated summer chapel in town and was using the Grange during the winter months. Bishop Hall of the Diocese believed the funds from the sale of the Bear Island Chapel could be used by the Meredith church to acquire a parish house.

Dr. Sauerbrunn first learned that the Chapel was for sale in February 1954, but purchasing it was not feasible for the islanders. The situation carried into the summer of 1954 without resolution. In July, things took a fortuitous turn. St. John's was visited one Saturday by the wife and son of the Chapel's founder, Reverend Forbes. The son, John Forbes, was visiting the lake from his home in California, and his mother had come up from Philadelphia. Neither had visited St. John's since the late 1930s. Thereafter, John Forbes stepped forward to lead the effort to save the Chapel.

John Forbes was a naturalist, conservationist, and educator who eventually became one of the best known and most respected men in his field. Over the course of his career, he helped establish more than 200 natural science museums and at least a dozen other museums around the country. In 1953, Time magazine referred to him as the 'Johnny Appleseed' of natural museums.

At the July 1954 visit to the Chapel, John and his mother, Ellen, were shocked to discover the 'For Sale' sign on the door. The personal nature of the shock for John was compounded just hours later when his mother died of a heart attack after returning from the Chapel to Birch Island.

Forbes jumped headlong into the effort to save the Chapel. He immediately understood both the dynamics of the situation and the Episcopal politics of it. He turned his immense energies into developing a plan to keep St. John's as a viable entity without having to buy it. For their part, the Sauerbrunns quickly understood that John Forbes was far better placed to lead the effort to save the Chapel.

To begin, Forbes gathered the support of various Episcopal clergy who had previously been involved with the Chapel. He also developed a comprehensive plan for funding and operating St. John's going forward, submitting it to the Bishop. The plan contained all of the elements that Forbes had learned in his non-profit museum efforts around the country. It also included full affiliation with the Episcopal Diocese.

However, Bishop Hall was not swayed by Forbes' plans. Undaunted, Forbes and others then took their case to the Trinity Episcopal leaders in Meredith. They strongly emphasized the damage in goodwill that would result if the Meredith church insisted on selling St. John's. Given the unexpected and unwelcome pressure being felt in his office, Bishop Hall became anxious to resolve the issue. He traveled to Meredith where he met with the Vicar, the Building Committee, and other representatives of the Meredith Trinity church. This meeting proved to be decisive. John Forbes and the other Episcopalians had convinced them that a forced sale would not be worth the headaches that would likely follow. They agreed to forestall the sale of the Chapel for one year to let the island organization "prove its worth."

With the Bishop's approval in hand, the Chapel leadership group convened a meeting in New York City and established the St. John's-on-the-Lake Association on December 15, 1954. Dr. Sauerbrunn was elected president of the new organization, and John Forbes was chosen as secretary. During the summer of 1955, a full schedule of services was well received by vacationers. Total attendance over nine Sundays was 639. The Association also built the first church dock in Deep Cove that summer. The Diocese remained supportive of the Association after the first year of operation. "It is quite apparent from your communications," wrote Bishop Hall, "that St. John's-on-the-Lake has had a splendid summer in every respect. I rejoice with you in the good work which has been accomplished and the promise for the future which prevails."

Following the resignation of John Forbes in 1956, the Association became largely dependent upon the leadership of Dr. Sauerbrunn. He willingly filled that role. His close group of friends constituted the core of a ready-made congregation. They also comprised the lion's share of contributing members. The Chapel continued to enjoy success throughout the latter 1950s. Reverend Martin handled the ongoing challenge of arranging the schedule of clergymen. Each season included a different mix of ministers; but the mix of denominations consisted almost entirely of Episcopalians and Methodists, the latter coming from ministers who summered on Bear.

By the end of the summer of 1959, the St. John's-on-the-Lake Chapel was seemingly firmly established. It had five seasons of successful operations under its belt. It was financially solvent and had built up an excellent following among islanders and some mainlanders as well. But it soon became apparent that the underpinnings of the Association were quite fragile.

The vulnerability of the Chapel organization was laid bare in 1960. The Sauerbrunns had moved to Texas during the fall of 1959 when Bert was recruited to lead a ground breaking effort in the field of nuclear medicine. Not long after the move, he had suffered a heart attack. This combination of events forced the Sauerbrunns to step back from their active leadership of the Association. In their absence, the Association lost direction and drive. There was no one else with the inclination or the time who came forward. As a result, there was no formal schedule of services held at St. John's during either 1960 or 1961. The situation took a dire turn for the worse after Labor Day 1961 when the Chapel was severely vandalized. The harm done by the vandals was extensive, although it was concentrated in the tower section.

Prompted by the vandalism and the continued inactivity of the Association, Methodist ministers Stanley Hopper and William Wallace stepped forward in 1962 to revitalize the Association. They began the process by reaching out to John Forbes. In June 1962, Forbes, Hopper, and Wallace called for the first meeting of the Association since probably July 1959. Their initiative was met with enthusiasm among people who had been involved with the Chapel in years past.

In short order, a full slate of clergymen was lined up for eight Sundays during 1962. Five

were Methodists, three of whom (Hopper, Wallace and Sorenson) were Bear Islanders. The other three were Episcopalians. Just as important as reestablishing a formal schedule of services, the Association also faced the major task of repairing the Chapel. Between the vandalism and 25 years of neglect, the tower needed substantial work; the cross was in danger of falling off of the roof; and the roof of the sanctuary required replacement. All of these things were accomplished before the end of the year. Thus, the St. John's-on-the-Lake Association was back on its feet by the end of the 1962 summer season. As an exclamation point to the effort, the board purchased an 1897 Estey organ for the Chapel. It was carried up the steep trail from Deep Cove for the last service of the year by the boys from Camp Lawrence.

The mid-1960s marked an inflection point in the mission of the Association. Ever since it

Dr. Hopper's island study which he built in 1949.

was established in the 1950s, there had existed an undercurrent of dissonance between the formality of Episcopal rites and the preferences of the non-Episcopalians who comprised most of the congregation. The board determined to alter the religious orientation of the Chapel. Stanley Hopper led the process of change. Dr. Hopper was an ordained Methodist minister, a poet, and a theologian who in the 1950s helped found and became the dean of the first United States graduate program in theology and literature at Drew University. Dr. Hopper saw in the Chapel its potential to play a broader role in the religious lives of all of those on the lake. His vision was to formally change the philosophy of the Association from its outwardly denominational orientation as an Episcopal Church to an organization that was truly interdenominational (one autonomous from any single or specific denomination). This decision to shift was broadly welcomed within the Association.

The commitment to this shift became apparent in 1965 when Dr. Hopper was elected president of the Association. By 1966, the schedule of clergymen had changed markedly to reflect the new philosophy. It included only two Episcopal services. Of the other seven, four were led by Methodists, and one each was led by a minister from the Presbyterian, United Church of Christ, and Catholic denominations.

As the Association embarked on this path away from the Episcopal Church, one last obvious disconnect remained. The Episcopal Diocese still owned St. John's. The Association leadership reached out in 1967 to Reverend William S. Cooper, ironically the Vicar of the Meredith Trinity Episcopal Church, for his insights into how to approach the ownership situation. The outreach bore fruit. Reverend Cooper recommended that the Association incorporate and then buy the property from the Episcopal Diocese for $1.00. He also recommended that the purchase contract contain a clause that ownership would revert back to the Diocese should the Association cease operating the Chapel as a place of worship.

The Association approached Bishop Hall with the plan. He gave it a favorable review, and he even advised the Association to proceed with its incorporation. The following summer (1968), the Association moved full speed ahead with the interdenominational plan. The services schedule for the summer did not include a single Episcopal service. Whether this resulted from conscious planning or simply the challenge of scheduling, the implications were unmistakable. More telling, after 41 years, the Association removed the word 'Episcopal' from the masthead of its schedule of services. Furthermore, the organization was legally incorporated in October 1968 as the St. John's on-the-Lake Chapel Association. Its Articles of Agreement stated its intention "to maintain a summer chapel providing services of worship and ministering to the religious needs of all interested summer residents of Lake Winnipesaukee, New Hampshire."

The following summer, in July 1969, the Association formally re-approached Bishop Hall with the request to purchase the Chapel. Bishop Hall responded that he would present the request to the Trustees at their annual meeting in February 1970. But by January 1971, the Diocese still had not come forth with its approval. The delay caused consternation among the Association officers who re-sent the request to buy the Chapel to Bishop Hall. Two months later, the Bishop responded with an answer. He had presented the proposal to the Standing Committee, but in a "joint decision" they had rejected the deal, desiring that the property remain in the name of the Diocese. The Bishop's letter came as a complete shock to the Association leadership.

Thereafter, the issue of ownership languished for some time without further substantive discussions. In 1973, whatever dialogue the Association had with the Diocese ended when Bishop Hall retired. He was replaced by Bishop Philip A. Smith. In September 1974, leading members of the Association reopened the dialogue with Bishop Smith in Concord. But the meeting did not elicit any definitive response. Another attempt to get action on the issue was made during the summer of 1975, but still nothing came of it.

Then the following summer (1976), the Association president, Duane Keeler, received some shocking news in a surprise phone call from Reverend Joseph Boudreau, a member of the Diocesan Board who had once preached at the Chapel. He informed the Association that the Diocesan Board of Directors had discussed selling the Chapel property to one of its members for use as a vacation home. Association leaders quickly arranged an emergency meeting with Bishop Smith. Bishop Smith immediately consulted with his various advisory groups, drawing the crisis to a

(Photo courtesy of Randy Barba)

conclusion. In late summer 1976, the Episcopal Diocese agreed to sell St. John's to the Association for $1.00 with a reversion clause.

The Association leaders took a unique approach to 'raising' the $1.00 purchase price. They solicited one cent from 100 different people (many of whom were children) thus bestowing upon the community the first-hand sense of ownership in the Chapel. The following summer, Bishop Smith attended a July service at the Chapel to formally convey the deed to the Association. The timing was nearly perfect. The service marked almost to the day the 50th anniversary of the first service at St. John's.

St. John's has prospered ever since. The Board was gradually expanded, and the financial resources of the organization were slowly improved. Most apparent, summer services have been held every year without interruption, remaining true to the interdenominational charter adopted during the 1960s. All of this was accomplished through the efforts of a committed core of vacationers drawn from a variety of summer places including Bear, Birch, Beaver, Meredith Neck, and Moultonborough Neck. Today, the Chapel remains a vibrant memorial to all who have touched its steps, worshipped in its sanctuary, or simply enjoyed its presence. It is the quintessential chapel in the woods.

Camp Nokomis-led service on the lawn.

Chapter Thirty-Six

The Methodists and the Camp Meeting[1]

Members of the Methodist faith played an especially large role in bringing the vacation era to the northwestern part of Lake Winnipesaukee. In the 1870s, they were the first group responsible for developing the Weirs into a summer resort. In the 1880s and 1890s, other groups of Methodists purchased Jolly, Birch, Steamboat, and Pine islands where they subdivided and sold lots largely to other Methodists. The movement also strongly influenced the first summer colony on East Bear Island. The phenomenon was not a coincidence. It had deep roots in the history of Methodism that ran back to the early 1700s.

Methodism refers to the denomination of Protestant Christianity that developed from the teachings of John Wesley in England. Wesley and his brother, Charles, were devout Anglicans who tried to live a holy life systematically. Their methodical application of the strictures of the church led fellow students to derisively call them 'Methodists'. During the 1730s and beyond, the Wesley brothers and others, most notably George Whitefield, began to do missionary work in the United States, but their fervency led many churchmen to exclude them from preaching within their established churches. In response, Whitefield traveled up and down the entire east coast, spreading the word in fiery style to audiences of thousands. His open air 'revival' type meetings drew large numbers of frontiersmen and women as well as people from among the poorer classes. They welcomed the message that emphasized that God accepted all men, not just a chosen few. Francis Asbury was sent to America in 1771 to carry the message further. He became a legend within the church. Beginning at age 26 and self-educated, he rode on horseback all over the United States during the next 45 years —some 275,000 miles—spreading the word at camp meetings.

In 1784, the Methodist Episcopal Church was formally established in the United States. Drawing upon its roots, the meeting place of the religion was not the typical church building but the outdoor camp setting. Like Asbury, preachers followed their own 'long trail' while administering to a widely dispersed flock. They were 'circuit riders' who were completely dedicated and always very poor themselves. The 'camp meeting' became part of the bedrock of Methodism. There were over six hundred camp meetings held in 1818 and almost 1000 in 1820. By 1840, the church had grown to almost 800,000 members from only about 15,000 in 1784.[2] Interestingly, the camp meeting was never an official part of the Methodist organization; it was a locally-controlled practice.

In time, regional groups of clergy established permanent camp meeting grounds. Originally rough and rustic, the permanent camps became more organized after the Civil War.

---

[1] The following discussion is based upon: <u>University in the Forest</u>, by John T. Cunningham, 1972 and "The Camp Meeting on the frontier and the Methodist Religious Resort in the East—before 1900," by Charles A. Parker.
[2] Disagreement over slavery led to the secession of almost 500,000 southern Methodists in 1844.

Numerous Camp Meeting Associations were formally incorporated. They were comprised of anywhere from a dozen to perhaps twenty-five Methodist ministers and laymen. The Associations were chartered by state legislatures as stock companies for the purpose of establishing and developing permanent outdoor meeting grounds. They purchased land for the camps and divided them into lots which were then leased, rented or sold to adherents. And they imposed strict regulations upon residents and visitors.

These camps became very popular, and their emergence dovetailed closely with the growing momentum of the vacation era. They were inexpensive, and they were considered safe places to take the entire family. The camps offered a variety of ways to enjoy a vacation place. Some people became owners of a cottage at the camp; others rented a cottage or very often a tent; and still others would stay at local hotels. The cottage owners were often preachers, lawyers, and businessmen whose families spent the entire summer on the grounds.

One of the earliest incorporated Methodist camp meetings was established in New Hampshire. In the mid-1860s, leaders of some 20 churches in New Hampshire incorporated the Lisbon Camp Meeting Association and established a camp near the Vermont border. The group of clergy

Methodist camp shorefront at the Weirs c. 1906.

included several from central New Hampshire churches as well as those from churches located further north. In the early 1870s, the organizers concluded that they needed to find a location that was more convenient for their members. They decided that access by rail was critical to any new location. After investigating alternatives, they determined that the Weirs offered the best place to establish the new camp because of its railroad station and waterfront property. In 1873, they incorporated a new organization, the Winnipesaukee Camp Meeting Association, and bought a five acre parcel just north of the railroad depot at the Weirs.[1] The arrival of the Methodists was the first major step in transforming the Weirs from a simple backwater passenger station into a destination in its own right. The Methodist camp at the Weirs flourished well into the 20th century, and the buildings in the now-privatized area still reflect its imprint.[2]

It was this camp meeting ethos that inspired other groups of Methodists from southern New England to establish their own formal and informal associations on some of the islands in Winnipesaukee. Their stories can be found in the following chapter.

---

[1] B/P 64/147. The date on the deed is not legible, but a hand written log book kept by the secretary of the Winnipesaukee Camp Meeting Association shows the purchase was made in 1873. The group held its first annual meeting there in September 1873. (p. 7). The log book is found at the Winnipesaukee Museum. See also, Lake Village Times, August 16, 1873, p. 2 and August 30, 1873, p. 3 for articles about the new camp.

[2] New Hampshire had an important role in the early development of the Methodist church. The Methodists in the United States did not believe in formal education for their ministers until 1841 when the first such theological teachings began in New Hampshire at the Newbury Biblical Institute. In 1847, the school was moved to Concord, NH. It was subsequently moved to Boston in 1867 where it ultimately became Boston University's School of Theology.

Part VII:

The Early History
Of
Other Islands

Chapter Thirty-Seven

The Early History of Other Islands

The Early Background

In the 1700s, the islands of Lake Winnipesaukee were of only minor interest to the Masonian Proprietors. Given their huge land holdings, they had far more important things to work on. In 1750, the islands briefly got some attention when the Masonians voted that all of the islands in the lake should be divided amongst themselves in their standard 15 equal shares; but there was no follow up. Of course, it did not matter in 1750, because there were still no colonial settlers in the Lakes Region.

In 1770, as settlements began to take shape, the Masonians again took up the question of allocating the islands. They commissioned a survey which was undertaken in 1772 by James Hersey. He produced a map of the lake showing the larger islands and the acreage of each. Of note, his map gave names to only seven of the islands, including Bear, Governor's, Long, Wentworth (now Timber), Fisher's (now Welch), Rattlesnake, and Barn Door.[1]

The Numbered Islands

Despite the survey, the Masonians still did not immediately address the issue of allocating the ownership of the islands amongst themselves. It was not until 1781 that they finally did so. The 35 largest islands were divided into 15 'lots' for drawing purposes. Each lot consisted of roughly 250 acres. The largest islands (Bear, Cow, Rattlesnake, and Long Island) were divided into more than one lot.[2] The smaller of the 35 islands were grouped into various other lots. All of these islands were subsequently referenced as the 'numbered' islands. In the absence of names, the deeds of sale always referred to them by the Masonian lot number of each.[3]

---

[1] Unlabeled, original copy of Hersey's map contained in Maps of the Masonian Proprietary, vol. 5, pp. 48-49, State Archives.
[2] Bear, Cow, and Rattlesnake were divided into two lots each. Long Island was divided into five lots.
[3] It appears that it was not until 1858 that all of the larger islands finally had names. Many of them picked up names randomly prior to that date as they were purchased by local farmers. In 1858, William Crocker completed his comprehensive survey of land owners on every part of the lake for the WLCWMCo. This included all the islands. Crocker included names for all of the larger islands. Many of these were doubtlessly pre-existing, but he may have created some of them himself to clearly identify the property. Among those names that changed later were Little Rattlesnake (now Sleepers), Red Head (Treasure), Smiths (Round), Follett (Camp), and Spindle (Oak). See 1858 map of Winnipesaukee by William Crocker, NH State Archives.

The table below shows the allocation of the numbered islands:

Lot #	Masonian Proprietor/Owner	Island
1	Thomlinson & Mason	E. Rattlesnake; Barndoor Islands; Sleepers; Diamond
2	Mark H. Wentworth (d. 1785)	N. Rattlesnake
3	Solly (d. 1785) & March	Welch
4	Wallingford	Long Island, Five Mile, Six Mile
5	Wibird (d. 1765)	Long Island
6	Meserve et al	Long Island
7	D. Peirce (d. 1773)	Long Island
8	Jaffrey (d. 1802)	Long Island
9	Rindge (d. 1740)	Jolly, Birch, Steamboat, Round, Lockes, Mark
10	Packer	South Bear
11	Atkinson (d. 1779)	North Bear plus part of South Bear
12	Odiorne (d. 1748)	Pine, Stonedam
13	John Wentworth	Three Mile; Big Beaver, Blackcat; Hull; Blueberry; Ragged; Pitchwood; Nine Acre; Whortleberry; Sandy; Dow; Chases; Farm
14	Moore	N. Cow; Little Bear; Timber
15	Moffatt	S. Cow

The Unnumbered Islands

Left unaddressed was the allocation of the other 235 or so 'unnumbered' islands in the lake. Since they were not part of the drawing, they were owned jointly by default by all of the Masonian Proprietors. With the passage of time, the ownership shares were passed down to heirs when a Proprietor would die. Since the original group of Proprietors was established in the 1740s, the number of living Masonians had dwindled almost entirely by the end of the 18th century.

Some time before 1812, the entire group of unnumbered islands was acquired by Samuel Abbot of Tuftonboro.[1] Abbot was one of the original township proprietors of Tuftonboro; but when

---

[1] The deed of sale to him was not found. B/P 8013/517 shows Abbot as the owner in 1812.

and from whom he bought the islands is not known.[1] In 1812, Abbot sold them to Josiah Sawyer, a Tuftonboro blacksmith.[2] Sawyer maintained ownership of the unnumbered islands until his death at mid-century. In 1850, Sawyer's estate administrator, John Blaisdell Jr. of Gilford,[3] sold them to four Gilford men: Thomas Plummer, John Thyng, John Potter, and James Plummer.[4] In 1855, these men sold them to George Goss and Henry Doan of Gilford, with Doan buying out Goss soon after.[5] In 1858, Doan sold the unnumbered islands to Abraham Morrison of Gilford, who six years later, in 1864, sold them to George W. Sanders, also of Gilford.

George W. Sanders maintained ownership of the unnumbered islands for years afterwards. At the time he purchased them, he owned a 600 acre farm in Gilford as well as Round Island and Timber Island. Sanders' interest in the islands was largely business-related rather than speculative. He wanted them for their wood and timber supplies as he was the owner of a large lumber business in Gilford.[6]

Sanders drowned in December 1903 while ice fishing at his Glendale camp. His heir, Joseph S. Sanders, sold the unnumbered islands to his brother, J. Frank Sanders of Laconia, in 1907.[7] In 1912, the latter sold the package of unnumbered islands to Fullerton Wells of New York City who immediately moved them into a corporation called the Lake Winnipesaukee Company, of which Wells was president.[8] The deed listed by name 212 islands that purportedly made up the unnumbered islands.[9]

By this time, some of these islands had already been sold, including, Goose, Loon, Horse, and Ozone. It appears there were perhaps only 10 islands that were sold (or 'resold') by the Lake Winnipesaukee Company (LWC). As Wells' lack of success in selling his trove suggests, ownership of many of the unnumbered islands passed by other means to people who were active on the lake.

In a few cases, some people simply 'assumed' ownership in a process legally known as 'adverse possession'. This was a natural outgrowth of the circumstances. During the 1800s, most of the small islands were unoccupied. Many were too little to be of much or any value to anyone during the pre-vacation era.[10] By the mid-1800s, a few active lake men found value in them primarily as fishing camps. That motive became increasingly prevalent after the Civil War.

---

[1] Various people from the Seacoast became involved in buying up the 'undivided' shares from the heirs of the Masonian Proprietors. This was a massive task. There was common and undivided land in every township. The unnumbered islands were a subset. One of the people, who made it his business to acquire undivided as well as divided land, was Nathaniel Appleton Haven who, for example, purchased the ownership rights of Thomas Packer on Bear Island among many other rights.

[2] BCRI, B/P 8013/517.

[3] This was the same John Blaisdell who had leased Lots 1 and 2 on Bear Island to Waldo Meloon at this time.

[4] B/P 26/331.

[5] B/P 25/201; 25/202; 26/347; 26/348.

[6] B/P 30/234; 40/301; 51/255. Meredith tax records periodically showed that he stored log booms on the ice at various points around the lake. At one point in 1874, he was declared bankrupt, although that did not affect his ownership of the unnumbered islands. B/P 57/471; B/P 55/450.

[7] B/P 120/119 and 133/81.

[8] B/P 133/207; 133/359; 133/366.

[9] See B/P 133/359. This was the first listing of these islands. The earlier deeds only referenced 'the unnumbered islands' generally. Most of the smaller islands did not receive names until the late 19th century when lake people and vacationers became interested in owning them.

[10] Most were too small for seasonal grazing or logging.

Under the long established legal concept of 'adverse possession' (aka squatters' rights), a person may claim ownership of a property if: he has occupied it without the consent of the owner; taken possession of it as demonstrated by acts such as living there, building a house, logging it; etc.; his presence is open for anyone to see; and his presence has existed for at least 20 years.

There was one case in which adverse possession was used as the formal basis of a claim. It was spelled out in the deed when, in 1889, Charles F. Brown sold Breezy Island to Levi Ward and Leroy Gould.[1] It was stated within the deed of sale that:

"Said Brown having entered upon said island in A.D. 1852 and has always claimed the island as owner since and has exercised rights as an undisputed owner since the above mentioned time, having gone upon said island and cut the wood there from, from time to time and has exercised such other rights and privileges over said island as are necessary to gain valid title to realty by adverse possession for a long number of years, namely twenty years."

Purchased or assumed, numbered or unnumbered, the following pages provide a brief discussion of the early history of many of the islands. Most are located near Bear Island, but some of the larger islands further afield are also included. In most cases, the discussion focuses upon the pre-vacation era ownership. The research into most of them is fairly superficial, given the book's focus on Bear and the constraints of time. As a result, there are numerous gaps in the chains of ownership. But the summaries provide some useful context within which to balance the Bear Island experience, and they also—hopefully—will provide a basis for further research by interested parties. The islands are listed alphabetically, although some are treated in groups.

Other Island Histories

Beaver Island Group (Big Beaver, Beaver, Middle Beaver, and Little Beaver)

The Beaver Islands originally consisted of five islands. There are four today: Big Beaver, Beaver, Middle Beaver, and Little Beaver. Sometime during the 1900s, two of the islands were connected by a causeway to form Middle Beaver. The islands are located northwest of Three Mile Island. The name 'Beaver' was probably given to the group c. 1858 when the surveyor for the Lake Company completed his map of Winnipesaukee. The channel between Big Beaver and the other three was (and still is cyclically) a natural habitat for beavers.

Big Beaver is by far the largest. It was part of Masonian Lot #13 drawn by John Wentworth in 1781, while the others were among the 'unnumbered' islands.[2] John Wentworth's original right to

---

[1] B/P 81/573. The language in the deed was very likely written by Charles Brown's brother, John, who was a lawyer in Washington D.C. The entire Brown family owned several islands on Winnipesaukee during the 19th century.
[2] This was not the John Wentworth who became governor of New Hampshire in 1766.

to Lot #13 devolved to Joshua Langdon, the highly regarded patriot from Portsmouth, who represented the state in the Continental Congress and later served as governor of the state.[1] He sold it to his son, John Langdon Jr. in July 1809.[2] In August 1811, Langdon Jr. sold all of his Winnipesaukee islands to Edmund and Catherine Roberts of Portsmouth.[3] Roberts sold Big Beaver to Timothy Robinson in 1834.[4] Timothy was an inn keeper in Lowell, MA.[5] In 1859, Robinson sold these islands to a Meredith farmer, David Robinson.[6] Apparently a fairly wealthy man, he owned farmlands in the upper Neck portion of the Third Division, near the schoolhouse lot (L26).[7] Robinson presumably would have used the islands for seasonal grazing and wood. He held on to them for varying lengths of time. The first to go were the three middle Beaver Islands (now Middle Beaver and Little Beaver). These were the least useful to Meredith farmer due to their small size.

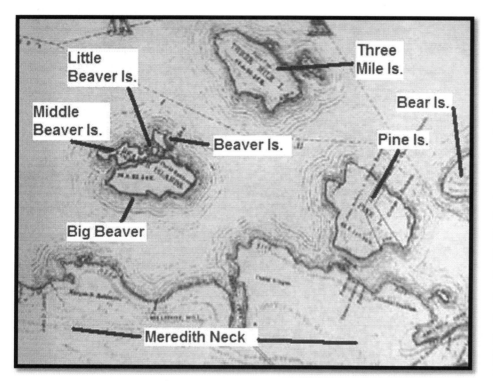

David Robinson sold Big Beaver to Levi Leach of Meredith in February 1866.[8] Leach was a Meredith Neck farmer who owned the island for 21 years. After moving to Franklin, NH, Leach sold it in 1887 to Samuel Kingdon of Somerville, MA.[9] Kingdon, a fairly colorful figure, began the vacation era on Big Beaver about the same time that Solomon Lovejoy was making his first vacation sales on North Bear. Kingdon was a newspaper editor for the *Boston Evening Transcript,* among other papers. He enjoyed the island immensely. After his death in 1902, Big Beaver was inherited by his nieces and nephews, who sold a half interest in it to Harry C. Francis of Philadelphia in 1904.

---

[1] Langdon briefly owned Governors Island in the late 1790s after he foreclosed on a mortgage loan he gave to John Cushing.

[2] SCRD B/P 61/255.

[3] SCRD B/P 67/559. The language in the deed references the islands as being in Tuftonboro. This is interesting since none of these islands had been incorporated into any of the towns around the lake. Six eventually became part of Tuftonboro. Some additional confusion around this deed trail arises because there is an 1813 deed in which Roberts resells the same property back to Langdon, but Roberts later sale of these islands suggests that the resale to Langdon was part of a mortgage transaction.

[4] See B/P 9015/553, referencing this sale. The original deed sited is Strafford County Registry B/P 161/523. It is not found online.

[5] See B/P 9015/551.

[6] The deed of sale was not found, but Timothy Robinson was listed as the owner on Crocker's map of the lake in 1858. David Robinson's ownership in 1859 is derived from later deeds.

[7] See B/P 35/347 and 43/557.

[8] B/P 43/557. An excellent history of Big Beaver Island, laying out the modern era, was written in 1973 by Alexander Standish: "History of Beaver Island (1781-1973). This can be found on-line at Winnipesaukee.com.

[9] B/P 77/172.

Francis gained full ownership of it in 1905. Thereafter, he began a more extensive vacation development of the island.

Beaver Island is the second largest of the group and located southeast of the others. David Robinson held on to this island the longest, finally selling it in 1869 to John F. Clough. With this purchase, John became one of the earliest vacationers on the lake. He probably used it primarily as a fishing camp. John (b. 1841) was one of four sons of John and Ellen Clough who had moved to Meredith in 1843. He had three brothers, William (b. 1840), Frank (b. 1851), and Edward (b. 1860).[1] John was also a Civil War veteran, a member of the 12th NH Volunteer Infantry. He was wounded at the battle of Chancellorsville, the same battle in which Oliver Bickford was captured and 10 other Meredith men were killed. He mustered out of the army in 1863, apparently due to his wounds.[2] He returned to Meredith and became a butcher, living with his parents. By 1880, he moved to Manchester to find another career. Still in possession of Beaver Island, he sold a half interest in it to his older brother, William, in 1881.[3] By this time, William was living in Nashua, NH, where he had become the editor of the *Nashua Telegraph*.

John and William maintained ownership of Beaver until 1893, when they sold it to their youngest brother, Edward H. Clough.[4] Edward was also living in Manchester, where he had built a very successful business career that included owning a coal delivery company and serving as postmaster for the city. But Edward had kept Meredith close to his heart, building a house at the base of Meredith Bay, situated at the junction of Pleasant Street and the D.W. Highway.[5] In later life, he was responsible for cleaning up the bay and building the stone retaining wall. Clough Park was named after him. Beaver Island remained in the hands of Edward, and then his widow, until 1975.[6] In all, the property was owned by members of the Clough family for 106 years.

David Robinson sold the three islands that became **Middle** and **Little Beaver** to Meredith farmers, William P. Smith and William T. Fogg, in February 1859.[7] Smith and Fogg were not interested in owning the islands for personal use; the next year, in October 1860, they sold them to James M. Prescott and Charles S. Prescott.[8] The latter two had purchased two-thirds of Pine Island just a few years before. The Prescotts owned the two Beaver islands for 12 years, but after James passed away, Charles S. sold them to the fourth Clough brother, Frank, in 1872.[9] Frank only owned the islands for three years. In 1876, he sold them to his brother, William.[10] Four days later, William sold a half interest to his brother, John.[11]

[1] Hanaford, p. 157. All four of the boys came to own some of the Beaver Islands at one time or another.
[2] Ibid.
[3] Deed not found. Reference found in B/P 91/135.
[4] B/P 91/135.
[5] B/P 174/31. The seller was Harriett Moses who ran a summer school on Horse Island during the early 1900s. This house is now the Lakeside Deli and Grille.
[6] B/P 658/365.
[7] Deed not found. Sale information contained in B/P 35/347.
[8] B/P 35/347.
[9] Deed not found. Sale information contained in B/P 60/467.
[10] B/P 60/467.
[11] B/P 60/475.

William and John held joint ownership of the islands until 1881 when William sold his half to John.[1] About a month later, John sold the islands to Frederick Chauncey, a young (29) 'dyer' who was living in Meredith.[2] Chauncey was a native of Newfoundland and probably came to Meredith Village to work in the Hodgson hosiery mill. He owned the islands for four years, presumably using them as a fishing camp.

In 1885, he sold them to Samuel Hodgson who was the owner of the Meredith hosiery mill.[3] An Englishman by birth, Hodgson had migrated to the United States in 1866. He had worked in a dye house in Lowell, MA, for a year or so before following his employer to Lake Village. He started his own manufacturing business there in 1870. In 1875, the Meredith Mechanics Association, which owned the village canal and water power system, lured Hodgson to Meredith where he became the largest employer in town.

Hodgson held on to the smaller Beaver Islands for four years. He was perhaps the owner responsible for building the causeway that linked the two islands that now form Middle Beaver Island.[4] In 1889, he sold them to Elias Russell, a professor at the state normal school in Worcester, MA.[5] Russell's tenure on the islands was relatively short. In 1903, he sold them to Charles A. Weaver, a physician from New Boston, NH.[6] In 1905, Dr. Weaver sold the smallest of of his islands to Frank Frisselle, a newspaper editor from Manchester, NH.[7] This became Little Beaver Island. The Frisselle family owned the island for 25 years.[8]

Birch and Steamboat Islands

In 1781, Steamboat and Birch were joined as a single, unnamed island.[9] It was part of the group of islands that made up Lot #9 drawn by the Masonian Proprietor, John Rindge. The other islands in the lot were Jolly Island, Mark Island, Lockes Island, and Round Island. After John Rindge died in 1786, his estate administrator, Daniel Rindge, disposed of his assets to pay off his debts. He sold Lot #9 to John Peirce, a Portsmouth merchant whose father, Joshua Peirce, was one of the original Masonian Proprietors.[10] After John Peirce died in 1814, two of his three sons, Joshua Winslow and Mark Wentworth, became the Executors of his will.

---

[1] B/P 74/554.

[2] B/P 75/434.

[3] B/P 75/440.

[4] This assumption is based upon the comparative language in his deed of purchase (references three islands) and his deed of sale (references two islands). See also B/P 111/55 that suggests the same islands were involved in these sales. On the other hand, a hand drawn map attached to the 1905 B/P 111/55 deed shows three separate islands.

[5] B/P 82/153.

[6] B/P 111/55.

[7] B/P 116/301

[8] Meanwhile the Weaver family continued to own Middle Beaver until 1940. During their tenure, they called the island 'Tizdoc's Island', presumably as in 'it is doc's'. See, B/P 248/21.

[9] They show as a single island in Hersey's 1772 map of the lake. NH State Archives, Fruit Street. See also the 1840s 'true copy' in State Papers, Vol. 29, p. 587.

[10] In the late 1780s, John Peirce was appointed the Collector of Taxes by the Masonians. When some Masonians did not make payments, Peirce auctioned off their land holdings. The heirs of Masonian Thomas Wallingford were among those who did not pay. In April 1789, Peirce auctioned off his island holdings (Lot #4) that included part of Long Island, Five Mile Island and Six Mile Island. B/P 9004/434. John Peirce also personally acquired the Masonian's island Lot #14 that included Timber, Little Bear, and part of Cow Island.

In 1841, while still a single island, it was given the name Steamboat after the *Belknap* sank in a storm in the cove on the eastern side. In 1851, Steamboat became two islands when the new Lakeport dam was built, causing the lake level to rise by several feet. The larger of the two became known as Birch Island before the end of the decade, the name probably given to it by John Brown.[1]

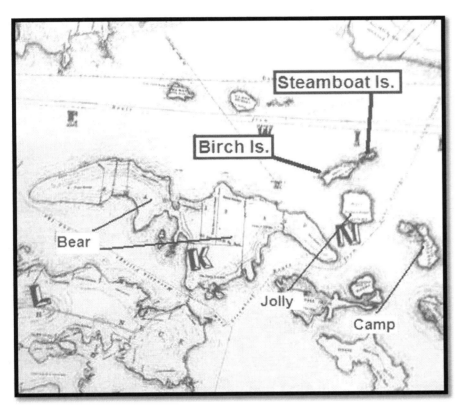

John Brown acquired the islands at some point prior to 1858.[2] Brown was a farmer from from Poplin, NH who had moved his family to Long Island in 1821.[3] Both islands were sold to to or inherited by Brown's oldest son, George K., in the latter 1860s.[4] George K. had as much much or more involvement with the islands on the lake as anyone during the latter 1800s. For example, in 1855, he acquired Camp Island from his father.[5] He built a cottage there in 1881, believed to be the first such camp built on any Gilford, NH island.[6] He also acquired a one-sixth share of Six Mile Island. In 1867, he acquired half of Cow Island, and then he bought the other half in 1871.[7]

George K. Brown was most likely attracted to Birch and Steamboat for several reasons. He was interested in them as wood lots and also for seasonal pasture. Their small size made the latter somewhat problematic, but the Browns may have rotated their herds among the smaller islands that they owned.[8] Another motive was their likely use as a fishing camp, something that George and his brothers apparently enjoyed a great deal.[9]

---

[1] See Crocker's1858 map of the lake. The name Birch was very slow to catch on. The 1860 Woodford map of Belknap County still showed only one island called Steamboat. Burwell's 1907 map showed both islands, labeled Steamboat or Birch and Little Steamboat. The 1909 USGA map labeled it Steamboat Island. A 1903 'Bird's Eye' map of the lake by George Walker also used only the name of Steamboat for it, although it showed both islands. Burwell's 1911 edition of his map finally identified the islands as Birch and Steamboat.
[2] John Brown is shown as owning them on William Crocker's 1858 map.
[3] B/P 9009/137.
[4] No deeds of sale were found online in regard to these purchases. John Brown died in 1867.
[5] B/P 26/334.
[6] Gunstock Parish, p. 246.
[7] Carroll County Registry B/P 53/525; ??
[8] Three of the Brown brothers, George, Frank, and Charles were all early steam boaters, starting in the 1850s. See, for example, Blackstone, Farewell Old Mount Washington, p. 19. They could tow barges to transport their cattle to seasonal pastures.
[9] While not a focus of this research, fishing was a very big pastime during the 1800s.

In 1879, under the pressure of debt taken on to support the Long Island House which he began in 1874, George sold Birch and Steamboat to his brother, Charles, and his wife, Ellen.[1] Charles (1831 – 1913) and Ellen Brown had moved from Long Island to the Lake Village section of Gilford in the 1860s. Charles made his living in a variety of ways, but he was primarily a lumber dealer.[2]

In 1886, Charles and Ellen sold all of Steamboat Island and 65' on the easterly end of Birch Island to two Methodist ministers, George Bates and Walter Yates of Plymouth, MA, and Taunton, MA, respectively.[3] Reverend Bates and his family lived on the northern half of Steamboat, while Reverend Yates set up camp on the southern portion.[4] The transaction was noted the following year (1887) in the *Boston Journal*:

"The two steamboat islands in the middle of the lake have also been sold to those who contemplate their improvement. Upon the eastern point of the smaller of these, the old steamer *Belknap*, the first of such craft on these waters, was wrecked when towing logs. From this fact and also because from this point there is a fine view of the Belknap or Gunstock Mountains, the new owners of this island have renamed it Belknap."[5]

The two families shared Steamboat for several years. The Bates family summered in tents, while the Yateses built a house. But in November 1892, George Bates purchased Hawk's Nest Island located next to Three Mile Island.[6] A few months later, in September 1893, the Bateses sold their interest in Steamboat to Walter Yates.[7]

Prior to the departure of Bates, another Methodist minister, William Ward, of Niantic, CT, began exploring the possibility of summering on Winnipesaukee. He got together with Reverend Yates, who by this time was serving a Methodist church in nearby New London, CT. They began organizing a congenial group to purchase the rest of Birch Island. Yates had previously obtained an option to buy the rest of Birch. In addition to Yates and Ward, the group included Edward and Susan K. Luce of Niantic, CT; Mary Rogers of New London, CT; and Winslow and Mary Avery of Plymouth, MA.[8]

Luce was noteworthy of them. He was a former sea captain who had developed a profitable manufacturing business in Niantic. Moreover, he was very active locally and nationally

[1] B/P 65/137. This is the purchase that included Camp Island and one-sixth of Six Mile Island.
[2] 1880 census and 1901 Laconia City directory. But Charles seems to have been a man in search of a career. In 1870, he called himself a 'grocer' (1870 census); in 1880, he was a 'wood dealer' (1880 census); in 1884, his occupation was 'steam yacht' (1884 Laconia Directory); and in 1900, he said he was a 'capitalist' (1900 census).
[3] B/P 76/250.
[4] Birch Island, by Emery L. Bradford, July 1936. An unpublished 'Account of the Birch Island Camp Company'. This account has a wealth of detail that forms the basis for the discussion below.
[5] Boston Journal, April 16, 1887, p. 5.
[6] B/P 88/497.
[7] B/P 91/202.
[8] Bradford, p. 2.

in the Methodist church. In 1880, for example, he had donated the land and money to build a new parsonage for the Methodist Episcopal Church in Niantic, CT.[1]

In August 1893, the group incorporated the Birch Island Camp Company (BICC), and it purchased the rest of Birch Island from Charles and Ellen Brown.[2] The purchase included two small buildings (one known as "the Old Camp"), presumably erected by George or Charles Brown as a winter fishing shack.[3] The following year, in May 1894, the BICC commissioned a survey of the island and developed a subdivision plan that established 12 shoreline lots.[4] The interior was maintained as common land as was the natural cove on the eastern end (this became a communal boathouse in the 1920s).

The BICC also developed fairly elaborate Articles of Association and Incorporation that established specific regulations for its members. Much of the focus was upon preserving the environment and respecting the privacy of the other members. One other provision was also noteworthy: "No intoxicating liquors shall ever be manufactured, landed or sold on these Islands for use as a beverage."

Following incorporation, Reverend Yates maintained ownership of Steamboat. Luce, Ward and Avery each bought two of the 12 lots on Birch, and Rogers purchased one. The four built houses on their lots in 1894 and 1895, getting the Birch Island colony well underway. In 1896, five more vacationers purchased lots. Two of the five were Methodist ministers from the New England Southern Conference, Reverend Francis H. Spear of Attawaugan, CT, and Reverend J. Thomas Everett of New Bedford, MA. Also in 1896, the island's steamboat wharf was built under the auspices of Charles Brown.[5]

By 1897, Birch had become a very active summer place. In addition to lot owners, some dozen other families annually rented houses on the island for several weeks each year.[6] During these years, the shoreline was slowly built out, with the last house built around 1906.

From its earliest days, Birch and Jolly Islanders held regular Sunday services, alternating between the two islands. Eventually, an open-air chapel was built on each of the islands. In 1897, they began holding vesper services in their boats between the islands before sunset.

"Captain Luce would anchor his cat boat in some quiet spot either in the lee of Birch

---

[1] History of New London County, Connecticut, D. H. Hurd editor, p. 563. This is the Edward Luce who started the East Bear Island colony in 1903.
[2] B/P 90/156. About half of the funds for the purchase came from the first lot sales, and the rest was borrowed from Captain Luce's wife, Susan. Bradford, p. 3.
[3] This old camp was located next to the island's wharf location.
[4] See attachment to B/P 90/156 for a copy of the plan.
[5] Previously, Birch Islanders had to row to and from Jolly Island to connect with the steamers.
[6] The group had originally met while vacationing at the Weirs in the early 1890s. When they heard that houses had been constructed on Birch, they all agreed to summer there. In 1910, they learned that a favorite picnicking spot in Far Echo cove on Moultonborough Neck had come on the market for vacationers. They all bought lots there. See Kenneth L. Carvell, A History of the Far Echoes Colony at Lake Winnipesaukee, 1997, pp. 4-6.

or Jolly Island from which the going down of the sun could be seen. He usually had on board the 'baby organ'... Other row boats would gather around, tying each to each, and with someone to 'lead', the old hymns would be sung."[1]

Vesper services off of Birch Island.

Blackcat Island

Blackcat (originally two words: Black Cat) is the 14th largest island in the lake at 75 acres.

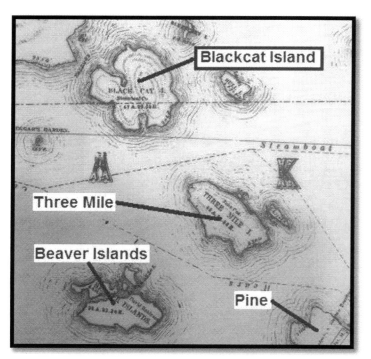

It is located in the northeast section of Winnipesaukee near Moultonborough Neck and Center Harbor. Estimated in the 1772 Hersey survey to be only 32 acres in size, it was also one of 12 islands that comprised Lot #13 in the Masonian Proprietors' lottery in 1781.[2] It was drawn to the original right of John Wentworth. It was not among the earliest 'named' islands. It was originally called Morrill's Island by those who lived nearby, probably based upon the name of a local farmer who squatted on it during the very early 1800s.

The early ownership of Blackcat is not without some twists and turns. John Wentworth's original right to Lot #13 devolved to Joshua Langdon, the highly regarded patriot from Portsmouth, who represented the state in the Continental Congress and later served as governor of the state.[3] He sold it to his son, John Langdon Jr. in July 1809. In

---

[1] Bradford, Birch Island, p. 26. See also, Carvell, Far Echoes Colony, p. 6.
[2] Lot #13 included Three Mile, the Beavers, Hull, Blackcat, Blueberry and Pitchwood along with the Tuftonboro islands of Ragged, Whortleberry, Dow, Nine Acre, Chases, and Farm.
[3] Langdon briefly owned Governors Island in the late 1790s after he foreclosed on a mortgage loan he gave to John Cushing.

August 1811, Langdon Jr. sold all of his Winnipesaukee islands to Edmund and Catherine Roberts of Portsmouth.[1]

Roberts apparently did nothing with Blackcat over the next several years, although he did not neglect his island holdings entirely. In 1819, for example, he sold three of his Tuftonboro islands.[2] In 1823, he appears to have mortgaged nine of the islands, including Blackcat, to Henry Rice of Boston.[3] But while Roberts was busy elsewhere, Blackcat had drawn the interest of a local Moultonborough farmer named Ezekiel Hoits. Hoits took possession of the deserted island, presumably for its seasonal grazing and wood. How long he used the island is not known, but it was long enough to establish a claim of ownership. In August 1822, he sold it to John Coe of Center Harbor.[4] Coe maintained ownership of it for five years before selling it in January 1827 to Nathan Bunker, another Moultonborough farmer.[5]

Summarizing this sequence of sales in 1855, a Moultonborough town officer, Shadrack Brown, wrote that Hoits "pretended to own the island by way of common land (i.e. adverse possession)." He went on to say that Hoits initially sold the island to one 'Morrill' but also noted that it became the property of John Coe of Center Harbor and "another man named Deans" at some later point.[6]

The sale by John Coe to Nathan Bunker is the last deed found before the mid-1840s. Neither Bunker nor Deans seems to have executed registered deeds on the property thereafter. And it appears that Shadrack Brown was more or less correct in his assessment of the legality of the would-be owners. The island legally belonged to Edmund Roberts. In 1834, Roberts sold "Black Cat" (and the Beaver Islands) to Timothy Robinson, the inn owner from Lowell, MA.[7]

Robinson held on to Blackcat for several years. Finally, in 1846, he sold Blackcat to his brother, Bradbury Robinson of Meredith.[8] Shadrack Brown referenced this transaction as well. He wrote that 'Black Cat' was sold to Bradbury Robinson after the latter "went to Portsmouth to obtain a better title, (and) he there obtained some kind of a title from a brother of his by the same name who kept Tavern in Portsmouth pretending that he had a title from the original proprietors…"[9]

---

[1] SCRD B/P 67/559. The language in the deed references the islands as being in Tuftonboro. This is interesting since none of these islands had been incorporated into any of the towns around the lake. Six eventually became part of Tuftonboro. Some additional confusion around this deed trail arises because there is an 1813 deed in which Roberts resells the same property back to Langdon, but Roberts' later sale of these islands suggests that the resale to Langdon was part of a mortgage transaction.
[2] CCRD 101/542.
[3] B/P 9010/135. Like the 1813 Langdon deed, this reads as a clean sale, but the later sale of some of these islands by Roberts suggest that this was a mortgage.
[4] SCRD B/P 115/91.
[5] B/P 9011/385.
[6] Letter from Shadrack H. Brown to Joshua W. Pierce, February 27, 1855. Peirce papers, NH Historical Society. Brown was concerned because islands like Blackcat had not been annexed to any town yet and therefore the owners were not being taxed. Brown wrote that Deans "exchanged his title (to the island) with someone for an old horse."
[7] B/P 9010/135. This was the first time the name 'Black Cat' appears in the documents, allegedly derived from the sighting of a black cat on the island.
[8] CCRD B/P 11/113. By that time, the island's acreage was listed by Robinson as 72 acres, much closer to its actual 74 acres.
[9] Brown to Peirce, Feb 27, 1855.

Regardless, Bradbury Robinson had apparently wanted Blackcat so he could resell it. Within two weeks of his purchase, Robinson sold it to George A. Sanders of Gilford and William Hoyt of Moultonborough.[1] But by this time, the Moultonborough tax assessor, Hosea Sturdevant, Sturdevant, claimed that Blackcat was part of that town and therefore subject to taxation. A few months after Robinson made his sale, Sturdevant brought the town's claim for back taxes to Robinson's attention. Robinson took the path of least resistance and paid $2.90 in back taxes to settle the issue.[2]

The ownership situation on Blackcat remained straightforward thereafter. Sanders and Hoyt held on to Blackcat for seven years, presumably using it for grazing and as a wood lot. In 1853, they sold it to the Winnipesaukee Steamboat Co. (WSC).[3] Its primary interest in Blackcat was for its wood which was transported to Center Harbor to fuel the steamers when they landed there.

The WSC owned Blackcat for 43 years. It finally ceded the island to the Concord & Montreal Railroad in July 1896 as part of a liquidation of the business in full satisfaction of a claim against it by the railroad amounting to $37,849.25.[4] The Concord & Montreal owned Blackcat for four years, again probably most interested in its wood. In May 1900, it sold the island to the wealthy Dumaresq family that had developed the giant Moultonborough Neck estate known as Kona Farm.[5] The Dumaresqs owned the island for 25 years. They sold it in 1925 to two Massachusetts men, Augustus Doty and Ross Whistler.[6] Whistler sold his share to Edward Townsend the following year, and thereafter Townsend and Doty owned the island for 28 years. Over that period, they brought Blackcat into the vacation era, adding docks, boathouses, and dwellings as part of a joint, private estate.

The island's future changed markedly in 1958 when Doty and Townsend sold it to William and Olive Chipman of Action, MA.[7] Within a couple of years, the Chipmans decided to subdivide and sell lots on the island. They commissioned the first of several subdivision plans in 1961. Initially, they created and sold a few large parcels. Eventually, over the course of the 1960s, the island was transformed. A bridge was built connecting it to the mainland, and vacation lots were sold around the entire island.

---

[1] CCRD B/P 9/390.

[2] CCRD B/P 11/95. The entire issue of jurisdiction over the islands continued to fester throughout the mid-1800s. The smaller islands had not been formally annexed to any of the towns. Therefore the owners of those islands contended that they could not be taxed by any of the towns. Sturdevant appears to have taken his own initiative with regard to Blackcat, but the issue was not resolved.

[3] BCRD B/P 22/143.

[4] CCRD B/P 106/283.

[5] CCRD B/P 114/128.

[6] CCRD B/P 173/40.

[7] BCRD B/P 393/393.

Camp Island

Camp Island was one of the unnumbered islands.[1] As such, its ownership theoretically passed through at least some of the chain of people who purchased them, beginning with Samuel Abbot before 1812. Before the mid-1800s, the island was occupied by a local farmer named Samuel Follett, from whom it derived its first known name as Follett Island. It is possible, perhaps even likely, that Follett purchased it from one of the early owners of the unnumbered

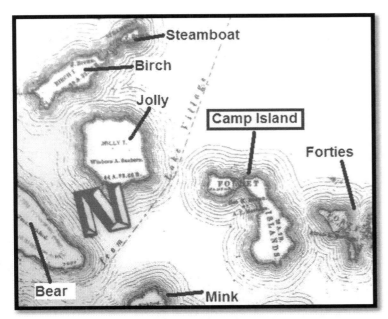

islands. Regardless, sometime before 1855, it came to be owned by John Brown of Long Island.[2] In December 1855, John Brown sold the island to his son, George. The deed noted that the island was known as Samuel Follett Island or Uncle Tom's Island at that time.[3] The island continued to be known as Follett Island at least through the 1940s, while its small neighbor became known as Little Camp during the 20th century.

George K. Brown owned the island until 1879 when he sold it to his brother, Charles, and his wife, Ellen Brown.[4] The island remained under the ownership of the Charles Brown family for decades thereafter. After Charles Brown's death in 1913, full ownership passed to his wife, Ellen, and then to their daughters, Dora and Anna, after Ellen's death in 1929. When Dora died in 1935, her half ownership was inherited by her daughter, Edna Nolan.

In 1947, Anna and her niece, Edna, reached an agreement to divide Camp Island and Little Camp Island between themselves. Anna received Little Camp and the northerly portion of Camp, and Edna was given ownership of the southerly portion of Camp Island.[5] In 1949, Anna sold her portion of Camp Island to her husband, Mortimer.[6] By then the couple was separated or divorced. Mortimer subsequently sold his holdings on Camp to John Stephenson in 1977.[7]

---

[1] Camp consisted of two islands, Little Camp and Big Camp. We will address them together as Camp for the most part.
[2] We have found no record of a sale to or by Samuel Follett or to John Brown. The Masonian map of the islands, annotated in the late 1840s, does not indicate any ownership or activity on Camp Island or the Forties but its focus was on the numbered islands. (State Papers, Vol. 29, p. 587).
[3] B/P 26/334. Crocker's 1858 map refers to Camp and Little Camp as Follet Island.
[4] B/P 65/137.
[5] B/P 304/242; 304/549; 304/550.
[6] B/P 722/346
[7] B/P 722/346.

On the southern portion of Camp, Edna Nolan followed a far different path. She commissioned a subdivision plan in 1955.[1] Several lots were sold off to vacationers over the ensuing years. Edna and her husband, Joseph, kept one of the properties for themselves. In 1963, they transferred half interests in it to their son, Robert, and daughter, Ruth, while reserving a life-estate in the property.[2] In 1985, Robert sold his interests in the island to Ruth. Ruth died in 2006, but her family still retains ownership of the southern end of the island. At more than 164 years (pre-1855 – 2018), this appears to be the longest ownership tenure of any extended family on any island in the lake.

Carry Cove Islands (Rock, Shepherd, Palmer, and Little Pine)

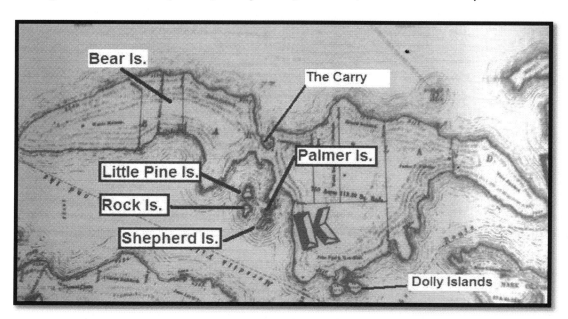

There are four very small islands located in the Carry cove on the west side of Bear Island, facing Meredith Neck. They are known today as Rock, Shepherd, Palmer, and Little Pine. In the early days, they were unnamed and routinely referred to as "the Carrying islands". Over the course of the 19th century, individual names were periodically applied, usually referencing the name of the current owner. Their early history is rather obscure and most likely unrecorded given their relative insignificance during the 19th century. None of the early Bear Island farmers ever owned them. They were too small to provide good grazing and offered little other value. These islands, however, began to draw attention during the last two decades of the 19th century when the vacation era began on the lake.

Rock Island was one of the first Carry Islands to be occupied. The second largest, at just over one acre in size, it was purchased around 1894 by Henry Batchelder.[3] Batchelder was a trustee of the Methodist Episcopal Church at the Weirs.[4] He put up a building—probably a fishing fishing shack--there shortly after its purchase. He sold it in 1900 to Benjamin P. Foster, a stone mason from Waltham, MA.[5] The island became known as Foster's Island for a long time

---

[1] Plan 9/602.
[2] B/P 430/370.
[3] The deed was not found, so we do not know the previous owner, but it was probably George W. Sanders.
[4] See B/P 90/135.
[5] B/P 103/451.

thereafter. It was not on the Fullerton Wells' Lake Winnipesaukee Company list of unnumbered islands. Foster built the still-standing house on the island c. 1920. Following his death, the island was willed to Clarence Whitney and his wife, May Foster Whitney.[1] They owned the island until 1946 when it was sold to Joseph and Gertrude Cox of Rochester, NH.[2] At that point, the deed referred to it only as "one of the Carrying Islands." The Cox family sold it to the current owners, the Goldberg family, in 1973.[3] By then, the island was known as Rock Island.

Little Pine Island was apparently the second of the Carry islands to be occupied. It is the largest of the four at something just over one acre. It was initially occupied before 1901 by two men from Center Harbor, James M. Thompson and Frank P. Farrar, although there is no history of when or from whom they acquired it.[4] In 1901, they sold it to Charles and Hattie Cushing, farmers who lived on Meredith Neck, across from the island.[5] In keeping with the practice of the day, it became known as Cushing Island for some time thereafter. The succeeding ownership trail was not found. It is presently owned by the Greater Boston YMCA. It was not listed by Wells among his unnumbered islands in 1912.

Palmer Island was also initially occupied during the 1890s. It is the smallest of the four Carry islands at just one-tenth of an acre in size. Its first known occupant was John H. Morrison of Meredith who acquired the island presumably in the mid-1890s.[6] Naturally, it was called Morrison Island. The Morrison family moved to Concord, NH but retained ownership of the island until 1938.[7] The name of the island was changed to Palmer Island in 1957 when the current owner acquired it. It was not on Wells' list of unnumbered islands.

Shepherd Island[8] is the third largest in the cluster at almost a half acre in size. Early on, it was not known by any particular name. It was not listed by Wells among his unnumbered islands in 1912. It was purchased before 1904 by Frederick E. Gilford, a Gilford, NH resident, who had acquired one of the nearby Dolly Islands before 1890. Gilford apparently built a "small and dilapidated building" on Shepherd.[9] In 1904, Gilford sold it to E. C. Mansfield.[10] Mansfield and his wife retained ownership of it until their deaths. It was then sold in 1942 to the Mansfields' granddaughter, Mary, and her husband, C.K. Plancon. It had become known as Cub Island by

[1] B/P 218/30. See also B/P 218/57.
[2] B/P 327/317.
[3] B/P 619/107.
[4] It seems likely that they bought it from George W. Sanders.
[5] B/P 105/399. Hattie Cushing was a great granddaughter of Robert Bryant, Bear's first settler. She was the daughter of Nancy Bryant Clark who was the daughter of Robert Bryant Jr. This is derived from Old Meredith and Vicinity, p. 92.
[6] Current Meredith tax records suggest the tiny camp on the island was built in 1895.
[7] B/P 236/176; 236/197.
[8] This is the proper spelling of the island's name. See B/P 1261/926. Meredith tax records incorrectly show it as Shepard Island.
[9] B/P 112/305.
[10] B/P 112/305.

this time.[1] The island continued to be called Cub into the 1990s.[2] The name was changed to Shepherd c. 1993, presumably by members of the Funkhouser family who own it.[3]

Cow Island

At some 520 acres, Cow Island is the third largest island in the lake after Long Island (1120 acres) and Bear Island (780 acres). The origins of the island's name are not known. It was not among the handful of islands that received names in 1772 when James Hersey surveyed the large islands on the lake for the Masonian Proprietors; nor was that name in currency in 1789 when it was still being referred to in the deeds as "island Number fifteen."[4] It appears likely that the island was given its name c. 1799 when it was annexed to Tuftonborough by the state legislature, although there is no known logic behind the name choice.[5]

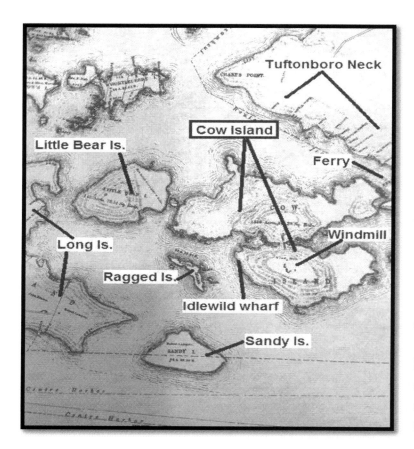

Similar to his assessment of Bear and some of the other islands, Hersey's survey of Cow Island was woefully inadequate. He determined that it had only a total of 291 acres. As a result, the severely underestimated northern section (said to be just 41 acres compared to its actual 300 or so acres) was coupled by the Masonian proprietors in 1781 with Timber Island and Little Bear Island to form Lot #14. The southern section of Cow (estimated at 250 acres but actually about 220 acres) formed all of Lot #15.

Lot #15 was among the first to be sold after the drawing. John Moffatt, the Masonian proprietor who had drawn the lot, died in 1786, leaving his estate to his daughter, Catherine. She and an administrator, Joshua Beckett, sold undivided halves of Moffatt's portion of

---

[1] B/P 267/400. The sale did not make reference to any buildings on the island, although the Meredith tax records suggest Mansfield had built the existing house on the island around 1920.

[2] B/P 1187/492.

[3] 1261/926. The name was changed during a transfer of the property within the Funkhouser family. The Funkhousers acquired it in 1954.

[4] See an original copy of Hersey's map in Maps of the Masonian Propriety, Vol. 5, pp. 48-49, held in the State Archives. A copy completed by Jeremiah Libbey in August 1818 is found in the same volume, pp. 44-45. The latter was annotated with notes as late as 1866. For the 1789 reference, see BCR B/P 9002/582.

[5] Laws of New Hampshire, Vol. 6, Second Constitutional Period 1792-1801, pp. 620-621. At this juncture, it appears that the island was still unoccupied. The annexation occurred at the same time Bear and Stonedam were annexed to Meredith and Governors was annexed to Gilmanton. Bear was unoccupied at the time as well.

Cow Island in 1789 to Samuel Sherburne of Portsmouth and Timothy Emerson of Durham.[1] Both men were real estate speculators. In 1809, Emerson sold his half to Ichabod Libbey of Tuftonboro.[2] Libbey maintained his ownership for only a few years before selling it to William Batchelder, a farmer from Salem, MA, in 1814.[3] Batchelder also purchased Samuel Sherburne's half of Lot #15 in 1814,[4] and he acquired the Lot #14 section of Cow as well around this time.[5]

In 1815, Batchelder sold a one-third interest in the entire island to Nathan Batchelder of Louden, NH,[6] and the two owned the island jointly for seven years. Neither of the Batchelders occupied the island while they owned it. A relatively poor Tuftonboro farmer, Jonathan Thompson, lived there instead.[7] Early occupation of Cow was not surprising given its size and the relative ease of access to it. There is a narrow waterway, known as the Barber's Pole, between the southeastern end of the island and Tuftonboro where a ferry was eventually established.[8]

The remains of the mill on Cow Island, c. 1890s.

The Batchelders held on to the island until 1822 when they sold it to John Prince of Roxbury, MA.[9] With the arrival of Prince, the history of Cow Island took a turn that was very different from any other island on the lake. He was a very well off 'gentleman farmer' who owned a large mansion in Jamaica Plain, Massachusetts. Prince was an active member of both the Massachusetts Horticultural Society and the Massachusetts Agricultural Society. He developed specialized gardens and orchards, and he was known for the specialty varieties of apples and pears that he grew on his estate.[10]

Prince purchased Cow Island to raise

---

[1] SCR B/P 25/26; 115/240.
[2] SCR B/P 62/284.
[3] SCR B/P 114/398.
[4] SCR B/P 78/614.
[5] The deed for this sale was not found. With regard to Lot #14, it was drawn in 1781 to the right of Daniel Peirce and Mary (Peirce) Moore. Mary Peirce Moore was the wife of the original Masonian Proprietor, Colonel Samuel Moore. They were childless, and Samuel died in 1748. His rights as a proprietor fell to his wife, Mary, but his place among the Masonian Proprietors was taken by Mary's brother, Daniel Peirce. Daniel and Mary were the children of the Masonian Proprietor, Joshua Peirce. Daniel Peirce's son, John Peirce, inherited it after Daniel died in 1773. After John died c. 1814, his estate fell into the hands of his estate administrators, his sons Mark Wentworth Peirce, Joshua Winslow Peirce, and Daniel Hale Peirce. They presumably sold the Cow Island portion of Lot #14 to Batchelder. They later sold both of the other Lot #14 islands, Little Bear Island (in 1817) and Timber Island (in 1823). BCR B/P 9010/15; 9007/550.
[6] Referenced in SCR B/P 115/350.
[7] Tuftonboro Inventory Records, 1818 -1838, Town Clerk's Office. Town inventory reports list his presence on the island, and they also indicate that he owned very little in the way of livestock.
[8] See Crocker's 1858 map of Winnipesaukee.
[9] SCR B/P 115/350.
[10] See: The Memorial History of Boston, 1630-1880, p. 622; The Massachusetts Agricultural Repository and Journal, 1819, p. 13.

pure bred cattle and sheep. He did not personally live on the island to take care of his herds. Around 1825, he hired Paul R. Pillsbury of Boscawen, NH, to manage the farm for him.[1] The developed part of the property amounted to three acres of tillage, eight acres of mowing, and 25 acres of pasturage in 1826.[2] During the 1820s, Prince imported cattle—called Alderneys-- from the British Isle of Guernsey.[3] Prince's island farm became home to a small but growing herd ranging from four to nine head.[4] More significantly, Prince bought the island to raise prized Merino sheep. By 1830, he had a herd of 250 head.[5] The next year the total was up to 370.[6] In recognition of his herd, Prince renamed Cow "Moreno Island."[7]

As an innovative farmer, Prince probably had Pillsbury build the well-known windmill on Cow that was used to grind grain for himself and some of the Long Island farmers.[8] Prince owned Cow Island until 1834, when he sold it to two colleagues from the Massachusetts Agricultural Society, Elias Hersy Derby and Henry Andrew.[9] They transferred it to Derby's son, Elias Hasket Derby, within a few months.[10] Derby continued the 'gentleman's farm' on the island but without the sheep. Prince must have sold his entire flock, because there were no sheep on Cow Island in the ensuing tax inventory reports. Derby presumably maintained an Alderney herd during his ownership of Cow.[11]

Derby kept the island until 1844 when he sold it to another Newton, MA 'gentleman', Samuel Bean.[12] Bean owned it for 17 years. He sold it James Littlefield, a farmer from Dover, NH, in 1861.[13] He owned it until 1867, when it was sold two more times. First, Littlefield sold it to

---

[1] Pillsbury appears in the Tuftonboro tax records for the first time in 1826. All of the inventory figures for Cow Island and Prince during this period appear after Pillsbury's name. See also, The Guernsey Cattle. Introduction to America.

[2] These totals held constant until the pasturage was expanded to 30 acres in 1830.

[3] See, The Guernsey Cattle. Introduction to America, www.jersey.dk.dk/hill.htm; remembermamaicaplain.blocspot.com/2008/05/gentlemen-farmers-of-jamaica-plain-took.html, referencing the American Federalist Columbian Centennial, Oct 11, 1823 and The Alderney Cow. John Prince is referred to as a seafaring Captain but the article goes on to refer to a brother who owned the farm on Winnipesaukee. It seems probable that his rank of Captain resulted from his position in the militia. The Alderney were kissing cousins of the highly prized Guernsey cattle if not simply an alternative name for them. In the early 1820s, people outside the Channel Islands used the term 'Alderney' to describe all cattle from the islands. In all cases they were prized as pure breds and not widely exported until years later. In The Guernsey Cattle. Introduction to America, a New Hampshire farmer noted in his diary that Prince imported "Alderneys, sometimes called Guernseys."

[4] Tuftonboro, Town Inventory Records 1826-1829. The timing of his introduction of the Guernsey to Cow Island is often put at c. 1831. However, Prince already owned some in the early 1820s. He had advertisements for the sale of an Alderney bull circulating in Massachusetts 1823, less than one year after he purchased Cow Island.

[5] This was the first year that New Hampshire town inventory reports specifically included sheep.

[6] Tuftonboro, Town Inventory Records 1830 and 1831. These were huge numbers. The largest herds in Meredith, for example, rarely exceeded 50.

[7] B/P9014/191. The Merino sheep, as discussed earlier in the book, were the prized breeds of the Spanish at the beginning of the century. The Merino and the Alderney (and/or Guernsey) were in keeping with Prince's focus on the 'best practices' in agriculture and farming.

[8] The timing of Pillsbury's arrival on Cow and the building of the grist mill are usually—and erroneously-- placed around 1812. The source of this information appears to have been W.S. Hawkes whose book, Winnipesaukee and About There, appeared in 1887. (See p. 43.) He also wrote several newspaper articles under the pseudonym, Republican, in 1885 and 1886, covering much of the same ground. Hawkes information about Cow came from George K. Brown's brother, B. Frank Brown, who ferried Hawkes around the lake for a week in 1885. Frank Brown grew up on Long Island, so he was seemingly a pretty good source. On the other hand, his family did not arrive until 1821, and Frank was not born until 1832. Everything Frank knew was hearsay.

[9] B/P 9014/191.

[10] SCR B/P 161/598.

[11] Herd sizes could not be determined because town Inventory report categories were altered in 1833 to show only total values rather than numbers of animals.

[12] CCR B/P 5/255.

[13] CCR B/P 39/401.

Blake Folsom, who then immediately sold it to Long Islanders, George K. Brown and Horace Lamprey. Cow was finally in local hands.[1]

George K. Brown was the son of Long Island farmer, John Brown. At the time of this purchase, George was also the owner of Camp, Steamboat, and Birch Islands. In 1871, he bought out Lamprey's undivided half of Cow.[2] Brown apparently used Cow to pasture sheep and and cattle, as well as for a wood lot, for many years thereafter.[3]

By 1874, George Brown began pledging Cow Island as collateral to obtain financing for the Long Island Hotel, which he established that year. He took out a $1000.00 mortgage from the Lake Village Savings Bank.[4] In 1878, he borrowed another $1000.00, giving a second mortgage on Cow to a private financier, David Sawyer of Belmont, NH.[5] And in 1879, he gave a third mortgage on Cow to Dana Brown to secure an existing loan of $1379.00.[6]

By the early 1880s, Brown was in trouble. In 1882, David Sawyer took him to court for lack of repayment. Sawyer received a judgment against Brown, and the court ordered Brown's arrest and seizure of the property in lieu of payment.[7] In 1885, Sawyer sold his loan and control of Cow Island to Clark Wentworth, a Long Island neighbor of Brown.[8]

With Wentworth now in control, the use of the island took a significant turn in 1891. He leased the island to John M. Dick who established Camp Idlewild on it.[9] John Dick renamed the island 'Manhannock', perhaps thinking it would have a more romantic appeal to families than Cow.[10] Regardless, the campers of Idlewild were apparently not the only children using the island. For example, a group from the Cambridge (MA) School of Manual Training (later Rindge School) spent five weeks camping on the island during the summer of 1892.[11]

Wentworth retained ownership of Cow until his death in 1900. The following year, 1901, Wentworth's executor sold the mortgage rights to Cow Island to Herbert A. Blackstone, who happened to be married to George K. Brown's daughter, Malvina.[12]

---

[1] CCR B/P 51/429; 53/525.
[2] CCR B/P 64/455.
[3] Hawkes, Winnipesaukee, p.34.
[4] CCR B/P 64/22.
[5] CCR B/P 71/367.
[6] CCR B/P 72/439. This loan was originally taken in 1876.
[7] CCR B/P 79/310. The first mortgage was presumably paid off before or during the foreclosure on the island.
[8] CCR B/P 71/367.
[9] The timing is based upon camp history. Idlewild was the first boys' camp established on the lake.
[10] This name was used in camp brochures and picked up by the Boston & Maine Railroad in its 1903 map of the lake. In the 1930s, the Guernsey Association got the NH legislature to change the name to Guernsey Island, but it was changed back in common usage to Cow Island many years later.
[11] Boston Herald, July 24, 1892, p. 13.
[12] CCR B/P 71/367. After George K. Brown died in 1903, his heirs formalized the Blackstone ownership of Cow Island by selling whatever residual rights they had via their inheritance to Malvina. CCR B/P 125/341. Malvina's ownership subsequently transferred to her husband after her death in 1917. BCR B/P 150/267.

By this time, the island was also being used by a group of outdoorsmen who had built the lake's first houseboat, the *Waungon*. Comprised of hunters and fishermen from the Boston and the Lakes Region, they created an organization known as the Cow Island Club. One of their members was Ralph Brown of Long Island, and his family connections made it possible for the club to build a house on Cow Island to use for hunting and as a fishing base.[1] In 1902, for example, the Boston Herald's summer gossip column noted that two Boston families would be staying at the "Cow Island Club house," one for two weeks and the other would be "spending the summer."[2]

By 1921, John M. Dick was ready to retire. He reached an agreement with Herbert A. Blackstone to purchase the southern part of the island where the main camp buildings, wharf, and beach were located (about 200 acres).[3] Then in short order, Dick turned around and sold the the camp and property to a newly-formed corporate entity, Camp Idlewild Inc., organized in Cambridge, MA, by Ed Roys.[4]

For more than two decades thereafter, Camp Idlewild was apparently the only entity occupying Cow Island, even though it only owned the southern part. Things began to change after World War II. In 1947, Herbert A. Blackstone sold the northern portion of Cow to two developers from Laconia, Paul Binette and J. Felix Daniel.[5] The two men sold a few lots in 1948 and then devised a 200 lot subdivision plan for the northern portion in early 1949. These lots began to be sold in the years thereafter.

Meanwhile, Camp Idlewild continued to enjoy the southern end of the island until the mid-1970s. In 1975, Roys finally closed the camp after 84 years of operation. He commissioned his own subdivision plan for that portion of the island, selling six acre lots to vacationers and carving out as common land a substantial amount of the interior along with the wharf and beach area.

Diamond Island

Diamond Island was part of Masonian Lot #1, along with Sleepers Island, the Barn Door islands, and the eastern end of Rattlesnake Island. It was unnamed on Hersey's 1772 map. By the 1820s, it was known as Diamond Island.[6] As one 1880s observer put it, "it was a green conical island, called Diamond (because of) its shape."[7]

---

[1] Blackstone, Farewell Old Mount, pp. 69-70. The club sold the boat in 1897. The purchasers converted it into the house boat *Iris* that was rented to vacationers on Bear Island and Three Mile Island among other places around the lake.
[2] Boston Herald, August 10, 1902, p. 27: "Mr. and Mrs. E.L. Fitzhenry of Boston are spending the summer at Cow island, with headquarters with the Cow Island Club." Fitzhenry owned a 'machinists' company in Boston during the early 1900s. (Boston Chamber of Commerce report, 1919). "W.C.Paine and family of Boston are at Bear Island for a stay...after which they will go to the Cow Island Club house for ... two weeks."
[3] CCR B/P 160/304.
[4] CCR B/P 160/309. The purchase price of $35,000.00 was taken back in paper by the Dicks who received $7000.00 each year through 1925.
[5] CCR B/P 251/301.
[6] See 1824 deed, B/P 9010/355.
[7] Hawkes, Winnipesaukee, p. 42.

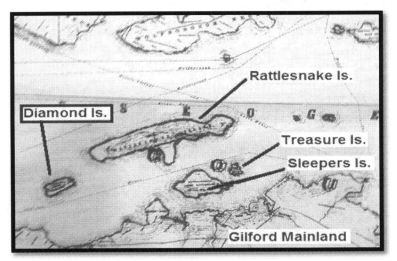

Lot #1 was drawn to the original right of Thomlinson and Mason. Their right went through a number of hands before ending up in the possession of Harry Long of England and Nathaniel A. Haven of Portsmouth.[1] Long was a relative of Thomlinson, and his interests in New Hampshire were represented by Mark W. Pierce. Haven was very active in acquiring islands and mainland properties of various Masonian proprietors.

Diamond did not draw the interest of anyone until 1824, when James Ames of Gilford acquired it from Haven and Peirce.[2] Ames owned a large farm on the Gilford mainland just opposite the island,[3] and the island provided seasonal grazing pasture and wood. Ames owned

Postcard of the *Lady of the Lake* at Diamond Island.

the island for six years. He sold it in 1830 to a neighbor, Benjamin Thurston.[4] Thurston held on to Diamond for five years, before selling it to Nathaniel Folsom, a Gilford blacksmith, in 1835. Folsom owned the island for the next 30 years.

In 1865, the use of Diamond changed dramatically. The Winnipesaukee Lake Steamboat Co. (WSC) purchased the island from the aging and infirm Folsom just three months after Appomattox brought an end to the Civil War.[5] The WSC saw an opportunity to enhance its passenger business on the *Lady of the Lake* by providing a new, unique destination for tourists.[6] In 1866, it built a hotel on Diamond Island that was open year round.[7] Prior to the new hotel, all of the *Lady's* passenger business revolved around passage between mainland ports at the

---

[1] See, for example, B/P 9014/97, regarding the sale of another Lot #1 island, Sleepers (listed as Flanders).
[2] B/P 9010/355.
[3] Ames had purchased this farm from Mark and Joshua Peirce in 1820. B/P 9009/385.
[4] B/P 9012/518.
[5] B/P 42/119. Nathaniel Folsom died that same month, July 1865. He was buried in Gilford's McCoy Cemetery.
[6] The ownership of the *Lady* during the latter 1800s is not entirely clear. The Winnipesaukee Steamboat Co. (WSC) leased the *Lady* to the BC&MRR in 1851, but in subsequent years it appears that the Steamboat Co. actively operated it. In 1862, the company sold it to George Clough of Concord, NH. By 1871, it was back in the hands of the WSC. By 1893, it was on lease again to the Concord and Montreal RR. See Boston Herald, August 2, 1862, p. 1 and July 2, 1893, p. 23. This is a topic that requires a lot more research.
[7] Regarding the year it was built, see Independent Democrat, December 28, 1865, p. 3; July 19, 1866, p. 3; and August 1, 1867, p. 3. The first citation is a notice that the hotel will be built 'next summer'. The latter notes the Diamond Island House was "newly built and finished last year. " Postcards of the hotel, that appeared years later, erroneously listed the date as 1861.

Weirs, Center Harbor, and Wolfeboro. The boat also promoted 'excursions' (day trips) around the lake with the only island stop being Bear Island.

Diamond Island now became a major destination point on the lake. A Lowell, MA, newspaper noted in 1867, that "Diamond Island is a popular place of resort for picnic parties and other excursionists, an excellent hotel being kept there, which is well patronized."[1] Another newspaper article touted its presence, concluding that "those who wish to spend a few days in a quiet retreat, or in excursions, picnics, parties, and the like, we know of no place with better conveniences, or more attractive and agreeable, than Diamond Island."[2] The WSC hired the very capable and well-liked Warren W. Rider to manage the hotel. He lived there year-round, and the hotel became popular with winter fishermen who preferred its comforts "to roughing it."[3]

DIAMOND ISLAND HOUSE IN 1861

The island's prominence became such that it was included in 1874 among the five key stops made by the steamers as they "constantly ply between …Weirs landing ,… Meredith, Alton Bay, Wolfeborough, Diamond Island, and other places around the lake."[4] The Diamond Island House House suffered a bit of a setback in 1870 when Rider died of typhoid fever. His local obituary summed up his popularity:

"Our pen moves unwillingly to record the death of Warren W. Rider, which occurred at Diamond Island on Monday. Ever since that spot has become a favorite resort of pleasure parties and summer visitors, Mr. Rider has had charge of the hotel, and by a geniality and courtesy rarely equaled, had made multitudes of warm friends, and we believe not enemies. The announcement of his death will cause a throb of genuine sorrow in many a heart and many a traveler over our beautiful Lake…"[5]

Over the next several years, the hotel's management changed with regularity. By the latter 1870s, the hotel apparently lost favor with the general public, having become a haven for gambling and drinking, two pastimes that were deeply frowned upon by the broad population.[6]

---

[1] <u>Lowell Daily Citizen and News</u>, August 24, 1867, p. 2.
[2] <u>Independent Democrat</u>, July 19, 1866, p. 3.
[3] <u>Independent Democrat</u>, January 28, 1869, p. 3. Also, <u>Lake Village Times</u>, September 14, 1872, p. 1.
[4] <u>Statistics and Gazetteer of New Hampshire</u>, 1874, p. 87.
[5] <u>Lake Village Times</u>, July 30, 1870, p. 3.
[6] The temperance movement was becoming increasingly stronger around this time. The Women's Christian Temperance Union was founded in the U.S. in 1874, and the Salvation Army was established in the U.S. in 1880. The NH state legislature, for example, passed a law in 1874 making it illegal to gamble on steamboats and railroads. <u>Lake Village Times</u>, August 22, 1874, p. 3.

The hotel remained in operation through the summer of 1880. In December of that year, the Winnipesaukee Steamboat Company sold it and the island to Winborn A. Sanborn, the former WSC shareholder and former captain of the *Lady*.[1] Sanborn made the purchase so he could move the hotel to the rapidly growing Weirs. He arranged to have the hotel cut in half and hauled across the ice that winter. It was rebuilt in the spring of 1881, opposite the Weirs railroad station.[2]

Diamond Island House reincarnated at the Weirs as the Sanborn Hotel c. 1881.

Diamond Island continued to be owned by the Sanborn family for many years after the hotel was moved. Winborn Sanborn died in 1882, and his estate was inherited by his daughter, Ellen, who was married to John S. Wadleigh, the captain of the *Lady* by that time. Ellen owned Diamond until her death in 1898. After the hotel was removed and until Ellen passed away, there are no records of any regular inhabitants on the island. Picnickers visited periodically, stopping at the old wharf until it rotted away.

Probably not long after Ellen's death, Diamond was acquired from her estate by a family friend, Fred W. Hoyt of Fernandina Beach, FL.[3] He owned the entire island until his death in 1935. It is not known how he used it. Diamond was then sold by Hoyt's estate administrator to Frederick C. Spooner of Lincoln, MA.[4] Beginning in 1945, Spooner began to carve out lots for other vacationers; but in contrast to almost every other island situation, he chose to lease the lots with an annual payment of $150.00. Spooner executed six such leases between 1945 and 1961. He changed his approach in the 1970s. After completing a subdivision plan, he sold off 28 lots around the island between 1971 and 1978.[5]

Dollar Island

Other than a passing fisherman or canoeist, tiny Dollar Island played no part in the settler era. The island was probably given its name in 1858 when Crocker completed his map of the lake for the Lake Company.[6] Dollar's early ownership trail followed the path of the other

---

[1] B/P 67/320. Sanborn was the captain of the *Lady* for several years beginning in 1862, was quite familiar with Diamond as it stopped there daily.

[2] It was called the Weirs Hotel after it was sold following Sanborn's death in 1882. Sanborn's huge farm was located on the Gilford side of the Weirs channel, so he was in close touch with the growth taking place at the Weirs. His estate became part of the Interlaken development some years after his death.

[3] No deed of sale was found, but circumstances strongly suggest this conclusion. Hoyt purchased Ellen Wadleigh's farm in Laconia from her Executor in October 1898 (B/P 101/170); and he owned Diamond when it was next sold in 1935. No record was found of any intervening owners between 1898 and 1935.

[4] B/P 220/1.

[5] All of this information is found in the Belknap County Registry of Deeds under the Grantor listing for Fred Spooner.

[6] The name is on his map, the first instance that it is found in the records. One must assume it was named after the silver dollar because of its shape.

unnumbered islands, coming into the hands of George W. Sanders in 1864.[1] Thereafter, there is no record that Sanders sold it. Very possibly, Charles F. Brown 'assumed' title to it in 1879 when

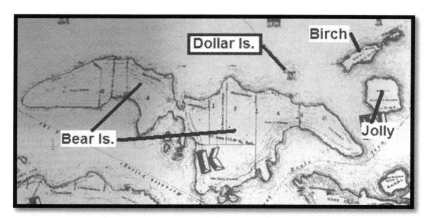

he purchased Birch and Steamboat from his brother, George. In 1886, Charles sold it to Reverend Walter J. Yates the same day he sold Steamboat Island to Yates.[2] Yates owned Dollar for six years and then sold it in 1892 to Henry B. Quinby of Gilford, NH.[3] Henry B. and his wife, Octavia, built the first house on the island.

Henry Quinby was one of the better known people who owned property on the islands during the late 1800s. Referred to as Colonel, he became the manager and treasurer of the Cole Manufacturing Company in Lake Village in 1883 when his father-in-law, Benjamin J. Cole, retired.[4] In the late 1880s, he began a very active career in state politics, serving in the House (1887-1888), the Senate (1889-1890), and the Executive Council (1891-1892). In 1909, he was elected Governor of New Hampshire, serving one term.

The Quinby family owned Dollar for some 20 summers, until 1912, when they were informed by Fullerton Wells' Lake Winnipesaukee Company that their original purchase was not legal. Apparently having no appetite to dispute it, the former Governor bought it (again) from Wells.[5] Henry B. eventually passed the ownership of Dollar to his son, Henry C. Both Henry B. and Henry C. died during the early 1920s. In 1927, Henry C.'s wife, Florence, sold Dollar to Edgar Caffall of Brooklyn, NY.[6] The island remained in the Caffall family for 48 years before they they finally departed the lake in 1975. Ownership of the island changed hands twice since then.

Dolly's Islands (Dolly, South Dolly, Little Dolly, and Penny)

In the late 1800s, these small islands were simply known collectively as the Aunt Dolly Islands.[7] Today, they are known by four names: Dolly Island, South Dolly Island, Little Dolly Island, and Penny Island.[8] These islands entered the summer era during the 1880s, although the the exact timing is uncertain. By 1890, there were five separate camps on them, nearly all occupied by local men from Gilford.

---

[1] B/P 40/301.

[2] B/P 76/205. See the discussion of Birch and Steamboat, above.

[3] B/P 88/209.

[4] The Illustrated Laconian (1899), pp. 48-49.

[5] B/P 134/360.

[6] B/P 182/233.

[7] See, for example, the 1891 deed, B/P 85/574. No individual names were given to them.

[8] The Meredith tax records incorrectly show addresses for only two islands, Dolly and Penny, with the latter encompassing South Dolly Little Dolly, and Penny.

The Dolly Islands were not among the numbered islands when the Masonians drew their lots in 1781. Ownership of them, therefore, moved along when the group of unnumbered islands was sold during the 19th century. George W. Sanders acquired them in 1864.[1]

Dolly Island is the largest of the four at about two acres in size. It is located to the

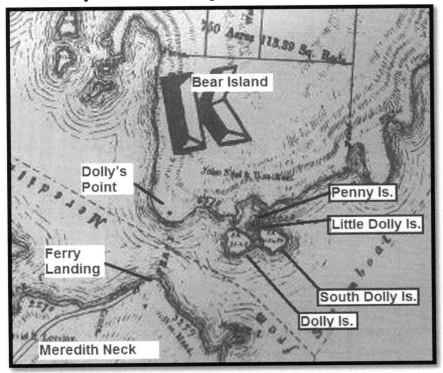

north of the others. The first known owner was Clinton E. Banfield, who acquired it sometime during the 1880s.[2] There is no record of when or from whom he bought it, but in all likelihood, he purchased it from George Sanders.[3] Banfield was a a machinist who lived in Lake Village with his wife, Sarah. Very early on, he built a small, one-room cottage there.[4] By the latter latter 1880s, he owned his own steam boat, making him one of the earliest vacationers to have one. The Banfields owned the island for more than 30 years. Clinton died in 1925, and his wife sold the island the following year.[5] Thereafter, ownership passed through five different owners and now resides with the Katzens. A second lot on the island was subdivided in 1948.[6]

South Dolly is the second largest in the group at 1.5 acres. Its early deed trail is also quite murky. By the 1880s, it was owned by George A. Sanders, a son of George W. Sanders. George A. Sanders used the island during the summers, along with Frederick E. Gilford, who lived on the island with him. They built one of the earliest houses found on the islands near Bear.[7] Both men were from Gilford, NH, and they undoubtedly used it as a fishing camp.

---

[1] Some or all of the Dolly Islands might have been part of Bear Island until 1851, when the Lakeport dam was improved and the lake level rose.

[2] See reference in B/P 83/256.

[3] None of these islands appeared on Fullerton Wells list of unnumbered islands in 1912, suggesting that they had all been sold legitimately.

[4] The one room cottage is still part of the existing house on Dolly Island.

[5] B/P 176/211; 179/216.

[6] B/P 300/243.

[7] Meredith's on-line tax card for 6 Penny Island (an incorrect identification) states the house was built in 1880.

In 1890, George A. Sanders sold South Dolly to Fred Gilford.[1] He was originally from Manchester, NH, where he was a machinist with the railroad. By 1900, he was living with his family in Concord, NH. In 1923, Gilford sold South Dolly to Harry C. Richardson, of New York City, who owned it until 1947.[2]

Little Dolly, about one half acre in size, was apparently occupied illegally during the 1880s by George W. Sherwell of Gilford, NH. At the time, the island was owned by a group of seven people, led by John and Sarah Ames of Charlestown, NH. Their ownership basis was not found. In 1891, they sold the island to the aforementioned George Sherwell.[3] George's brother, Harry, was also living on Little Dolly at this time.[4] George Sherwell owned South Dolly until his death, after which his widow, Sadie, and his daughter, Dora, sold it in 1927 to Harry C. Richardson, the same man who had purchased South Dolly in 1923.[5] Richardson owned it until 1947. Today, Dolly, South Dolly, and Little Dolly are all owned by the Katzen family, with the exception of the second lot on Dolly Island.

Penny island is the smallest of the four and barely large enough to support a tiny camp. The island was acquired in 1907 by J. Frank Sanders when he purchased all of the remaining 'unnumbered islands' from the heir of George W. Sanders. In 1911, J. Frank sold it to Harry E. Sherwell of Laconia, who had been summering next door on Little Dolly with his brother, George, since the 1880s.[6] Sherwell and his wife owned the island until 1941.[7] It was sold three times thereafter (1941, 1961, and 1963), ending up in the Linstrom family.[8]

Five Mile Island

Five Mile Island was part of the Masonian Lot #4 as designated in 1781.[9] It was given its name sometime between 1837 and 1847, presumable by its then owner, John Brown.[10] The name is derived from the island's distance from Center Harbor. The lot was drawn to Thomas Wallingford in 1781, but he passed away not long afterwards. All of his Masonian land rights devolved to John Peirce. In 1789, Peirce sold all of Wallingford's Masonian lands to John Cushing of Berwick, ME, including his island holdings in Winnipesaukee.[11]

---

[1] B/P 83/256. The seller in this case was George A. Sanders, not the George W. Sanders who owned all the unnumbered islands. This was the same Fred Gilford who sold Shepherd Island to E. C. Mansfield in 1904. Gilford and Mansfield bought undivided halves of Timber Island in 1903. Gilford sold his half of the island to Mansfield in 1917.

[2] B/P 169/190. See also, B/P 83/256 regarding his living on Little Dolly.

[3] B/P 85/574.

[4] See B/P 83/256.

[5] B/P 183/131. See also,. B/P 183/133.

[6] B/P 131/432.

[7] B/P 253/206.

[8] B/P 253/206; 417/516; 436/59. An intra-family sale between Linstroms in 1972 left sole ownership in the hands of Carl Linstrom. B/P 582/127.

[9] The majority of the acreage that comprised Lot #4 was on Long Island. Five Mile and Six Mile were also part of the lot.

[10] In 1837, when John Brown bought Daniel Follett's half, Five Mile and Six Mile were still simply referred to as two small islands. (SCR B/P 172/240). When Brown sold Five Mile in 1847, he used the name 'five mile' to describe that island. Presumably Six Mile was named by then as well. (B/P 43/240). The inspiration for the name probably stemmed from Three Mile Island which was the first island to be named based upon its distance from Center Harbor.

[11] B/P 4/434. Lot #4 consisted of a parcel on Long Island as well as Five Mile and Six Mile.

In 1821, Cushing sold Five Mile (along with part of Long Island and Six Mile) to John Brown and Daniel Follett.[1] In 1837, John Brown bought Follett's share of Five Mile and Six Mile.[2]

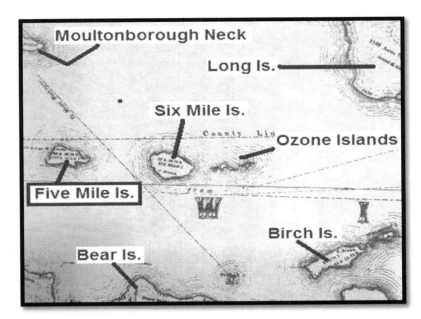

Mile.[2] In 1847, after 26 years of using it it as seasonal pasture and a wood lot, Brown sold it to George W. Brawn and Rufus Smith, both of Moultonborough.[3] Brawn and Smith also presumably wanted the island for grazing and wood. Smith eventually sold his half interest to Brawn. Brawn died in the 1880s.

In 1887, his wife, Mary, sold Five Mile to the ubiquitous Charles F. Brown and Levi Ward, a physician. Both men were living in Gilford then.[4] Ward bought out Brown, and then in 1896, Ward sold Five Mile to John H. Dow and Henry B. Quinby, the future New Hampshire Governor who had purchased Dollar Island in 1892.[5] The two men built a house in the small cove facing Bear Island.

In 1903, Quinby purchased Dow's half interest in the island.[6] Five Mile was owned by the Quinby family for 56 years thereafter, the last member being Henry B.'s daughter, Candace Q. Maynard, who died in 1952. The executor of her will sold it at auction to George Brigden.[7] The island changed hands several times in the following years, but it was rarely occupied by summer residents. The house gradually crumbled after years of neglect. A new wharf was built on Six in the latter 1980s, but the next winter's ice quickly laid waste to it. In 1998, the island was purchased by the Lakes Region Conservation Trust.[8]

Goose Island

Goose is a tiny island located in the channel between Pine Island and Meredith Neck. Like almost all of the other tiny islands, its early history is unknown. The first owner of

---

[1] B/P 9009/137.
[2] SCRD B/P 172/240.
[3] B/P 43/240. Brawn was the early farmer who presumably gave his name to Brawn Bay. His farm was located at the base of that bay. The bay was so-named by 1858 at the latest. Rufus Smith was Brawn's neighbor at the base of the bay.
[4] B/P 77/56.
[5] B/P 105/469.
[6] B/P 110/552.
[7] B/P 337/323.
[8] B/P 1472/515.

record was the Pine Island Outing Club. There is no information about when or from whom the PIOC bought the island. The founders of the Pine Island Club had acquired Pine Island in 1888, and it is possible that they simply assumed ownership of Goose at that time.[1]

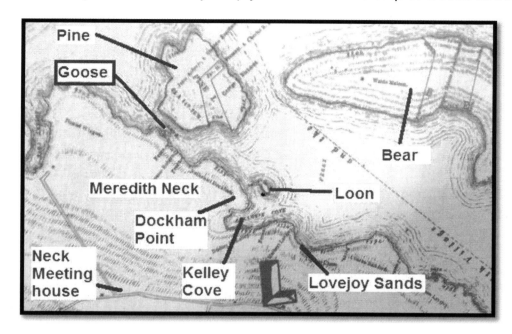

The PIOC sold Goose (aka Pine Cone Island) to Nellie B. Follett in November 1906.[2] Follett had recently purchased the Neck shorefront property opposite Goose.[3] By then, a house was already in place on Goose. In addition, the New England Telephone and Telegraph Company had placed a pole on the island in 1902 to facilitate getting its wires to Pine and Bear.

The ownership of Goose was contested in 1912 when Fullerton Wells' Lake Winnipesaukee Company acquired all of the unnumbered islands. Wells' company asserted its ownership of the island and insisted that Follett 'repurchase' it. Follett complied.[4] Follett's mainland property is now The Oliver Lodge at 92 Powers Road. Goose is still part of that property.

Governors Island

Governors Island was given its name in the early 1700s when it was apparently granted to New Hampshire's then-Lieutenant Governor, John Wentworth, during the 1720s. Wentworth never visited the island, given the absence of colonial settlement in the region prior to the 1760s. In 1766, another John Wentworth, the grandson of the former Lieutenant Governor, was named provincial Governor of New Hampshire. He was deeply invested in the expansion of the colony both for political and personal reasons. In the latter regard, his interests in the Lakes Region focused upon Kings Wood (Wolfeboro) where he established a summer estate—the 'first' vacation home in New Hampshire--in 1767. In July 1772, after the completion of James Hersey's survey of the lake, the Masonian proprietors granted "Governours Island" to John Wentworth.[5]

---

[1] John S. Roberts was the seller of Pine Island. He owned the mainland property on the Neck across from Goose.
[2] B/P 119/323. The PIOC gave Follett a confirmatory deed in 1910. B/P 130/187.
[3] B/P 118/343.
[4] B/P 142/510. Wells' deed of sale to Follett indicates that the island was listed as Arlington Island, "sometimes called Goose Island" on its list of unnumbered islands.
[5] State Papers, vol. 29, p. 553.

The Masonian Proprietors were close associates of Wentworth, sharing numerous family ties as well as business and real estate interests. They were always cognizant of currying his favor.

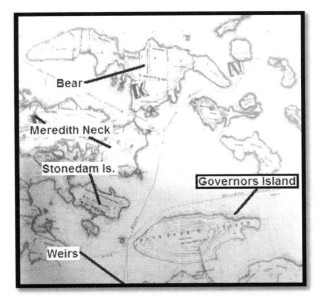

John Wentworth never visited Governors Island either. It was confiscated by the state legislature in 1778, along with all of his other property, after Wentworth fled the country at the outbreak of the Revolution. In 1780, the island was sold by the Probate court to John Cushing, a merchant from Boston. Cushing obtained a mortgage from John Langdon to finance the purchase.[1] Cushing was apparently unable to repay the loan, and the property was foreclosed by Langdon. In 1797, Langdon sold it to one Lemuel Bickford Mason, who was residing on Governors Island at the time of the sale.[2] Mason was said to be a Revolutionary veteran who had squatted there after the war.

Two years later, in 1799, Mason sold the island to Eleazer Davis.[3] Davis was a wealthy farmer who owned upwards of 700 acres in Alton.[4] Eleazer Davis retained personal ownership of Governors Island for two years. Then, in March 1802, he sold 200 acres on the western side to his son, Nathaniel.[5]

Nathaniel made Governors his homestead farm. His lot was just across the channel from the mainland. In 1803, he built a road from the mainland shore, opposite his land on Governors, to the main road running to the Weirs. At that point in time, the water level between the island and the mainland was low enough for crossing by horse or wagon but too deep in places to make the trip easy. In 1807, Nathaniel built a bridge across the shallow channel. In 1808, he sought and received approval for the bridge from the state legislature. Nathaniel acquired the rest of the island from his father in 1813.[6]

Nathaniel eventually developed a large farm on the island with various ancillary operations such as barrel making and blacksmithing. His estate was also a source of supplies for

---

[1] B/P 9001/433.
[2] B/P 9003/183.
[3] B/P 9003/184. Governors Island was annexed to the town of Gilmanton in 1799. It became part of Gilford in 1812 when that town was carved out of Gilmanton.
[4] See Fisher to Davis, B/P 9003/183. Two months after Davis bought Governors Island, he purchased Rattlesnake Island. See B/P 9004/481 and the vignette on Rattlesnake further below.
[5] B/P 9005/304. There is an oft-repeated story that Eleazer Davis bought the island for "his reckless, scapegrace" son, Nathaniel, to give him something to do. See, for example, the New England Farmer, August 13, 1870, p. 1.
[6] B/P 9006/424.

other settlers. Dolly Bryant reputedly rowed to Governors Island to stock up on rum and other necessities.

Nathaniel was apparently a good citizen. In 1816, the 'year without a summer', his farm was still productive, and he provided other settlers with wheat at standard cost.[1] By the latter 1820s, the name of the island changed to Davis Island. In 1831, Nathaniel purchased Lots 7 and 9 on Bear Island to give him an additional wood lot and seasonal pasture. He sold Lot 7 on Bear in 1833 to Dolly Nichols son, Robert, but continued to own Lot 9 for years thereafter.[2]

In the late 1830s, Nathaniel became an ardent follower of William Miller who gained increasing numbers of adherents during the decade as a result of his belief that the Advent (the physical coming) of Christ was going to occur in 1843.[3] Davis convened 'camp meeting' type services on the island, and the founder, William Miller, led some of them.

In time, Nathaniel began to incorporate his sons into the island farm. He sold 107 acres of it to Franklin in 1837, who in turn sold it to his brother, Eleazer, in 1849. In 1850, Nathaniel sold Eleazer an additional 75 acres on the island. [4] The Davis era on Long Island ended in 1857. In January, with his health failing, Nathaniel and his son, Eleazer, sold their lands on the island in separate transactions to George Smith of Meredith and David Plummer of Concord, NH.[5]

Ownership of 'Davis Island' underwent a number of changes in the succeeding years. In 1858, David Plummer bought out George Smith.[6] There were several more owners, including Smith Neal[7] and James H. Plummer, before it was sold in 1872 to Isaac Morrill and James Brown. In 1883, then sole owner, Isaac Morrill, leased it to Stilson Hutchins of Washington DC. The lease was converted to a sale in 1887.[8]

Hutchins' arrival coincided with the early evolution of the summer era around the lake. He was the editor of *The Washington Post*. In 1885, he built a huge mansion on the island's heights with a grand view towards the Weirs. He also built a road along the shoreline and another along the inland crest. Hutchins stocked his estate with Shetland ponies, a herd of pure bred Jersey cows, and several hundred sheep. About 1893, he leased his property to Charles Sleeper who ran the Hotel Sanborn (aka Hotel Weirs) at the Weirs. Sleeper called the Hutchins mansion Terrace Hall and developed plans to lease it out during the summer season.[9] In 1903, the German embassy rented the mansion for the summer.

---

[1] In that vein, he was apparently similar to Reuben Whitten of Ashland who is remembered for feeding many of the townsfolk whose crops failed during 1816.

[2] He finally sold it in 1854.

[3] Arthur W. Spalding, Origin and History of Seventh-Day Adventists, vol. 1.

[4] B/P 12/79; 14/66.

[5] B/P 8012/79; 9016/514-516; 8014/66; 28/197; 28/198.

[6] B/P 30/402.

[7] This was the same Smith Neal who owned half of Bear Island Lot 9 in 1855.

[8] B/P 72/11; 77/288.

[9] Boston Herald, July 2, 1893, p. 23.

Hutchins' mansion c. 1900 (courtesy of the Thompson family)

By the 1880s, the name of the island had reverted back to Governors Island.[1] It was sold by Stilson Hutchins to his son, Lee, in 1904. When Lee died in 1927, it was willed to Ramon Penn of Boston. In February 1928, Penn sold it to The Hayes Recreational Communities, a Maine-based corporation owned by Clifford Hayes, a real estate developer.[2]

Hayes had big plans for the island. In 1929, he created an extensive subdivision plan for his so-called "Governors Estates". He borrowed $50,000 from a syndicate of three banks to fund the endeavor.[3] But the purchase by the Hayes Communities came just in time for the stock market crash and the Depression. The endeavor fell on difficult times. The Stilson mansion burned in August 1935, one year after the Bear Island House suffered the same coincidental fate. In 1935, the mortgage holders foreclosed on Hayes.[4]

In 1937, the banks began to actively sell residential properties on the island in an effort to recoup their funds. By the end of 1940, they had sold 52 separate parcels.[5] In 1940, the growing population formed its own island organization, Governor's Island Winnepesaukee (sic) Inc. (GIW). With the onset of the war, lot sales naturally dwindled. Only three lots were sold from 1942 through 1944; then in 1945 the number jumped to 19.[6]

---

[1] See Hawkes, <u>Winnipesaukee</u>, p. 35.
[2] B/P 185/501.
[3] B/P 191/492.
[4] B/P 218/67.
[5] B/P 283/439.
[6] B/P 283/439.

View of the *Mount* at the Weirs with the Hutchins mansion and Governors Island in the background.

With its post-war population growing rapidly, the Governor's Island Winnepesaukee, Inc. organization gained in strength. In May 1946, it purchased all of the remaining unsold parcels on the island from the bank group.[1] Thereafter, the island population continued to expand, and Governors became one of the more exclusive locations on the entire lake. The GIW Inc. eventually morphed into the Governor's Island Club, which became the managing entity of the private island community. By the early 1960s, there were some 40 permanent houses on the island and another 90 summer homes. By 1992, the combined total had reached 156, and by 2015, it approached 200.[2]

Horse Island

Horse Island sits just across the channel from the Dolly Islands, very close to the Neck (old Lot 82). Its name is said to derive from a long-ago incident in which a Neck farmer's horse fell into the lake while being barged to Bear Island, swam to the little island, and refused to leave it.[3] The island's early ownership history is unknown, beyond being part of the unnumbered islands. As such, George W. Sanders would have been the owner of record in the late 1880s. Given its small size, Horse Island was of interest to no one during the farming era. In 1896, William O. Tuttle, a Newton, MA vacationer, purchased the Meredith Neck point lot opposite the island.[4] There is nothing to indicate that Tuttle bought Horse then or any time thereafter.[5] It appears that he simply 'assumed' ownership of it.

Sometime between 1896 and 1906, Tuttle sold Horse Island to Robert Moses, a tinsmith and fishing devotee who lived in Meredith.[6] By spring 1906, there was a house standing on the island.[7] The building on the property was or became a unique two- story, round structure.

---

[1] B/P 283/439.
[2] Governor's Island Club website.
[3] Hawkes version of the story has it that the horse drowned off the island. Hawkes, Winnipesaukee, p. 46.
[4] B/P 95/595. The seller, Smith Paine, had purchased this part of the Neck from long-time Neck settler, William S. Mead, only the month before.
[5] Horse Island was one of the names on Wells' list of unnumbered islands in 1912.
[6] No deed was found to document the sale to Robert Moses. Tuttle's ownership and sale to Moses are referenced in B/P 121/253; 121/583; 122/240.
[7] B/P 122/240. Among other things, the deed indicated that the island was also called 'Wambeek' Island. Meredith Inventory report for 1906 shows the "Moses sisters" owned Horse Island & cottage.

Horse Island c. 1907. (Courtesy of the Thompson family)

In 1907, Robert Moses (by then 70) sold 1/4th shares in the property to each of his three daughters, Hattie Moses, Mildred Woodman, and Flora Moulton. Hattie sold her share to Flora

Fishing party at Horse Island early 1900s. Robert Moses on the left.

the following year.[1] The island was used at least in part as a summer camp by Hattie Moses, a Summit, N. J. resident, who taught summer school in Meredith. She occasionally brought some of her summer students to the island by boat for swimming and enjoyment. In 1908, and some summers thereafter, the students included Mei-ling and Ching-ling Soong, the young daughters of a wealthy Chinese family who were in the country for schooling. Hattie noted about Mei-ling: "While in Meredith she was fond of boating, canoeing, swimming and having trips by motor boat to Horse Island, near Bear, and other places for picnics."[2] Years later Mei-ling became the wife of Chiang Kai-shek, and Ching-ling became the wife of Sun Yat-sen.[3]

The ownership was consolidated again in 1913, when Flora sold her half interest to

---

[1] B/P 122/240; 121/253; 121/583; 122/265. Despite Hattie's withdrawal, for years beginning in 1907, Meredith tax records list only Hattie Moses as owner of the island.

[2] Van Veghten, <u>Meredith Bay</u>, p. 45.

[3] Van Veghten, <u>Meredith Bay</u>, pp. 42-50.

Mildred, giving Mildred a 3/4th ownership interest along with Robert Moses 1/4th interest.[1] For a time thereafter, the island was the summer home to Camp Winnipesaukee, a school for boys that operated year round under the leadership of Hattie Moses.[2] Mildred and her father apparently enjoyed a fruitful time of it for many years. They even managed to almost survive the Depression. But in 1939, their resources ran out. It may be that the hurricane of 1938 devastated the island and leveled their house. The bank foreclosed on them. Poetically, the island was sold out of foreclosure, not to brand new owners, but back to Hattie Moses and Mildred Woodman.[3] They owned the island until 1955, when it was sold to the owner of the mainland property nearby.[4]

Jolly Island

In 1781, Jolly Island (then called Foley Island) was part of a group of islands that made up Masonian Lot #9 drawn by John Rindge.[5] After Rindge died in 1786, his estate administrator, Daniel Rindge, sold Lot #9 to John Peirce. After Peirce died in 1814, Jolly Island ended up in the private hands of his sons, Joshua Winslow Peirce and his younger brother, Daniel Hall Peirce. They retained ownership of it well into the 1840s despite at least two offers to buy it and Round Island (one in 1837 from George Sanders and the other in 1839 from Nathaniel Davis of Governors Island).[6] By the 1840s, the island was known as 'Jolly', although the circumstances of the naming are not known.[7] In any case, Jolly apparently was not entirely deserted during the years of Peirce ownership. According to one source writing in the 1840s, a squatter, Levi Sanborn, was actively 'improving' the island.[8]

Finally, in 1846, the Peirce brothers sold Jolly to Winborn A. Sanborn of Gilford.[9] Sanborn Sanborn was a well known figure around the lake.[10] Born in 1811 and raised on a farm in Gilford, he moved to Salem, Massachusetts around 1830. He became a sailor, working on a merchant clipper that made a 12 month round trip to Bombay, India. He returned to New Hampshire soon thereafter. In 1833, he became the captain of Winnipesaukee's first steamer, the *Belknap*. In 1835, his wanderlust got the better of him again. He left New Hampshire, first for Virginia and then St. Louis, for a few years. He returned to the captaincy of the *Belknap* for a few years in the

---

[1] B/P 138/84. As of 1910, Robert Moses was living with Millie and her family in Meredith. They mortgaged the property with the Laconia Savings Bank, perhaps to fund the camp. B/P 136/17.
[2] "Meredith," The Granite Monthly, Vol. 46, Jan-Feb, 1914, p. 42.
[3] B/P 238/399.
[4] B/P 360/465. This deed makes no mention of a building on the island.
[5] The other islands in the Lot were Steamboat Island, Mark Island, Lockes Island, and Round Island. The derivation of the name 'Foley' was not found.
[6] The name Jolly is found in this 1846 deed: B/P 8008/551. See also comments on map, Masonian Division of the Winnipesaukee Islands, found in State Papers, Vol. 29, p. 587. The personal ownership was an anomaly for the Peirce brothers. Joshua and Mark had sold every other island their father had purchased, including Lockes Island, Little Bear Island, Timber Island, Round Island, part of Cow Island, and Mark Island (of which Mink Island was still a part). Daniel Hall Peirce was only part of the Mark Island sale.
[7] B/P 8008/551.
[8] See comment on map, Masonian Division of the Winnipesaukee Islands, found in State Papers, Vol. 29, p. 587. Levi Sanborn had purchased Mark Island in 1840 and Mink Island in 1841. Squatting was not unheard of. Two men, James Follett and Levi Shaw, were identified as having squatted on Round Island before 1820.
[9] B/P 8008/551.
[10] Almost all of the biographical information about Winborn Sanborn is drawn from: Hurd, The History of Merrimack and Belknap Counties.

latter 1830s, before once again departing, this time to take up engineering. He served as the lead engineer on two ocean steamers, the *Decatur* and the *Ohio*, before illness forced him to return home to Gilford. It was apparently at this juncture that Jolly Island beckoned him. Perhaps he saw in it the magical healing powers that summertime on the lake provides.

Winborn Sanborn owned Jolly until his death in 1882. But there is nothing to suggest that

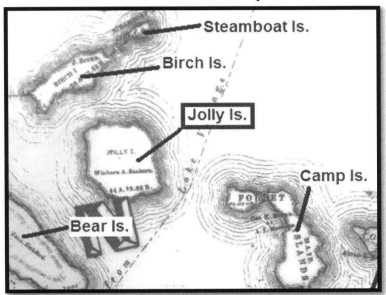

he made use of the island to any great extent. For example, he did not build a house or fishing camp there. Over the course of the three and a half decades that he owned the island, he was quite active around the lake. In 1851, he oversaw the construction of the second major passenger steamboat on the lake, the *Dover*. It was built for the Boston and Maine railroad to compete with the *Lady of the Lake*. Sanborn became its captain in 1852, when it took to the waters. He wintered on his Gilford farm which was located on the shore at the mouth of the Weirs channel. By 1863,

Sanborn had switched allegiances, becoming the captain of the *Lady*. In the early 1870s, he moved to Florida where he established a lumber business. He again returned to Winnipesaukee in 1878, and yet again became the captain of the *Lady*. In 1880, he purchased Diamond Island enabling him to move the hotel to the Weirs where it was called the Sanborn Hotel.

Sanborn died in February 1882. Ownership of Jolly Island was inherited by his daughter, Ellen, who was married to John S. Wadleigh, the captain of the *Lady* by then. In 1891, Ellen sold Jolly to Charles S. and William F. Davis.[1] The two were brothers and Methodist ministers who were living in Bristol, Rhode Island when they made the purchase.[2] For several years previously, previously, they had camped on Long Island at the farm of a family friend, Minnie Wentworth. When they heard the island was for sale, they leaped at the opportunity.[3] The following summer, 1892, they convinced two others, John P. Arnold of Middleboro, MA, and Reverend Walter Ela of Fall River, MA to visit the island with them. Having piqued the interest of their visitors, the Davis brothers then developed a plan to subdivide the island and sell lots to like-minded associates. They hired E.S. Ellis of Bourne, MA, to do the work. He completed a survey of Jolly in September 1892, dividing it into nine shorefront lots while leaving the interior land as a common 'Reservation', abutting all of the shore lots.[4]

---

[1] <u>Jolly Island: One Hundred Years, 1893-1993</u>, Jolly Island Centennial Committee, June 1993. Re the Davis' purchase, B/P 86/343.
[2] By 1893 Charles Davis was living in New Bedford, MA, and William Davis was in Middleboro, MA.
[3] Mary Donsker, <u>The Story of Welch Island Through 1945</u>, p. 13.
[4] Plan of E.S. Ellis, Sep 1892, Book 5, Page 328, Belknap County Registry of Deeds.

While awaiting the final survey in 1892, the families stayed at the Long Island Hotel or camped in tents on the island. They brought a carpenter to the island and had two cottages built.[1] By August the following summer, Jolly was "covered with cottages, and they (were) all filled with happy campers." There were six houses and some tents occupied by seven Methodist ministers, their families, and a few other guests.[2] That summer, ownership of the lots was also formalized. Charles and William Davis jointly owned one lot. They sold another to John Arnold and a third to Walter Ela and Augustus Holmes.[3] Among the new vacationers, Walter Ela was also a Methodist minister from southern New England who had responsibility for a church in Danielsonville, CT. Augustus Holmes was Ela's son-in-law and a bookkeeper. John P. Arnold, on the other hand, was the principal of the grammar school in Middleboro, MA, where William Davis had a church in 1893.[4] Two years later, in May 1895, another vacationer was added to the budding list of Jolly Islanders. This was Harrison T. Borden of New Bedford, MA, where Charles Davis had his church.[5] Younger than either of the Davises, Borden (28) was perhaps the carpenter who built the first homes on the island.

Four of the remaining five lots on the island were sold by the Davises during 1896 and 1897. In all cases, Methodist clergy were involved in the purchases. They included Emma Gifford (soon to be wife of Reverend R.E. Schuh) of Cottage City, MA; Reverend Benjamin F. Simon of New Bedford, MA; Reverend Charles A. Stenhouse of Taunton, MA; and Reverend Andrew J. Coultas of Fall River, MA. The last of the nine lots was sold in 1905 to Ella Bartholomew and her husband, Reverend James L. Bartholomew, of Manchester, CT.[6]

Not long after settlement, the ministers began holding religious services on the island in keeping with the Methodist camp tradition. This later evolved into an open-air chapel in the center of the island and the sharing of evening vespers with Methodists from Birch Island. A steamboat wharf was built in the mid-1890s on the southwestern side to facilitate travel to and from the island. Prior to the mail boat route which started in 1902, travel was provided by smaller steamers that usually ran between the wharf at Long Island and the Weirs.[7]

Charles and William Davis left the island within a few years of its being built out, although their reasoning is not clear. In 1903, William Davis became interested in nearby Welch Island, at that time uninhabited and much larger. He was finally able to purchase a lot there in 1906.[8] In the

---

[1] Boston Herald, Aug 6, 1892, p. 13 mentions "two handsome cottages" on Jolly. Charles Davis and William Davis shared a house and Walter Ela and Augustus Holmes shared the other one that year.
[2] Boston Herald, August 27, 1893, p. 12. The Methodist ministers were the two Davis brothers, and reverends Simon, Carlton, Stenhouse, Ela, and Bartholomew.
[3] For the former, B/P 96/529. For the latter, B/P 90/283. The deeds contained provisions requiring the burning or burial of all waste so the lake water would not be contaminated.
[4] His connection to the Davises has not been determined.
[5] B/P 96/549. Borden does not appear to have had a familial connection to the Davises nor was he a clergyman. The Borden family continues to own the property on the island, the only one with a direct connection to the founding families.
[6] B/P 96/509; 98/82; 98/85; 98/87; 98/89; 98/97; 98/97; 115/349.
[7] The Island was not along the main routes of the *Mt. Washington*. The *Lady of the Lake* was no longer active, having been retired in 1893. By this time, there were numerous small, private steamers on the lake, many of them built and operated out of Long Island.
[8] B/P 118/306.

the same year, Charles was transferred to Minnesota. The combination may have prompted the Davis brothers to sell their property on Jolly.[1]

Long Island

Like almost every other island in the lake, the history of Long Island is known only in the broadest of strokes. Given its size and complexity, Long Island deserves a book of its own. What follows is a brief and spotty history of the island to provide at least some perspective on it.

Long Island is the largest island in the lake at 1186 acres. It was one of the seven islands given a name on James Hersey's map in 1772. The Masonian proprietors divided it into five lots (#4 through 8 on the list of 15 lots) in 1781. Lot #4 included the southwestern end of Long Island as well as Five Mile and Six Mile. Lots #5-8 consisted solely of Long Island property. The island was annexed to the town of Moultonborough in 1799, before anyone settled on it. Although it was not heavily settled early on, Long Island was more attractive to prospective farmers than any other island in the lake. In addition to its sheer size, it was relatively flat, offering extensive opportunities to develop large pastures and cultivated fields. Had it been part of the mainland or incorporated into Moultonborough earlier, it almost certainly would have been settled in the 1770s when the town was initially inhabited.

The first settler on Long Island was John Dow, a Pittsfield, NH, cooper who purchased 116 acres of Lot #8 in 1804.[2] The acreage was the southwesterly half of the lot, so it did not encompass the northeastern end of the island nearest the mainland. Yet, Dow undoubtedly utilized the tip of the island to get back and forth to the mainland, for all practical purposes establishing the first ferry.[3]

The next farmer to settle on Long Island was John Boody who purchased lot #7 around 1810.[4] He was followed by the families of John Brown and Daniel Follett, who were brothers-in-law. They jointly bought Lot #4 in 1821.[5] Brown was from Poplin, NH, and Follett was from Gilford. The two men divided the lot in half, with Follett taking the southwestern end facing Sandy Island and Brown owning the parcel to the northwest of Follett.[6] Follett, however, did not stay long. He sold his half to Brown in 1826, and Brown subsequently sold it Robert Lamprey in 1832. Most of Lot #5 was sold to Brown in 1837.[7]

---

[1] B/P 118/327.

[2] SCR B/P 52/22. The seller was John Jeffries of Boston. He was the guardian of the minor son of George Jaffrey who drew lot #8 in 1781.

[3] Dow's situation on Long Island was similar to Robert Bryant's on Bear Island. They both settled on the section of the island nearest the mainland. The Long Island ferry was used until the late 1860s. The first bridge was finished in 1868.

[4] No deed of purchase was found. In re the timing, see transcript "Long Island Tour," by Frank E. Greene and Bill Depuy, May 20, 1996, Moultonborough Historical Society and the transcript "Long Island of the Past," by Philip Parsons and Clark Myers, June 8, 1987. Both can be found at the Moultonborough Library. The red Boody farmhouse is the oldest house still found on the island.

[5] SCR B/P 108/524 (BCRI 9009/137). They also jointly owned Five Mile and Six Mile as a result.

[6] SCR B/P 133/35. SCR B/P157/334.

[7] SCR 172/115. He bought 200 acres.

Lot #6 came into the hands of the extended Brown family before 1843.[1] The other lots on

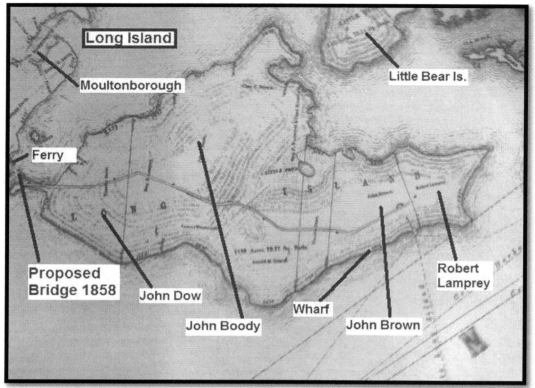

the island were settled a few years later, many by members of the Wentworth family. By 1858, there were nine separate farms on Long Island.[2] And like the situation on Bear Island, all of them became connected through the intermarriages of their children.

During the 1800s, Long Island was the home to some of the most successful farmers in the state. John Brown became famous for his King Philip corn (aka "the Brown corn");[3] his wife, Catherine, became well known for making up to 700 pounds of cheese each year; and Robert Lamprey was also recognized for the huge crops of corn he grew each year. John Boody became famous for his potatoes and corn crops.[4]

A road was developed from the ferry across the entire island to Lot #4 after the Browns arrived. Probably during the 1840s, John Brown also built a wharf (known as Front Wharf or Brown's wharf) on the south side of the island so he could tap into the commercial traffic provided by the gundalows, horseboats, and the *Belknap* before 1850.[5]

After the Civil War, the Long Island farmers began the same slow transition away from farming experienced by everyone else in the state. In 1874, John Brown's son, George K. Brown, turned the family farm into the Long Island Hotel. It became the center of activity on Long Island for years thereafter. The hotel could accommodate 50 guests, and it also served as a post office beginning in 1878. George Brown sharply improved the road down to the family wharf

---

[1] CCR 21/137.

[2] See Crocker's 1858 map which gives the names of the farm owners and has a notation about the possibility of a bridge. The bridge was not built until 1868, although there were petitions for one as far back as c. 1820.

[3] For some first-hand perspective on the popularity of Brown's corn, see a letter from Warner, NH farmer, Levi Bartlett in *The New England Farmer*, November 5, 1870, p. 1.

[4] See: "Windermere: A Jewel on Long Island," written c. 1910 by Dr. Frank Greene. Reprinted in the <u>Weirs Times</u> and found on the Lake Winnipesaukee Historical Society website (lwhs.us). This article is the basis for much of the 19th century history on Long Island.

[5] The timing of the wharf is not known. Edward Blackstone implies that it was in existence before 1849 when the *Lady of the Lake* first took to the lake. E. Blackstone: <u>Farewell Old Mount Washington</u> (1969), pp. 17-18.

where numerous large and small commercial steamers, led by the *Lady of the Lake* and the *Mount Washington*, stopped several times a day bringing tourists, supplies, and mail. The location was a beehive of activity with people and boats coming and going constantly. Another hotel, the Island Inn (aka Blake's Hotel), was developed in the middle of the island in 1879. It became successful as well.[1]

Front Wharf with steamers *Mt. Washington* and *Lamprey* docked.

Several Long Islanders entered the boat manufacturing business beginning in the 1850s. Many of the best known, smaller commercial steamers were built and/or owned by the Browns, the Lampreys, the Wentworths and the Blackstones on Long Island during the latter half of the century.[2] In many respects, the island was the steamboat capital of Winnipesaukee.

The island was very popular with tourists, and the Brown's Hotel was kept very busy. According to Reverend Hawkes in 1887, that hotel "has been crowded with guests, overflowing into the farmers' chambers, into tents and occasionally with cots in the great barn." By 1892, one correspondent noted that "there are more visitors to Long Island each year than (to) all the other (islands) combined... All of the large steamers make landings here, and it is truly a busy place through the summer months."[3]

[1] "Windermere," (lwhs.us). Rice, "Long Island."
[2] Blackstone: Farewell Old Mount, pp. 17-50.
[3] The Boston Herald, July 24, 1892, p. 13.

Long Island wharf with the road leading to the Long Island Hotel c. 1874.

In the mid-1890s, this all began to change. The Lampreys' old farm on the southern end of the island was purchased by Dr. Alonzo Greene who developed his Windermere estate on it. Greene's brother also acquired extensive property on the island and built a large mansion called Roxmont Castle. Other parcels gradually changed hands during the early 1900s. The number of summer home owners gradually accelerated thereafter, although, like Bear, most of the development did not take place until after World War II.

Loon Island

Loon is located near Kelley Cove and Shep Brown's Boat Basin.[1] It is a small island about two acres in size. It was acquired by Ede T. Gordon, a blacksmith and farmer from Laconia, some time before 1901.[2] As with so many other local men who acquired the small islands around Bear, he probably used it as a fishing camp. He built the first house on the island. In October 1901, Gordon sold the island and its tiny satellite island (where the mail boat stops) to Elias A. Bryant of Stoneham, MA.[3] Loon became one of the stops for the new mail boat service on the lake in

Mailboat at Loon Island, early 1900s.

---

[1] For its location, see map above in re Goose Island.
[2] We were unable to find any information about when or from whom.
[3] B/P 107/181.

1902, and it remains one today.

Originally from Francestown, NH, Bryant was a Civil War veteran who was a musician in the 4th NH Volunteer Infantry Regiment.[1] After the war, he moved to Boston where he was a printer. In1899, he purchased land in Gilford from George Merrill. By then, Bryant had his own steamboat and had also acquired land and a boathouse in the Weirs channel.[2] He built a new house on Loon in 1906.[3] In 1912, it was one of the islands that Fullerton Wells listed among the 212 unnumbered islands he acquired, but there is no indication that Wells ever tried to assert his claim of ownership. Elias died c. 1930, and his wife, Abbie, sold Loon Island the next year to Maxine Woodring.[4] It has changed hands a couple of times since then.

Mark Island

Well before the first colonial settlers came to the Lakes Region, Mark Island was one of the best known islands on the lake because of the steep hill that dominates its profile.[5] Legend

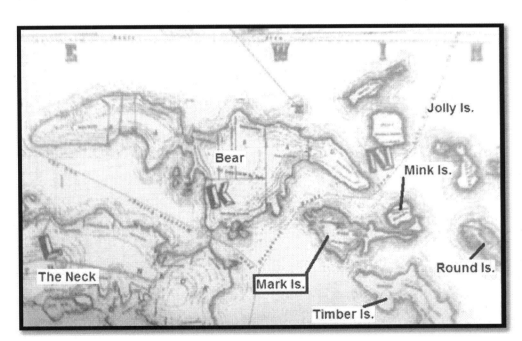

has it that the Abenaki kept it cleared of trees to use as a lookout. The hill was probably used by the colonial militia for similar purposes during the last two French and Indian wars, and the island's name derived there from. It later became a key navigational aid for early boaters. The name was picked up by George Hersey during his survey of the islands in 1772.

In 1781, Mark was included in Masonian Lot #9, and it was drawn to the right of John Rindge. The right passed to John Peirce and then was inherited by his sons, Mark W., Joshua W., and Daniel H. Peirce. In March 1824, the Peirce brothers sold Mark Island to George Sanders of Gilford.[6] Eleven days later, Sanders sold an undivided half to Samuel Sanborn, also

---

[1] He served for three years and left a diary of his service.
[2] In 1905, Bryant sold the boathouse and land to South Bear vacationer, James Aiken. B/P 115/219.
[3] The Boston Herald, July 1, 1906, p. 30.
[4] B/P 201/20.
[5] The hill is 177' above the lake, about the same height as the highest point on South Bear.
[6] B/P 9010/538. B/P 9010/233.

of Gilford.[1] The two men jointly owned the island for the next 13 years. As with other island owners, they probably used Mark for seasonal pasturage, timber, and as a wood lot.

In 1837, Samuel Sanborn sold his half to Isaac Sanborn, also of Gilford.[2] The ownership of Mark was unified in 1839 and 1840, when Sanborn and Sanders sold their halves to Levi Sanborn.[3] Levi held on to the island until 1846, when he sold it to yet another Gilford farmer, Gilman Small.[4] Gilman Small owned Mark until his death in 1849. He was survived by his wife, Polly, and two children, Mark and Mary. Polly retained her right of dower (her 'widow's thirds') in Mark Island, while the rest of it was divided between the two children. In 1866, a guardian, Thomas Weeks, was appointed to dispose of Mark Small's half interest in the island. Weeks sold it to Henry H. Sleeper and Josiah F. Robie, both of Gilford.[5] Thus, as of 1866, half Mark Island was owned by Sleeper and Robie, and the other half was owned by Mary Small. Polly Small still retained her right of dower.

The ownership remained in this configuration until the late 1870s. In March 1878, Josiah Robie sold his share to his son, George, who also lived in Lake Village.[6] The following year, Henry Sleeper's share was sold to the Winnipesaukee Lake Cotton and Woolen Manufacturing Company (WLCWMCo.) by a court agent handling the affairs of the deceased and bankrupt Sleeper.[7] Mary Small still retained her half interest, while Polly Small still had her right of dower.

Mary Small's half interest in Mark Island was finally sold in July 1880 after she was decreed insane. A guardian, Frank Rollins, was appointed to oversee her affairs, and he sold her part to the WLCWMCo, giving the company a three-quarters ownership position.[8] Three years later, in March 1883, the WLCWMCo. sold its interest to George Robie, the owner of the other quarter interest.[9] Robie immediately sold half of the island to Abigail Hutchinson of Gilford.[10] At the end of all of these transactions, Robie and Hutchinson jointly owned Mark Island, although Polly Small still retained her right of dower. Ownership of Mark Island remained this way until 1891 when Polly Small passed away. Her death left the island cleanly in the hands of Robie and Hutchinson. They owned it for another 18 years.

In May 1909, Mark Island finally transitioned to the vacation era when Robie and Hutchinson sold it to George K. Webster, a Rhode Island business executive who had purchased a sizeable amount of lake front property on the lower Neck (Lot 82) in 1897.[11] Early on, Webster had three houses and a wharf built on the northeastern side of the island, looking out between

---

[1] B/P 9010/653.
[2] B/P 9016/566.
[3] B/P 9018/99; 9018/260.
[4] B/P 8010/294.
[5] B/P 44/29.
[6] B/P 63/384.
[7] B/P 71/70.
[8] B/P 71/82.
[9] B/P 71/90-91.
[10] B/P 71/72.
[11] B/P 125/526. Re the Neck: B/P 98/216; 107/94.

South Bear and Mink towards the Ossipees.[1] He also commissioned a survey of the island in 1909 and developed a nearly 100 lot subdivision plan for it.[2] But Webster managed to sell only two lots before his death in 1922.[3]

Ownership of the island was inherited by his two daughters, Marion Dawley and Mildred

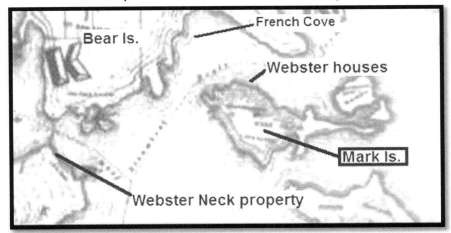

Kenyon, who also inherited his property on the Neck. They immediately repurchased one of the two lots sold by their father.[4] father.[4] Thereafter, they maintained ownership of the island (except for one lot) for another 18 years. In 1940, they sold their holdings to the Mark Island Development Corp., an entity formed by Gustav Beiswenger of Elizabeth, NJ,

Gertrude Tourtellot of Media, PA, and Eleanor Crinnion of Plainfield, NJ to develop the island. The buyers' timing, of course, was not propitious.

In 1944, the corporation made its only sale, but it was a large one. It sold the southern-facing points (Long Point and Deep Cove Point) to George and Margaret Wells of Laconia.[5] The Wells were also real estate speculators. But they were only able to sell one lot in 1947, and that was the last until 1956. Their lot sales picked up very rapidly during the late 1950s and into the early 1960s as the southern end of Mark became built out with vacation homes.

The Mark Island Development Corporation, on the other hand, apparently made no other sales on the large, northern end of the island. It was dissolved in 1951 with its assets moving into the hands of the three original principals. Nothing happened after that for another 10 years until Gustav Beiswenger purchased the interests of the other two owners in 1961.[6] Even then, over the next almost 20 years, Beiswenger did not sell any of the 60 or more subdivided lots he owned. It was not until the early 1980s that lot sales accelerated again. This continued into the 21st century as the island was gradually built out.

---

[1] The three houses are now part of #20 Mark Island. The houses were for George and his two daughters.
[2] See B/P 271/269 for a map of Webster's subdivision plan.
[3] B/P 135/427; 165/384.
[4] B/P 165/356.
[5] B/P 271/269.
[6] B/P 416/505. Gertrude Tourtellot married Gustav Beiswenger in later years.

Mink Island

Before 1831, Mink Island did not exist. It was actually part of Mark Island. As such, it was part of Masonian Lot #9 drawn to John Rindge in 1781. Ownership passed from Rindge to John Peirce and then to two of his sons, Joshua and Daniel, in 1814. When the new, improved dam was built in Lake Village in 1831, the lake level rose, creating a channel and a new island. Before the latter 1850s, it did not have a name. It was simply referred to as 'a certain small island' near Mark.[1] By 1858, it was known as Mink Island, probably given the name by William Crocker during his survey of the lake. Even then, the name was not widely accepted or used. Deeds still referred to it as the 'small island' near Mark. In 1880 and 1883, the deeds called it Little Birch Island.[2] It was not until 1912 that the name Mink Island appeared again.[3]

With regard to ownership, in 1841, the Peirces sold Mink to Levi Sanborn, the Gilford farmer who had purchased Mark Island in 1839-1840.[4] Sanborn owned Mink Island for eight years, selling it in 1849 to two Bear Island farmers, James Bickford and Theophilus Dockham.[5] Bickford soon bought out Dockham, and, in November 1851, he sold Mink to Andrew Gray of Meredith.[6] Gray held the island only briefly, selling it the next summer to another Bear Islander, Eleazer Bickford Jr.[7]

Eleazer owned Mink Island for 12 years. During most of those years, he was serving as pilot of the *Lady of the Lake*. He was still unmarried and living with his parents on Bear Island. Presumably, Mink offered seasonal pasturage and wood resources. Eleazer finally sold Mink to Thomas Appleton in 1864.[8] Appleton was a Lake Village manufacturer who had purchased Three Mile Island a year earlier. But Appleton went bankrupt in 1867, and a court appointed administrator sold off his assets the following year. In May 1868, Mink Island was purchased by two busy island investors, George H. Robie and Charles F. Brown, who were close neighbors in Lake Village.[9] In 1883, Charles encountered financial difficulties, and his wife, Ellen, took ownership of his half of the island.[10]

George Robie and Ellen Brown continued their joint ownership of the island until 1912. In that year, George sold his half interest in Mink Island to his daughter, Lillian Robie Webster of Laconia.[11] Thereafter, the dual ownership of Mink continued unchanged for another 17 years.

---

[1] See, for example, the 1852 deed B/P 105/244.
[2] B/P 67/331 and 71/527.
[3] B/P 133/244.
[4] B/P 8001/63.
[5] B/P 105/168.
[6] B/P 105/173. The deed from Dockham to Bickford was not found.
[7] B/P 105/244.
[8] B/P 40/121. Eleazer had recently married and moved to Gilford.
[9] 1892 Atlas, p. 267.
[10] B/P 47/447. Brown had run into financial troubles in 1880 that almost cost him his ownership of not only the island but also his property in Lake Village. In 1878, he mortgaged his properties to Samuel Osgood in exchange for $700.00. He defaulted on the loan, and in 1880 Osgood obtained a judgment against Brown authorizing the sheriff to seize Brown's properties.[10] Brown's wife, Ellen, resolved the problem in 1883 when she settled Osgood's claim, by then in the hands of David Sawyer, for $429.00.
[11] B/P 133/244.

Ellen Brown passed away in 1929, leaving the family's interest in Mink Island to her two daughters, Anna Chandler and Dora Wilder.[1] Dora passed away in 1935, and her ownership interest in Mink Island was inherited by her husband, George, and her daughter, Edna.

The ownership changed within both families in 1936. George Wilder deeded his interest to his now married daughter, Edna Nolan.[2] Edna and her aunt, Anna Chandler, now owned the Brown's half of Mink Island. When George Robie's daughter, Lillian Robie Webster, passed away in 1936, the Robie half of Mink became the property of her daughter, Olive Webster Page. This ownership structure was modified again in 1948 when Anna Chandler transferred her ownership to her daughter, Lillian C. Sanborn.[3]

Thus entering the 1950s, Mink Island was still entirely owned by third generation members of the Brown and Robie families that originally purchased it in 1868. The situation entered another state of flux in the late 1950s. First, Edna Nolan sold her one-fourth share of the island in separate transactions to families unrelated to either the Browns or Robies, ending a 90 year string of joint ownership. She sold one-eighth to Allen and Nina Veazey and the other one-eighth to Gerald and Myrtie Wheeler on July 4, 1958.[4] In 1959, the two new families developed a a subdivision plan of the island in conjunction with the Brown/Robie-related majority owners, Lillian Sanborn and Olive Page.[5]

The island was slowly built out thereafter. The Brown's heir, Lillian Sanborn, sold her remaining interests in 1972, ending 104 years of ownership by the Brown family lineage.[6] The Robie's heir, Olive Page, remained an owner until her death in 1989. Her property was inherited by her son, J. Douglas Page, who finally sold it in 1996, ending 128 years of ownership by the Robie lineage.[7]

Pine Island

Pine Island is the 15th largest island in Winnipesaukee at 72 acres. The island got its name prior to 1827, although the origins of the name are not known. Pine was combined with Stonedam Island in 1781 to form Lot #12 in the allocation of the largest Winnipesaukee islands amongst the Masonian Proprietors.[8] Lot #12 was drawn to the right of Jotham Odiorne. However, Odiorne had died in 1751. Odiorne's Winnipesaukee islands ended up in the hands of Portsmouth 'Gentlemen,' Peter Pearse and Daniel Treadwell, whose wives were daughters of Odiorne.[9] It was not until 1827 that they finally sold Pine Island to Caleb Lovejoy, who purchased

---

[1] See B/P 306/263.
[2] B/P 221/4.
[3] B/P 306/263.
[4] B/P 389/33; 389/34.
[5] BCRD Plan B/P 13/974. B/P 399/467; 399/469; 399/471.
[6] B/P 587/320.
[7] B/P 1394/835.
[8] Back in 1772, James Hersey had estimated its size at only 42 acres.
[9] See B/P 9002/120-124 for the 1780 division of most of Odiorne's assets (although not the islands). Odiorne's heirs were his daughters, Mary and Mehitabel.

purchased it for seasonal grazing and wood lot purposes.[1] The purchase made sense for Caleb whose Neck farm was located nearby on the northern end of Lot 78.

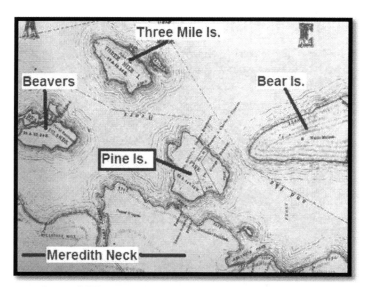

Caleb owned Pine until his death in 1841. It was sold at public auction the next year by his son and estate administrator, David Lovejoy, to three other Neck farmers, Moses Chase, John Roberts Jr., and Stephen Boardman Jr.[2] They informally divided it into three parcels, including the northwest end facing Three Mile Island; a middle section; and a southeast section facing down the lake between Bear Island and the Neck.[3] Stephen Boardman Jr. took control over the northwest end of the island.[4] He owned the Pine acreage for nearly 30 years, finally selling it in 1871 to Noah Davis of Gilford.[5] The middle portion of Pine Island was allocated to John Roberts whose Neck farm was located right across the channel from Pine. His ownership of the parcel is muddled somewhat by conflicting deeds, but through a series of transactions, this parcel moved from his hands to Thomas Chase to Madison Chase and finally to James M. Prescott and his brother, Charles, in 1855.[6] The Prescotts maintained ownership of it until James died in 1873.

The southern end of Pine was allocated to Moses Chase in 1842. After he died in 1847, his wife sold the parcel to Thomas Bickford, the son of Bear Island veteran, Brackett Bickford.[7] In In 1851, Thomas sold the parcel to his cousin, Ebenezer Bickford, who had a farm near Advent Cove.[8] After Ebenezer died in 1857, his wife, Almira,[9] sold the acreage on Pine to another son of of Brackett Bickford, George S.[10] George did not own the property for very long, selling it in 1859 to James M. and Charles Prescott.[11]

---

[1] There is one uncertainty in the ownership trail, the logic of it notwithstanding. There is an 1834 deed that, by its description, shows a Portsmouth man, Edmund Roberts, selling what is clearly described as Pine Island (i.e. 42 acres, island #12) to Timothy Robinson of Lowell, MA. (B/P 9010/135). The deed, however, refers to it as Black Cat, although that island was smaller and part of lot #13. The deed trail suggests that the Roberts deed to Robinson did in fact intend to sell Black Cat and not Pine. The sale of Pine to Caleb Lovejoy was never contested. B/P 9011/405 (SCR 132/138).

[2] B/P 8/209.

[3] Various deeds show this three parcel division, but there are at least two others that reference ownership in terms of an 'undivided one third' share. Regarding the former, see, for example, Sarah Chase to Thomas Bickford, Feb 1848, B/P 17/74. In re the latter, see John Roberts to John S. Roberts, Apr 1860, B/P 34/62. See also B/P 37/300.

[4] This is the Boardman who had donated the land on the Neck for the Meetinghouse just a few years earlier.

[5] B/P 52/420. Boardman's sale came three years after he had acquired the nearly 90 acres that comprised Dolly's Point (old Lot 9) on South Bear Island which provided him with far more grazing land than the small parcel on Pine offered. For his part, Davis was primarily interested in the island's timber.

[6] B/P 25/99; 25/100. In the 1860s, John Roberts still claimed ownership as seen in deeds among family members. B/P 34/62; 36/368; and 37/300.

[7] B/P 17/74.

[8] B/P 18/88.

[9] Almira was the daughter of Eleazer Bickford Sr. and grew up on Bear Island. She was Ebenezer's cousin.

[10] B/P 31/583. George S. Bickford was Almira's brother-in-law and her cousin.

[11] B/P 31/559.

With this last sale, some two-thirds of Pine was owned by the Prescotts. They maintained ownership of it until 1873. James M. Prescott passed away, prompting Charles to sell out. The acreage was purchased jointly by John S. Roberts and Noah Davis, the latter of whom had purchased the northwestern end of Pine from Stephen Boardman in 1871.[1] In 1882, John S. Roberts bought out all of Noah Davis' interests in Pine, giving him ownership of the entire island.[2]

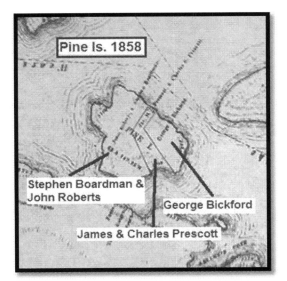

The farming era on Pine continued thereafter for another six years. In 1888, Roberts sold it to four Methodist ministers from Massachusetts.[3] The four were William E. Huntington of Newton, William I. Haven of Malden; James H. Humphrey of Reading; and Joseph W. Dearborn of Stoneham. They had become aware of the island's availability through William Haven who had vacationed on Hawkes Nest Island nearby.[4]

Huntington was the best known of the four. After growing up on a farm in Illinois, he had served in the Civil War. He then prepared for the ministry at Boston University where he received his S.T.B. degree (Bachelor of Sacred Theology). After being a pastor for eight years, he was named the Dean of the Boston University College of Liberal Arts in 1882 at the age of 38. He was holding this position at the time of the purchase of Pine Island.[5] The other three men were also Methodist clergymen, although none gained the distinctions of Huntington. Haven's background included an education at Boston University, but his pedigree stemmed from his father, the Methodist Episcopal Bishop Gilbert Haven, who was a prominent figure in the abolition, temperance, and women's rights movements.[6] Their numbers on Pine were augmented by their extended families as well as by other Methodist ministers, including E.M. Taylor, W.L. Thirkield, and Fred H. Knight. They were joined a few years later by Reverend Wesley O. Holway and Reverend Joseph H. Mansfield.

In 1892, the original owners incorporated the Pine Island Outing Club (PIOC) and sold the island to it.[7] By this time, there were apparently two houses on the island, probably one on the

---

[1] B/P 56/154. John S. was the son of the earlier Pine Island owner.

[2] B/P 69/137. As part of the sale, Davis retained the right to all of the timber on the island for three years.

[3] B/P 79/120. See also, "Pine Island in the Early Days," by Mrs. Fred S. Knight, undated manuscript, Moultonborough Library.

[4] Knight, "Pine Island," p. 1. Mrs. Knight erroneously states that Haven owned Hawkes Nest. In 1891, it was owned by Winfield Hawkes. See below, under Three Mile Islands.

[5] He later became president of Boston University. "A People's History of the School of Theology/Boston University," www.bu.edu/sth-history.

[6] Bishop Haven was familiar with the lake as well. In 1875, he made a presentation at the Methodist camp at the Weirs. Springfield Republican, April 21, 1875, p. 7.

[7] B/P 99/490.

northwestern end (now #8 Pine) and one on the southeastern end (now # 61 Pine).[1] In 1898, the PIOC commissioned C. H. Sleeper to prepare a survey and subdivision plan of the island. The survey resulted in a 20 lot subdivision with the center of the island left as a 10 acre communal center (called the 'ellipse' or the 'oval'). On May 3, 1901, the PIOC sold all 20 lots to its members and their families. Twelve of the lots were purchased by nine different Methodist ministers, including Reverend Edward Taylor, Reverend James H. Humphrey, and Reverend Wilbur Thirkield. Reverend Thirkield was a Methodist Bishop originally from Ohio. His wife, Mary, was the daughter of Bishop Gilbert Haven and sister of fellow Pine Islander, Reverend William I. Haven.

Another very prominent member of the PIOC was Wesley O. Holway. He was a Harvard graduate and Methodist minister who enjoyed a long and successful career as a Navy chaplain. He organized the Navy Temperance League among many other initiatives. His two daughters, Bertha and Edith, both joined him on Pine. Bertha married Charles Fletcher, and they bought a lot to the west of Holway.[2] Edith married a successful investment banker and automobile advocate, Lewis R. Speare. They bought the lot (now #61) on the other side of Holway.[3] In addition, Lewis Speare's brother, E. Raymond Speare, purchased the lot next to his brother. Another organizing member of the PIOC who purchased more than one lot was Robert F. Raymond. While not a minister, Raymond was a Harvard educated lawyer whose brother was president of the Methodist Wesleyan University in Connecticut. He was a staunch prohibitionist and became president of the American Bible Society.[4]

Mail boat passing Pine Island in the background. H.O. Whitney boathouse is the large structure on the left. It was torn down c. 1950. The small boat house to the right of it is still there.

---

[1] Meredith tax records, 1892 (MHS Archives) reference the two houses. Current Meredith tax cards indicate that both those houses were built in 1890. The cards also indicated another house on the western side of the island (#1) was built in 1891.

[2] Holway had purchased the lot and perhaps built the house (#59 now) where the mailboat docked beginning in 1902.

[3] Their lot on Pine was acquired a few years later by Arthur Whitney who built a huge boathouse there. Edith and Lewis Speare also purchased extensive property on the Neck, more or less facing Pine Island. Speare owned a steamboat, the *Falcon*, which was "one of the finest appointed private yachts on the lake." The Boston Herald, July 8, 1900, p. 27.

[4] Richard Herndon: "Men of Progress: One Thousand Biographical Sketches and Portraits of Leaders in Massachusetts," New England Magazine, 1896.

In keeping with its roots, the PIOC included several restrictions in all of the deeds of sale. These included, among other things, a prohibition against making or selling "intoxicating liquors"; forbidding any type of manufacturing operation; a limitation of two dwelling houses per lot; a banning of any horse stables or pig sties; and the requirement that sanitary conditions be maintained.[1]

Thus, by the end of 1901, Pine Island had fully transitioned into the vacation era. Over the following years, the now private lots changed hands regularly. But Pine continued to be a summer haven for clergymen throughout the 1900s.[2] The history of that process is for someone else's telling.

Rattlesnake Island

Rattlesnake is the fifth largest island in the lake at 368 acres. The name was in use as far back as 1772 when James Hersey completed his survey of the lake for the Masonian Proprietors. The island was given the name because rattlesnakes inhabited it.[3] Hersey's survey estimated the size of the island at 290 acres. The Masonian Proprietors divided it in two parts for drawing purposes in 1781. A 40 acre parcel on the eastern end was included in Lot #1 along with the Barndoor Islands, Sleepers Island, and Diamond Island. Lot #1 was drawn to the original right of Thomlinson and Mason. The remainder of Rattlesnake (then estimated at 250 acres) comprised all of Lot #2, which was drawn to Mark Hunking Wentworth.

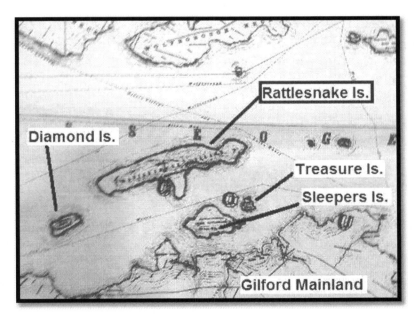

Mark Hunking Wentworth died in 1785. His estate was inherited by his wife, Elizabeth, but she died not long thereafter. The estate ultimately was passed to her four grandchildren. In1797, they worked out an agreement among themselves regarding the division of the assets. Rattlesnake Island (Lot #2) became the property of Francis Gore and his wife, Annabella, who

---

[1] See, for example: B/P 106/342.

[2] Among others were Reverend Henry Hitt Crane, Bishop G. Bromley Oxnam, and Reverend Kenneth Rose.

[3] An 1848 newspaper article references the "craggy hill' on the island that is "the abode of the venomous reptiles." It says an early settler had "the vocation of a snake hunter" and caught the rattlesnakes for their venom which was valued as "a remedial agent." The Boston Evening Transcript, October 14, 1848, p. 4. The Lake Village Times reported on September 26, 1868 that a visitor to the island killed a nine foot long rattlesnake. An 1860 article reported that several rattlesnakes were killed there during the summer. Aurora of the Valley (VT), October 27, 1860, p. 1.

lived in England.[1] In 1799, the Gores sold Lot #2 to Eleazer Davis of Alton.[2] Davis owned this lot for 26 years, presumably using it for seasonal grazing and as a wood lot. In March 1826, he sold his entire 250 acre parcel to John Davis of Alton.[3]

The early ownership of the 40 acres on the eastern end of Rattlesnake (part of Lot #1) is not clearly known. The original rights of Thomlinson and Mason ended up in the hands of Harry Long of England and Nathaniel A. Haven of Portsmouth.[4] Long was a relative of Thomlinson, and his interests in New Hampshire were represented by Mark W. Pierce. Haven, as we saw in connection with Bear Island, was very active in acquiring islands and mainland properties of various proprietors. Sometime along the way, the Lot #1 portion of Rattlesnake was acquired by one George Brown of Portsmouth. In June 1826, he sold it to William Nutter of Salem, MA.[5] Sometime before 1830, the Lot #1 acreage on Rattlesnake was sold to John Davis, the owner of the rest of the island.[6] In June 1830, Davis sold the entire island to Nathaniel Rogers, a farmer from Wolfeboro.[7]

The trail again becomes murky after this sale. Rogers owned the property for 10 years before selling an undivided two-thirds of it to Alpheus Sweat (or Swett) of Tuftonboro in June 1840.[8] Sweat was a lumber man who presumably valued the island for its timber. Ten years after after that, in December 1850, David Rogers, the son of Nathaniel, sold the remaining one-third interest to George Whitten of Wolfeboro.[9] Whitten apparently quickly sold his 1/3 of the island to Eleazer Barker and William Barker, Wolfeboro and Alton residents, who just as quickly flipped it to James Worster of Meredith.[10]

The appearance of James Worster was the beginning of a saga on Rattlesnake (and on neighboring Sleepers Island) that lasted until the late 1870s. In 1852, James Worster leased his interest in Rattlesnake to his daughter, Susan W. Worster, of Meredith.[11] In 1854, Susan, by then living in Concord, NH, sold her lease to three Concord men, Abraham Bean, Enos Blake, and Robert Corning.[12] A year later, those three sold the lease to George O. Worster, the brother of Susan and the son of James.[13]

---

[1] B/P 9002/532; 9002/535.

[2] B/P 9004/481. This was the same Eleazer Davis who purchased Governors Island the same year. Davis had dealt with other Wentworth heirs from England in 1797, when he bought land in Alton. B/P 9003/183.

[3] B/P 9011/193. John Davis was perhaps a son of Eleazer Davis.

[4] See, for example, B/P 9014/97, regarding the sale of another Lot #1 island, Sleepers (listed as Flanders).

[5] B/P 9011/140. This transaction seems suspect because Brown listed the acreage sold at 200 (vs. the 40 acres owned), and the price was exceptionally high compared to the amount paid by Davis three months earlier.

[6] No deed trail was found to document the sale.

[7] B/P 9013/253.

[8] B/P 9018/244. The deed does not indicate it was a sale of 2/3, but Rogers next transaction suggests that to be the case.

[9] B/P 23/256.

[10] See B/P 17/489 and 18/540, 18/51 and 18/52 deeds in which Worster gave a mortgage to the Barkers on the 1/3 undivided share of the island. The deed places Worster in Meredith but the 1850 census lists his residence as Dover. His presence in the latter location makes good sense in light of later events.

[11] B/P 21/91. It appears that James made a living by leasing out properties around the region. See, B/P 21/92.

[12] B/P 23/227.

[13] B/P 25/219.

In 1855, George Worster apparently purchased the other two-thirds of Rattlesnake from David Rogers.[1] That year he used the island as collateral for a $2800.00 mortgage loan from James Littlefield of Dover, the proceeds of which were probably used to make the purchase.[2] The mortgage was rewritten in 1858.[3] The collateral packages used in the mortgages reflected both George's one-third interest and his newly acquired two-thirds interest in the island, a distinction that came into play during the latter 1860s.

Whatever his plans for Rattlesnake, George Worster's financial situation deteriorated by 1866. He apparently first tried to deal with this in May of that year by transferring ownership of the island to his wife, Mary J.[4] Nevertheless, in September, James Littlefield, the mortgagee, sued George and won a judgment against him, relating to the one-third interest in the island. Assessors were sent to Rattlesnake to value it, and the sheriff was ordered to seize the property in lieu of payment. Littlefield was awarded the one-third ownership in the property.[5]

In October 1866, George Worster took another defensive step, notwithstanding his apparent sale of Rattlesnake to his wife the previous spring. He sold the remaining two-thirds of it to his mother, Sarah Worster, of Concord.[6] George apparently used a small portion of the proceeds in 1868 to repay Littlefield the amount due regarding the one-third portion of the island, thus recovering that part of it.[7]

All of Rattlesnake now theoretically belonged to George's mother, although the mortgage to James Littlefield on the two-thirds portion of the island remained in place. The Worsters managed to stay above water for the next decade, but at some point during that period they once again fell behind in their payments on the Littlefield mortgage. How soon thereafter is not clear. James Littlefield passed away in 1871. It is likely that the mortgage arrearage fell between the cracks as his estate affairs were being worked out. James had left everything to his several children, many of whom had moved to New York.

But the mortgage issue did not go unnoticed forever. The children, as trustees for the estate of James Littlefield, sued George Worster for non-performance under the mortgage. In June 1878, they won a judgment against him and foreclose ensued.[8] The Littlefields took possession of Rattlesnake. They maintained ownership of it for the next 22 years. In July 1900, they sold the island to Henry F. Libby, a dentist from Boston but a native of Tuftonboro.[9]

---

[1] We have not found this deed, but events suggest the timing of this purchase. It is possible that Rogers had sold it to another party who sold it to Worster about this time.

[2] B/P 25/246. Worster also used the island as collateral for a $126.88 loan from the County of Merrimack in 1861. B/P 36/257.

[3] B/P 31/391.

[4] B/P 44/7.

[5] B/P 44/530.

[6] B/P 44/479.

[7] B/P 47/93.

[8] B/P 63/647.

[9] B/P 104/524.

The Libby family owned Rattlesnake for decades thereafter. In 1910, Henry entered into a deal with lumbermen Henry Yeaton of Alton and Clifton Loring of Medford, MA, selling all of the trees, wood and logs on the island and giving them six years to do the work.[1] Some years later, Henry Libby apparently sold an interest in the island to his brother, Arthur A. Libby. After the deaths of the two in the 1940s, Rattlesnake was inherited by their children, Arthur Jr., Madeleine, and Gordon. They had no enduring interest in it, selling the island in 1950 to Joseph I. Melanson.[2]

Joseph Melanson maintained sole ownership of Rattlesnake for a little more than ten years. In February 1961, he sold it to the Rattlesnake Island Corporation, a newly formed Wolfeboro outfit established to develop it.[3] The process was a slow one given the inherent obstacles in establishing summer cottages on the steep banks and deep water shores of much of the island. It was not until 1971 that a subdivision master plan was created for the island. Shorefront lots were sold all around it thereafter with the exception of the eastern end (part of the old Masonian Lot #1). The latter was sold by a large land holder, Charles Pardoe, in 1982 to the Lakes Region Conservation Trust.[4]

Round Island

Round Island is the 20th largest in the lake at 43 acres. In 1781, it was among the several islands designated as Masonian Lot #9, drawn to the right of John Rindge.[5] As with the other islands in that lot, ownership devolved to the Peirce family, ending up in the hands of Mark W. and Joshua W. Peirce in 1814.

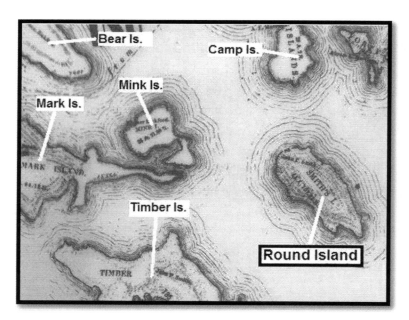

During the early 1800s, the island was occupied by squatters, Levi Shaw and James Follett.[6] In 1819, the Peirce brothers sold the island, still unnamed, to Samuel Thompson of Gilford. Thompson actively occupied the island seasonally for pasture and timber. In 1828, he sold an undivided half of it to James Hoit of Gilford.[7] Thompson

---

[1] B/P 128/153. Libby was paid $17,000.00.
[2] B/P 320/439.
[3] B/P 421/113.
[4] B/P 835/666.
[5] Like almost all of the islands in the lake, James Hersey had underestimated its size, putting it at 18 ½ acres.
[6] B/P 9012/614. This was presumably the same Follett whose name was attached to Camp Island during the early 1800s.
[7] B/P 9017/346. In 1858, James Hoit lived next to Winborn Sanborn on the point opposite Governors Island.

reserved all of the wood and timber for himself, but he allowed Hoit to clear up to half of the island for "pasture land."

In 1829 and 1830, Hoit and Thompson sold their halves to Gilford's John Pick Smith, who had purchased Timber Island in 1823.[1] Thompson reserved the right to take as much wood as he desired during his lifetime. The island was still unnamed at this juncture, although in some places it was referenced as Samuel Thompson's island.[2]

John Smith owned the island for 30 years, during which time it became known as Smith's Island.[3] His primarily interested in it was perhaps seasonal sheep grazing. In December 1860, John Smith sold "Round Island" to his son-in-law, George W. Sanders, the Gilford lumberman who had acquired several other islands during this period.[4] Sanders borrowed heavily to finance his ventures on the lake and in Gilford near the Weirs Bridge. By 1874, he was overextended and grasping at straws. He tried to keep things afloat by selling Round Island, Timber Island, and numerous mainland parcels to the WLCWMCo., but the sales were subject to mortgages held by the Laconia Savings Bank ($6000.00) and John P. Smith Jr. (also about $6000.00).[5] Not long after, Sanders was forced into bankruptcy, and the bank eventually took possession of Round Island. In December 1877, John P. Smith Jr. purchased the island, executing deeds with both the bank and with George W. Sanders.[6] John P. Smith Jr. owned Round Island for the next nine years. In September 1886, he sold it to George H. Robie.[7] One year later, in September 1887, Robie sold it to David Folsom of Revere, MA.[8]

The last sale brought Round Island into the vacation era, but it was not acquired with the intent to create a massive subdivision. Folsom did nothing with it for several years. Then in 1895, he sold off a two acre parcel on the southern end to Charles H. Sanborn.[9] That was the only subdivision made on Round. The rest of the island remained in the Folsom family which has built several well-spaced houses around the shore. They have enjoyed Round Island for 112 years.

Sandy Island

Sandy Island was originally part of Masonian Lot #13 drawn to John Wentworth. It came under the ownership of Edmund and Catherine Roberts of Portsmouth before 1823.[10] Roberts apparently sold the island to Benjamin Young Esquire who in turn sold it to Joseph McIntire of

---

[1] B/P 9012/501; 9012/557. Smith was very active on the islands. He purchased Welch Island in 1841. B/P 1/440. His farm was near Sanders Cove and Smith Cove in Gilford.
[2] See the annotated copy of Hersey's map, State Papers, Vol. 29, p. 587.
[3] See Crocker's 1858 map of the lake.
[4] B/P 36/494. Sanders gave Smith a mortgage on it, Timber, and other properties in 1862 to secure a $4500 loan. B/P 36/518.
[5] B/P 57/589.
[6] B/P 63/184; 63/198. For some reason, Smith paid Sanders $325.00. The bank deed did not state the price paid by Smith.
[7] B/P 76/285. This is the same George Robie who was active on Mink and Mark islands. The spelling of his last name is given as Roby in this deed. (As an aside, Hawkes Winnipesaukee, p. 70, stated that Round was still owned by George Sanders c. 1886, revealing the challenge of taking as gospel information from period pieces like his book. He was probably repeating what Frank Brown was telling him.)
[8] B/P 78/140.
[9] B/P 95/509.
[10] It was one of the islands pledged by Roberts to Henry Rice in 1823 when Roberts obtained a mortgage loan. B/P 9010/138.

Tuftonboro in 1829.[1] Sometime thereafter, the ownership of Sandy made its way to another Tuftonboro farmer, Robert Sweat (or Swett). After he passed away in the early 1840s, his daughter, Harriett Piper, sold it in 1846 to William Swett, yet another Tuftonboro farmer.[2]

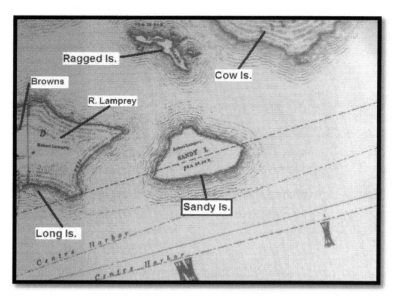

In 1851, William Swett sold Sandy Island to Robert Lamprey, the owner of the southern end of Long Island at that time.[3] Lamprey used it as an extension of of his farm, pasturing cattle, developing a garden, growing potatoes, and harvesting the wood.[4] He maintained ownership of it it until his death in 1886. His estate administrator, Lanson Lamprey, then sold Sandy to John S. Brown, a son of John Brown 2nd who owned the farm next to the Robert Lamprey farm on Long Island.[5] John S. Brown was living in Washington D. C. by this time. He died in c. 1897, leaving Sandy Island in equal shares to his wife, Mary, and his three children, Agnes, Edith and Arthur. Edith sold her one-quarter share to Agnes in 1897.[6] Mary's share also made its its way into Agnes's hands. Arthur sold his one-quarter share to his cousin, Walter A. Brown, the son of Benjamin 'Frank' Brown in March 1899.[7]

This flurry of sales among family members in March 1899 was probably precipitated by the Greater Boston YMCA. It was interested in establishing a family camp on the island. The administrators of the Y approached the Browns about leasing the island. A deal was struck for an annual payment of $100.00. The camp enjoyed so much success that the Y bought Sandy the following year and has owned it ever since then.[8]

Six Mile Group (Six Mile, Little Six Mile, and the Ozones)

Six Mile Island is one of six Winnipesaukee islands that derived its name from its distance from Center Harbor. The name came into usage between 1837 and 1847, perhaps given by its owner, John Brown.[9] The island is about 19 acres in size. It was part of the

---

[1] SCR B/P 140/442. No deed was found for the sale to Young.
[2] CCR B/P 8/461. The Swetts were undoubtedly related to Alpheus Swett, the Tuftonboro lumber man who owned part of Rattlesnake Island during the 1840s.
[3] CCR21/154.
[4] See, for example, B/P 54/289, in which Lamprey references in 1869 the cattle and wood uses. See also, Walter Jones, The Sands of Time: Sandy Island Camp, YMCA of Greater Boston (1998), p. 4.
[5] CCR B/P 90/570.
[6] CCR B/P 109/73. Sale reconfirmed in 1899: CCR B/P 111/457.
[7] CCR B/P 111/323. Walter was living with Arthur and his family in Washington D.C.
[8] Jones, The Sands of Time, pp. 4-5.
[9] In 1837, when John Brown bought Daniel Follett's half, Six Mile and Five Mile were still simply referred to as two small islands. (SCR B/P 172/240). When Brown sold Five Mile in 1847, he used the name 'five mile' to describe that island. Presumably Six Mile was named by then

Masonian Lot #4 as designated in 1781.[1] The lot was drawn to Thomas Wallingford, but he passed away not long afterwards. All of his Masonian land rights devolved to John Peirce. In 1789, Peirce sold all of Wallingford's Masonian lands, including his island holdings in Winnipesaukee, to John Cushing of Berwick, ME.[2] In 1821, Cushing sold Six Mile (along with the rest of Lot #4) to John Brown and Daniel Follett.[3] In 1837, ownership of the island shifted entirely to John Brown, who owned it until his death in 1867.[4]

Six Mile was inherited in six equal shares by John Brown's five living children (George, John, Benjamin [known as Frank], Charles, and Arvilla) and the heir(s) of his other son, Perley,

who died in 1864.[5] The ownership began to be consolidated in 1879, when George sold his 1/6th share to Ellen R. Brown, the wife of Charles Brown.[6] Two years later, in 1881, their brother, John, bought the share of his sister, Arvilla Lamprey.[7] Five years after that, in 1886, John S. purchased the 1/6th share of his brother, Frank, and he purchased the 1/3rd share owned by Charles and Ellen Brown.[8] As a result of these purchases, John S. Brown owned 5/6ths of Six Mile, and the heirs of the deceased Perley Brown owned the other 1/6th.

The ownership remained divided along those lines until the 1890s when John S. Brown died.[9] It appears that he divided his ownership in Six Mile into four equal shares going to his wife, Emmaline; his daughters, Agnes and Edith; and to his son, Walter. In 1897, Edith sold her share of the island to Agnes.[10] In 1899, Walter sold his share to his cousin, Arthur S. Browne, the son of Benjamin Frank Brown.[11] Sometime thereafter, Emmaline apparently sold her shares to Arthur as well.[12]

By the early 1920s, the ownership of the island was divided between Arthur Brown (5/12th), Agnes Brown Croxall (5/12th), and seven heirs of Perley Brown (1/6th), including his son,

---

as well. (B/P 43/240). The inspiration for the name probably stemmed from Three Mile Island which was the first island to be named based upon its distance from Center Harbor.

[1] The majority of the acreage that comprised Lot #4 was on Long Island. Five Mile and Six Mile were also part of the lot.

[2] B/P 9004/434.

[3] B/P 9009/137.

[4] SCRD B/P 172/240.

[5] This is made clear in various deeds detailed below. Perley was a Civil War victim.

[6] B/P 65/137. The sale also included Birch, Steamboat, and Camp islands. This was the period in which George was having some financial issues.

[7] B/P 76/295.

[8] B/P 76/296; B/P 7611.

[9] I have not found the details of his death or of his will.

[10] B/P 99/273.

[11] B/P 101/431. Arthur was a D.C. lawyer who was living with Walter at the time of this sale. Towards the end of the 19th century, some of John Brown's grandchildren added an 'e' to their last name (hence Browne) apparently to give it an original British spelling.

[12] I have found no support for this conclusion. It is assumed based upon the later settlement of the island's ownership.

John Parker.[1] A dispute arose in 1922 among the three parties regarding the disposition of the island. It pitted Arthur against the others. The dispute dragged on until 1932, when a court appointed commissioner was authorized to sell the island and divide the proceeds among the owners. Six Mile was sold in July 1932 to Sarah Ransom of New Jersey.[2] The sale ended 111 years of ownership by the Brown family. The Ransoms maintained ownership of the entire island until 1958 when a large portion of the shoreline was sold to vacationers, Arthur and Martha Tucker.[3] In the years that followed, several vacation lots were carved out along the southeastern southeastern shore.

The ***Ozones* and *Little Six Mile Island***: To the east of Six Mile Island, there is a string of three (in the early days considered four) small islands. The island nearest Six Mile is named Ozone Island and is part of Meredith. The other two islands are part of Moultonborough. They are called Little Six Mile Island (next to Meredith's Ozone) and a second Ozone Island. Historically, ownership of these islands traces back to the Brown family of Long Island. The basis of that ownership is unknown. The islands were not part of Masonian Lot #4 that John Brown purchased in 1821 with Daniel Follett. They were unnumbered islands and theoretically belonged to the block of such islands that changed hands at various times during the 1800s. It appears that John Brown 'assumed' ownership of them, although it is possible that he purchased them at some point.[4]

Ownership of Meredith's Ozone Island followed the same path as outlined for Six Mile Island. It was part of the court sale in 1932 that left it in the hands of Sarah Ransom in 1932.[5] Ransom sold the island to Arthur and Martha Tucker in 1958 at the same time she sold them her house and land on Six Mile.[6] The Tuckers gave Ozone Island to the Audubon Society in 1973.[7]

The two Moultonborough islands in the group, Little Six Mile and Ozone, had very different paths. Their ownership was passed among the Brown family members through the 1890s, just as Six Mile Island was. Through some process, they ended up solely in the hands of John S. Brown's daughter, Agnes E. Croxall.[8] On January 21, 1916, Agnes sold Little Six to Marion Ely of East Orange, NJ.[9] She sold Ozone (then unnamed) to Emma Whittier of Stoneham, MA.[10] By then, there was a small camp or cottage on it.

---

[1] B/P 204/275.
[2] Ibid.
[3] B/P 393/360.
[4] No deeds of sale to John Brown were found regarding these islands.
[5] B/P 204/275.
[6] B/P 393/360.
[7] B/P 625/208.
[8] Presumably the small islands were sold by siblings and cousins at the same time Six Mile was sold. But the small islands did not end up in dispute. At some point Arthur S. Browne and the heirs of Perley Brown apparently sold their interests to Agnes. Brown Croxall.
[9] CCR B/P 150/255. At the time, it was also known as Crescent Island. There was no mention of a camp at this time.
[10] BCR B/P 145/210. It is not known why this deed was registered in Belknap rather than Carroll County.

Sleepers Island

Sleepers Island was originally called Flanders Island in the survey of the lake done by James Hersey in 1772.[1] At 113 acres, it is the tenth largest island in the lake. Hersey had estimated its size at 79 acres. The Masonian Proprietors combined it with the eastern end of Rattlesnake, Diamond Island, and the Barndoor Islands to comprise Lot #1 in the 1781 lottery. It was drawn to the original right of Thomlinson and Mason.

The early ownership trail of Sleepers is not known. The island did not draw any interest until well into the 1800s. By then, its title had passed most likely through a number of hands, including Nathaniel A. Haven. By the early 1830s, its ownership was divided, one half among Haven's heirs and the other half with Harry L. Long of England.

In January 1833, David Glidden Jr. of Alton acquired the two halves of Sleepers in separate transactions.[2] Glidden quickly brought in other owners. In June 1833, he sold undivided one-third shares to Abner Morse of Alton and Nehemiah Sleeper of Alton.[3] As was typical, the three men probably used the island for seasonal grazing and as a wood lot.

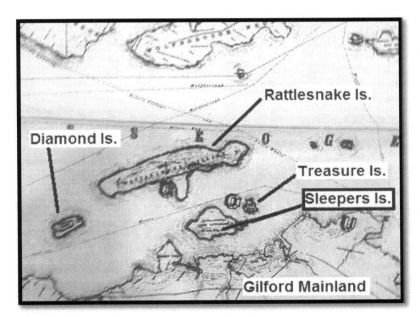

In 1838, Glidden and Morse decided to sell their one-third interests. The new owner was George W. Sanders, the ever-active Gilford lumber man.[4] He now shared ownership of the island with Nehemiah Sleeper. Six years later in 1844, Sanders sold one-third ownership shares each to John Sleeper and Jonas Sleeper.[5] Four years after that, in 1848, John and Nehemiah Sleeper departed the island, selling what they described as one-half of the island to George Sleeper of Gilford.[6] Jonas Sleeper owned the other half. George and Jonas owned the island jointly for more than 20 years. By 1858, the island had come to be called Little Rattlesnake.[7] It was also during this period, that the name Sleepers became attached to it.

---

[1] There was a local Alton farmer by the name of Flanders whose name may have been used to identify the island.
[2] B/P 9014/97. This was not the first time local folks had taken notice of it. Enoch Small of Alton had laid claim to it sometime before, alleging that he had authorization from Nathaniel Haven and Mark W. Peirce. His claim was not upheld. See B/P 9014/124.
[3] B/P 9014/155.
[4] B/P 9017/1; 9017/191.
[5] B/P 10/32; 29/537.
[6] B/P 50/255. They had owned two-thirds. It appears they sold part of their interest to Jonas Sleeper before selling the one-half to George.
[7] See Crocker's 1858 map of Winnipesaukee.

Iin October 1869, George and Jonas Sleeper sold their shares to Sarah W. Worster.[1] Sarah was the wife of James Worster, who had purchased Rattlesnake in 1850.[2] At the time of this purchase, Sarah received a mortgage loan of $1400.00 from James Littlefield of Dover, some $400 more than the purchase price. Littlefield was the same Dover, NH, farmer who owned the troublesome Rattlesnake loans of Sarah's children.[3] By 1877, Sarah had fallen into financial difficulties. The children of the deceased James Littlefield sued Sarah for lack of performance under the loan. They won a favorable judgment in June 1877 and took ownership of the island.[4]

The Littlefield children owned Sleepers Island until 1894, when they sold it to William Hale of Boston and Edward Hale of Brookfield, MA.[5] William bought out Edward in 1896.[6] By this time, time, the island was called both Sleepers Island and Little Rattlesnake Island. Around 1913, Edward Hale built the signature castle that still stands as a unique landmark on the island.

The island was sold to Ivar Swenson of Arlington, MA in 1939.[7] Swenson maintained complete ownership of the island until his death. In 1962, John Swenson sold it to the Sleeper Island Corporation.[8] Soon after, the corporation subdivided the island's shorefront and numerous numerous vacation lots were sold during the 1960s.

Stonedam Island

Stonedam is the eighth largest island in the lake at 141 acres. It was included in the 1781 island lottery held by the Masonian Proprietors, becoming part of Lot # 12, along with Pine Island. Lot #12 was drawn in the name of Jotham Odiorne who had died years before in 1751. Lot #12 ended up in the hands of Peter Pearce and William Treadwell, the husbands of Odiorne's daughters.[9]

Sometime before 1797, Stonedam was sold, presumably by Pearce and Treadwell, to Francis Adam Bowman. Bowman took up residence on the island, making him one of the earliest islanders on the lake.[10] In 1797, Bowman sold 60 acres to Benning Wilkinson, a farmer from Alton.[11] Before 1799, one or both of these men built a dam (or perhaps a bridge with granite abutments on either side), connecting the island to Meredith Neck.[12] The dam gave birth to the

---

[1] B/P 50/287; 50/288.
[2] Sarah briefly became owner of Rattlesnake. She was also the mother of George and Susan Worster who struggled with mortgage debt on that property throughout the 1860s and 1870s.
[3] B/P 50/281.
[4] B/P 62/472.
[5] B/P 92/229.
[6] B/P 96/491. A confirmatory deed was given in 1904. B/P 112/85.
[7] B/P 238/460.
[8] B/P 428/43.
[9] The early deed trail for Stonedam after the lottery was not found. Odiorne's estate was divided amongst a handful of heirs in 1780, including his wife and two daughters. See B/P 9002/120-124. Their ownership of Pine Island is clearly documented. There is no deed trail including them for Stonedam, but it is assumed that they got ownership of it as part of the package.
[10] It made sense that Stonedam was the earliest large island to be occupied because it was located so close to the mainland.
[11] See B/P 9008/41. This is the oldest deed found involving Stonedam Island.
[12] The Neck property was part of Lot 80 which was not (at least legally) occupied at the time.

name of the island which was in use in 1799 when the island was annexed to the town of Meredith.[1]

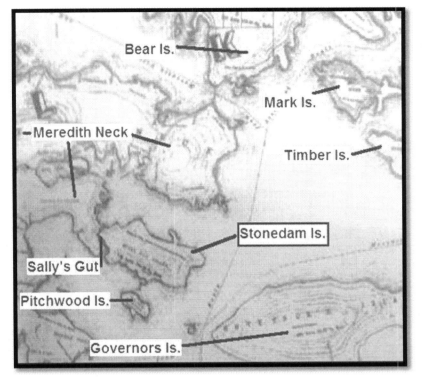

The ownership trail runs dry for many years thereafter. Some time before the 1840s, the island was purchased and divided equally between Ezekiel Dow and Josiah Perkins. Dow had moved to Meredith from Deerfield, NH, in 1810.[2] Perkins arrival in town had preceded Dow by several years. The two lived in the First Division, just north of the Weirs, a location that was in close proximity to each other and to the island. Presumably, they were interested in the island for seasonal grazing and wood.

Dow died in 1849, leaving his share of Stonedam to his son, Lorenzo Dow, of Somerville, MA.[3] Lorenzo quickly sold his share to his brother, Jonathan G. Dow, who lived on part of their father's original farm in the First Division.[4] Perkins died a few years later, leaving his share to his sons, Abram and Josiah. In 1858, Abram sold his interest to Josiah.[5] Thus, the island was once again equally divided between Jonathan Dow and Josiah Perkins who were First Division neighbors on the mainland, just like their fathers had been.

This status quo was maintained until Josiah Perkin's death in the latter 1870s. His undivided half interest in the island was inherited by two wings of the family. In 1878, each group sold their shares to their relative, David P. Perkins of Manchester, NH.[6] David held onto his share of Stonedam for several years. The records become a little murky, but it appears that sometime before 1884 he sold half of his share (¼ of Stonedam) to two of Josiah Perkins daughters, Emeline and Sarah (Sally).[7] In late 1884, the Perkins family members all finally sold their interests in Stonedam to John Edgerly.[8] This was the inflection point for the island as it began the transition from the farming era to the vacation era.

---

[1] See: Laws of New Hampshire, Vol. Six, Second Constitutional Period, pp. 620-621.
[2] See B/P 9006/10; 9006/175.
[3] Ezekiel had already sold his part of his mainland farm to Lorenzo in 1843. B/P 5/185 and 186.
[4] Jonathan Dow was a neighbor of John and Joseph Neal who bought Lot 9 on Bear Island in 1838.
[5] B/P 45/283.
[6] B/P 65/189; 65/190. David Perkins was related to Josiah but it is not clear in what way. David Perkins also bought half of the Josiah Perkins farm on the mainland at this time.
[7] These sales are suggested by transactions that occurred in 1884.
[8] B/P 73/432; 73/411; 73/413. David sold a ¼ share while Emeline and Sally each sold 1/8 shares.

John Edgerly (b. 1846) was a Laconia farmer who was born and raised in Meredith's Second Division. He acquired the family farm in 1868, just before his father passed away. He sold it soon thereafter and moved with his mother and siblings to Concord, NH. In the following years, he apparently became quite successful. By 1880, he was retired. His Meredith roots made him very interested in the lake for vacation purposes. In 1880, he had purchased a one acre mainland lot with more than 650' of frontage on Winnipesaukee from Josiah Perkins. The lot was located somewhat north of the Methodist camp at the Weirs, between the David P. Perkins portion of the Josiah Perkins farm and the farm of Jonathan G. Dow.[1]

John Edgerly and Jonathan Dow maintained undivided ownership of Stonedam for the next ten years. In 1894, Dow sold his undivided half to the Meredith Shook & Lumber Company.[2] Five years later, in 1899, Edgerly acquired the lumber company's half, not for money, but for "a lot of standing timber, (and) trees on Stone Dam Island, delivered to the corporation."[3]

John Edgerly and his wife, Emma, owned all of Stonedam Island for another 26 years. Finally, at the age of 80, Edgerly sold the island in 1925 to Robert D. Judkins of Long Beach, California.[4] Judkins was a banker who was raised in Manchester, NH. He owned the island until his death in 1933. The following year, his wife, Jessica, sold Stonedam to Thomas E. P. Rice of Meredith.[5] A wealthy town resident, Rice and his wife, Margaret, had also purchased the mainland property where the bridge to Stonedam had once stood and is now the eastern entry point to Sally's Gut.[6] They also owned various other properties on the lake, and Margaret was known for the Morgan horses she raised on the Neck on the original farm of Neck settler, Joseph Mead.

The Rice family owned the entire island for nearly 50 years before deciding in 1981 to sell it to developers who had plans to reconnect it to the mainland at the old bridge location. When word got out about the possibility of subdivision, the recently formed Lakes Region Conservation Trust, led by Birch Island's John Forbes, rallied in an effort to buy the property. Given less than a week to raise $650,000, the LRCT quickly marshaled support and reached an agreement with the Rice family to buy about 80% of the island. The deal was closed in March 1982.[7] Members of the Rice family continue to own about 28 acres on the southern end of Stonedam.

[1] B/P 66/541. In 1883 and 1885, Edgerly also purchased three lots in the Methodist camp at the Weirs. B/P 75/30; B/P 74/530.
[2] B/P 93/261.
[3] B/P 103/537.
[4] B/P 173/173.
[5] B/P 215/449.
[6] As an aside, the use of the term 'gut' was common during the late 1800s to describe narrow waterways between islands or between islands and the mainland. It was not a reflection on Sally's appetite. See Hawkes, _Winnipesaukee_, p. 37.
[7] B/P 820/20. See also, _Nature's Keeper_, pp. 150-154 for an account of the efforts made by John Forbes and the LRCT.

Three Mile Island Group (Three Mile, Hawks Nest, Rock, and Nabby)

At 47 acres, *Three Mile Island* was one of the large islands that the Masonians included in the lottery of islands in 1781. It was part of Lot # 13 that also included nine other islands.[1] The lot was drawn to the original right of John Wentworth. Lot 13 ended up in the hands of the Portsmouth merchant, Edmund Roberts, sometime before 1823.

In 1826, Roberts sold Three Mile Island to Joseph Senter of Meredith. The origin of the island's name found its roots in the deed of this sale. Roberts described the property as "a certain island numbered thirteen in the Winnipisiogee Lake, so called …being about three miles from Centre Harbour…"[2] The description morphed into a formal name sometime thereafter.

Joseph Senter was a blacksmith who lived just west of Center Harbor bay in what was then still part of Meredith. He was the son of Moses Senter, one of the earliest farmers to settle near the bay, and the nephew of Revolutionary Colonel Joseph Senter, who had settled earlier than Moses above the bay in what was then known as the Moultonborough Addition.[3]

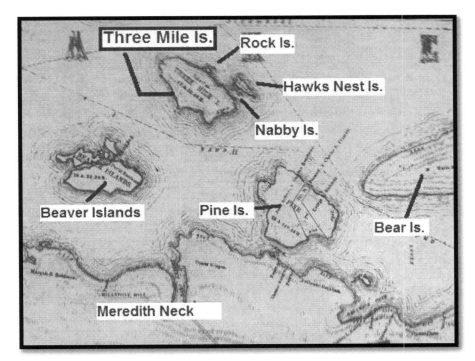

Joseph Senter presumably used Three Mile for seasonal grazing and timber. He died in 1849. After his death, the island passed to John Coe, a well known entrepreneur who gained ownership of several islands during this period. Coe was married to Joseph's niece, Lavinia. Coe retained ownership of Three Mile until his death in 1861. His estate administrator, Nathaniel Upham, subsequently sold Three Mile to Frank Brown in October 1862.[4]

---

[1] The other nine were Beaver, Hull, Blackcat, Pitchwood, Whortleberry, Dow, Farm, Chase, and Ragged.

[2] B/P 9011/274. Center Harbor became a place of note c. 1787 when the postal system gave it the name when new mail routes were being established throughout New Hampshire. It was a major cross-roads location, thus necessitating that the 'place' be identified. The area was the nexus of three towns, including Meredith, Moultonborough, and New Hampton, although the lake frontage belonged to Meredith and Moultonborough. The town of Center Harbor was carved out of New Hampton in 1797. The new town did not have any land on Winnipesaukee. The Meredith portion of the bay was not annexed to the town of Center Harbor until 1873.

[3] Moses farm was in Meredith on D3/Lot 9. B/P 9002/32.

[4] B/P 37/592.

Frank Brown was one of six children of the early Long Island settler, John Brown.[1] He did not hold on to Three Mile for very long. He sold it in September 1863 to Thomas Appleton of Laconia.[2] Appleton owned a manufacturing operation in Lake Village but was also interested in the islands.[3] In the late 1860s, Appleton's business took a turn for the worse, and he went bankrupt. His assets were sold off in 1868, and Frank Brown repurchased Three Mile.[4] Thereafter, Brown owned Three Mile for almost three decades. His interest in the island was most likely seasonal pasture and timber. He did not build on it.

In July 1895, Frank Brown sold Three Mile and its tiny neighbor, **Rock Island**, to Mary Eastman of Concord, NH.[5] She and her husband, Edson, were members of the Appalachian Mountain Club. In November 1899, Mary donated two and one-third acres of Three Mile to the AMC.[6] The following summer, July 1900, she donated another three acres to the club.[7] The same day, she sold 10 more acres of the island to Rosewell B. Lawrence, of Medford, MA, who was the secretary of the AMC.[8] In February 1901, Lawrence sold this parcel to the AMC after a successful fund raising effort was undertaken to recoup Lawrence's cost.[9] On the same date, Mary Eastman also donated the small parcel on the southern end of the island that she had retained. She included Rock Island in the donation.[10]

Three Mile developed into a core holding of the AMC. It became the organization's 'camping' headquarters. Major improvements occurred fairly quickly. The AMC commissioned the building of the main lodge in 1900; the boathouse in 1901; and an observation tower in 1902. The island was in constant use every summer thereafter. In 1903, one visitor captured it this way:

> "As the visitor comes to this place on the steamer *Mt. Washington*, one of the picturesque sights of the lake is witnessed at Three-Mile island. On this island, which is the summer home of the Appalachian Club, are pitched a large number of tents, where since early in the season many of the club members have been enjoying out of doors life under canvas."[11]

---

[1] He was born and raised on Long Island and "spent his life lumbering, rafting and boating on the lake." He later bought a farm on the mainland in Moultonborough. During the latter 1800s, he and his brother, Charles F., were very active on the lake, acquiring ownership of Hawks Nest, Six Mile, Mink, and Camp Island. By the 1880s, Frank had acquired a steam boat, the *River Queen*, and was providing excursions for private parties. The latter included week long tours around the lake for camping and fishing on the largely deserted islands. See, W.S. Hawkes: Winnipesaukee (1887), pp. 35, 41, and 46.

[2] B/P 38/586.

[3] He also bought Mink Island in 1864.

[4] B/P 78/404.

[5] B/P 94/535.

[6] B/P 103/339.

[7] B/P 104/471.

[8] B/P 104/556.

[9] B/P 105/490.

[10] B/P 105/509. With specific regard to Rock Island, we have found is no further detail to add to its history. As a tiny (3/10ths of an acre), unnumbered island, it got the attention of no one during the first nine decades of the 19th century. It appears that Frank Brown 'assumed' ownership of it after he bought Three Mile Island in 1868. Rock Island first appears in the deeds when Brown sold Three Mile to Mary Eastman in 1895.

[11] Boston Herald, August 23, 1903, p. 28.

Hawks Nest Island (referred to as Little Three Mile occasionally in the late 1800s) is a small island about one and a half acres in size. It is located next to Three Mile Island. **Nabby Island** is a very small island between Hawks Nest and Three Mile. Like so many of the small islands in Winnipesaukee, the early ownership of the two is unknown. It would appear that Frank Brown also 'assumed' ownership of them after he bought Three Mile Island in 1868. In December 1886, Brown sold both to Winfield Scott Hawkes of South Hadley, MA.[1] In concern over the title, Hawkes insisted that Brown include a clause that the purchase price would be refunded if Brown's title were vacated by the Masonian Proprietors or the state.[2]

Hawkes was a Congregational minister who had purchased a lot (#432) on Bear Island in 1886.[3] He was also the author of the railroad sponsored book, Winnipesaukee and About There, There, that was published in 1887 to attract vacationers to the Lakes Region. While doing his research, Hawkes was ferried around the lake for a week by Frank Brown. Around 1888, Hawkes built a fishing cabin on Hawks Nest.

In November 1892, Hawkes sold the two islands to George H. Bates, the Methodist minister from southern Massachusetts who had purchased and then sold half of Steamboat Island.[4] After George Bates died in 1907, his widow, Abby, and one of his daughters sold the islands to George's other daughter, Adella W. Bates of Boston, the following year.[5] Thereafter, Adella maintained ownership of the two islands for another 56 years. She died in c. 1964, around the age of 94. She left Hawks Nest and Nabby to the Appalachian Mountain Club.[6]

Timber Island

Timber Island is the ninth largest in the lake at 136 acres. It was not given a name at the time of James Hersey's survey on which it was listed as having 110 acres. In 1781, it was combined with Little Bear Island and the northern section of Cow Island to comprise Masonian Lot #14. The lot was drawn to the original right of Daniel Peirce and Samuel Moore, both of whom were deceased by the time of the drawing. Ownership immediately devolved to John Peirce, and then after his death in 1814, it became the responsibility of two of his sons (who were his estate administrators), Mark W. and Joshua W. Peirce.

The island remained in their hands for the first two decades of the 19th century. During this period, it came to be known as Timber and/or Wentworth Island. In 1823, it was finally sold by the Peirce brothers to John Pick Smith of Gilford.[7] He owned the island for the next 33 years,

[1] The name 'Hawks Nest' was already in use when the island was sold to Winfield Hawkes.
[2] B/P 76/529. Reverend Hawkes must have learned of the Browns propensity for 'assuming' ownership of small islands. This is the only deed found that includes language like this.
[3] B/P 76/231.
[4] B/P 88/497.
[5] B/P 123/369.
[6] See Meredith Tax Inventory for Non –Residents, 1965, MHS Archives which notes the bequest.
[7] B/P 9010/15. Smith also bought Round Island in 1829 and Timber Island in 1841.

during which time he used it for seasonal pasture and timber.[1] Smith used the island so extensively for sheep grazing that the cove on the eastern end of it became known as "Sheep Yard Cove".[2] Smith's interest in its timber was evident at the end of his ownership in the mid-1850s. According to one passer-by, the island was "utterly devoid of growth of any kind, and barren enough to deserve some (other name than Timber)."[3]

John Smith sold Timber to his son, John Jr. in 1856.[4]

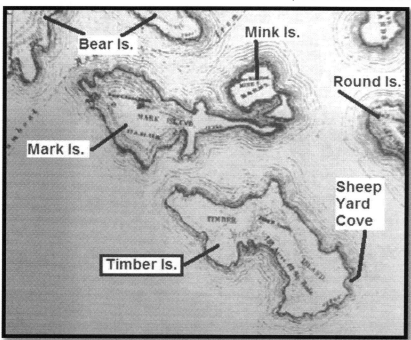

Soon after, John Jr. built a small house in Sheep Yard Cove, but he did not own Timber for very long. By 1862, he sold it to George W. Sanders, the lumber man from Gilford, who also acquired a great deal of mainland real estate from John Jr.[5] As part of the sale of Timber, John Jr. reserved his ownership of the small house. George W. Sanders was interested in its wood (such as it was), although he probably used it for seasonal grazing as well.

Sanders owned Timber for 12 years. By 1874, however, he was financially overextended. He tried to keep things afloat by selling Timber Island, Round Island, and numerous mainland parcels to the WLCWMCo.; but the sales were subject to mortgages held by the Laconia Savings Bank ($6000.00) and John P. Smith Jr. (also about $6000.00).[6] Not long after, Sanders was forced into into bankruptcy. The bank eventually took possession of his properties and auctioned them off.[7] The fate of Timber through this process is not known. Like Round Island, it presumably ended up back in the hands of John Smith Jr.

However, by the 1880s, the ownership of Timber somehow ended up being owned by George Sander's wife, Sarah, who was the sister of John Smith Jr. She sold it in 1889 to Alfred

---

[1] There is one point of confusion about his ownership. An 1829 transaction seems to indicate that Smith and Samuel Leavitt, acting as guardians for the children of Thomas Thompson (a neighbor of Smith), had sold ½ of Timber Island to Daniel Blaisdell of Gilford. B/P 9013/226. But the registry has no deed showing that Thompson purchased the interest in Timber from Smith nor are there any follow up deeds indicating that Blaisdell ever sold it thereafter. Whatever the case, by 1856, John P. Smith owned the entire island.
[2] See B/P 86/411. This is cited in an 1891 deed, decades after the sheep boom ended. The continuation of the name suggests that it was well established during the first half of the decade.
[3] The <u>Boston Traveler</u>, August 11, 1857, p. 4.
[4] B/P 27/247.
[5] The deed of sale was not found. Ownership is confirmed in an 1862 deed from Sanders to Smith in which Sanders gives Smith a mortgage. This was not their first transaction. In 1860, Sanders had purchased extensive real estate holdings from John Jr,. including Round Island. B/P 36/494.
[6] B/P 57/589.
[7] See <u>Lake Village Times</u>, March 7, 1874, p. 3; March 14, 1874, p.3; and June 13, 1874, p.4.

Roberts, a blacksmith from Concord, NH.[1] Roberts was the first pure vacationer to own the island. He quickly sold undivided quarter shares to Melvin Roberts and Omar Shepard, both also from Concord.[2] Soon after, Alfred and Melvin Roberts built a house in Sheep Yard Cove.[3] The Roberts group enjoyed summering on Timber until 1903. They sold it in September of that year in undivided halves to E.C. Mansfield and Frederick E. Gilford.[4]

The two new owners were interested in keeping Timber undeveloped. It was not until 12 years later that they finally subdivided off a single lot to anyone. In 1915, they sold 100' of frontage on the westerly end to Arthur Hellstrom, a Laconia machinist.[5] Two years later, in 1917, Fred Gilford sold his half of the island to E.C. Mansfield, bringing virtually the entire island under his ownership.[6]

The ownership remained with Mansfield for the next 26 years. It was not until 1943 that Timber resurfaced on the market. Mansfield had died in 1937, and his wife had died in 1939. It took several years to sort out the process by which their estate would be sold. In 1943, Daniel Eaton was appointed Administrator of the estate. His first step, in his individual capacity, was to acquire the single, subdivided lot that was originally sold in 1915.[7] Having gained complete control of the island, Eaton sold all of Timber to an entity called Skyhaven Inc. of Rochester, NH, in August 1943.[8] Skyhaven was the creation of William Champlin Jr., the son of the founder of the Champlin Box Company in Rochester.[9] In 1946, Skyhaven sold the island to Champlin.[10]

The Champlin family was among Rochester's most prominent and philanthropic. William Jr. was an active conservationist, having, for example, a 185 acre forest in Rochester named in his honor.[11] With this in his background, it is no surprise that Champlin resisted any urge to subdivide the island during the first four decades he owned Timber. Finally in 1991, Champlin created a multi-part strategy to address its future.[12] He subdivided it into four parcels. The largest parcel, at 126 acres, encompassed the vast majority of the island. Champlin gave a conservation easement to the Lakes Region Conservation Trust to preclude any development on it.[13] The other three parcels were located on the southeast, southwest, and northeast corners of the island. They were set aside for single family homes.[14] Despite the subdivision, Timber remained

---

[1] B/P 80/288. In 1892, Alfred bought a small lake front lot in Thompson's Cove on the Gilford mainland. B/P 87/505.
[2] B/P 80/464; 80/477. Omar's wife was a Roberts.
[3] Omar deeded his interest in the house to Melvin in 1891. B/P 86/411.
[4] B/P 111/140 and 111/160. Mansfield, of course, had purchased old Lot 9 on Bear a few years before, in 1898. Gilford had owned property on the Dolly Islands since the 1880s. Mansfield gave a mortgage loan to Gilford to finance his purchase. B/P 111/94.
[5] B/P 144/321.
[6] B/P 148/210.
[7] B/P 264/125. The place had been sold by Hellstrom in 1930 to William Emerson. (B/P 196/1210. Emerson died c. 1940. His wife sold the place to Eaton in 1943.
[8] B/P 264/274; 264/380.
[9] Champlin made box shook and locked-cover, wooden boxes among other things. It was founded during the early 1900s.
[10] B/P 290/423
[11] Martha Fowler article, Rochester Historical Society, June 2011.
[12] Plan L15-069, BCR.
[13] B/P 1193/159.
[14] The southeast corner was the location of the original small house and the Roberts place. The southwest corner was the location of the original Hellstrom place. The parcel was the largest of the three at five acres. Each of the three lot owners enjoyed a 1/3rd interest in the conservation land.

entirely in the hands of the Champlins for an additional ten years. After the death of William Champlin, the three lots were sold to vacationers in 2004-2005.[1]

Treasure Island (fka Red Head)

Treasure is a tiny island located next to Sleepers Island. It was known as Red Head Island until the late 1930s.[2] It was an unnumbered island during the Masonian era and therefore not part of the 1781 lottery. Its first known owner was George W. Sanders who acquired it sometime before 1838.[3] In December of that year, he sold it to David Glidden of Alton, a transaction that occurred at the same time Sanders acquired two-thirds of Sleepers Island from Glidden and Abner Morse.[4]

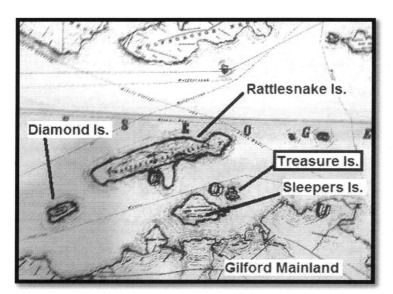

Sometime over the ensuing years (perhaps in the 1840s), the ownership of Red Head passed from Glidden to Jonas and George Sleeper, who also became joint owners of Sleepers Island in 1848. In October 1869, George and Jonas sold Red Head to Sarah W. Worster.[5] As with Sleepers and Rattlesnake, Red Head was apparently mortgaged to the Littlefield family. When financial troubles beset the Worsters, Red Head became part of the island properties taken over by the Littlefields. In October 1878, Judith Littlefield sold the island to Charles Foss of Alton.[6] Foss owned it for 15 years before selling it in 1893 to J. Edward Burtt of Malden, MA.[7]

Burtt owned it for 20 years, selling it in 1913 to L. Theodore Wallis, a Brookline, MA, schoolteacher.[8] Wallis changed the usage of the island for years to come. He established a private camp for boys that he called Mishe Mokwa.[9] The camp prospered for more than two decades before succumbing to the Depression in 1938. Reminiscent of Camp Passaconaway on Bear Island during that period, Wallis borrowed heavily to sustain the camp before it finally failed.

---

[1] B/P 2021/189; 2044/335; 2231/055.

[2] It was also known as Birch Island in 1892. See 1892 Atlas, town of Alton.

[3] When and from whom he acquired it are not known. This might have been Sanders first island purchase. It was a time frame well before he acquired all of the unnumbered islands.

[4] B/P 64/264. The deed was not filed with the Registry until 1878.

[5] B/P 50/256. She bought Sleepers Island from them at the same time. The deed suggests 'Red Head' consisted of nine acres.

[6] B/P 64/277.

[7] B/P 90/254.

[8] B/P 137/296. In 1912, Wallis had purchased shore frontage on Bear Island, hoping to establish a boys' camp there. In 1915, Wallis also bought nearby, tiny Cub Island. It was called Black Island then.

[9] See the Lake Winnipesaukee Historical Society website, lwhs.com, regarding this and some other camps on the lake.

The mortgagors foreclosed in 1937 and 1938, and the island, still known as Red Head, was repossessed.[1]

In August 1938, the island received new life when it was sold to the Boston Council of Girl Scouts.[2] The Council incorporated Camp Treasure Island to own and operate a Girl Scout camp on the island. The name changed from Red Head Island to Treasure Island as a result. Camp Treasure Island flourished for many years. The camp finally closed in August 1964, when the Girl Scouts sold the island to Willetta and Forrest Manchester of Canton, MA.[3] The Manchesters developed a subdivision plan for the island in 1966 and began selling off shorefront lots thereafter.[4] The island now consists of 17 vacation lots with the center of the island held separately.

---

[1] See B/P 231/275; 234/267 among others.
[2] B/P 235/171. Cub Island was sold with it.
[3] B/P 445/484.
[4] B/P 471/235.

Appendix:

Family Trees

Robert Bryant

John Bickford

Paul Nichols

Theophilus Dockham

Caleb Lovejoy

Waldo Meloon

Robert Bryant Family

Robert Bryant (c.1744-1830) Joanna Stevens (c.1745-1840)		

V

John (1769-1847) Eleanor Bickford	Robert (c.1770-.1850) Abigail Bickford (c.1779-1865)	Dorothy (Dolly) (1780-1858) Joseph Nichols

V — V — V

Priscilla (1811-1882) Jonathan Bickford Jr. (179 3-1880)	Abram (1810-1876) Mahala Bickford (1812-1901)	Robert M. Huldah Jones
Sarah R. Samuel Swain	Priscilla C. (c.1816-?) William Holmes	James (d. 1913)
Joseph B.	Nancy B. (c.1797-1850) Thomas Clark (c.1809-?)	George (d. 1862)
John S.		(Daughter)
Samuel B.		

John Bickford Family

John Bickford (c.1742-) Phebe Johnson (c.1743-)			

Jonathan (c.1766-1859) Abigail Page (1769-1859)	John (c.1768-)	Eleanor (c.1770-) John Bryant (1769-1847)	Eleazer (1774-1873) Sally Swain (1783-1866)

Lydia (1789- Parker Nichols (1804-1883)	Priscilla (1803-1886) John Nichols (c.1815-)		Priscilla (1811-1882) Jonathan Bickford Jr. (1793-1880)	Charles (1809-1893) Augusta Chase (1811-1881)
Brackett (1791-c1850) Mary Bryant (c.1801-)	James S. (1802-1888) Lucinda Bryant (1805-1876)		Sarah R. Samuel Swain	Eleazer (1822-1904) Ann Blaisdell (1835-1894)
Jonathan (1793-1880) Priscilla Bryant (1811-1882)	Abigail (1810-1886) John Russell		Joseph B.	Almira (1825-1891) 1.Ebenezer Bickford (m.1852) 2. Smith E. Dockham (m. 1859)
Phebe (1796-) Nathaniel Nichols	Mahala (1812-1901) Abram Bryant (1810-)		John S.	3. Stephen B. Dockham (m. 1861)
John P. (1798-) Nancy Bryant	Eleanor (1814-) Jesse Lovejoy (1814-)		Samuel B.	
Ebenezer (1800-1883) Ruth Clark				

Paul Nichols Family

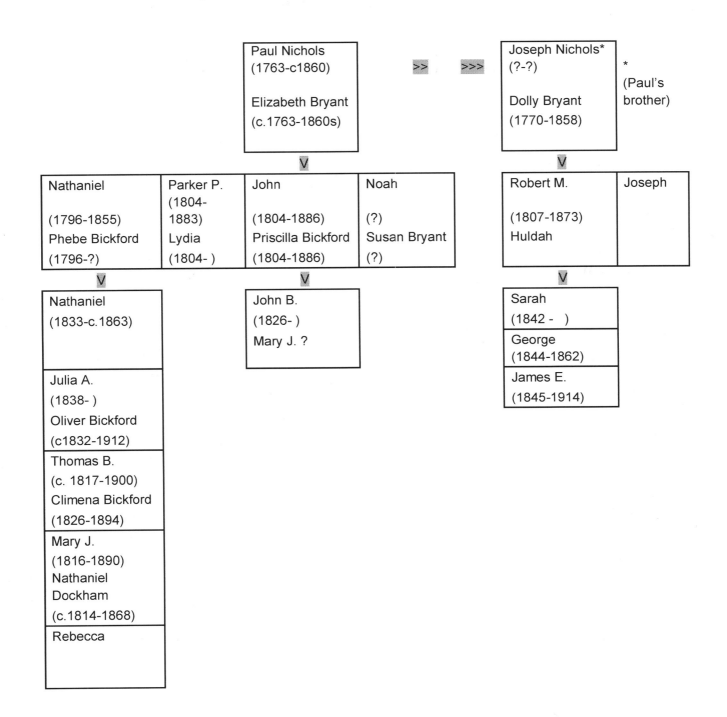

Theophilus Dockham Family

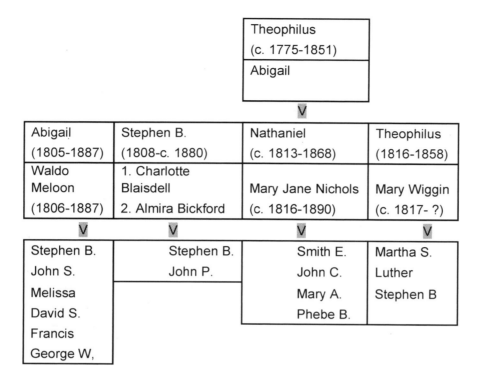

Theophilus (c. 1775-1851)
Abigail

V

Abigail (1805-1887)	Stephen B. (1808-c. 1880)	Nathaniel (c. 1813-1868)	Theophilus (1816-1858)
Waldo Meloon (1806-1887)	1. Charlotte Blaisdell 2. Almira Bickford	Mary Jane Nichols (c. 1816-1890)	Mary Wiggin (c. 1817- ?)

V   V   V   V

Stephen B. John S. Melissa David S. Francis George W,	Stephen B. John P.	Smith E. John C. Mary A. Phebe B.	Martha S. Luther Stephen B

Caleb Lovejoy Family

			Caleb Lovejoy (1749-1841) Eliza Kimball (?)				
∨							

Jesse (1814-1881) Eleanor Bickford (1814-1880)	David R. (1805-1875) Belinda Chase (1815-1897)	Herbert (1818-1897) Hannah Clark (1814-1872)	Martha P. (1807-?) McDaniel Lovejoy (1802- ?)	Mehitabel (1806-?) Thomas Chase	Nathan (1805-1828)	Sarah R. (1812-1875)	Nancy (1816-?)
∨	∨	∨					

Ezra (1841-1919) Martha Glines (1843-1879)	Fred W. (1852-1875)	Cyrus (?-1897) Nancy Roberts					
Solomon (1844-1924) Sarah Lizzie Wiggin (1857-1936)	Emeline	∨					
	Mary J.	∨					
	Stillman	∨					
	James H.	∨					
∨	Jerusha	∨					

Ralph (1884-195?)	Ellen A.	Susan Eva (1870-1929) John W. Wiggin					

Waldo Meloon Family

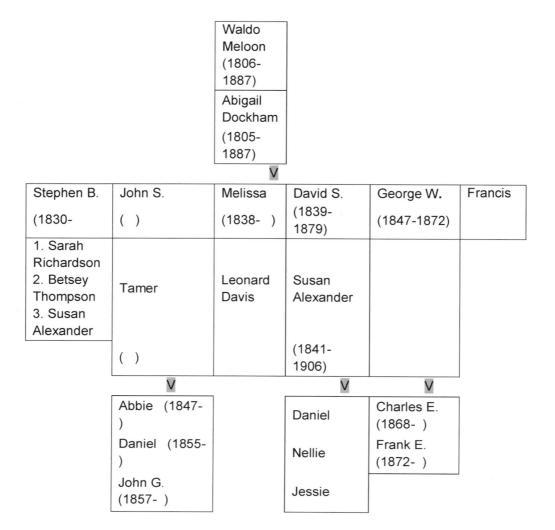

Acknowledgements

This book has been several years in the making. Along the way, I discovered a large number of people whose love for the lake and whose interest in its history mirrored my own. I am deeply indebted to them for the many contributions they made to this work. Without them, the end result would have been decidedly poorer.

Critical editorial work was done primarily by Linda Hopper, Nancy Scanlon, and Sharon Doyle, all of whose insights and efforts are most greatly appreciated by the author.

The all- important pictures were provided by a variety of sources. Many of them are acknowledged within the contents of the book. Perhaps foremost, I would like to thank the Thompson and Wright families for sharing their photographs that were taken by their forebears around the turn of the 20th century. This trove represents the finest collection of early pictures that I came across. Its breadth helps to illuminate a great deal of Bear Island history. It seems only appropriate that they would have this collection, given that the lineages of the two families are the longest still residing on Bear Island.

Additional photographs came from a wide range of people. These include current or former islanders Roger Dolan, Becky Dolan Fuller, George Mayo, Jocelyn and Bill Wuester, and Janet Ochs. Others who were kind enough to provide photos include Randy Barba, David Ames, Austin Hollis, and Bill Hemmel. The latter's aerial pictures capture the beauty of the lake in ways that can be found in no other way. Several of the local historical societies were also extremely helpful in providing pictures. The Meredith Historical Society was foremost among them. Other important contributions came from the Laconia Historical Society and its partner, the Gale Library, as well as from the Moultonborough Historical Society and Library.

Further I want to acknowledge some other individuals who provided additional sources of information, including Ellee Thompson, Naomi Wright Taylor, Jane Rice, Rudy Van Veghten, Leslie Hopper Keeler, John Edgar, David Cail, Warren Huse, John and Margie Krietler, Randy Harold, David Warren, and Fred Clausen. There are many others who contributed to this book in a variety of ways. I am most grateful to all of them.

With regard to original historical resources, we are fortunate that the Meredith Historical Society had the foresight to save the town tax and inventory reports. In many ways, they comprise almost the only primary source of information available about much of early Meredith. We would also like to thank the Meredith Town Clerk for providing access to the very early records of the town's selectmen.

We would also like to thank the Town Clerks of Gilford and Tuftonboro for their assistance in providing access to town inventory and tax records from the 19th century. These prized documents have often simply sat gathering dust and taking valuable space, but they are vital to the understanding of our history.

In addition, valuable information was found in the widely divergent collections housed at the following locations and depositories: the Strafford County Registry of Deeds; the New Hampshire State Records and Archives (Concord); the New Hampshire Historical Society (Concord); the New Hampshire State Library (Concord); the Meredith Town Library; the Moultonborough Town Library; and the Laconia Gale Library. I am indebted to the staffs of each of them for their assistance in researching this book. In addition, the Winnipesaukee History Museum was also very helpful in providing source material that could be found nowhere else. I am very grateful for the time and effort provided by many individuals at each of these organizations. Their commitment to the Lakes Region's history is quite remarkable, and their willingness to help with this project was instrumental in its success.

Note on Sources

<u>Abbreviations</u>**:**

      BCR: Belknap County Registry of Deeds (Laconia)
      BCRI: Belknap County Registry of Deeds (Internet)
      CCR: Carroll County Registry of Deeds (Ossipee)
      SCR: Strafford County Registry of Deeds (Dover)
      B/P: Book/Page

The historiography of Meredith and Bear Island is rather limited. We have not found any diaries or extensive correspondence. Little original research has been done over the years. Most of what was done occurred in the 1880s when E. Hammond Hurd edited <u>The History of Merrimack and Belknap Counties</u>. Chapters about Meredith and Laconia contained some original research, although hardly extensive given the breadth of the topics. In the 1920s, Mary Neal Hanaford compiled her book, the <u>Meredith, N.H.: Annals and Genealogies</u>. It contains a wealth of birth, death, marriage, and other historical information about Meredith and other towns, but it did not attempt to provide a coherent history. About the same time, <u>Old Meredith and Vicinity</u> was published, containing some excellent pieces of history and original research. Again, given the breadth of the topic, it did not delve deeply into the history of the town.

<u>Deeds</u>

For the most part, I relied extensively on property deeds in developing this book. Thanks to the British influence and the rule of law, real estate transactions were required to be registered with the county Registry of Deeds. Prior to 1841, Meredith and the Lakes Region were part of Strafford County. The Registry housing these deeds is located in Dover. In 1841, Strafford was divided into several smaller counties with Meredith and the western part of Winnipesaukee falling into Belknap County. The Belknap Registry of Deeds is in Laconia.

Belknap County digitized all of its deeds, including those that preceded its formation in 1841. These deeds may be accessed on line from the Registry's website. The online availability of deeds made researching this book infinitely easier. It also presented some minor challenges in finding some of the deeds. The online deeds dated before 1841 are not found using the book and page numbers originally used in Strafford. In the digitization process, more than one deed usually ended up appearing on the same page. As a result, more than one deed appears when using the online database for this early period. When accessing online deeds from before the formation of Belknap County, one must use a 90 prefix along with the book and page number found in the online index. The Strafford deed book and page numbers are located at the bottom of each individual deed. The online index uses the same prefix, with 'grantor' listings found under book 9020, and 'grantee' listings found under book 9019. Then when a particular listing is identified, the 90 prefix is used to get to the book listed in the index. For example, the index may list a particular deed as 1/10. To get to it, one needs to input the information as 9001/10. That page will appear with two or three deeds on it. The grantor and grantee parties are given so one can easily identify the deed sought.

The online system has another quirk for the earliest deeds after the formation of Belknap county. While the index system has straightforward dropdown boxes covering various date ranges for grantors and grantees, the book and page search requires that a prefix of 80 be applied to books numbered one through fifteen. For example, if a particular deed of interest is found in the index with the book and page listed as 5/19, the online search for that deed is entered as 8005/19. Starting with book 16, the '80' prefix is not necessary. One can simply enter book 16, page 19.

Census Information

Prior to 1850, the US Census information listed only the head of a household. No other names were given. The 1850 census was the first to list the names of each member of a household. In some cases but not always, census information was also presented geographically rather than alphabetically. This provided real insight into where people were living, based upon their neighbors. Unfortunately, the census information for New Hampshire gathered in 1820 and 1890 was lost.

Bibliography

Allport, Susan: <u>Sermons in Stone: The Stone Walls of New England & New York</u>, Countryman Press (2012).

Anderson, Carol Lee: <u>A History of the Belknap Mill</u>, The History Press (2014).

Aron, Cindy S.: <u>Working at Play, A History of Vacations in the United States</u>, Oxford University Press (1999).

Bartlett, Ira: <u>History of the Twelfth Regiment New Hampshire Volunteers in the War of the Rebellion</u>, Concord (1897).

Bear Island Conservation Association: <u>Bear Island Reflections</u>, (1989).

Benton, C. and Barry, S.F.: <u>A statistical View of the Number of Sheep in the Several Towns and Counties.</u> Folsom, Wells, and Thurston (1837).

Blackstone, Edward H.: <u>Farewell Old Mount Washington: The story of the steamboat era on Lake Winnipesaukee</u>, The Steamship Historical Society of America (1969).

Burgess, Gideon and Ward, J.T.: <u>Free Baptist Cyclopaedia</u> (1889).

Carter, Nathan F.: <u>The native ministry of New Hampshire</u>, Rumford Printing Co., Concord (1906)

Carvell, Kenneth: <u>A History of the Far Echoes Colony at Lake Winnipesaukee</u>, Morgantown, West Virginia (1997).

Clark, Charles: <u>The Eastern Frontier: The Settlement of New England, 1610-1763</u>, Alfred A. Knopf (1970).

Crocker, William P.: <u>Map of Winnipesaukee, May 1858</u>, NH State Archives, vault.

Dalzell, Robert F.: <u>Enterprising Elite: The Boston Associates and the World They Made</u>, W.W.Norton & Co. (1987).

Daniels, Jere: <u>Colonial New Hampshire, A History</u>, KTO Press (1981).

Donsker, Mary: <u>The Story of Welch Island Through 1945</u>, (1984).

Farmer, John and Moore, Jacob: <u>A Gazetteer of the State of New Hampshire</u>, Concord (1823).

Fogg, Alonzo J.: <u>The Statistics and Gazetteer of New Hampshire</u>, D.L.Guernsey (1874).

Forbes, Ripley: "Gone But Not Forgotten. Island Legend Ernest H. Abbott 1888-1964," <u>The Weirs Times</u>, October 13, 2016.

Garvin, Donna-Belle and James L.: <u>On the Road North of Boston</u>, University Press of New England (1988).

Greene, Frank E., "The Story of Two Brothers: J.A. and F.E. Greene," Moultonborough Public Library Collection (1985).

Greene, Gardiner: "Windermere on Long Island," Moultonborough Public Library Collection (1979).

Hanaford, Mary E.: <u>Meredith, N.H.: Annals and Genealogies</u>, The Rumford Press (1932).

Hawkes, Winfield S.: <u>Winnipesaukee and About There</u>, Boston and Lowell R.R. Passenger Department (1887).

Haynes, Martin A. ed. <u>Historical Sketches of Lakeport, New Hampshire</u>, Lakeport (1915).

Hayward, John: <u>Gazetteer of New Hampshire</u>, John P. Jewett (1849).

Heyduk, Daniel: <u>Meredith Chronicles</u>, Charleston, S.C. (2015).

Heyduk, Daniel: <u>Stories in the History of New Hampshire's Lakes Region</u>, N. Charleston (2017).

Heald, Bruce: <u>Postmaster of the Lake</u>, The Meredith News (1971).

Holden, Steve: <u>The Old Country Store</u>, Moultonborough (1991).

Hurd, D. Hamilton editor: <u>The History of Merrimack and Belknap Counties, New Hamshire, J.W. Lewis & Co. (1885).</u>

Hurd, D. Hamilton, editor: <u>History of New London County, Connecticut</u>, J.W. Lewis & Co., Philadelphia (1882).

Hurd, D. Hamilton, Editor: <u>Town & City Atlas of the State of New Hampshire State 1892</u>, Boston (1892).

Huse, Warren: <u>Laconia</u>, Dover (1995).

Huse, Warren: <u>The Weirs</u>, Charleston (1996).

Huse, Warren: <u>Lakeport</u>, Charleston (1999).

Jager, Ronald: <u>The Fate of Family Farming</u>, University Press of New England (2004)

Jager, Ronald: <u>Last House on the Road</u>, Beacon Press (1994).

Kennard, Jim: "Horse Powered Ferry Boat discovered in Lake Champlain," July 2, 2005, <u>www.shipwreckworld.com</u>.

King, Thomas Starr: <u>The White Hills: Their Legends, Landscapes, and Poetry</u>, Boston (1860).

Lane, Charles: <u>New Hampshire's First Tourists</u>, The Old Print Barn (2007).

Mead, Edgar T.: <u>The Up-Country Line</u>, The Stephen Greene Press, Brattleboro, VT (1975).

<u>New Hampshire Provincial and State Papers</u>, Vols. 1-40, G.E. Jenks, state printer.

Nylander, Jane: <u>Our Snug Fireside, Images of the New England Home, 1760-1860</u>, New Haven (1993).

Parker, Benjamin F.: <u>The History of Wolfeborough New Hampshire</u> (1901).

Puffer, William: "Log Book of the Homeless Wanderers," unpublished manuscript.

<u>Reminiscences of Meredith</u>, Meredith Historical Society (1987).

Rice, Jane: <u>Bob Fogg and New Hampshire's Golden Age of Aviation</u>, Portsmouth (2012).

Rogovin, Larry: <u>A History of Three Mile Island Camp</u>, Three Mile Island Camp publisher, undated.

Spalding, Arthur Whitefield<u>: Origin and History of Seventh-Day Adventists</u>, Vol. I, Review and Herald Publishing Corporation (1961).

<u>Special Report on the history and present condition of the sheep</u>, US Bureau of Animal Husbandry, Dr. D.E. Salmon, Washington (1892).

"Twenty-Five Years of Kuwiyan: A History as Told at the Last Council Ring of 1934," donated by John D. Link in 2005, file cabinet, Meredith Historical Society.

Van Veghten, Rudy: <u>The History of Meredith Bay</u>, Meredith (2015).

Vaughan, Charles W.: <u>The Illustrated Laconian, History and Industries of Laconia, New Hampshire </u>(1899).

Vermont Merino Breeders' Association: <u>Spanish Merino Sheep, Their Importation from Spain, Introduction into Vermont and Improvement Since Introduced</u>. The Free Press Association, Burlington, VT (1879).

Wessels, Tom: <u>Reading the Forested Landscape</u>, The Countryman Press (1997).

Wessels, Tom: <u>Forest Forensics</u>, The Countryman Press (2010).

Wilcomb, Edgar H.: <u>Winnipesaukee Lake Gleanings</u>, (1923).

Willan, Mildred: "Bear Island, New Hampshire in the Twenties," unpublished family history (1982).

Whittier, Horace G.: <u>Historical Sketches of Lakeport, New Hampshire, Formerly Lake Village, Now the Sixth Ward of Laconia</u>, Martin Alonzo Haynes (1915).

Wyatt, Harold: <u>Early New England Farming: Tools and Techniques</u>, Meredith Historical Society (1999).

Made in the USA
Middletown, DE
27 September 2020